Encyclopedia of
GEOGRAPHICAL FEATURES
in World History

Europe and the Americas

Encyclopedia of

GEOGRAPHICAL FEATURES

in World History

Europe and the Americas

James R. Penn

ABC-CLIO

Santa Barbara, California
Denver, Colorado
Oxford, England

Library of Congress Cataloging-in-Publication Data
Penn, James R.
    Encyclopedia of geographical features in world history : Europe and the Americas /
James R. Penn.
        p. cm.
    Includes bibliographical references and index.
    1. Historical geography. I. Title.
    G141.P43   1997
    911—dc21   97-24437
                                                                                CIP

ISBN 0-87436-760-3

02 01 00 99 98 97   10 9 8 7 6 5 4 3 2 1

ABC-CLIO, Inc.
130 Cremona Drive, P.O. Box 1911
Santa Barbara, California 93116-1911

Typeset by Letra Libre

This book is printed on acid-free paper.
Manufactured in the United States of America

For April and Eric

CONTENTS

PREFACE

This work is not a gazetteer or geographical dictionary, but rather a compendium of selected geographical features that have rich historical associations. The features in this A–Z reference book have been selected according to certain definite but flexible criteria. All have played an important role in the historical development of Europe and the Americas.

I began this project by reviewing a number of high-school and college texts on Western history and civilization. I eliminated places where events occurred but the landscape didn't appear to play a significant role, such as towns where treaties were signed, or certain battlefields such as Borodino or Waterloo. Other battlefields, including Thermopylae, Salamis, and Trafalgar, can be found here because the terrain or water body was relevant to the battle. The list of entries excludes political units, obsolescent or present-day, unless the underlying geography warrants an entry. No towns, cities, counties, duchies, principalities, states, or countries are covered as primary entries.

The intended audience for this book is the general public, high-school students, college students, or anyone interested in improving his or her geographical and historical literacy. American students' test scores in both these subjects have reached rock bottom, and I would gladly contribute any small amount I can to improving the public's knowledge in these areas.

This work makes no claim to be exhaustive, but it is comprehensive. There are entries for North America, Mexico and Central America, the Caribbean, South America, and all parts of Europe, including Russia as far east as the Ural Mountains, the traditional boundary with Asia. The book is no substitute for that most valuable reference work, an atlas, and I recommend the reader have a good atlas at hand when reading what I have to say about these places. I had *Goode's World Atlas,* 19th edition, 1995, constantly at my side as I wrote the entries in this book. One could do worse than use the long-lived work of the University of Chicago professor J. Paul Goode, who started producing a set of world regional maps in standard format bound in book form for Rand McNally (the Chicago publisher that got its start publishing train schedules) as early as 1922. The work is widely available in paperback for about the price of a good dinner and should last a lifetime. Other atlases will also serve to orient the reader and provide additional material for study.

Anyone who has attempted to write a similar geographical reference work knows about the nagging difficulties of multiple and changing place-names. Rebecca Ritke, working for ABC-CLIO, has standardized the geographical names as much as possible against *Merriam-Webster's Geographical Dictionary* (1997), a readily accessible and modestly priced book.

My general attitude toward the important matter of how to conceive the relationship between the physical environment and historical development (see the Introduction for a fuller treatment) is that a complex, reciprocal relationship exists between nature and people, and that this blend gets incorporated into the landscape through time (i.e., natural landscapes evolve into cultural landscapes). The cultural landscape in turn affects human behavior. In this way the cultural landscape is just as much natural (i.e., tangible) as the so-called natural landscape, which in most cases is not pristine.

It is truly a pleasure to acknowledge the many debts I've incurred during the course of preparing this volume. The seed of the idea came from wide-ranging conversations over coffee with Louisiana State University (LSU) geography professor Dr. Roland Chardon. I also benefited while at LSU from contact with Dr. Sam Hilliard, who—like me a Wisconsin alumnus—learned a lot during the course of a fine career about the need to pay careful attention to the material landscape and managed to convey it to me, however indirectly.

This set the background but not the beginning of the book. Transferring my residence and employment (and book collection) 40 miles to the east of Baton Rouge, to Hammond, Louisiana, I began to peddle my expertise around the Piney Woods before Dr. Bill Robison, a history professor at Southeastern Louisiana University (SLU), pointed me in the direction of this book's publishers. Before long

I had signed a contract and was working on a project that, I wouldn't be honest if I didn't say, at times I wondered whether I could see through to the end. The idea of an entire encyclopedia written by one person is a bit daunting. For his efforts on my behalf I would like to thank Bill, all the same.

Henry Rasof at ABC-CLIO saw this book through its early stages and contributed some well-received criticisms of early drafts. Other staff at ABC-CLIO helped in countless ways to bring this work to fruition, particularly Todd Hallman, Connie Oehring, Sue Ficca, and Liz Kincaid. My wife, Laura, ably drew the maps and assisted me in numerous other ways. I had wanted Dr. Robert Gohstand, professor of geography at the University of California–Northridge, to contribute entries on Russia, which he was unable to do, though he did send a sample entry on the Valdai Hills that was helpful. Dr. Jesse Walker, Boyd Professor of Geography at LSU, kindly contributed photos he took on his many trips around the world; Jesse is as widely traveled as Mark Twain and just as literate. Dr. Sam Hilliard and Dr. Robert West also contributed some photographs. I benefited from conversations with Robert ("Buck") Thomas, a student at SLU, about the importance of key land gateways and maritime choke points in European history. Finally, Scott Brady kindly allowed me to use parts of his recently completed dissertation (1996) on transisthmian routes in Central America in general and the Comayagua Depression in Honduras in particular.

For any errors or omissions, spells of turgidity, or lapses into obscurantism, I take complete responsibility.

James R. Penn

INTRODUCTION

Try though we might to be scientific and objective, we are part and parcel of a larger world. Our needs are satisfied, our interests fulfilled, in the world around us. We speak as if the natural world were a proxy of our selves, even our bodies: the *face* of the mountainside, the *eye* of the storm, the *lip* of the canyon. To make this observation is not so much to plead for a subjective approach to geographical study as to recognize that the places discussed in this volume are of interest to us today, and that many of them have been commented on for centuries, even millennia. We cannot help taking an interest in the landscape, nor should we try to deny our intimate relationship with nature.

The further I went with this project, the stronger grew the impression that I was going to my sources—regional studies, historical monographs, and reference works—in pursuit of treasure. The gold was the richness of history, the silver the value of place. I had to fashion a method to extract the wealth (research technique) and to bring it back to the surface (writing style). I confess to a somewhat idiosyncratic style, but I wanted my entries to be interpretive as well as descriptive. I have at various times considered this book to be modeled on *Van Loon's Geography,* a serious but lightly written popular work; Fernand Braudel's classic *The Mediterranean and the Mediterranean World in the Age of Philip II,* which relies heavily on geography; Voltaire's *Philosophical Dictionary,* a wide-ranging, satiric compendium of Enlightenment wit; and the time-honored Victorian reference work *Brewer's Dictionary of Phrase and Fable.*

I don't consider the events chronicled here in their geographical settings mere anecdotes or just so much detail. This material can be trivial only if we have lost contact with our past. I am mindful, however, of what Dostoevsky once said: "As soon as you begin to describe something, you cease to be a philosopher."

I must put forward some considerations about how I view the relationship between the physical environment of climate, terrain, soils, and vegetation and historical development. The age-old question of the relationship between nature and culture cannot be answered in a set of postulates. I think when the reader finishes reading this book—or some of its entries—my methods will be apparent. Nevertheless, some explanation may be essayed here, at the beginning.

Academic geographers have exhibited two extremes in how they have viewed this relationship. Environmental determinists, exemplified by such early twentieth-century American geographers as Ellsworth Huntington and Ellen Semple, considered the physical environment to be the primary determinant of human behavior and historical development. Most geographers today rightly reject the rigidity and narrowness of this approach. Since about 1960, a new orthodoxy termed *spatial analysis* has emerged, partly to replace environmental determinism but more to replace what was perceived as a naive regional approach—the consensual approach in the 1940s and 1950s, fostered by Richard Hartshorne's not-so-naive *Nature of Geography* (1939). Spatial analysis begins with a flat, featureless plain, bringing human beings into play only so far as they behave according to a simple economic principle: the minimization of time, distance, or, in more recent models, risk.

It is probably obvious where my bias lies. I am doubtful of the value of a study that purports to find hexagons on the landscape that really don't exist. Nor can I follow an approach that conceives the relationship between culture and nature so narrowly that it borders on racism (twentieth-century European fascisms always had an aspect of this kind of environmentalism). I try to steer a middle course through the perils of these two approaches. Nature offers possibilities for human settlement and sets limits, but humans react or adjust to these given conditions differently according to their way of life. This view is in agreement with the French tradition of possibilism as advocated by Paul Vidal de la Blache (1845–1918). Rational, economic motivation has a large role to play, especially in modern life, but it is the task of the historical geographer to show worlds other than just today's and to demonstrate the processes of change that brought us to the brink of the present.

The encyclopedia consists of 166 alphabetically arranged entries that range in length from about 200 to about 1,800 words. Each entry treats the people,

events, battles, and influences associated with the geographical feature. Most entries contain references at the end for further reading, and a complete bibliography can be found at the back of the book. Cross-references within entries are indicated by boldface, and *See also* references are used when a relevant cross-reference is not made directly in the narrative.

Certain terms and concepts, mostly in the areas of geology and geomorphology, need to be introduced and defined here because they crop up repeatedly in the text, and it would be easier to begin by setting down their meaning so the reader starts with some basic knowledge. A term that I will have recourse to is *physiography*. Though somewhat old-fashioned and sometimes used synonymously with *physical geography* or *geomorphology*, the word more properly refers to the study of natural regions—the totality of the terrain, climate, vegetation, and soils that make up a place's physical environment. Some examples of physiographic features or natural regions that I treat in this book are the Paris Basin, the Colorado Plateau, and the Scottish Highlands.

The terrain of many places in Europe and the Americas has a geological structure consisting of alternating layers of sedimentary rocks of differential resistance to erosion that are inclined to the surface. Dipping hard rock layers form ridges, one side being steep (the escarpment, or scarp) and the other gentle (the dip slope, or as it is known in England, the down). Soft rock layers erode to form a broad valley (in England, a vale). Although the geographic pattern made by the hills varies from region to region, northern France, southeastern England, western Russia, and the coastal plain (Atlantic and Gulf) of the United States all feature this kind of low, asymmetric hill known as a *cuesta* (wold in southern England).

Geologists refer to the processes of mountain building in certain periods as *orogenies*. The older rocks of the Appalachians and the central European plateau lands (Hercynian Uplands) are lower in elevation and rounder in form than the relatively young rocks of the Rocky Mountains and the Alps because there has been more time for the erosive action of wind, water, and ice to bring them down and smooth

chronologies I have used sparingly, assuming no knowledge about this admittedly important matter. The specialist geologist will surely sigh upon reading this comment, but the information is widely available and can be obtained without much effort. On occasion I have referred to specific time spans, as, for instance, the Pleistocene epoch (extending roughly from about two million to about ten

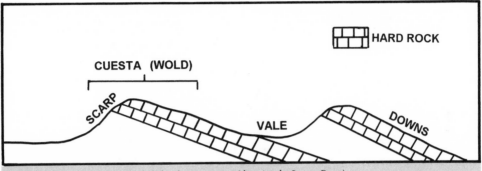

Cuestra terrain, with some English landscape terms *(drawing by Laura Penn).*

them off. The Alpine orogeny, which occurred about 44 million years ago, elevated not only the Alps proper in Switzerland and upper Austria (and some parts of France and Italy) but also much of southern Europe, all the way from the Cantabrian Mountains in Spain to the broken hill lands of the Balkans, as well as rejuvenating (that is, reelevating) older uplands of the Hercynian orogeny.

A *massif* (French) is a large mountainous mass, usually of resistant volcanic or crystalline rocks, that has nearly uniform physical characteristics and stands out conspicuously in the landscape. The best examples covered in this book are the Massif Central and the Armorican Massif in France.

The geological names for eras, periods, and epochs and their corresponding

thousand years ago and corresponding with the advance and retreat of continental ice sheets). The movement of ice was such an important shaper of landscapes in the northern parts of Europe and North America that it has been given a separate entry, under the title *Würm (Wisconsinan) Glaciation.*

One of the most spectacular glacial landforms is a *fjord,* an inundated glacial trough. Fjords, common on the west coasts of landmasses in the higher midlatitudes, formed when rising sea levels caused by the melting of Pleistocene ice sheets flooded the mouths of river valleys that had been previously carved into U-shapes by glacial ice.

Other terms will be introduced as needed. Remember to open your atlas. Good sailing!

M A P S

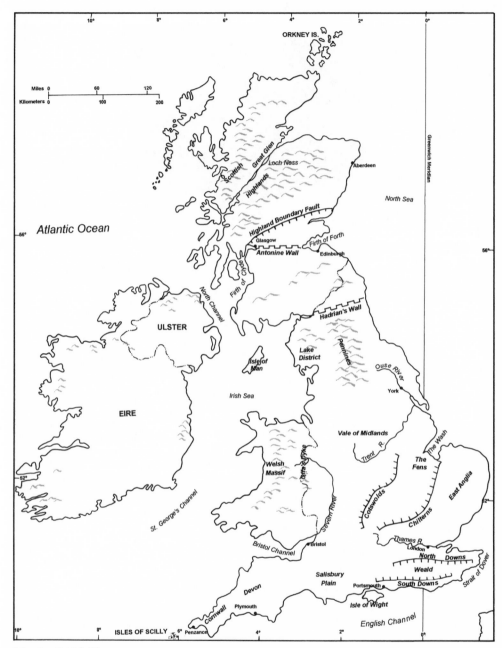

Map 1   British Isles

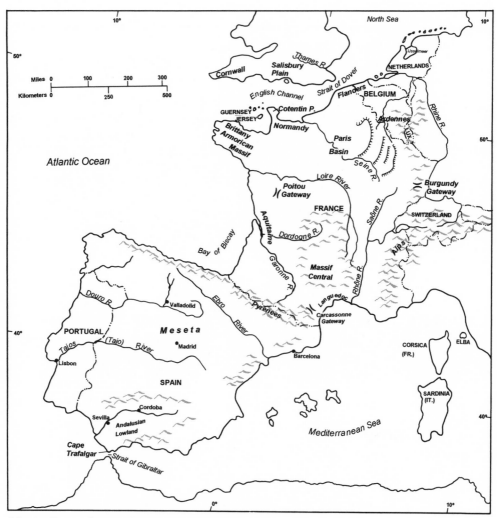

Map 2　France, the Low Countries, Spain, and Portugal

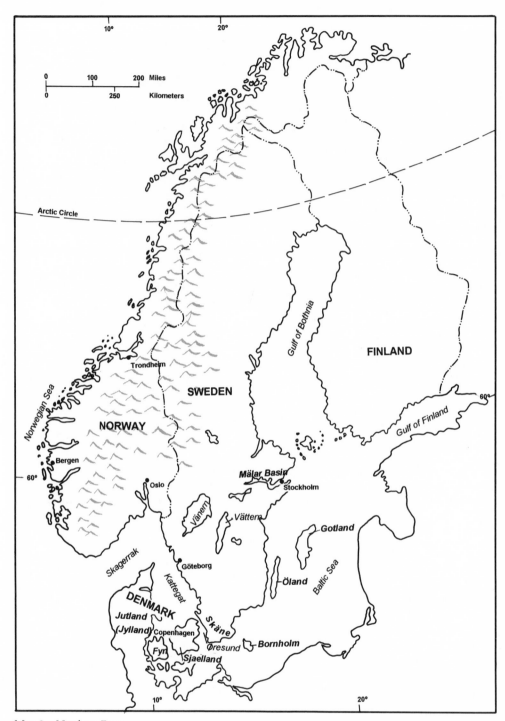

Map 3   Northern Europe

Map 4   Central and Eastern Europe, Italy, and the Balkans

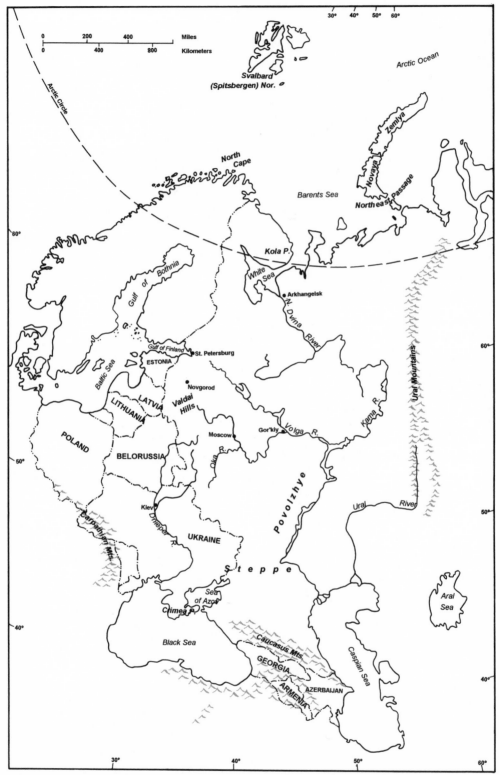

Map 5   Russia and neighboring countries

Map 6   South America

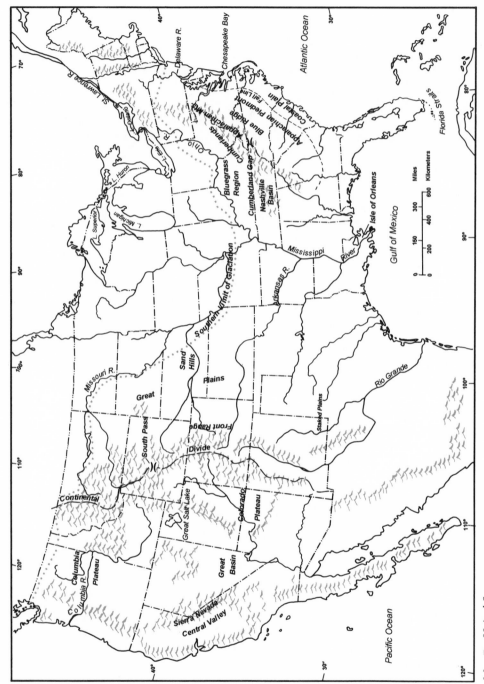

Map 7   United States

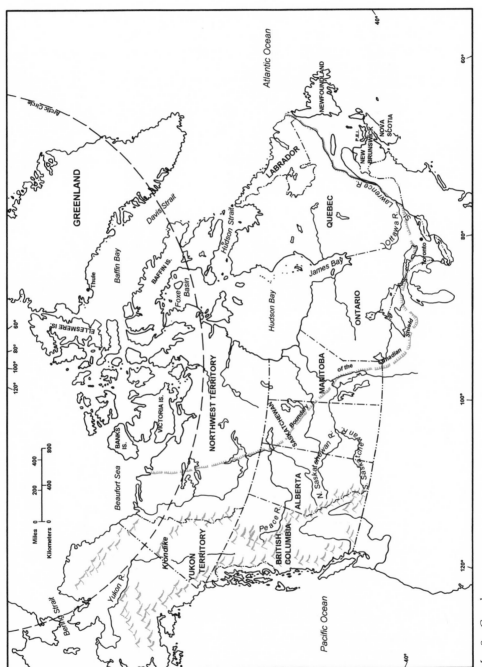

Map 8   Canada

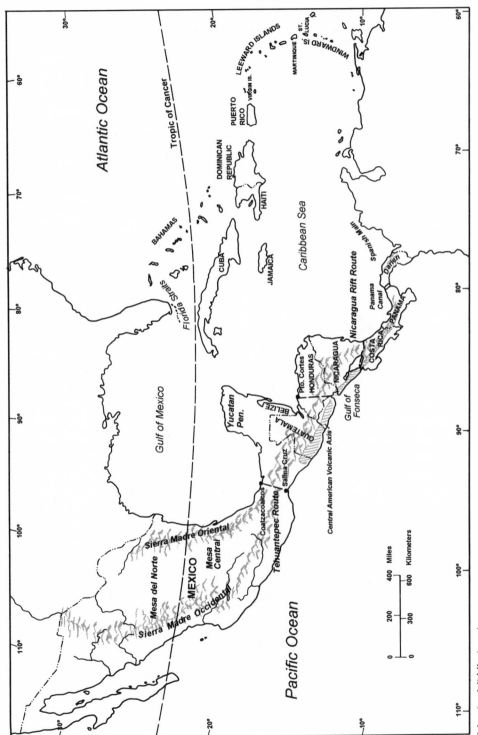

Map 9   Middle America

ABRAHAM, PLAINS OF

The middle years of the eighteenth century saw the revival of an intense rivalry between Great Britain and France for control of the North American continent. In 1745 England seized the fortress of Louisbourg on Cape Breton Island, in Acadia (French Nova Scotia). The treaty that concluded the War of Austrian Succession (1744–1748), however, restored Acadia to the French. Both sides cynically viewed the Peace of Aix-la-Chapelle as a mere truce and made preparations for their next armed encounter.

Tensions only increased in the 1750s as settlers moved, slowly at first, then in a wave, across the trans-Appalachian frontier, whose imperial attachment was as yet uncertain. A three-way competition emerged between the French settlements to the north, the British colonies along the eastern seaboard from Virginia to Massachusetts, and the newly settled Ohio country. Thus, it came as no surprise when Great Britain declared war on France in May 1756. The armies were more nearly matched than the navies, as the Royal Navy had already established its preeminence on the seas, at least against the navy of any single country. The French commander, General Louis Montcalm, with fewer men and resources, tried to disguise an essentially defensive strategy of holding onto the Saint Lawrence Valley by making forays south of Lake Ontario, but finally chose to take his stand on the rock where a century and a half earlier Champlain had established the city of Quebec, at the head of navigation on the Saint Lawrence.

Quebec was not a scientifically constructed fortress like Louisbourg, but it did have strategic high ground, especially from the high cliffs about Cape Diamond. But further downstream the low Beauport flats were vulnerable, as was the stretch upriver above Cap Rouge. The British general James Wolfe worried Montcalm, who was entrenched for about six miles (ten kilometers) along the north shore of the St. Lawrence River, between the rivers St. Charles and Montmorency, by sailing British ships back and forth in front of the old city. Montcalm expected the attack to come from above or below the city, but only posted a small picket on the breaks in the cliffs at Anse-au-Foulon, which gave access to the nearly level Plains of Abraham. These rolling lands lay adjacent to the upper part of the city.

A seriously ill Wolfe was the first man ashore in the early hours of 13 September 1759. After overpowering a sleepy guard, the British scrambled up steeply pitched hills and reached the level ground above. The Plains of Abraham more nearly resembled a parade ground than the forest trails and strategic heights that the French preferred in their battles with the English. Sternly disciplined and deployed in the classic square formation, the British held their ground, even as the French made a ragged attack in the early morning. At forty paces as ordered, the two long lines of redcoats discharged a crashing volley, before which the French soon broke and fled. Wolfe, in his moment of glory, had been shot and was dying, even as Montcalm's black horse carried its mortally wounded master back into the city through the St. Louis gate.

The French had been beaten before, but only at the fringes of New France. This time the key corridor of the Saint Lawrence had been penetrated and taken; thus, at the Treaty of Paris signed in 1763 after the French and Indian War, or as it is known in Europe, the Seven Years War, France ceded to Great Britain all of its North American possessions except Louisiana west of the Mississippi, and New Orleans, which had passed to the Spanish by secret agreement during the war. In addition to their American colonies, the British now had a monopoly in India and Canada; everything seemed to be going their way, for the moment.

Further Reading: Donald Creighton, *The Story of Canada,* Toronto: Macmillan, 1959.

ACTIUM

This promontory and ancient town in western Greece located at the southern end of the entrance to the Ambracian Gulf was the site of one of the climactic battles of ancient history, for it was here in 31 B.C. that Octavian (Augustus) defeated the combined sea and land forces of Mark Antony and his Egyptian ally, Cleopatra.

Following the assassination of Julius Caesar in 44 B.C., Octavian and Antony found themselves on opposite sides in the struggle for control of the Roman world.

In early 31 B.C. Octavian dispatched Agrippa across the Ionian Sea to take the Greek city of Methone in the western **Peloponnese.** After so doing, Agrippa then advanced north, in the direction of Mark Antony's main force, which was encamped at Actium. The site, located just opposite modern Préveza, contained vestiges of ancient temples, including one dedicated to Apollo that dated from the fifth century B.C. About the same time, Octavian crossed from Brundusium on the heel of the Italian boot to Macedonia (across the Strait of Otranto), closing on the Roman province of Epirus from the north.

By the first of September in the year 31 B.C., the Romans had assembled a fleet of 400 ships against 230 Egyptian ships. It was believed at the time that the large, oared Egyptian ships had the advantage over the lighter, more maneuverable Roman ships. In the ensuing battle of 2 September 31 B.C., fought offshore near Actium, the Roman fleet under Agrippa avoided ramming tactics but sideswiped their opponents, crushing their oars and boarding them. When the news arrived that Cleopatra had abandoned her squadron, and soon after, that Antony had deserted too, the battle turned into a rout. Most of Antony and Cleopatra's fleet surrendered or was destroyed. The way was now open for Octavian to consolidate his rule: He adopted the new name Augustus and became the first Roman emperor. He built the town of Nikopolis just south of where his camp had been, to commemorate his victory. The Romans held the Actian games here every four years to celebrate this decisive turn in their history.

AEGEAN ISLANDS

These islands scattered between Greece and Turkey from the **Dardanelles** to the island of Crete were a meeting ground for disparate early Bronze Age cultures and a studded lane across the Aegean highway in classical times. Today they are a zone of conflict between essentially Greek peoples of western culture and the eastern-influenced Turkish population.

The islands are for the most part partially submerged remnants of the mainland, featuring outliers of the downthrust

The name Aegean has been variously described as having derived from a city with a similar name in Euboea; from Aegeus, the father of Theseus, who drowned himself in the sea, believing his son had been slain by the Minotaur; from Aegea, an Amazon queen who likewise drowned in the sea; and from the Latin word *oega,* or goat, referring to an island in the sea that looked like a goat lying down. This diver-

View of Thíra (Santorini), one of the crater-islands of the Cyclades, showing white buildings on the edge of the crater in the main town *(photo by Jesse Walker).*

limestone fold systems displayed in Anatolia, in the Dinaric Range of the former Yugoslavia, and in peninsular Greece. Evidence of vulcanism can be detected on a number of the islands, such as at Milos in the Cyclades, where a deep basin that was formed by the drowned crater of a volcano serves as an excellent harbor.

The original name for the Aegean Sea was Archipelago, or Chief Sea; but in time, *Archipelago* came to be applied to the islands in the sea, while today the word refers to any large group of islands.

sity of explanations well illustrates that the origins of place-names are often impossible to ascertain.

The islands are so numerous and geographically diverse that they must be addressed individually. However, one might point to several common elements: (1) Lacking important mineral resources and agricultural potential, the islands have derived their significance from their relative location at a cultural crossroads. (2) Those islands nearer to Asia Minor frequently have been subjected to changes and disturbances associated with the movement of peoples and with political pressures along a major land corridor connecting southeastern Europe and the Middle East, in contrast to islands farther west, which lay closer to peninsular Greece and thus have enjoyed comparative immunity from these shocks (although they have been more subject to disturbances arriving via the open sea from Italy and western Europe).

Lying closest to mainland Greece are the island arcs of the *Cyclades,* or *Center Islands,* which structurally are seaward prolongations of the ridges of Attica and Euboea. In antiquity these islands were thought to be grouped in a circle around Delos, an especially important early site although it was also the smallest island in the group. Delos does not in fact occupy a central position—it is nearer to one end of the northern chain—but the island was accorded symbolic centrality because it was the legendary birthplace of Apollo. It became an important early commercial center on the basis of its crossroads location and its sanctified site. After the Persian wars (490–479 B.C.), Athens's rise to hegemony was signaled by the alliance of many of the Aegean Islands in the Delian League, which evolved into the Athenian Empire. The treasury of the Delian League was housed at the temple of Apollo on Delos until it was removed to Athens in 454 B.C. Larger islands in the Cyclades include Andros in the northern arc, and Naxos and Paros, which are nearly encircled by smaller islands, in the southern arc. South of the southern arc are the crater-islands of Milos (where the famous Venus statue originated) and Thíra (Santorini), the latter still volcanically active (Thíra last erupted in 1925–1928).

Farther removed from mainland Greece and spread over a wider area are the appro-priately named *Sporades.* A small northern cluster of these islands (Skíros, Skiathos, Skópelos) is essentially a continuation of the crystalline ridges of Thessaly, which extend all the way back to Mt. Olympus. The northern Sporades are not particularly productive, lying at a distance from the main sea-lanes between Greece and Asia Minor; as a result, they have not featured as importantly in history as have the other islands. In contrast, the southern Sporades, a large group of scattered islands in the eastern Aegean between Samos and Crete, have been an important geographical focus of conquest, colonization, and trade since the Bronze Age. Among these is the Dodecanese (the Twelve) group, first described under that name as an administrative subdivision of the Byzantine Empire about A.D. 730. The largest and most important island in this group (which actually includes about 20 islands and islets) is Rhodes, close up against the Turkish coast and at the southeastern margin of this maritime region. As in the case of the Cyclades, a variety of types of geological structure and bedrock can be found, including crystalline massifs, limestone terrain honeycombed with subterranean water channels, and volcanic craters that continue the activity of the southern Cyclades. The city of Rhodes, located on the largest island in the group, was a flourishing commercial center in ancient times, controlling the carrying trade between Greece and Asia Minor as well as the coastwise trade between Asia Minor and the Levantine cities through an eastern gateway. In the Bronze Age, Rhodes was a Greek stepping-stone both to the coast of Asia Minor and to the larger islands to its north and inshore (e.g., Cos, Samos). Unification of the different seaboard communities in 408 B.C. set the stage for the strengthening of a political system that successfully resisted the more powerful city-states of Athens and Sparta. One of the **Seven Wonders of the Ancient World** was the colossal bronze statue dedicated to the Greek sun-god Helios that stood at the entrance to the harbor in Rhodes. For many years, the island was under Byzantine rule. Then the Knights of the Hospital of St. John of Jerusalem, retreating from Palestine after the fall of Acre, established themselves here from 1310 to 1522. The Knights abandoned their original function of ministering to the sick and infirm and reorganized as a military order charged with defending western Christianity against Islam. They remained in Rhodes until at least 1522, when the island was overrun by Ottoman Turks, who held political sway until 1912. Italy then established control of these islands, which did not pass to Greece until after World War II in 1947. The early importance of Rhodes can be seen from the fact that the population of the port during Roman times—past its heyday—has been estimated at half a million.

The Greek-administered *Aegean Islands* group includes three large inshore islands just off Asia Minor, north of the Dodecanese—Samos, Chios, and Lesbos. Important as stepping-stones in the Greek migration to Anatolia, these islands later provided strong resistance to the Turks both before and after the fall of Constantinople (A.D. 1453), not because their people were particularly courageous but because they had become protectorates and outposts of the powerful Italian city-states of Genoa and Venice (Chios as early as 1172). The expulsion of Greeks from the Anatolian mainland in 1922 left many cut off from their farms and trading posts, which lay beyond the narrow channels that separate these islands from the Turkish mainland.

The *North Aegean Islands,* in what was once called the Thracian Sea, include Thá-sos, Samothrace, Imbros (Turkey), and Bozcaada (Turkey). Their strategic significance is that they control the main passageway between Europe and Asia across the Dardanelles. Ancient Athens considered it necessary to secure control of the port and mainland dependencies of Thásos in order to avert further Persian aggression. Imbros and Bozcaada are situated like sentinels on either side of the entrance to the Dardanelles, one of the reasons the North Atlantic Treaty Organization (NATO) considered it important to include Turkey in its post–World War II alliance.

Further Reading: R. L. N. Barber, *The Cyclades in the Bronze Age,* Iowa City: University of Iowa Press, 1987; John L. Myres, *Geographical History in Greek Lands,* Westport, CT: Greenwood, 1974 (orig. pub. Oxford: Clarendon Press, 1953).

AGRI DECUMATES

The Roman frontier was extended beyond the Alps early in the first century A.D. to secure the Italian peninsula against invading Germanic peoples. No defensible boundary could be found among the moraines and dissected outwash plains north of the Alps until the Danube was reached. The Danube was marshy, flood prone, and difficult to cross—hence defensible. The Romans therefore selected the Danube in combination with the previously secured Rhine as the limit of the Roman Empire; they quickly went about establishing a fortified *limes,* or frontier. The Rhine-Danube frontier would last for the next four centuries.

Trajan abandoned a purely riverine frontier in A.D. 83, when he expanded into the area known as the Agri Decumates in southwest Germany. This region included lands in the upper Rhine valley on the east side of the river as far as the crest of the **Black Forest** (Schwarzwald, in

German). The virtue of this policy was that in addition to shortening the frontier and improving communication between the armies on the Rhine and Danube Rivers, it included within the imperium the densely settled and fertile **Rhine Graben** on both sides of the river, as well as opening up promising lands on the lower Main and Neckar Rivers. Legionary camps lined the frontier like knots on a string, promoting what we would today call economic development by attracting resources and providing manpower. Retired legionnaires were given land warrants to settle this newly occupied region, a policy anticipating the U.S. government's granting of bounty warrants to veterans in the nineteenth century. German *foederati*—tribes allied with the Romans—were given lands in exchange for military protection against other German tribes (well illustrating the attempted Roman policy to divide and conquer). Much of the settlement network of what is today Baden-Württemberg was established during Roman times, with the creation of a dense pattern of villas, forts, towns *(civitates),* and cities *(coloniae).*

The Germans were generally held outside the imperial boundaries of the Rhine-Danube except in the neighborhood of the Agri Decumates. That the Rhine frontier was not considered final is suggested by Augustus's attempt to extend the line of Roman control outward as far as the Elbe River. The loss of three legions in an abortive campaign (A.D. 9) convinced Augustus to abandon this effort, and the frontier in the west remained stable from A.D. 83 to the loss of the Agri Decumates in A.D. 273. It has been argued that the invading Alemanni occupied the same sites and cultivated the same ground as had the Romans. If this is true, it presents the unusual situation in western Europe of a continuity of settle-

ment from Roman to German occupancy. In general, with some cities as exceptions, sites and settlements were disrupted with the fall of Rome. The historical taproot in southwestern Germany may go even deeper: There was a strong substratum of Celtic population in this region, as attested by the frequency of Celtic place-names and the presence of a number of Celtic archaeological sites.

The Rhine frontier held until Suevi and Vandal tribes crossed the frozen river in the winter of A.D. 406. Following the puncturing of the frontier, the Alemanni, whose homeland previously had been the Agri Decumates, moved into Switzerland, Alsace, and Burgundy. The period of the great migration of the German peoples (*Völkerwanderung*), around A.D. 400–600, furthered the mixing of Romano-Celtic and Germanic peoples that had begun in this important corner of southwestern Germany.

ALPINE PASSES

Stretching in an arc from the French Riviera through Switzerland to the Wienerwald (Vienna Woods) on the banks of the Austrian Danube, the Alps are one unit in a broader mountain system of southern Europe dating from an orogeny (mountain-building process) that occurred about 40 million years ago. Included in the extensive Alpine System are the **Pyrenees** Mountains, the **Carpathian** Mountains, and the various ranges of the Balkans. The Alps proper, the highest mountains in Europe, constitute sizable amounts of land in France, Italy, Switzerland, and Austria, and extend into the territory of Germany and Yugoslavia. The Romans thought the name referred to their word *albus,* or white, on account of the snow in the Alps, but actually it was derived from the Celtic *ailp,* or mountain. In fact, local residents use the word *alp* or *alm* to refer to the high mountain meadows above the tree line, which have been an important part of the Alpine pastoral economy.

Though impressive in appearance, the Alps have never served as a complete barrier, except perhaps in prehistory. The north-south mountain ridges have been severed by the headwaters of the Rhine, Rhône, and other major rivers. Pleis-

as "magnificent traitors." A cavalcade of figures in European military history have made their way across the Alps through these passes: Roman generals, Germanic invaders, and the armies of Charlemagne and Napoleon I.

The western Alps, in eastern France and southwestern Switzerland, have the highest elevations, with deeply incised valleys and large remnant glaciers. One of

The Matterhorn, the most famous mountain in Europe, is located on the border between Switzerland and Italy *(photo by Jesse Walker)*.

tocene glaciers, extending farther down valley in the western Alps than at present, opened up broad U-shaped valleys that have acted as corridors linking the north Italian plains to German lands. A number of low passes and water gaps have been in use since ancient times. Though clearly an important factor in the cultural division of Europe and in climatic variation, the Alps have never been a defensive bulwark. The Italians living south of the mountains consider them a natural border yet refer to them

the best-known associations of a geographical feature with a historical event can be found here. It is believed that the *Little Saint Bernard Pass* (7,178 feet or 2,188 meters) was the route taken by the Carthaginian general Hannibal in 218 B.C. when he crossed the Alps with a cavalry of elephants and 30,000 men in his invasion of Italy. Also in the vicinity of the western Alps is the *Col de Tende* (6,143 feet or 1,872 meters), which was, until the French Revolution, the chief trans-Alpine pass for wheeled transport.

Control of the *Mont Cenis Pass* (6,834 feet or 2,083 meters) promoted the fortunes of Savoy-Piedmont, which also safeguarded the Great Saint Bernard Pass in the central Alps until the nascent Swiss confederation took it over. Other important passes in the western Alps include *Maddalena Pass* and *Montgenèvre Pass* (some scholars think Hannibal may have taken this route).

The central Alps likewise have a number of historically important pass routes. Perhaps most famous is the *Great Saint Bernard Pass* (8,110 feet or 2,472 meters) on the Swiss-Italian border, linking Valais canton with the Valle d'Aosta, Italy. Frequented by Romans and Gauls, the route was crossed by Charlemagne, Emperor Henry IV, Frederick Barbarossa, and Napoleon I. It had been a boyhood dream of Napoleon's to outdo the heroes of antiquity, and his passage across the Great Saint Bernard in 1800 as part of the second Italian campaign, with a fully equipped army including a large number of cannon, may have eclipsed Hannibal's earlier remarkable feat. The pass was named in memory of St. Bernard of Menthon, who, around A.D. 960, established a hospice along the route and trained dogs to bring comfort to people who lost their way in snowstorms. The **Saint Gotthard Pass** (6,935 feet or 2,114 meters) in southern Switzerland is the most direct route between Milan and the Rhineland, and it has been heavily used since the Middle Ages. Encompassing large stretches of river and lake transit, the pass route skirts Lake Lucerne. A showdown over its control in the thirteenth century led to the first Swiss confederation. Other important passes in the central Alps are the Simplon, Maloja, Stelvio, Splügen, Lötschberg, Grimsel, Furka, and Arlberg Passes.

The principal crossing in the eastern Alps is the *Brenner Pass* (4,500 feet or 1,372 meters) linking the **Po Plain** and the **Bavarian Plateau** across Tirol, which straddles both sides of this important pass. Used as a trade route since antiquity, the Roman road north of Innsbruck, the capital of Tirol, branched toward Augsburg and Regensburg (but not to Munich, which is a more modern town). The strategy of Napoleon's first Italian campaign (1796–1797), which was the earliest demonstration of his military prowess, hinged on an attempt to command the exits from the Brenner Pass. The major battles against the Austrians concentrated on the quadrilateral fortresses in Lombardy—Peschiera, Verona, Mantua, and Legnago—which are all located on or near drainages that find their way back to the Brenner. *Thurn Pass* (4,175 feet or 1,272 meters), in the Kitzbühel Alps of western Austria, permitted a relatively easy crossing between Tirol and Salzburg. *Semmering Pass* (3,215 feet or 980 meters) lies along the principal connecting route between Venice and the **Vienna Basin.** Crossing a lower part of the eastern Alps and making use of longitudinal (east-west) valleys, this route was relatively easy, though somewhat long.

Further Reading: Griffith Taylor, "Trento to the Reschen Pass: A Cultural Traverse of the Adige Corridor," *Geographical Review* 30 (1940), pp. 215–237.

ALTIPLANO (BOLIVIAN)

The highlands of the **Andes** attain their greatest width, at approximately 40 miles or 64 kilometers, near latitude 18° S, between Arica on the Pacific Coast and Santa Cruz on the eastern plains. An extensive series of elevated intermontane basins between the Cordillera Occidental and the Cordillera Oriental form the Bolivian Altiplano. The Altiplano is not a single continuous plateau surface, as it is sometimes portrayed, but consists of a number of separate basins at different levels, divided by mountain spurs. The Altiplano is ringed with raised benches and floored with the sediments of shrunken or extinct lakes, testimony to wetter conditions during the Pleistocene epoch.

Most of the population of Bolivia clusters at the humid northern end of the Altiplano, around Lake Titicaca or in basins and valleys of the Cordillera Oriental. Even though Lake Titicaca has an elevation of 12,507 feet (3,812 meters) above sea level, making it the highest large lake in the world, temperatures do not drop as much as one might expect at night or in winter, due to the moderating effects of the marine influence. As a result, maize (corn) and wheat can be cultivated successfully along the lake's margins. A population concentrated in the Titicaca basin gave rise to an ancient civilization whose temple ruins can be seen on the promontories and islands of the lake. The conquest of this densely settled agricultural district was one of the first steps in the expansion of the Inca Empire in the century before the Spanish Conquest. The legendary creation of the first Inca by the sun-god around A.D. 1200 was believed to have occurred on an island (the Island of the Sun) in Lake Titicaca. The early Incas left the Altiplano and wandered northward, looking for suitable agricultural lands, eventually settling in the valley of Cuzco, reportedly due to its excellent agricultural soils. This central place—the name of which meant Navel of the World in the native language of the Incas, Quechua—became the royal capital and cultural hearth of an empire that eventually stretched from southern Colombia to central Chile, incorporating a territory spatially equivalent to the Roman Empire from Britain to Persia.

The establishment of Spanish control in the Titicaca basin did not greatly alter the subsistence patterns or the rhythms of life of the Indians, who yet today represent the vast majority of the population. The international boundary between Bolivia and Peru, which transects this densely settled agricultural district, has little meaning for the local people, a fact that shows how little external political forms have influenced ancient ways. Even the Incas had difficulty imposing their tongue on the local population, and the native language of the Titicaca area, Aymra, has experienced something of a comeback.

The world's highest large city, La Paz, is the administrative capital and commercial center of Bolivia. It is literally located in the Altiplano rather than on it. The site of the city is a chasm cut by headward erosion of an Amazon River tributary, the Río La Paz, as it extended westward from the cordillera out onto the Altiplano. At an elevation of 12,000 feet (3,658 meters) above sea level, the city lies 1,400 feet (427 meters) below the rim of the Altiplano. The Indians shunned this inhospitable trench, but the Spaniards chose it as the site of a city due to its accessibility to the colonial route from Lima to the silver mines of Potosí, which crossed Lake Titicaca on the southwest side, passing across the Altiplano very near the chasm. The sunken valley offered shelter from the winds, though cramped space and rarefied air have made this a difficult location for a capital city. Several large salt flats or *salars* can be found on the Altiplano, such as the Salar de Uyani and the Salar de Coinasa, but these are not generally well inhabited.

Its connection to the fabulous silver mines of Potosí gave the Bolivian Altiplano major historical importance. It has been estimated that from the time that silver deposits were first discovered by the Spanish in 1544 to the beginning of the seventeenth century, about half of all the silver produced in the world came out of the Bolivian peak of Cerro Rico, with Potosí at its base. The "royal fifth" that was taken by the Spanish treasury played a crucial role in the monetary and economic history of western Europe.

AMAZON BASIN

Stretching almost 4,000 miles (6,437 kilometers) from its headwaters as an icy rivulet in the Andes Mountains of southern Peru to its fifty-mile-wide outlet on the Atlantic Ocean, the Amazon River is truly a river of superlatives. Though not the longest river in the world (the Nile is longer), it carries more water in its channel than any other river—in fact, more than the combined flow of the next eight largest rivers. At Óbidos, in the lower valley, the river carries ten times the volume of water that flows past Vicksburg, in the lower **Mississippi River Valley.** Draining a territory almost as large as the 48 contiguous U.S. states, the Amazon is the only river in the world to drain large portions of both hemispheres. The large discharge of the river compared to other rivers is explained by its equatorial location: For most of its length, the Amazon's course approximately parallels the equator (with the main channel lying a little to the south), and its broad drainage basin is the convergence zone between the moisture-laden northeast and southeast trade winds. This produces a general tendency for lifting in the atmosphere, which combines with convectional heating due to the high sun to produce an abundance of precipitation year round, without the seasonal aridity that prevails on the margins of the Tropics.

The vast Amazonian region is therefore home to the largest tropical rain forest (*selva*) in the world, with an almost inconceivable biotic diversity. Though appearing monotonous from the air, the forest in many places contains more than 100 species of trees in one square mile, and the number of species of birds, fish, amphibians, reptiles, and most of all insects, is astounding. Nineteenth-century naturalist Henry Walter Bates discovered no less than 14,712 species in the region, of which 8,000 were new to science. Tropical rain forests—of which the Amazon basin is the largest unit—occupy only six percent of the world's land surface but are believed to contain more than half of the earth's plant and animal species. The Amazon basin alone accounts for 30 percent of the world's 9,040 bird species. The number of butterfly species boggles the mind: In the Río Madre de Dios drainage in southeastern Peru, researchers have identified 1,209 butterfly species in a single hectare, about 2.5 acres (Wilson, 1992). Surprisingly, there are few large land animals in Amazonia compared with the forests of Africa.

The Amazon River begins in northern Peru, at the junction of two northeast-flowing streams, the Ucayali and the Marañón. At this point the river is a sluggish, lowland stream, with an extremely low gradient. As the river passes Iquitos, a major town of the upper valley and a center of navigation for oceangoing vessels with a draft of less than fourteen tons (even though it is 2,300 miles, or 3,701 kilometers, from the sea), the river turns east and enters Brazilian territory, picking up a number of longer tributaries, especially from the south. Between the Brazilian border and the influx of the Río Negro, the river meanders across a vast floodplain 50 miles (80 kilometers) wide with an intricate network of channels, oxbow lakes, and islands, and appropriately the river takes on a different name here: Solimões (maze). Below Manaus (which is actually located on the Río

Negro just above the Amazon), the wide valley narrows until at Óbidos and Santarém river bluffs conspicuously border the floodplain, representing tabular remains of younger sedimentary formations that overlie the crystalline **Guiana Highlands.** Below the influx of the Xingu, the valley broadens again until it reaches the Atlantic Ocean, branching around the Switzerland-sized island of Marajó. Because of the gradual submergence of the coast in eastern Brazil, the Amazon is embayed. The strong currents and tides of the Atlantic sweep the yellow, silt-laden waters of the Amazon out to sea for hundreds of miles and along the coast as far as the Guianas, but prevent the creation of a true delta. Located on the southern distributary, the Pará River, just below the influx of the Tocantins River is Belém (Bethlehem), the major entrepôt and gateway to the Amazonian region.

The first European to sight the Amazon was the Spanish commander Vicente Yáñez Pinzón, who had earlier been in charge of Columbus's *Niña.* Pinzón explored the river's lower part and was the first to experience the awesome power of the tidal bore called the *pororoca* (big roar), which travels as far as 500 miles (800 kilometers) upstream. Real exploration began with the voyage down the river from the Napo by the Spanish explorer Francisco de Orellana in 1540–1541. He is credited with naming the river after his fanciful description of female warriors seen along the banks, or it has been suggested as a result of linguistic confusion when an indigene used the native term, *amassona* (boat destroyer), probably referring to the dangerous tidal bores. Early Portuguese explorers gave the name O Rio Mar, the River Sea, to the vast complex of waterways that constitute the basin.

Though most of the valley lay to the west of the line agreed upon between the Spanish and Portuguese powers and confirmed by the pope and was therefore Spain's by right, the 1637–1638 explorations of the Portuguese Pedro Teixeira, in conjunction with the wanderings of the *bandeirantes* fanning out from São Paulo into the backcountry at about the same time, brought most of the basin into legal, if not always effective, Portuguese occupation.

Settlement remained sparse throughout much of the nineteenth century, when naturalists and scientists traversed the region in pursuit of knowledge and samples to send back home. Among the large group of scientific travelers were Charles Darwin, Alfred Russel Wallace, Louis Agassiz, and Henry Walter Bates. Although the great naturalist and geographer Humboldt did not travel in the valley (he was more interested in climbing the peaks of the Andes), he did discover the waterway that links the two great river systems of northern South America: the Casiquiare River, which joins the upper Orinoco to the Amazon via the Río Negro. The Amazon was mostly left to scattered native tribes of the Tupi-Guaraní linguistic stock, who gave colorful names to its numerous tributaries and subtributaries. One of the major obstacles to settlement was that although the main stem of the river was navigable thousands of miles into the interior, major tributaries were blocked by a series of rapids and cascades where the rivers came off the crystalline uplands of the Brazilian and Guiana Highlands.

In the 1850s regular navigation on the Amazon was authorized by Emperor Dom Pedro II. After the American Civil War a colony of Confederates moved to the Santarém region of Brazil, and as the country did not outlaw slave-owning until 1886, the colony established plantations and grew cotton for the export market. Though steamboats plied the waters of the Amazon after 1866 and made regular stops at the Santarém colony to pick up small amounts of cotton for distant markets and to deliver imported merchandise, it was the collection of wild rubber in the upper valley in the late nineteenth and early twentieth centuries that was to result in a brief boom in Amazonia. Manaus became the chief entrepôt of the rubber industry, boasting its own opulent opera house. After 1912, the rubber market was captured by the newer, more productive Southeast Asian plantations, which had got their start with imported Amazonian seed. Later experimental plantations operated by the Ford Company (the U.S. automobile manufacturer) at Fordlandia and Belterra, along the Tapajós River, failed as a result of leaf blight.

Renewed interest in scientific exploration at the turn of the century led Theodore Roosevelt to travel in rough fashion down an isolated and uncharted tributary of the Amazon, the Rio da Dúvida (River of Doubt)—the Rio Roosevelt on today's maps. Accompanying Roosevelt on this six-month expedition was a rising star of the Brazilian political imagination, Cândido Mariano da Silva Rondon. Rondon is most important during this time for his Strategic Telegraph Line connecting Cuibá in southern Mato Grosso to present-day Porto Velho, an engineering feat perhaps matched only by Roosevelt's nearly contemporaneous Panama Canal. Rondon, who gave his name to Brazil's western territory (now state), was responsible for projecting Brazilian settlement from the southern rimlands of the Amazon basin in the *sertão*, or backland, into the valley proper. For too long, some argued, the Brazilian population had been "scratching along the sea like crabs," a vivid but accurate description of

this peripheral settlement pattern, made by Father Vicente do Salvador, a seventeenth-century Franciscan friar who was one of Brazil's first historians. President Getúlio Vargas (governed in 1930–1945 and again in 1951–1954) was only echoing the public will in his campaign to occupy the interior in a "march to the west." Indian cultures and the natural environment receded before the inevitable onslaught of guns, gold, and asphalt. Vargas's elected successor, Kuscelino Kubitschek, continued the expansion of settlement, moving Brazil's capital from Rio de Janeiro out onto the semiarid central plateau of Goiás and creating the planned city of Brasília. The military rulers who followed Kubitschek in the 1970s and 1980s were responsible for extensive clearance of the forest and destruction to the native peoples and the environment, but they were continuing a policy whose origins went back at least a century. It is estimated that from 1978 to 1990, 105,320 square miles (272,779 square kilometers) of forest were cut in the Brazilian Amazon. Mini gold rushes sprang up everywhere like mushrooms; in 1991, there were more than 1,850 gold digs in Amazonia. Thousands of newcomers streamed into Rondônia every day along the infamous Highway BR-364, which provided the main access route. Migration peaked in 1986, when 167,000 newcomers arrived. The Belém-Brasília Highway and the Trans-Amazon Highways opened up other parts of the valley.

Much of the region in the Amazon administrative region is not species-rich rain forest but unlovely bush and squat forests. The land was cleared for soybean cultivation with the aid of tax breaks and financial incentives, turning Brazil into a major soybean exporter. But soybeans have gone the way of rubber, gold, and other primary products—downward in price—preventing long-term stability on the land. Examples of successful and nonexploitive occupancy exist in the region, as in the case of the Japanese, who colonized the eastern Amazon early in the twentieth century and have introduced intensive cultivation of Indian spice pepper and jute. Even the Japanese are struggling today, caught up in the vicissitudes of the world market, but they are often considered innovators in developing polycultural plots by making use of a variety of native nuts, oils, and woods in a sustainable, ecologically sensitive agricultural strategy.

See also: Tordesillas Line.
Further Reading: Paul A. Colinvaux, "The Past and Future Amazon," *Scientific American,* May 1989, pp. 102–108; Mac Margolis, *The Last New World: The Conquest of the Amazon Frontier,* New York: Norton, 1992; Loren McIntyre, "Amazon: The River Sea," *National Geographic,* Oct. 1972, pp. 445–494.

ANDALUSIAN LOWLAND

The air of this ancient Spanish kingdom is as redolent of history as of Mediterranean rosemary and basil. Long occupied by the Moors, who controlled parts of the Iberian Peninsula for seven centuries, the southern Spanish cities of Córdoba, Seville, and Cádiz evoke images of olive-skinned women being courted by chivalrous men amid plashing fountains in the plazas of old towns. The depression formed by the valley of the Guadalquivir River (from the Arabic *al-wadi al-kabir,* or great river) is an embayment of an ancient sea, which is evident from inspection of its funnel shape—broad along the coast and tapering toward the interior. The head of navigation today is at Seville, 50 miles (80 kilometers) from the coast. The outlet of the Great River has been choked by large amounts of sediment draining from the uplands, especially the

heavy winter runoff, which has produced extensive, largely uninhabited marshlands (Las Marismas) below Seville. The broad, fertile lowland of the Guadalquivir River and its many affluents lies to the south of the Sierra Morena range, which in turn bounds the great central plateau of Spain. In the other direction, to the south, are the foothills of yet other east-west trending sierras that stretch all the way to the Mediterranean, culminating in the snow-capped Sierra Nevada (highest peak, Mulhacén, at 11,417 feet or 3,480 meters).

The Guadalquivir depression, with a climate akin to Africa's, can be quite hot in summer. The fertile alluvial soils, with irrigation, can yield a rich harvest of olives, grapes, and sugarcane, as well as providing good pasture for horses and cattle (bulls for the corrida are bred in this region). The upland margins of the nearby sierras offer opportunities for the grazing of pigs on the mast of oak woods or for the harvesting of the thick, corky bark of the native Cork Oak for bottle stoppers.

The province of Andalusia (Andalucía, in Spanish) is one of the oldest seats of civilization in western Europe. An attractive lowland situated between two mountain ranges, the Great River's basin has been a focus of settlement and a gateway to the Iberian Peninsula since ancient times. Phoenicians occupied the region as early as the eleventh century B.C., drawn westward by the silver and lead found in the surrounding sierras. They founded coastal colonies, most notably Gadir (now Cádiz) and perhaps also the inland town of Tartessus, which is thought by some to have been named for the biblical Tarshish. Following on the heels of the Phoenicians, the ancient Greeks and Carthaginians set up colonies for trade and settlement in the region. In the third century B.C. the Romans merged all of southern Spain into the province of Bætica. The Roman Bætis (Guadalquivir River) flowed like the Rhône into a lake, the Lacus Ligustinus, before deltaic sedimentation filled it in, forming the Marismas, which were only recently brought under cultivation. Under imperial Rome, a high level of cultural achievement was attained, and the native language yielded to a form of Latin. Roman ruins in the

of orchards and vineyards *al-Andalus*. Lying between Africa and Europe, at the intersection of seaways connecting the Atlantic to the Mediterranean, the region became a major center of civilization, learning, and trade during the golden age of medieval Islam. In A.D. 900, when Paris was but a small cluster of people located on a defensive island in the Seine (see **Paris Basin**), Córdoba—the capital

Olive groves south of Seville, Spain *(photo by Jesse Walker)*.

area (for example, the bridge at Córdoba) testify to the empire's lengthy rule. Bætica contributed a number of notable statesmen to the empire, including the Emperors Trajan and Hadrian and the philosopher Seneca.

Islam also has left a noteworthy imprint on the cultural landscape. From A.D. 711 on, when Arab armies crossed the narrow **Strait of Gibraltar** and seized control of the entire Iberian Peninsula, the Moorish influence in architecture, habits, and speech penetrated deeper and lasted longer than in any other Spanish region. The Arabs called their new realm

of Moorish Spain—had a population of 500,000 and a library of 400,000 books.

The Islamic impetus was checked by the Christian reconquest (Córdoba in 1236, Grenada in 1492), but the Moorish influence and a semioriental character persist to this day. The Andalusia of both past and present is enveloped by a sharp Iberian nostalgia, well captured in the words of Arab poet Ibn Said al-Maghribi:

> From tears of remembrance,
> I know no surcease,
> What madness to leave you,
> Fair al-Andalus!

Triumphant Christianity shaped and surmounted the Arab fundament as mosques were converted to cathedrals. The Castilian impress was most conspicuous in the large estates carved by Spanish grandees out of their newly occupied domain. Some of the region's agrarian problems, including a lack of petty proprietors and a large number of tenant farmers with relatively little motivation for capital

1900 a decline set in, due to phylloxera on the vines and a drop in mining output. Today, the storied land that gave us flamenco dancing and the rules of the corrida receives agricultural subsidies from the European Union. In the 1960s and 1970s, many Andalusian men traveled to Germany, Switzerland, and France as guest workers, but this is a less attractive opportunity today, with many of the Eu-

A cork oak tree being harvested in a Mediterranean woodland, Portugal *(photo by Jesse Walker)*.

initiatives, originated from the manner in which land tenure relationships were imposed after the Christian reconquest.

Seville became the staging place for voyages of discovery and colonization in the New World. The ancient Phoenician port of Cádiz, located to one side of the outlet of the Guadalquivir to avoid silting (Marseilles has a similar location on the Rhône Delta), experienced a golden age as long as trade with the American colonies and the Philippines remained active. In contrast, the prestige of the interior city of Córdoba declined, and the long shadow of its Roman and Moorish past became as oppressive as the summer heat.

During the nineteenth century the region prospered due to the expansion of mines, new metallurgical works, and the cultivation of cereals and wines; but in

ropean economies prone to recession. The region's greatest economic asset may be its heritage, as attested to by the large number of tourists who visit its fabled cities every year.

See also: Meseta (Spanish).
Further Reading: Howard La Fay, "Andalusia: The Spirit of Spain," *National Geographic,* June 1975, pp. 833–856.

ANDES

Stretching more than 4,000 miles (6,437 kilometers) along the western edge of South America, the Andes are the longest and, on average, the highest mountain range in the world. This great mountain system parallels the west coast, extending from the southern tip of the continent at **Tierra del Fuego** to Colombia and Venezuela, along the southern rim of the Caribbean. The north end of the island of

Trinidad is considered an extension of this range. The Andes are not a single chain of mountains but rather a series of distinctive physiographic units. These units arose during the formation of a complex, faulted mountain system in fairly recent geological time, around the same time as the Alps and the Himalayas. The collision of the eastward-moving lithospheric plate underlying the Pacific only about 200 miles (322 kilometers) wide, except in Bolivia, where the **Altiplano** attains about twice that width. Though narrower than the western mountains of North America, they are considerably higher and crossed by relatively few low passes. Passes through the North American mountains can be found at elevations of six or seven thousand feet, but most of the passes over the Andes, es-

At the southern end of the Andes, the mountains form a political boundary between Chile and Argentina (*photo by Jesse Walker*).

Ocean and the westward-moving plate beneath South America has produced intensive vulcanism, faulting, and earthquake zones in this geologically unstable region. Although a relatively simple model of converging plates explains the general nature of the folded mountain system, the details of timing and structure of orogenic (mountain-building) events are complex. Much of the Andes consists of two parallel cordilleras, or mountain ranges, with a series of intermontane basins and plateaus between them. The Andes are relatively narrow, averaging pecially where they are most needed, require ascents to more than 10,000 feet (3,049 meters) above sea level.

In the southern section of the Andes the western slopes have been flooded, resulting in an indented, fjord-lined coast similar to the west coasts of Norway and British Columbia. Northward of 42° S, the single Andean range overlooks the Central Valley of Chile. Only north of 35° S do the Andes begin to exceed 10,000 feet in elevation. Near 23° S, where Argentina, Chile, and Bolivia meet, the Andean system widens to form the Altiplano, enclosed between two mountain ranges, the Cordillera Occidental and the Cordillera Oriental. In Peru the central basins are smaller but are overshadowed by the great snow-capped volcanic peaks of Chimborazo and Cotopaxi and other volcanoes that have been active in recent times. After being somewhat constricted in width in Peru and Ecuador, the Andes splay out in Colombia and Venezuela to enclose low-level basins and river valleys, including the Magdalena River valley, the Bogotá Basin, the Cauca River valley, Lake Maracaibo, and the Gulf of Venezuela.

The formidable topographic barrier of the Andes has effectively blocked exchange of people and goods between the eastern and western parts of the continent. The high civilization of the Incas in the century before the Spanish Conquest stretched out along the Andean chain from Ecuador to central Chile, incorporating the coastal lowlands to the west and inching into the forbidding jungle of the Amazon headwaters to the east.

Around A.D. 1200, the Incas were lords of a relatively minor agricultural state in the central valley around Cuzco. In 1438 the ninth Inca and first Emperor, Pachacuti, and his son, Tupa Inca, began to consolidate and extend Inca control, so that by 1520 the Inca Empire was as large and as well organized as Caesar's Rome. An ingenious system of post roads (the old Inca Road is still in use today), straw bridges (made famous by Thornton Wilder's *Bridge of San Luis Rey*), and relay teams of messengers resembling a pedestrian Pony Express tied together an imperium known as Tahuantinsuyu, the Four Quarters of the World. The terracing of slopes and construction of long-distance irrigation canals supported an intensive agriculture, adding to the surplus controlled by the Incas.

In 1532 the Spaniard Francisco Pizarro with an army of only 62 cavalrymen and 106 foot soldiers conquered the Incas by exploiting civil strife to gain allies just as Cortés had done to conquer Mexico. There is little evidence for, but considerable interest in, the idea that some Inca nobles may have withdrawn from the royal capital at Cuzco to the nearby haven of Machu Picchu, the famous "lost city" of the Inca discovered by the Yale anthropology professor Hiram Bingham in 1911. Located some 2,000 feet (610 meters) above the Urubamba River in a saddle between two pinnacles, Machu Picchu is graced with stone stairways, elaborate terraces, and an assortment of stone buildings of superior construction. The outpost had escaped the detection of the Spanish as well as later travelers, as its ruins became topped with an obscuring encrustation of jungle.

In the early nineteenth century, before the Himalayas were surveyed, it was believed that the highest peaks in the world were in the Andes. The German naturalist-geographer Alexander von Humboldt visited South America between 1799 and 1804 in the company of the French botanist Aimé Bonpland. In his quest to order the disparate facts of nature into a systematic, unified whole, Humboldt was particularly interested in the relationship between altitude and patterns of climate and vegetation. He climbed most of the way up Ecuador's highest peak, snow-covered Chimborazo (el. 20,702 feet or 6,310 meters). As Chimborazo at the time was thought to be the highest mountain in the world, Humboldt thought he had climbed higher than any previous explorer anywhere in the world. Some 30 years later, when he was still writing up the results of his South American trip, he was upset when he heard that British surveyors had climbed higher in the Himalayas. Nevertheless, the results of his Andean excursions made their way into the 30 published volumes based on his South American trip, including his celebrated five-volume study *Cosmos,* which is considered a pioneering work in modern geography. (Curiously, due to equatorial bulging caused by the greater centrifugal forces at low latitudes, Chimborazo is actually about two miles higher than Mount Everest if the peaks are measured from the center of the earth.) As a fitting conclusion to a century that had started with Humboldt's climbing of Chimborazo, in 1897 Matthias Zurbriggen and Stuart Vines first climbed the Aconcagua along the Chilean-Argentine border, at 22,835 feet (6,960 meters) the highest peak not only in the Andes but in the western hemisphere.

Further Reading: Isaiah Bowman, *The Andes of Southern Peru: Geographical Reconnaissance along the Seventy-Third Meridian,* New York: Henry Holt and Co., 1916; Harry A. Franck, *Vagabonding Down the Andes: Being the Narrative of a Journey, Chiefly Afoot, from Panama to Buenos Aires,* New York: Century Co., 1917.

ANIAN, STRAIT OF

Although a legend might have little basis in fact, it sometimes takes on a life of its own, inspiring actions and behavior that one must take into account in order to understand the breadth of historical experience. The premodern map of the Atlantic Ocean was dotted with mythical islands that might seem to matter only to a consideration of human subjectivity or parapsychology; yet no less an individual than Christopher Columbus, a genius at navigation, believed the hypothetical midoceanic island of **Antillia** would be a suitable stopping point on his western voyage and based his plans on this belief.

Early European explorers of the Americas did not know that these landmasses would turn out to be conjoined continents, as they searched for shortcuts across the Central American landbridge and through the Arctic Archipelago of northern Canada. Less well known than the search for the **Northwest Passage**— an easily navigable northern route that would permit access to the riches of the Orient—was the belief in a mythical Strait of Anian and its persistence on maps well into the eighteenth century.

The name derives from the Chinese province of Ania described by Marco Polo. A pamphlet published by Jacopo Gastaldi in 1562 contained the first mention by name of the Strait of Anian. Gastaldi cited a lost map of a contemporary Venetian geographer, Mateo Pagano, as his source of information. The first surviving map to depict the strait was the Zalterius Map, drawn a few years later, in 1566. The feature appeared regularly on world maps drawn after this time until the mid-eighteenth century.

This aquatic gateway was sought in both northern and southern approaches to the New World. A typical southern path was pursued by the Spanish captain Juan Fernández Ladrillero, best known for his voyages confirming Magellan's discovery of a strait across the southern end of South America. In 1540–1541, Ladrillero explored the west coast of Mexico, looking for but not discovering the Strait of Anian. In a deposition made in Colima, Mexico, in 1574 he stated, "[It is] certain and true that there is such a strait, and that it can be navigated." Other southern searches for the mythical shortcut looked for an extended embayment of the western Gulf Coast that would join a similar indentation of the California coastline, perhaps opening up from the Gulf of California. Given the explorers' assumptions about waterways penetrating far into the continent, it is easy to see how the belief in the mythical island of California arose.

Meanwhile, and partly driving these fruitless Spanish attempts to discover an easy way across the continent, were the activities of English and French explorers who were looking for passageways at higher latitudes. Here the search for the Strait of Anian overlapped with the pursuit of that other will-o'-the-wisp, the Northwest Passage. The Englishman Sir Humfry Gilbert in his *Discourse* (published in 1576 but written ten years earlier) adduced numerous "facts" and quoted multiple references to prove that the Strait of Anian not only existed but was practicable. Cutting through the smokescreen of the pedantic references, it seems that Gilbert believed in the strait because the Spanish did. Gilbert's publication—something of a public relations piece—was primarily used by Frobisher and others after him who were looking for a northwestern route to Cathay. A map attached to George Best's *True Discourse* of 1578, a summary of the three voyages of Frobisher along the east coast of northern Canada, showed an extremely broad "Frobussher's Straits," covering a larger area than the **Great Lakes,** being connected to a small Strait of Anian, which separated America from "Cathaia in Asia." Drake looked for the strait on his circumnavigation of the globe aboard the *Golden Hind* but did not find it (1578–1580).

The mythical strait persisted on maps well into the eighteenth century, until Vitus Bering in 1728 discovered the strait separating Asia from North America, which now bears his name. In the previous century, a Spaniard named De Fuentes (or De Fonte) claimed to have discovered the Anian passage in 1640, sailing through it to Hudson Bay, where he met a ship owned by a Mr. Gibbons of Boston, Massachusetts! Benjamin Franklin—in some ways a representative American of his day—even believed this hoax.

The story at this point follows the oft-recounted tale of the attempt to find the Northwest Passage—the one that actually exists—across the Canadian Arctic, even as it was realized that this was not the long-sought, easy route to the east. Highlights of this saga include the disappearance of Sir John Franklin's expedition in 1845, numerous later expeditions looking for Franklin, which coincidentally added to the knowledge of northern Canada, and the successful negotiation of the passageway by the Norwegian Roald Amundsen aboard the *Gjöa* in 1903–1905.

See also: Atlantic Ocean, Legendary Islands of; Magellan, Strait of.
Further Reading: J. G. Kohl, "Asia and America," American Antiquarian Society, *Proceedings,* October 1911, pp. 284–338; Sophus Ruge, *Fretum Anians,* Dresden, 1888.

ANTILLIA

By about 1350, almost all the major island groups of the Atlantic were known to the geographers and cartographers of western Europe. The Fortunate Islands of the Carthaginians and the Romans had been rediscovered and renamed the **Canary Islands,** while the nearby archipelago known to the Romans as the Purple Islands (Insulae Purpurariae) had been rediscovered as the **Madeiras.** Farthest from the mainland, the **Azores** may not have been known to the ancients; included on a 1351 map, the islands were not visited and settled until early the following century, when Portuguese mariners first landed on them.

In the early 1400s a legendary island west of the Azores began to appear on the *mappa mundi:* Antillia. A large, rectangular island, with its long axis oriented north-south, Antillia became a regular feature of maps for the next century and a half, a period roughly coinciding with the great Age of Discovery. Columbus stated in his book on the history and life of his father that the island of Antillia was located two hundred leagues (686 nautical miles) due west of the Canaries and the Azores. The respected cartographer Martin Behaim portrayed on his famous 1492 globe numerous scattered islands stretching from Cipangu (Japan), itself well off the coast of East Asia, along the Tropic of Cancer as far as Antillia and the well-known archipelagoes of the eastern Atlantic. Columbus probably did not see this globe before his first voyage in 1492, but he was familiar with Behaim's work, which displayed the geographical knowledge current at that time. Working with a restricted circumference of the earth by about 25 percent and deceived by the Florentine cosmographer Toscanelli dal Pozzo, who also subscribed to a "small earth" or "narrow Atlantic" hypothesis, Columbus made the obvious yet radical inference that the scattered islands of the Atlantic could be used as stepping-stones and way stations along the route to the Indies. Columbus thus believed that Antillia lay in the western Atlantic and could be used as a stopping point at midvoyage in crossing the western ocean. Though the island proved a phantom, it was by such imaginary geographies that the explorers of the dark Atlantic were drawn westward.

The basis of the legend takes us back to the medieval Catholic world of Iberia, when the Moorish infidels were on the point of overrunning Spain and Portugal. In A.D. 734, an archbishop from Porto in Portugal, along with six other bishops, sailed far out into the Atlantic and discovered and settled on an island where seven cities were founded—one for each bishop. In 1414 a ship from Spain was blown off course and approached very near this island, or so it was reported to geographers and cosmographers, who fixed it on their maps beginning with the 1424 nautical map of Zuane Pizzigano of Venice. The curious symmetrical shape of the island, with its regular, quadrilateral shape and seven evenly-spaced trilobed coastal indentations (one for each bishop's city), attracts the eye as one peruses European maps of the Atlantic during the next century and a half. Behaim's 1492 globe contained an annotation describing the emigrating bishops and the founding of the Sete Cidades, or Seven Cities, on a distant island. The Benincasa map of 1470 is representative of the large number of maps that continued to show this legendary island during this time. Curiously shaped like a miniature Portugal, Antillia lies due west of the Azores and well away from the recognized archipelagos of the eastern Atlantic. It is the largest island in a group including Saluaga to its north, another rectangular island with a regularly notched coast but smaller; and further north the two small islands of Taumar and Ymana. The seven cities of the interior are even named: Ansalli, Ansodi, Anhuib, Ansesseli, Ansolli, Aira, and Con (five of the seven begin with "An"). No one has explained the mystery of these place-names, though the name of the large island is generally regarded as a fusion of Portuguese *ante* (opposite) and *ilha* (island)—opposite or opposing island. Therefore, Antillia can be taken to mean an island lying opposite the European continent and in proximity to another continent, presumably Asia.

This legendary feature played its most important role in history in a letter received by Columbus around 1481, written by Toscanelli dal Pozzo, recommending to Columbus that he consider Antillia as a possible stopover and resting place on any trans-Atlantic voyage.

Antillia persisted on world maps throughout the sixteenth century. It can be found on Mercator's famous 1569 map, the first to use his famous projection, and on the 1587 Ortelius map, though by this time cartographers had moved the island farther south and farther out to sea and reduced it in size, as if to hedge their information. Not long after this the Seven Cities of Antillia disappeared from the map, retained only in a local name on St. Michael island in the Azores, where the name Sete Cidades refers to seven interior villages surrounding twin lakes occupying the crater of an extinct volcano. After European discovery of the New World, the legendary island's name was transferred to the islands of the West Indies, which the Dutch and French began to refer to as the Antilles. Some respected authors have maintained that the island of Antillia was not a legendary island at all but a record of pre-Columbian contact between Europe and the Americas (see Further Reading). Antillia was, according to this belief, none other than the large Caribbean island of Cuba.

Further Reading: William H. Babcock, *Legendary Islands of the Atlantic: A Study in Medieval Geography,* American Geographical Society Research Series, no. 8, New York: American Geographical Society, 1922; Donald S. Johnson, *Phantom Islands of the Atlantic: The Legends of Seven Lands that Never Were,* New York: Walker and Co., 1994.

ANTONINE WALL

Emperor Antoninus Pius (ruled A.D. 138–161) reoccupied Roman positions established by Agricola, and built between 140–142 a turf wall about 36 miles (58 kilometers) long, connecting the Firths of Forth and Clyde in the **Scottish Lowlands.** This forward position represented an advance on that of Antoninus's predecessor Hadrian, who had built his defensive perimeter, partly in stone, across the Tyne-Solway gap in northern England.

Antoninus modified the Hadrianic manner in a number of ways, not just in doing without stone. A large ditch was dug in front about 12 feet (3.6 meters) deep and 40 feet (12.2 meters) wide, but the rearward earthworks of the southern wall's Vallum—so impressive in conception but without the dramatic relief of the curtain wall—was absent. Like Hadrian's line, Antoninus's included a military road on its southern side and numerous associated forts. The forts were smaller and more closely spaced than Hadrian's, allowing flexible movement of troops from smaller garrisons. No turrets are apparent today, and only a single structure similar to the mile-castles of **Hadrian's Wall** is known to have existed in this wall. Antoninus's wall, like Hadrian's, was not a simple line for defensive attack. Both served more to control access to a militarized zone. Strategically, the line across the Scottish isthmus could be easily outflanked. In the east, Fife had to be practically encircled to prevent its use as a springboard to attack the Roman position. To the west, the southern bank of the Clyde estuary had to be strengthened. The fortified approach road through the pass of Darvel was the result of the need to occupy the Ayrshire coast, whence free Kintyre was only a short distance away. To give an example of the scale of occupation in Scotland and the extent of Roman commitment: In response to alarms during this period, the largest fort and pivot of activity, Newstead, received a cavalry garrison 1,000 strong (an *ala*). These regiments were even more valuable than legions, and their use suggests intense military activity in the north.

But the Romans knew, as they would have put it, that they were holding a wolf by the ears. The revolt of A.D. 155–158 and subsequent disturbances led them to withdraw to Hadrian's Wall along the Tyne. After A.D. 185 the Romans did not again occupy the northern line, and Antonine's Wall was abandoned. The forces of wind and water have removed any trace of this earthen bulwark, the northernmost limit of Roman rule.

See also: Hadrian's Wall.
Further Reading: I. A. Richmond, *Roman Britain,* 2d ed., Harmondsworth, Middlesex, England: Penguin, 1963 (orig. ed. 1955).

APENNINE MOUNTAINS

The backbone of Italy, this mountain chain has contributed to the regional diversity of the peninsula as well as to the political fragmentation of the Italian states, although it is the sole cause of neither.

The mountains are composed of sedimentary beds, primarily of limestone, that formerly occupied the ancient Tethys Basin (roughly corresponding to today's **Mediterranean Sea**), which were squeezed upward between the African Shield and the **Hercynian Uplands** of central Europe. The folds and fractures are geologically young, and as a result, erosion has not had enough time to sculpt the landscape into isolated peaks and sharp needles, but instead numerous upland basins, plateaus, and gorges prevail. Unlike the Alps, the Apennines (in Italian, Appennino) were not glaciated in Pleistocene times except in a few places, and therefore they do not possess the characteristic glacial features seen in the more elevated mountains to the north. The occurrence of earthquakes in this range even today, especially at the southern end, indicates that the forces of buckling and breaking have not entirely subsided.

There is a marked contrast between the eastern and western slopes of the range. To the east, the slopes are more gentle and are drained by a large number of unimportant streams flowing only a short distance to the Adriatic. The coastal plain on this side is either absent or extremely narrow, and combined with the monotonously straight coastline largely devoid of sheltered bays, it has not favored the development of towns and ports. On the western side, the relief tends to be somewhat chaotic, with undulating hills, plateaus that sometimes reach mountain stature, intermontane basins, and alluvial valleys. Only a few river systems exist, and they are extensively developed (Arno and Tiber). They drain west to the sea across a diverse region known as the Antiapennines, a name that is not geologically descriptive but merely refers to a diversity of terrain types, including the Tuscan Hills south of the Arno, the Maremma along the lower course of the Arno, and several extinct volcanic areas in Tuscany and around Rome.

The Apennines present a bewildering variety of landscapes. In the north, the mountains, which along most of their length lie near the east coast, curve across the peninsula, approaching the Ligurian shore in a sheer wall. The precipitous yet narrow screen that lies behind Genoa effectively separates but does not seal off the port from the major hinterland of the **Po Plain.** The most spectacular mountain scenery in this northern section comprising the Ligurian and the Tusco-Emilian Apennines is the metamorphosed limestone of the Apuan Alps, which rise in dazzling whiteness from the coastal plain, furnishing along its lower slopes the famous marbles of Massa and Carrara.

In the central Apennines the highest elevations of the range are attained, as limestone begins to predominate. Lying along the east coast, the mountains are separated from the sea by only a thin coastal strip, which has precluded major port or town development. From north to south, a series of characteristic landscapes succeed one another, from the karst (limestone) plateaus of the Marches in Umbria to the fortress-like features of Abruzzi. The highest elevations are obtained in this section in the massively uplifted Gran Sasso group (9,560 feet or 2,914 meters), which tower above the Adriatic foothills and show evidence of glaciation. The major features of relief in this central section are a series of roughly aligned horsts trending northwest-southeast, separated by intervening basins, which are sufficiently broad and verdant in places to have attracted significant settlement, such as in the green hollows of Aquila, Sulmona, and Avezanno.

In the south, the Apennines swing once more toward the west coast. Limestone maintains its dominance in the landscape until the Neapolitan and Lucanian Apennines, where argillo-schistose corridors lie athwart squarish limestone blocks. In the far south, in the Calabrian Apennines, a granitic toe protrudes from the limestone boot of Italy.

The name of the range may have been derived from the Celtic *pen* (equivalent to the Brythonic hill), but the Romans referred to the Pænine or Punic Mountains because Hannibal, the Carthaginian general, crossed these mountains in his invasion of Italy. The terrain and the soils of the Apennines are particularly subject to erosion due to the Mediterranean climate's wet winter conditions and to prolonged deforestation, which was already well advanced in ancient times. These two factors have been primary contributors to siltation, landslides (*frane*), and accelerated erosion. In the northern Apennines,

certain shales (*argille scagliosi*) are especially prone to gullying, known locally as *calanchi*. In the central Abruzzi section, a highly permeable limestone markedly improves the hydrologic regimes of rivers, reducing the high variability of streamflow and the frequency of flooding.

Many of the examples of deleterious human impact on the physical environment cited in what is considered the first systematic treatment of the subject (George Perkins Marsh's *Man and Nature, Or Physical Geography as Modified by Human Action,* 1864) came from the Mediterranean basin and Italy in particular, as Marsh served for a period as the U.S. minister to Italy. Ellsworth Huntington, an early twentieth-century American geographer whose name has been tarred by the environmental determinist label, used Italian examples similarly, to illustrate his thesis of the cultural debt to the physical environment. Although a number of geographic factors might be suggested as explanations for the tardy creation of a unified Italian nation-state, the distinctiveness of Italian identity and the variety of Italy's cultural landscapes cannot be traced directly back to the physical geography. For example, one might be tempted to consider the Apennines as a topographic obstacle that long isolated the Italian peoples and prevented (or at least delayed) their political unification. However, this would not be true, because numerous routes crossed the comparatively low elevations of the Apennines, even in imperial Roman times. The most important Roman road linking the Eternal City to the Po Valley was the Via Flaminia, which ran northeast past Perugia, across the watershed at Scheggia Pass in the direction of Rimini, where it joined a northwest-running segment leading past Bologna to the Po at Piacenza. The Appian Way (running southward) and the Salarian and Valerian Ways (both running east to the Adriatic) also crossed the Apennines. Railroad tunnels and highway passes today follow lines of accessibility already established in ancient times.

Further Reading: D. S. Walker, *The Mediterranean Lands,* London: Methuen, 1960.

APPALACHIAN PIEDMONT

The Appalachians are not a single, continuous mountain range but rather con-

Geologically, the Piedmont consists mostly of old metamorphic rocks with complex structures truncated at the surface, so that there is little evidence of rock structure in the landforms, which are characteristically rolling hill lands of only moderate relief. Steep slopes can be found in the valley sides of streams that are deeply incised into the plateau surface. The Piedmont gradually levels out to the

Prosperous farms in the Amish country of the Lancaster Plain, southeastern Pennsylvania *(photo by Jesse Walker).*

tain four major regions: the Piedmont Plateau; the **Blue Ridge;** the Ridge and Valley; and the Appalachian Plateau (also known as the Cumberlands or the Alleghenies). The easternmost part of the Appalachians consists of the Piedmont Plateau, extending almost 1,000 miles (1,609 kilometers) from southernmost New York to Alabama, where the region wraps around to the west. To the south, where the region is widest, elevations range from 500 feet (152 meters) at the **Fall Line** to about 1,000 feet (305 meters) at the foot of the western mountains.

north, with elevations in Pennsylvania and New Jersey of between 100 and 500 feet (30 and 152 meters).

In addition to igneous and metamorphic rocks, basins of unmetamorphosed sedimentary rocks that have been downfaulted into older crystalline formations make for more fertile soils and agricultural concentration in the Newark Basin, the Gettysburg Basin, the Culpepper Basin, and the Richmond Basin, all named after nearby towns. In the southeastern part of the region, from southern Virginia to Georgia, the less intensively metamorphosed slate that composes the Carolina slate belt predominates. Somewhat more prone to erosion than neighboring formations, the slate beds form slightly lower ground and wider valleys, which provide excellent reservoir sites, such as that on the Saluda River above Columbia, South Carolina, and on the Savannah River above Augusta, Georgia.

The eastern band of the Appalachians was a fertile, inviting land. In its northern parts, the rolling Piedmont is quite literally at the back door of major seaboard settlements like Philadelphia and Baltimore, located on or near the Fall Line, while further south where the coastal plain broadens, the Piedmont was farther removed from early colonists (nevertheless, it, too, was occupied by the time of the American Revolution). In the Middle Colonies the Piedmont represented the first agricultural frontier for westering settlers who had initially only secured footholds (perhaps better described as toeholds) at limited tidewater sites. From the **Chesapeake Bay** area came yeoman farmers and freed indentured servants to claim lands in the backcountry. The Blue Ridge was a formidable barrier, and after 1763 British imperial edict forbade settlement farther west, though the Shenandoah region was densely settled by the time of the American Revolution. The colony of Pennsylvania—"Penn's woods"—was particularly well advantaged by fertile lands on the Piedmont in the area surrounding Philadelphia. The Quaker colony lost some of its more purely religious purpose of providing a haven for persecuted English Protestant groups as it attracted an increasingly diverse group of non-Anglo immigrants, including continental Europeans. Scotch-Irish, Welsh, Germans of a variety of faiths, and many other national groups followed the southwest-trending Piedmont as far as the Carolinas and Georgia, giving the interior parts of these deep southern states a population noticeably different in composition from that of the coastal areas.

With the widespread adoption of Eli Whitney's cotton gin, the upland or short-fiber variety of cotton could now be cultivated at interior locations, where it could not have been grown previously due to the labor bottleneck at harvest time, caused by the difficulty of separating seeds from the tightly meshed lint or fiber. The first signs of the emerging cotton belt were on the interior coastal plain in eastern Georgia and west-central South Carolina and on adjoining land of the Piedmont. From there cotton spread north into North Carolina and southern Virginia, at which point further extension was restricted by the short growing season.

The cotton belt was never a single, continuous region but rather consisted of a number of distinct islands of specialization, which were often widely separated and did not constitute the majority of farmland even in the deep South. The Georgia-Carolinas region was perhaps the most geographically extensive tract of cotton-growing land in the antebellum South, although by the time of the Civil War, western and frontier areas in Mississippi (the Natchez District), Louisiana (the Baton Rouge–St. Francisville area), and eastern and southern Texas were beginning to overtake the eastern region.

The distinctive red-yellow soils of the southern Piedmont, derived from the deep weathering of granite and gneiss, are inherently quite fertile, but because of the high clay content they are prone to gullying and erosion. A combination of factors besides depleted soils and erosion contributed to the decline of cotton farming on the Piedmont in the post–World War II period. Many faulted the federal allotment program, which allowed farmers to cultivate only a restricted acreage that generally was too small to permit the profitable adoption of the latest equipment. In many cases, older and risk-averse farmers, equipment dealers, and processors just didn't want to spend the money on the unproven technology of mechanical cotton pickers and high-capacity ginning equipment. As western regions modernized and mechanized, farmers in the east switched to livestock or poultry, planted peach orchards, or began to grow trees as a tax writeoff. One of the key regions in the Old South had cast off its agrarian skin by the 1970s and increasingly sought its future in education, research, and high technology, as exemplified in North Carolina's Research Triangle.

Further Reading: Merle C. Prunty and Charles S. Aiken, "The Demise of the Piedmont Cotton Region," *Annals of the Association of American Geographers* 62 (1972), pp. 283–306.

AQUITAINE BASIN

The sedimentary basin drained by the Garonne River and its numerous tributaries, located west of the **Massif Central** and north of the **Pyrenees,** is the second largest lowland in France. It represents an extension of the belted **North European Plain** southwestward from the **Paris Basin.**

Ancient basement rocks dip to the south here and are covered by thousands of feet of younger sedimentary formations, including limestone that contributes to the soil's fertility. Recent sediments sluiced out of the Pyrenees fill the alluvial valleys and terraces of the lower courses of the Garonne and the Dordogne, as well as the banks of the Gironde estuary, which was formed by the junction of these two major rivers

just below Bordeaux. The conspicuous fan-shaped drainage pattern of the upper Garonne between Pau and Toulouse can be observed easily on atlas maps of France. Toulouse, the capital of the medieval province of **Languedoc,** lies along the upper Garonne and belongs, in the strict geographic sense, to the Basin of Aquitaine. A landscape of coastal lagoons, sand spits, and dune plains extends far inland, from Pointe de Grave at the mouth of the Gironde to the seaside resort town of Biarritz near the Spanish border. This coastal area, unimaginatively named Les Landes, is the locale—albeit somewhat accidentally—of the world's first large-scale conservation project. Napoleon planted a belt of pine trees in this sparsely populated region, with an eye toward ensuring a steady supply of the resins and tars he needed to keep his navy seaworthy. Today, this is the largest pine forest in western Europe, and it provides recreational opportunities as well as timber resources.

Natural routes connect the Basin to nearby physiographic units. The wide, sweeping corridor of the Carcassonne Gateway provides access in the direction of the Mediterranean. To the north, the **Poitou Gateway** passes through low massifs to connect the region to the Loire Valley and the Paris Basin. To the southwest, a strip of lowland at the western end of the Pyrenees allows passage into north-central Spain.

Julius Caesar conquered the local Aquitani tribes, an Iberian people occupying southwestern Gaul who may have been ancestors of the Basques. Under Augustus the province of Aquitani (Land of Waters, referring to the long seacoast and many rivers) extended north as far as the Loire. Bordeaux was a flourishing center already during the Roman period when it was known as Burdigala. Following the decline of Rome, the region was successively overrun by the Visigoths, the Arabs (briefly), and the Franks, before Charlemagne made it a secure part of his kingdom. The separation of Gascony for a time during the Middle Ages resulted in the appellation Aquitaine being applied only to the northern part of this historic province. This region acceded to England upon the marriage of Eleanor of Aquitaine to Henry II, Duke of Normandy, after he became king of England in 1154. Considering that the duchy of Aquitaine was one of the most powerful states in western Europe at the time, it is not surprising that the French tried to reclaim it, which they finally accomplished at the end of the Hundred Years War (1337–1453), after three hundred years of English rule. So much destruction of peasant life had occurred in this densely settled agricultural district as a result of the Hundred Years War that a folk saying in the Aquitaine Basin held that "the forests came back to France with the English." With the addition of Normandy and Aquitaine, and the access to the Atlantic that they afforded (England retained only the small coastal **Channel Islands**), France approximated its present-day boundaries. Only the Burgundy-controlled southeast remained to be incorporated into the French royal domain, and that would be done in short order.

ARDENNES, FOREST OF

This highly dissected tableland covering southeastern Belgium, a northern *département* of France, and much of the grand duchy of Luxembourg was the focus of important early industrial developments as well as the scene of major military engagements.

A natural borderland between French and Germanic realms, the Ardennes Forest rises to 1,600–2,300 feet (488–701 meters) in a series of old folded Paleozoic formations oriented along a northeast–southwest axis. The tableland is old, mature, and well planed, and constitutes a part of the **Hercynian Uplands,** which form a belt across the center of western Europe. The topography of the Ardennes is continued to the east by the Eifel plateau of Germany. The Latin name Arduenna Silva was derived from the Celtic *ard* (hilly or high).

The greater portion of this landform region is located in southeastern Belgium, a zone of uplands that contrasts markedly with the lowland districts of central and northern Belgium. The plateau is rugged enough so that the region traditionally has been considered one of difficult passage and a dead end. Most of the cities of the region are located along its margins or in the lowland corridor of the Meuse, an industrial valley.

The severity of the higher elevations is suggested by the near continental climate—at Bastogne, one of the few towns on the plateau, there are 145 days of frost a year. Most of the Ardennes is covered with spruce and beech woods, but peat-covered moorlands extend into shallow depressions called *fagnes*. The scattered population in the uplands is not very prosperous, but neither are they poor, as the pastoral, French-speaking Walloons have learned since the end of the nineteenth century to improve the soil and maintain the land as good pasture and meadow.

The most significant economic activity takes place in the cities, in the entrenched valleys that cross the plateau. A string of cities in the Sambre-Meuse corridor form a "black country"—an old industrial landscape based on exploiting the nearby Belgian coal fields. The Meuse River drains north from France through a narrow gorge before reaching Namur in Belgium, whence it flows eastward in a wide valley toward the Liege industrial concentration. The Sambre joins the Meuse, draining from the west at Namur. The east-west oriented Sambre-Meuse corridor is a 100-mile-long contact zone between the plateau and the central plain, with outcroppings of limestone and rich but buried coal seams.

Small-scale, traditional iron smelters had long made use of local iron-ore deposits and charcoal from the Ardennes Forest before modern development took place. (The region's long history in Europe is suggested by the fact that Shakespeare set the idyllic retreat of his play *As You Like It* in the Forest of Arden—a slightly disguised reference to the Belgian Ardennes, which the English bard would have counted on the better-educated members of his audience to recognize.) The first blast furnaces and large-scale metallurgy using steam on the continent operated in the district with the help of English technicians from the 1820s on. Later French and German industrial development was often directly based on these Belgian experiments.

The Ardennes also has been the scene of bitter fighting in many of the major wars of the past two centuries. The town of Sedan in the French Ardennes gained notoriety (at least among the French) as the result of two disastrous defeats in 1815 and 1870, the latter leading to the demise of Napoleon III and the end of the Third Empire. During World War I, the Battles of the Ardennes and of the Argonne (a southern extension of the Ardennes, in France) took place in this region, with U.S. General Pershing launching an offensive at the end of the war that took him from a line south and east of the Argonne to Sedan in the Meuse Valley before the armistice in 1918.

During World War II the Germans took the Meuse Valley early, but it was re-occupied by the Allies in September 1944, following the D-Day invasion of Normandy. Hitler's last counteroffensive—an act of sheer desperation—focused on the relatively unprotected Ardennes district in southeastern Belgium. This was the famous Battle of the Bulge (Dec. 1944–Jan. 1945). An 80-mile (129-kilometer) front centered around Bastogne was defended by outnumbered U.S. troops in the fog and snow of the Belgian winter. The battle was so called because initial Nazi successes created a large bulge in the Allied lines that threatened to engulf the troops. After six weeks of difficult fighting, U.S. troops drove the Germans back, but at a tremendous cost of life. The 77,000 Allied casualties represented the largest American loss on any battlefield in history, including Gettysburg. Winston Churchill called this battle "the greatest American battle of the Second World War."

See also: Armorican Massif; Rhenish Uplands.
Further Reading: David H. Lippman, "Bastogne Belatedly Besieged," *Military History,* Dec. 1994, pp. 30–37.

ARMORICAN MASSIF

These upland plateaus composed of ancient crystalline rock extend west from the **Paris Basin** in the historic provinces of Brittany and Normandy. The Precambrian and Paleozoic formations were strongly folded and metamorphosed to produce a rigid massif, whose general structure of undulating hills and broad intervening valleys trends east-west in the northern section (Cotentin or Normandy Peninsula) but diverges to the southeast in the southern section. The **Channel Islands** are emergent parts of the submerged portion of this massif.

The two largest peninsulas of western France jut out into the Atlantic like the jaws of an enormous beast at a place where the ocean meets the **English Channel**—a key to their strategic importance. The coastline is dominated by rocky cliffs, especially in Brittany, but along the northern coast of Normandy a broadly embayed stretch of shore between Cherbourg and Le Havre affords sandy beaches and a strip of coastal plain that were crucial to the D-Day (6 June 1944) landings by the Allies.

A distinctive *bocage,* or hedgerow landscape, prevails here, with live hedges surmounting earthen banks and surrounding pastoral plots. The settlement pattern is one of isolated homesteads in a checkered landscape of woods, copses, orchards, and fields, rather than nucleated settlement in the form of small villages and towns, except along the coast, which has long been a focus of tourists and travelers. The main cities of Normandy and Brittany lie outside the bocage of the Armorican Massif, along the lower Seine (Rouen and Le Havre are the major Norman cities) and lower Loire (Nantes is the most important city in Brittany). Besides accessibility and settlement, the region is distinguished from the rest of France by language: Breton, a Celtic tongue related to Welsh, is spoken in Brittany. The name of this colorful region, where traditional dress, clothing, music, and speech live on, was derived from that of the fifth-century British tribes who fled there from the Saxon invaders of southern England after the collapse of the Roman Empire.

Normandy and Brittany together comprised the northwestern part of the Roman province of Gallia Lugdunensis, previously known as Armorica (Aremorica). Home to five different tribes during the Roman occupation, the region was never thoroughly Romanized, and its name changed to Brittany with the arrival of Celtic tribes in the fifth century. Later,

the northern part was invaded by Norsemen (or Northmen), after whom the important medieval duchy of Normandy was named.

One of the largest and most important military invasions in history was launched across the English Channel from the Normandy coast by Duke William II (later called "the Conqueror") in 1066, and Normandy subsequently passed into English hands. Normandy was also a major bone of contention in the Hundred Years War, which may be surprising until one recalls that the historic region included the fertile lower Seine as well as the granitic Cotentin. France's claim to Normandy was finally confirmed in 1450, with the exception of the Channel Islands, which are still a British dependency.

Brittany's political history resembles that of Normandy, although its occupancy is even more ancient, as evidenced by the megalithic ruins at Carnac, where huge upright stones resembling those at Stonehenge (**Salisbury Plain**) line a two-and-a-half-mile-long arcade, bearing mute witness to a pre-Celtic society. Retaining autonomy from the Romans, the Franks, the counts of Anjou, and the kings of England, Brittany did not become part of France until a number of dynastic marriages in the sixteenth century tied the region to the Capetian monarchy.

A second cross-channel invasion some thousand years after the Norman Conquest—this time in reverse—landed on almost the identical stretch of beach near Bayeux from which William the Conqueror had cast off. The 6 June 1944 invasion of Normandy, with 176,000 men, 9,500 warplanes, 600 fighting ships, and 4,000 transports, was the largest military force ever assembled in one place. The choice of location for the amphibious landing and its eventual outcome were strongly affected by geographical factors: the presence of sand beaches; the absence of a cliffed shore, which would have provided a more secure line of defense; and the openness of the immediate onshore terrain, which prevented the isolation of the invaders. In the American sector, Utah Beach was on the leeward side of the Cotentin Peninsula, and its taking was less difficult than that of the more exposed Omaha Beach to the east, where high winds and waves created treacherous conditions. More than 1,000 American soldiers were killed taking Omaha Beach, above which today stand serried ranks of crosses in a memorial cemetery.

The coast of Normandy was the western flank of the heavily defended German West Wall, within striking distance of Allied fighter patrols. Once the Allies were onshore, however, the bocage country made their advance difficult, as the copses and woodlands that fragmented the terrain provided the Germans with easy cover and good ambush opportunities. The Allied tanks had difficulty surmounting the hedgerow embankments and often became moored aloft, exposing their vulnerable undersides to enemy fire.

A key region of the British sector was Caen, with its central locale surrounded by a dense network of small villages and roads. Here the landscape was open *campagne* rather than bocage. Under such conditions, the Germans were even better able to withstand British attack, and the town fell only after six weeks of vigorous attack.

After the capture of the plains of Caen and the Cherbourg Peninsula, the final breakout occurred to the south, as U.S. troops began on 3 July to advance east across a marsh belt south of the Cotentin Peninsula. The Germans took the high ground provided by resistant stumps of the Armorican bedrock at La Haye du Puits, at the Forêt de Mont Castre, and at St. Lô. But the U.S. forces and morale were too strong to stem the tide. The Yanks took St. Lô on 18 July, paused for a week of bad weather, and then launched the greatest mobile offensive of the war, leading to the most decisive military victory since Waterloo.

Further Reading: Stephen E. Ambrose, *D-Day, June 6, 1944: The Climactic Battle of World War II,* New York: Simon and Schuster, 1994; Arthur Davies, "Geographical Factors in the Invasion and Battle of Normandy," *Geographical Review* 36 (1946), pp. 613–631.

ATLANTIC OCEAN, LEGENDARY ISLANDS OF

In ancient Mediterranean cultures, the paradise where the blessed dead went to live was commonly held to lie beyond the **Strait of Gibraltar.** The belief in a western paradise was an important part of ancient Egyptian religion. The Elysian Fields of the Greeks were described as a winterless land of plenty, while the related Garden of the Hesperides was a place where the daughters of Hesperus guarded a tree of golden apples. The Romans knew of the **Canary Islands** and referred to them as the Fortunate Islands (Fortunatae Insulae). Various north European cultures, notably the Celtic, similarly had their legendary islands in the west.

By 1350, European explorers and geographers knew of the eastern Atlantic archipelagoes: the **Azores,** Canaries, and **Madeiras.** As the major European powers—Spain, Portugal, France, and England—sent their ships westward into the Atlantic Ocean beginning in the mid-fifteenth century, the islands of tradition were rediscovered and new ones found. The phantasmal islands were displaced westward and northward as geographical knowledge increased. Although some of these may have had an empirical basis in a report of a lost mariner or the like, all are today considered legendary. They persisted, however, on late medieval and Renaisssance maps, and thereby influenced people's behavior. Belief in their existence encouraged early explorers to venture out into the dark waters of the Atlantic. The islands were sought for what they intrinsically offered—blissful life and valuable resources—but also as possible stopover points on the way to greater riches.

Antillia, or the *Island of the Seven Cities,* was portrayed on maps as early as 1435. Cartographers showed the island as a large, rectangular landmass oriented from north to south, lying due west of the Azores. Columbus received correspondence in 1474 from the Florentine cosmographer Toscanelli dal Pozzo, who recommended that Columbus consider stopping over at Antillia on any possible trans-Atlantic voyage. The island (actually, group of islands) was believed to have been colonized by emigrating bishops from Iberia who sought refuge from Moorish invaders.

Atlantis, the sunken continent of antiquity, was not just a curiosity, as many believed what they read in Plato, that a great civilization had foundered and sunk into the sea with large loss of life, sometime before the rise of the ancient Greeks. Belief in this lost civilization whose geographic position was unknown but was usually assigned to the Atlantic was remarkably persistent. As late as the end of the nineteenth century, interest in Atlantean matters was sparked by the 1882 publication of the classic *Atlantis: The Antediluvian World,* written by Ignatius Donnelly (1831–1901), a populist U.S. congressman from Minnesota, who argued that Atlantis was the source of all civilizations and that fleeing Atlanteans had arrived in the New World long before

Columbus to establish "native" American cultures and civilizations, such as that of the Mound Builders of the Mississippi Valley. Rosicrucians and other mystical secret societies incorporated legends associated with Atlantis and other sunken continents into their religious beliefs.

Avalon was a mythical western island in the Celtic tradition, the place to which King Arthur was brought after he was mortally wounded in the Battle of Camlann. Geoffrey of Monmouth, writing between 1129 and 1151, referred to Avalon as Ynys Avallach (Isle of Apples). Avalon is the place where the magic sword Excalibur was forged (for a delightful modern version of the Arthur story, see T. H. White's *Sword in the Stone,* while the classic reference is Malory's medieval *Morte d'Arthur*).

The island of *Brazil,* or **Hy-Brazil,** was one of the most elusive of the mythic isles in the Atlantic. It was sometimes placed in the position of the Azores, other times off the west coast of Ireland. Navigators and explorers sought it for centuries but never found it. As a rumored rock off the coast of Ireland it persisted in the popular imagination until around 1865.

Buss Island had so many sightings, and even some landings, that it's hard to believe that a place with such a substantial historical record could have been imaginary. The island was first reported by one of the passengers on Frobisher's third voyage of 1578, which sought the **Northwest Passage** as a short cut to the riches of the Indies. The passenger was traveling aboard the *Emmanuel* (referred to also as the *Busse of Bridgewater,* after a busse, a type of fishing boat), which had separated from the fleet and was returning home when the passengers sighted a large island, which they named after their ship. The story was retailed in Richard Hakluyt's well-respected history of the English voyages of discovery. The Dutch navigator Henry Hudson in 1609 looked for the island at its reported location southeast of Greenland but did not find it. In 1671 John Seller's *The English Pilot* reported two different sightings of Buss Island. Captain Zachariah Gillam, en route to Hudson Bay in 1668, where he would establish the great trading company of the same name, likewise reported sighting the island. In 1675 the Hudson Bay Company went so far as to obtain a patent for possession of Buss Island from Charles II. After 1745 the island is referred to only as the "Sunken Land of Buss," having apparently followed Atlantis into the depths. As recently as 1904, the *Proceedings and Transactions of the Nova Scotia Institute of Science* reported the discovery of "the sunken land of Buss" along what turns out to be the Reykjanes Ridge, an underwater mountain chain extending from the Azores to Iceland as part of the Mid-Atlantic Ridge. Based on a reconstruction of the route of the *Emmanuel* voyage, the Buss Island legend could have originated from voyagers mistaking the southern coast of Greenland for a separate island. Errors of the kind were frequent at the time, as witnessed by numerous cartographic duplications.

The *Island of Cronus* was, according to legend, the place of exile to which the victorious Zeus assigned his defeated father, Cronus, one of the Titans. It was believed to lie west of the British Isles. The Roman Plutarch, in one of his lesser known works, *The Face in the Orb of the Moon* (dated around A.D. 75), described a pilgrimage that left Britain every 30 years to study and meditate on the island. The locale was a beautiful place where Cronus supposedly slept in a magic cave and was fed by birds, which brought him ambrosia, and attended by a mysterious court. The pilgrims came to the island to study important matters of philosophy and astronomy.

Frisland was a large island in the north Atlantic whose existence relates to the controversial narrative of the Zeno Brothers (1390s), based on a putative northern voyage in which these two Venetian noblemen were blown off course and visited Greenland and other unknown lands. Since the brothers were part of the Venetian elite, the publication of their narrative in a document dated 1558 was greeted with acclaim in Venice, establishing as it did the priority of the Venetians as discoverers of the New World over the claims of the Spanish and their navigator Columbus, who was after all from Genoa, Venice's archrival. On the 1558 *Carta da Navegar* accompanying the Zeno narrative, prepared by Nicolò the younger, Frisland is shown as a large island south of Islanda (i.e., Iceland), surrounded by other unknown and presumably legendary islands and lands, such as Icaria, an island to the west of Frisland, and Estotiland, which appears to represent the Labrador mainland. The fantastic nature of the Venetian claim was not rendered more sensible when the British countered with the claim that Frisland was already a possession of theirs, since King Arthur had discovered it in A.D. 530!

Saint Brendan's Island refers to the blessed Land of Promise of the Saints, reached in the sixth century by the Irish missionary monk Brendan, who ranged widely over the open seas in a curragh, a hide-covered boat resembling a bathtub. Persisting as late as 1759 on sea charts, the geographical feature is difficult to pinpoint. If one follows the Latin record of his voyage, the *Navigatio,* which didn't appear for more than two centuries after Brendan's death, the island could be anywhere between the Arctic and the Bahamas. As geographical knowledge increased, the island of Saint Brendan was ever farther displaced toward the margins of the map, and it eventually came to occupy the far northern waters between Newfoundland and Labrador.

Other saints besides Brendan had islands named after them. The legend of Saint Ursula, loosely based on an early Christian martyrdom about which little is known, tells how the daughter of a Breton king refused to marry a British king because he was a pagan, sacrificing herself and her 11,000 companions—all virgins—rather than submit to the Englishman. Variations and elaborations of the legend can be found, but it is sufficient for our purposes to note that Saint Ursula was believed to have made a long sea voyage out into the Atlantic along with her companions, traveling to Rome.

On his second voyage (1493), which was meant to colonize the new possessions and to explore further, Columbus landed on a Caribbean island. It was 3 November 1493, which was a Sunday, so he named the island *Dominica.* Proceeding to the northwest past the **Leeward Islands** of the Lesser Antilles in the direction of Hispaniola and Cuba, the great navigator found and named numerous islands until he came upon a large group of islands separated by narrow channels, against whose rocky coasts the seas beat relentlessly. Columbus, a man of intense faith, must have known of the works of another Genoan, Jacobus de Voragine, the author of *Lives of the Saints: The Golden Legend,* including its account of Saint Ursula. Exercising the right of the founder, the admiral named the largest island Saint Ursula, and the others the *Eleven Thousand Virgins.* No map ever showed Saint Ursula, but the islands ever since have been known as the Virgin Islands (possession today is divided between Britain and the United States).

Nor does this exhaust the list of legendary islands. We could add *Mayda,* a crescent shape near the shore of Brittany or Ireland, sometimes confused with Mam (the Isle of Man). The island of *Demonias* appears on sixteenth-century maps along the Labrador coast, occupying the mouth of the Hamilton Inlet. The haunting sounds emanating from this island, which gave it its name, may be the result of ice cracking and thawing in the spring. Let us not forget to mention *Fixlanda, Stokafixa, Grocland,* and *Drogeo*—a few more names selected from a group of apparently less pronounceable islands. We should not be too glib, though: Historians tell us that Sweden was once thought to be an island.

Further Reading: William H. Babcock, *Legendary Islands of the Atlantic: A Study in Medieval Geography,* American Geographical Society Research Series, no. 8, New York: American Geographical Society, 1922; Ronald H. Fritze, *Legend and Lore of the Americas before 1492: An Encyclopedia of Visitors, Explorers, and Immigrants,* Santa Barbara, Calif.: ABC-CLIO, 1993; Donald S. Johnson, *Phantom Islands of the Atlantic: The Legends of Seven Lands that Never Were,* New York: Walker and Co., 1994.

AZORES

This archipelago of nine islands in three groups about 900 miles (1,448 kilometers) off the coast of Portugal goes by the Portuguese name Ilhas dos Açores, or Hawk Islands, because its earliest discoverers found it inhabited by hawks and buzzards. Ranging in size from São Miguel (St. Michael), the largest island located in the eastern cluster, to tiny Corvo and nearby Flores in the northwest, the islands span some 300 miles (483 kilometers). They are volcanic in origin, with steep-sided, craggy shorelines. Lying along the eastern margin of the Mid-Atlantic Ridge, the islands are subject to tectonic activity, and a number of volcanic eruptions and earthquakes have been recorded. Fertile volcanic soils, mild temperatures throughout the year (temperatures are moderated by a current of the warm Gulf Stream), and abundant precipitation without a dry season contribute to high agricultural productivity, with rich yields of corn, sugar, and grapes in the lowlands and excellent pasturelands for cattle on higher ground.

The islands have been a way station and resting point for Atlantic travelers since they were first discovered in 1427 or 1431 by far-ranging mariners under the direction of the Portuguese ruler Prince Henry the Navigator. Their whereabouts may have been known to earlier peoples, perhaps to the ancient Carthaginians or the related Phoenicians, the greatest mariners of the classical and preclassical eras. Evidence for pre-Portuguese contact is scant and controversial, but we do know for sure that the islands first appeared on a map in 1351. They were uninhabited before Portuguese colonization began in 1445.

Lying near the 40th parallel, well within the belt of the midlatitude Westerlies, the islands were often visited by ships making the eastern crossing, which benefited by the prevailing breezes at their backs. Fresh water and provisions could be taken on at a midpoint in the long Atlantic crossing. Columbus is known to have stopped at Santa Maria, one of the islands in the eastern cluster, on his return voyage from the New World in 1493. Spanish galleons making the homeward journey routinely reprovisioned on what they called the Western Isles.

The islands were the sites of important naval battles between the English and the Spanish during the era of the Armada. The remote northwestern island of Flores, seldom visited due to its location away from the main routeways, derives its name from the luxuriance of its flowers.

Its fame, however, results from the naval battle fought in 1591 just beneath the cliffs and along the rocks of its southern coast. The famous sea fight of "the one and the fifty-three" (one British ship encountered a squadron of fifty-three Spanish ships) is memorialized in Tennyson's stirring ballad "The Revenge," whose opening line rings: "At Florés in the Azorés Sir Richard Grenville lay." The heroic English captain Grenville died aboard an enemy ship after the battle, as he watched his ship, *The Revenge,* sink, but he had destroyed so many Spanish ships during the battle that it was considered a major victory for the British and an important follow-up to their defeat of the Armada in 1588.

In the eighteenth century, New England whalers made stops here for supplies and to recruit extra crew. Açorianos learned traditional whaling techniques involving small boats (*canoa*) and hand-thrown harpoons, methods that have continued into the era of factory ships.

The United States maintains a NATO air base at Lages Field on the large central island of Terceira (this island gets its name from the fact that it was generally the third island visited on a typical crossing). Traditional livelihoods like fishing and farming have declined, and a large outmigration to the United States recently took place. Red-tiled roofs, terraced hillslopes, and attractive vineyards are becoming as much relics of the past as are the scenic, historic forts that dot the islands. Tourism vies with the export of agricultural crops as an earner of scarce foreign exchange. A movement for independence in the 1970s has given way today to an acceptance of the islands' status as an autonomous region within the Portuguese republic.

Further Reading: Don Moser, "The Azores: Nine Islands in Search of a Future," *National Geographic,* Feb. 1976, pp. 261–288.

BALKANS

See Vardar-Morava Corridor

BAVARIAN PLATEAU

In southern Germany, a fairly uniform slope extends north from the Alps as far as the Danube. These Alpine forelands of low hills with rounded slopes covered in grass are a result of glacial deposition. Although permanent ice fields today are found only far to the south, during the Pleistocene epoch glaciers ran down these valleys and spread out over the landscape.

Rivers fan out over the land surface, eventually draining into the Danube, which makes a big turn at its historical head of navigation, at Regensburg, where the river reaches its northernmost point. The southern district of scattered lakes with access to the high Alps (Germany's highest peak, Zugspitze, with an elevation of 9,720 feet or 2,963 meters, is located here) includes many tourist stops but is a traditionally poor region, consisting of villages with surrounding fields, cut into a mantle of spruce forests. The unglaciated portion of Bavaria (Bayern, in German), further north, up to the Danube, is one of the largest agricultural concentrations in south-central Europe, a region more characterized by hill lands and mountains.

To the west, the river Lech is an important natural and cultural divide. Beyond it, the landscape alters to the hillier and more varied Swabian Jura, which has the look and personality more of the Rhineland than of Bavaria.

To the north is another district that is part of present-day Bavaria but whose history is separate—Franconia. Franconia's terrain consists of sedimentary scarplands along the margin of another Alpine-era hill land—the Franconian Jura. The westward-flowing Main River, along with its tributaries, dissects this traditional German *Land* into several administrative districts on the basis of topographic position in the Main watershed: Upper Franconia (Bayreuth), Middle Franconia (Nürnberg), and Lower Franconia (Würzburg). In this direction Bavaria abuts the **Hercynian Uplands** of central Europe, including the forests of **Thuringia** to the north and the Bohemian Forest to the northeast.

The historic core of Bavaria lies to the south, between the craggy Alps and the Danube, on broad, rolling subalpine plateau land. Originally inhabited by Celts and conquered by the Roman general Drusus Senior in 15 B.C., the region was invaded by the Germanic Baiuoarii, who moved westward along the Danube to settle the region approximately between A.D. 490 and 520. Christianity was imported from the north by Scottish and Irish monks. Saint Boniface completed the work of establishing the church as a key institution, as he did elsewhere in Germanic central Europe.

The agricultural wealth of the region and its strategic position along the lines of communication between Italy and Germany have made it a coveted prize. Its boundary varied greatly throughout history, sometimes including territory in the Rhine valley (Lower or Rhenish Palatinate) and parts of present-day Austria. In the early medieval period, Bavaria became one of the five basic or stem duchies of Germany. In the tenth century the frontier march of the Nordgau or Upper Palatinate was added to its territory. In 1070, Emperor Henry IV granted the fief to Welf, or Guelph d'Este IV. The Guelph dynasty was to play an important role in the struggles from the ninth to the twelfth centuries of the German princes against the emperor, clashes that sometimes spilled over into Italy. As a reduced territory and political power, the duchy passed in 1180 to Otto of Wittelsbach, the founder of a dynasty that lasted until 1918.

Bavaria was strong as it entered the Reformation period and withstood the Protestant challenge. Maximilian I, Duke of Bavaria (1597–1651), headed the Catholic League in the Thirty Years War and was rewarded with the rank of elector. About 70 percent of Bavarians today are Catholics.

Although it had sided with Napoleon (at least until 1813, when his defeat was apparent), Bavaria proved to be a territorial winner at the Congress of Vienna (1814–1815). The result of Napoleon's reorganization of the political map of Germany was that Bavaria gained the traditional Frankish kingdoms of Swabia and Franconia while retaining the Upper Palatinate.

The rulers of independent Bavaria in the nineteenth century were prone to magnanimity and madness, the two sometimes being combined, as in the case of Mad King Ludwig (Ludwig II), who built the whimsical storybook castle of Neuschwanstein in southwestern Bavaria—seemingly the prototype for the Disneyland palaces. Though somewhat daft, the three Wittelsbachs who ruled Bavaria in the nineteenth century supported the arts and established Munich as a cultural center (and world capital of beer drinking), a reputation that still flourishes today.

The rural prosperity of the largest German state and the influence of the Roman Catholic church, which predominates except in the Upper Palatinate and in Middle Franconia, led to friction with the rising Protestant state of Prussia. Siding with Austria against Prussia in the Austro-Prussian War (1866), Bavaria was nevertheless forced to join the German Empire in 1871. Even as the chief German state after Prussia in the Second Reich, Bavaria retained strong secessionist tendencies.

In the twentieth century Bavaria has been home to extremist political movements of both the right and the left. After deposing the last Wittelsbach ruler, King Louis III, Kurt Eisner led a short-lived socialist republic before he was assassinated. A subsequent attempt by the communists to take power resulted in their bloody suppression by the German army. National socialism had its roots in Munich, where the party of "blood and soil" attempted unsuccessfully to seize power in 1923 (during what came to be known as the Beer-Hall Putsch). Catholic Bavaria, however, gave little support to the Nazis until Hitler acceded to power in 1933. After World War II, Munich benefited from its position as the largest city in the American zone of occupation.

Further Reading: James Bentley, *Bavaria,* London: Aurum, 1950.

BERING STRAIT

At its narrowest point, the water passageway separating the northeastern tip of Russian Siberia from the western end of Alaska's Seward Peninsula is 55 miles across (90 kilometers). The strait joins the Bering Sea, an arm of the Pacific Ocean, to the Chukchi Sea, which is part of the Arctic Ocean. Although its existence was long suspected, this strait separating

terest in the cossack's explorations for nationalist reasons.

As part of Peter the Great's quest to expand the Russian sphere of influence, the dying czar in 1724 chose the Danish explorer Vitus Bering to lead a major expedition to Kamchatka and to navigate the water passageway between Asia and America. In July 1728, Bering passed through the strait that has since borne his

A whale-jawbone cemetery fence on Point Hope, northwest Alaska, on the Arctic Ocean north of the Bering Strait *(photo by Jesse Walker).*

North America from Asia was first discovered by Europeans thanks to the Russian explorer Semyon Ivanovich Dezhnyov (1605–1672). A cossack leader, Dezhnyov sailed down the Kolyma River to the Arctic Ocean in 1648, then navigated along the Arctic coast before passing through the Bering Strait some 80 years before Vitus Bering. Knowledge of the strait did not achieve wide currency at this time due to Dezhnyov's poor report-writing skills, and his achievement did not really become widely known until twentieth-century historians revived in-

name. On 17 August he discovered the Diomede Islands, two islands only about two miles apart. Today one island is Russian, the other U.S. territory, with the International Date Line and a geopolitical fault line (at least from 1917–1991) separating them.

Bering's well-publicized discovery led to his being selected as commander of the Great Northern Expedition, which lasted from 1733–1742. On the return trip from this expedition, scurvy killed Bering, and he was laid to rest on Bering Island, in the Commander group of islands. On the basis of Bering's explorations, Russian interests in the fur industry had been established in Alaska, and Russian influence quickly spread down the coast of what is now western Canada and the Pacific Northwest of the United States.

The origin of the native peoples of the New World had been a conundrum ever since Columbus encountered decidedly non-European peoples on his first voyage of 1492. The Bible didn't seem to account for the people he mistakenly named Indians. Could God have created more than just the aboriginal couple, Adam and Eve? The answer seemed to be either the heretical notion of polygenesis (or multiple creations) or an account of migrations of Old World peoples to the Americas, which, because almost everyone imagined a seemingly impossible crossing of the Atlantic or Pacific Oceans, seemed equally bizarre. (Today ideas about extraterrestrial visitation and aliens would probably have to be assessed.) As early as 1590, the historian and ethnographer Father José de Acosta suggested that the Indians arrived from Tartary or Siberia in Asia. After Vitus Bering proved the existence of a narrow strait separating the two continents, numerous enlightenment scholars favored the idea of a migration from Asia across the Bering Strait. Thomas Jefferson in 1787 while writing *Notes on the State of Virginia* suggested the plausibility of an Asian ancestry for the native Americans. Samuel Haven (1806–1881) in his classic *Archaeology of the United States* (1856) strongly backed the Asian origin of American Indians. Rather like the purely theoretical notion of continental drift proposed by Alfred Wegener almost a century ago without any empirical evidence, the theory of Indian migration was correct, but it lacked any substantial proof. Unlike the idea of continental drift, which was pooh-poohed by geologists for the better part of a century, the "out of Asia" theory of native American origins became iron-clad orthodoxy.

The possibility of a land bridge connecting North America and Asia had been proposed as early as the late nineteenth century on the basis of the nearly identical plants and animals on either side of the strait. In 1934 the geologist R. A. Daly put forward the idea that sea levels had been as much as 300 feet (91 meters) lower during the Pleistocene ice age due to the locking up of so much water in the continental glaciers. A land bridge would have appeared in the shallowest parts of the Bering and Chukchi Seas beginning about 25,000 B.P. and ending about 10,000 B.P. This would have allowed the ancestors of the American Indians literally to walk from Asia to America. We now know that there were three major migrations giving rise to three distinct groups of indigenous people: the Paleo Indians, who traveled southward and spread throughout the western hemisphere; an Athabascan migration, which gave rise to the Indians of Alaska and the Yukon as well as some tribes that lived in the southwestern United States, including the Navajo and Apache; and a final migration, giving rise to the Aleuts and Eskimos of the North American Arctic.

Warmer temperatures by 10,000 B.P. led to rising sea levels and the submergence of Beringia (the name scientists have given to the temporary land bridge). In the subsequent period of warming after 10,000 B.P., ice-free corridors appeared between the glaciers of the Rocky Mountains and the Laurentide or continental ice sheet that spread southward from north-central Canada. These open corridors favored southward migration, as did the appearance of ice-free land along the maritime west coast, although the rugged and sinuous coastlines of present-day Alaska and British Columbia did not present easy migration routes. As deglaciation proceeded, it was natural for early Americans to move far southward beyond the influence of the cold conditions they had always known. By 11,500 B.P., the Clovis culture of big-game hunters (with distinctively shaped, large spearheads) had already spread across North America, reaching southern Argentina a thousand years later.

Thus, it is now known with some degree of certainty that the ancestors of the myriad cultures and tribes that populated the Americas before 1492 descended from a relatively small number of peoples who crossed the Bering land bridge in three migrations between 15,000 and 10,000 B.P. The old hypothesis of a land bridge where the Bering Strait is today has been substantially confirmed, though there is still plenty of controversy about the precise dating of sites and the interpretation of evidence.

Further Reading: Brian M. Fagan, *The Great Journey: The Peopling of Ancient America,* London: Thames and Hudson, 1987; Raymond H. Fisher, *Bering's Voyages: Whither and Why,* Seattle, Wash.: University of Washington Press, 1977; Ronald H. Fritze, *Legend and Lore of the Americas before 1492: An Encyclopedia of Visitors, Explorers, and Immigrants,* Santa Barbara, Calif.: ABC-CLIO, 1993.

BLACK FOREST

On the opposite side of the **Rhine Graben** from the French Vosges is the highly dissected upland of the German Schwarzwald, or Black Forest. Stretching northeast about 90 miles (145 kilometers) from the Rhine on the German-Swiss border, this heavily forested plateau with scattered pasturelands and urban areas occupies the southwest German state of Baden, extending into Württem-

berg. Roughly triangular in shape (with the broad end to the south), this terrain region contains the drainage divide between the Rhine and Danube river systems and is closely associated with German identity and consciousness of nature.

To the west, the Black Forest is sharply delimited by marginal hills that mark the edge of the Rhine basin. This boundary between highland and lowland is designated by the Alemannish term *Gau.* From the time of the Romans, who occupied the eastern side of the upper Rhine valley as far as the crest of the Black Forest, the focus of settlement has been on the western border of this heavily forested tableland of low rounded hills, deeply incised valleys, and sacred fir woodlands. The Breisgau in upper Baden around Freiburg, Kraichgau located in central Baden in the neighborhood of Karlsruhe, and the depression of the Ufgau, in which lies Pforzheim or Maulbronn Gate, all are fertile lands, each with its distinctive agricultural specialty, be it fruit, wine, or cereals. This region is the crossroads of middle Europe and has in the past century attracted considerable industry of the newer kind—electricity and chemicals rather than steel. To the east, the limit of the Black Forest is not so readily defined in terms of topography, as there is a long, gentle eastern slope that merges gradually into the Baar plateau of Württemberg.

The forest itself is situated on an asymmetrical block of gneissic rocks and intruded granites that is part of the **Hercynian Uplands.** The highest elevations are reached in the south-central part of the region, in the Feldberg (el. 4,898 feet or 1,493 meters), while to the north the heights culminate in the Hornisgrinde (3,819 feet or 1,164 meters). A major folding of the crystalline core of the mountains is apparent, running in a south-southwest—north-northeast axis, and giving the massif a distinctive appearance that is visible even on a small-scale atlas map. Younger sedimentary rocks including Bunter sandstones to the northeast and the Muschelkalk (shelly limestones) on the eastern and western border give rise to sharp contrasts in landform, vegetation, and settlement. (The Bunter sandstone is largely covered with fir forests, while the Muschelkalk is more open, with pastoral and arable land.) The foundering of the Rhine Rift Valley in the Tertiary, or most recent, geological period resulted in a series of step faults, which left fertile terraces ascending from the valley bottom to the highlands. Pleistocene glaciation covered the valley with alluvial gravels and windblown loess, into which the Rhine had cut a devious channel until regulation fixed a navigable course as far as Basel in 1905. In the mountains, closed ice caps extend downslope in both the Feldberg and Hornisgrinde districts, altering the landscape in characteristic ways (glacial lakes and U-shaped valleys), though not as dramatically as in nearby Switzerland.

In contrast to the "garden of Germany" on the Black Forest's western margin, its interior is among Germany's most inhospitable landscapes; this is still the most thickly forested district in southern Germany. Most cities, excluding small resort and industrial towns, are located along its periphery. Only in a few locales does the forest continue above the tree line at about 4,000 feet (1,219 meters), beyond which the conifers become dwarfed, giving rise to high moor and subalpine vegetation. The typical tree of the forest is the silver fir (*Pinus silvestris*). Spruce can be found on the light, sandy soils of the north. At lower elevations in the west and southwest a mixed forest of beech and chestnut predominates.

The general trend until about a century ago was for the area under forest to decrease as a result of cutting. Most of this clearance was to provide timber for a variety of purposes to the wood-deficient Rhine Delta and northern plains as well as to open up land for grazing (*Graswirtschaft*). Most of the soils are too thin, leached, and porous for crop cultivation, but the verdant high pastureland provides excellent forage for dairy cows.

Small industrial centers produce not only the celebrated cuckoo clocks and musical instruments that make this region well known throughout the world but also textiles, metal goods, and furniture, though many of these businesses were spun off as ancillaries to the main lines of production (for example, jewelry making, enameling, and screw manufacturing all were boosted by the needs of the clock industry). Originally, the making of brushes, clocks, and wood carvings was carried out on a domestic basis throughout the Schwarzwald as a sideline during the slow winter months. The first Black Forest clock using wooden wheels dates from 1680, while cuckoo clocks began to be made in 1720. The transition from domestic to factory production occurred during the nineteenth century, hastened by the customs union (*Zollverein*) in 1836 and German unification in 1871, both of which expanded market area. The first large factories making clocks were not established until after 1850.

The self-sufficient Black Forest peasant is as much a thing of the past as is the pristine and unspoiled environment. Large-scale industry has undercut the individual producer as surely as it has polluted the air with acid rain, which has devastated large parts of the forest, though the source of the pollution lies outside the district. As much as 50 percent of the fir trees in the forest have been damaged by industrial pollution, in one of the best-documented cases of the negative impacts of acid rain on forests. Germans revere their forests and make regular use of hiking trails. There are areas in the Black Forest where signs with the word *Sterben* (German for "death" or "dying") are posted, referring to the effects of pollution on this valuable natural resource.

the **Bosporus,** the Sea of Marmara, and the **Dardanelles.** The character of the northern coastline, with its lagoonal river mouths almost cut off from the sea by sandspits, and the steep, rocky margins to the south have caused port development to be less pronounced than along the highly indented, harbor-rich Mediterranean. The historical development of surrounding lands has been af-

The Black Sea coastal resort town of Sochi; the beach is mostly gravel, so sunbathing decks are provided *(photo by Jesse Walker).*

See also: Agri Decumates.
Further Reading: Alice F. A. Mutton, "The Black Forest: Its Human Geography," *Economic Geography* 14 (1938), pp. 131–153.

BLACK SEA
The skies above this large inland sea are often black and stormy compared to the clear, cloudless skies over the **Mediterranean Sea,** which explains how this body of water connecting Europe to Asia got its name. Known to the ancient world as the Pontus Euxinus (Hospitable Sea), it is joined to the Mediterranean by

fected by its accessibility to Europe, yet at a far enough remove that the region has been easily overrun by nomadic Turkic peoples of oriental customs and languages. The Russian culture that came to dominate the Black Sea lands once the Ottoman Empire collapsed bears the unmistakable imprint of internal tensions between the oriental and occidental worlds. It was not until the age of Peter the Great in the early eighteenth century, for instance, that the oriental kowtow went out of fashion among the Russian elite.

The sea is enclosed by Ukraine to the north, Georgia to the east, Turkey to the south, and Romania and Bulgaria to the west. Its principal feeders flow from the north and include rivers that begin with the letter D: the Danube, Dniester, Dnieper, and Don, the latter actually emptying into the Sea of Azov, which is connected to the Black Sea through the Kerch Strait.

The Greeks colonized the shores of the Black Sea between the eighth and the sixth centuries B.C., and the Romans under Hadrian charted its waters in the second century A.D. According to Greek legend, Jason sailed across the Black Sea on his way to Colchis, the land of the Golden Fleece. Its importance increased with the establishment of Constantinople in A.D. 330. Genoese merchants created trading colonies on the Crimean Peninsula, which juts out from its northern shore, in the thirteenth century, but the Ottoman Turks made it a Turkish lake until the eighteenth century.

By this time, Russian peoples had begun to move southward, as the Tatar khanate eased its grip on the semiarid steppe lands of Ukraine and the deserts east of the Caspian. The Black Sea is highly navigable and ice free the year around, an important consideration for the initially landlocked Muscovite kingdom. In the eighteenth century, Russia made significant territorial gains in the west and south at the expense respectively of Poland and of Turkey. Catherine the Great (reigned 1762–1796) succeeded where her ambitious predecessor Peter the Great (reigned 1682–1725), who had done so much to modernize Russia and extend its geographical domain, had failed. In the war of 1736–1739, Russia defeated the Turks, and thereafter it controlled much of the steppe lands; yet control of the key fort of Azov remained in

doubt as long as the Crimean Tatars, who were governed as a separate khanate, threatened Russian settlers on the frontier. After a series of wars, Catherine's armies finally seized the Crimea in 1783, thus extinguishing, after nearly five and a half centuries, the Tatar peril. In 1794 the empress founded a city on the Black Sea in her newly annexed southern territory. When she asked for suggestions in naming it, her advisers gave her 47 different names. Finally, someone suggested *Odissos,* perhaps in memory of Homer's epic poem, the *Odyssey.* She liked this idea but settled on a feminine form of the name, Odessa.

Russian advances in the nineteenth century led to confrontation with the west European powers over control of the Black Sea and access to the Mediterranean. With the slow decline of the Ottoman Empire during the nineteenth century, the Black Sea assumed a new strategic and geopolitical importance. It was a major setback to Czar Nicholas I's imperial aspirations when England and France defeated the Russians in the Crimean War (1853–1856), though the ruthless autocrat died before the signing of the Treaty of Paris (1856), which officially concluded the war by restricting Russian influence along the strategically important Black Sea–Bosporus route.

The spirits of the two ambitious eighteenth-century Russian rulers, Peter and Catherine the Great, and perhaps also of lesser emperors and empresses, might well have been stirred when a native of Georgia, one of the relatively recently annexed lands, by the name of Josef Stalin concluded an agreement in February 1945 with his Western allies Winston Churchill and Franklin Roosevelt at the Crimean resort town of Yalta, which effectively extended Soviet influence after World War II as far west as the banks of the Elbe.

Further Reading: Neal Ascherson, *Black Sea,* New York: Hill and Wang, 1995.

BLUE RIDGE

The easternmost and highest part of the Appalachian Mountains, the Blue Ridge lies between the Great Appalachian Valley and the **Appalachian Piedmont,** extending from southern Pennsylvania to northern Georgia.

The ridge is crossed by few passes or rivers, so settlers advancing from the east beginning in the mid-eighteenth century faced a formidable obstacle. Even if one crossed the Blue Ridge and reached the Great Valley, a series of linear ridges composing the Ridge and Valley Province of the Appalachians lay beyond. North of Roanoke River (Virginia), which crosses the mountain front forming a "water gap,"

The Smoky Mountains on the border between Tennessee and North Carolina, part of the Blue Ridge *(photo by Sam Hilliard).*

Beginning near Carlisle, Pennsylvania, as South Mountain—its name in Pennsylvania and Maryland—the prominent ridge of pre-Cambrian metamorphic rocks continues southward in Virginia as the Blue Ridge, with the Shenandoah Valley on its western side. In Virginia the Skyline Drive winds through Shenandoah National Park and connects southward with the 500-mile-long (805-kilometer) Blue Ridge Parkway, established in 1933, as far as the Great Smoky Mountains on the Tennessee–North Carolina border.

the Blue Ridge is generally narrow (10–15 miles or 16–24 kilometers wide) and linear. South of the Roanoke the ridge widens to as much as 70 miles (113 kilometers) in western North Carolina, where the geological structure is more complex and the highest elevations are attained. Mt. Mitchell, North Carolina (6,684 feet or 2,038 meters), is the highest peak east of the Mississippi. It was named after Elisha Mitchell, the North Carolina state surveyor who lost his life mapping the region in 1857. Elsewhere the Blue Ridge has average elevations in the 2,000–4,000-

foot (610–1,219-meter) range. Few rivers cut across the imposing wall of rock, a factor promoting town development where natural breaks occur: at Harpers Ferry, Virginia (Potomac River); Roanoke, Virginia (Roanoke River); and Lynchburg, Virginia (James River).

Settlement was confined to the eastern seaboard during much of the colonial period by the imposing obstacle of the Blue Ridge and the series of ridges that lay beyond the Great Valley. As a result of the northeast-southwest trend of the mountains, approximately paralleling the eastern coastline and lying transverse to migration paths, many pioneers crossed the Blue Ridge (or Blue Mountain) and then traveled southwest along the Great Wagon Road until they found a gap or pass in the mountains that allowed them to cross into Kentucky or Tennessee. The **Cumberland Gap** at the southwestern tip of Virginia is the most famous such pass. A "wind gap," it sits high and dry in the hills, providing an opening to Kentucky. People of Scotch-Irish, German, Welsh, and other non-Anglo extraction in southeastern Pennsylvania in the late colonial period followed the Great Valley south and were to become important components of the population of the upland South.

The ridges of the High Appalachians not only impeded the movement of people west but also blocked produce bound for urban markets to the east. Both the short-lived C&O Canal and its successor, the B&O Railroad, followed the Potomac corridor, slicing across the transverse ridges of the Appalachians to provide an outlet for western production.

The Appalachian Trail winds some 2,000 miles (3,219 kilometers) along the ridge from Mt. Katahdin, Maine, to Springer Mountain in northern Georgia, making a wide, well-marked footpath (the author once encountered a blind

hiker on one of the more accessible portions of the trail in the Great Smoky Mountains National Park). The southern Appalachians, where the highest elevations are found, offer beautiful scenery and numerous resorts catering to relatively well-to-do easterners, but the isolated hills and "hollers" have often been economically depressed and the mountain folk patronized by distant government bureaucrats charged with sustaining the rural standard of living. Mountain residents who have occupied remote valleys since prerevolutionary times still retain distinctive Elizabethan speech patterns and play traditional melancholy ballads accompanied by rural America's instrument of choice—the fiddle. This music has been commercialized, electrified, and transformed into today's country music.

BOHEMIAN BASIN

The historic province of Bohemia is the core area of the Czech Republic (the western part of former Czechoslovakia). It has as its natural basis a depressed plateau rimmed by units of the **Hercynian Uplands,** which have fostered a distinctive Slavic language and culture. The Bohemian Basin is a textbook example of the coincidence between a natural region and a political boundary, where a national identity arose behind the folk fortress of natural frontiers. (Another example often given is that of France, with the Pyrenees, the Alps, and a series of Hercynian units to the east serving as natural frontiers with Spain, Italy, and Germany, respectively, though the eastern frontier with Germany is notoriously porous.)

With elevations between 500 and 2,000 feet (152 and 610 meters), the dissected plateau of Čechy (in German, Böhmen) is surrounded by hill lands, and hence it is sometimes referred to as the "Bohemian Square," though the border to the east, of a different geological character, is lower and serves more to connect than to block access to an important adjoining corridor. In three directions, forested ranges divide the Czech homelands from other peoples who did not wish them well and often were much stronger: To the southwest, on the border with Bavaria, lies the Bohemian Forest; to the northwest, on the border with Saxony, are the Erzgebirge or Ore Mountains, whose name testifies to their mineral wealth; while to the northeast, on the present-day boundary with Polish Silesia, is the **Sudetes** (or Sudetenland), a border region that figured prominently in the buildup to World War II. To the southeast, the low plateau of the Bohemian-Moravian Highlands (Českomoravská Vrchovina) joins Bohemia to the Moravian depression, an important corridor connecting the Danube and the **North European Plain.**

None of these barriers are, of course, impenetrable, and in fact one of the great rivers of Europe, the Elbe, travels across the center of Bohemia before cutting a deep valley across the Ore Mountains just above the river's juncture with the northern plains near Dresden. When the southern Alpine ranges were elevated, in comparatively recent geological time, the entire Bohemian Basin and surrounding borderlands were rejuvenated, with the result that most of the streams in the region are tributaries of the north-flowing Elbe. The interior has been fractured and has sunk, with sedimentary ridges preserved as limestone plateaus and clay depressions at the foot of the escarpments. The entire basin is a mosaic of hills and depressions, ancient crystallines covered in places by sandstones, limestones, or marls.

The main wealth of Bohemia is concentrated at its center, along the Elbe, in the rich industrial district of the Polabi, or Plain of the Elbe. Two small depressions shelter the chief urban-industrial agglomerations; Plzeň (Pilsen) is in the middle of a fertile agricultural district with a small coal basin nearby, which was the basis of its early industrialization. The largest city and industrial center is Prague, whose name means "ford" (the site of the town is a shallow stretch of the River Vltava where crossing was easy). Iron and steel finishing industries, engineering, glass, textiles, chemical manufacture, and almost anything that can be conceived is made in the Prague manufacturing district, which benefits from its role as the political capital and the major cultural and commercial magnet.

The original inhabitants of the region, the Boii, or "terrible ones" (probably Celts) were displaced after the first century A.D. by the Germanic Marcomanni and Quadi. With the decline of the Roman imperium, Slavonic settlers in turn displaced these Germanic tribes in the fertile quadrilateral. Christianized by the Carolingians in the eighth and ninth centuries A.D., the region became an important duchy of the Holy Roman Empire, retaining a large measure of political autonomy and displaying notable cultural achievements during its golden age under Charles IV (1336–1378). Weakened by an early version of Protestantism (the Hussite Reform) and its violent repression, Bohemia came under Habsburg domination in 1526 (lasting until 1918) and gradually lost self-rule. Meanwhile, German incursions into the borderlands, and even into the basin itself, laid the seeds of future contention. The nineteenth-century movement for an independent Czechoslovak state (uniting the core region of Bohemia with adjoining

Moravia, and mountainous Slovakia farther to the east) reached its goal in 1918, under the able and intelligent direction of Tomáš Masaryk.

The strategic importance of Bohemia (and later Czechoslovakia) as a powerful central state in Europe is obvious when one looks at the map. According to an old saying, he who holds Bohemia commands Europe. Though history has not always upheld this assertion, there are numerous examples that do. Napoleon's victory at Austerlitz (1804) in the Moravian Corridor gave him command of central Europe. The attempt to appease Hitler with the Munich Agreement of 1938 led to the incorporation of the Bohemian stronghold into the Third Reich and the final upsetting of the delicate balance of power in Europe. Bohemia's position as an outpost of Slavic power in the West, or alternatively as a developed Western land in the midst of the less-developed, Slavic East, guaranteed its status as a keystone in the arch of European unity. Elongated in an east-to-west direction, Czechoslovakia took in lands extending from Bavaria to Ukraine. Behind a mountainous rim, the Czechs created a strength and moral independence that allowed them to survive the terrible time of troubles ushered in by the cession of the Sudeten borderland to the Nazis. (Bohemia-Moravia became a German protectorate during World War II.) Unnaturally aligned in the post–World War II period with the U.S.S.R., a country that had never been important in Bohemia's history, the two component parts of Czechoslovakia—Bohemia-Moravia and Slovakia—decided to go their separate ways after the collapse of communism. On 1 January 1993, Czechoslovakia split into the Czech Republic and Slovakia—two separate, sovereign nations—despite the opposition of writer Vaclav Havel,

Czechoslovakia's president and its most prominent fighter for independence.

BOSPORUS

Joining the Black Sea to the Sea of Marmara, this strategic waterway separates the European and the Asiatic portions of Turkey. Together with the **Dardanelles**, it was historically the major link between the **Mediterranean Sea** and the steppe lands of southern Russia and central Asia, and until Vasco da Gama pioneered the all-water route around Africa to the east, most of the trade with the Orient passed through Constantinople, which was situated at the southern end of the strait on the European side. Whether as Byzantium, the Greco-Roman town on the site until the fifth century; or Constantinople, founded as a second Rome by emperor Constantine and destined to become seat of another empire; or Istanbul in the twentieth century, the city commands the strait from a curved harbor (Golden Horn) indented into the northern end of a triangular promontory jutting out into the straits. Napoleon was so impressed by the site's centrality that he predicted it might one day be "the seat of universal sovereignty." The city and the strait have been a geographical pivot between the eastern and western world throughout history.

Nineteen miles (31 kilometers) long and half a mile to one and a half miles (0.8–2.4 kilometers) wide, the Bosporus is shorter and narrower than the Dardanelles, with which it should not be confused. (Historians often refer to the two together as the Turkish Straits or just the Straits.) The narrowest part of the Bosporus is approximately halfway between the Black Sea and Istanbul, where fortifications first built by the Ottoman Turks are still in place. The strait's name refers to the Greek myth of Io, the nymph, who was metamorphosed into a heifer to escape the clutches of an amorous Zeus, hence the name—Ox ford, or Bosporus. The Turks call it Istambul Boghaz (Strait of Stamboul) or Karadeniz Bogazi. The ancients knew it as Bosporus Thracius.

The Black Sea became a Russian rather than a Turkish lake, with the expansion of Slavic power southward in the eighteenth century. The further decline of Ottoman influence in the nineteenth century led to concern among the great powers about the possible control of the Turkish Straits by Russia. A major objective of England's during this period, and one that it shared with France, its traditional enemy, was the need to prevent Russia's possession or even coadministration of this marine chokepoint. Maritime England feared the expansion of Russia's navy into the Mediterranean and the creation of an unmatchable combination of a Russian-land-and-sea empire. In the disastrous Dardanelles Campaign of 1915, the Allies attempted unsuccessfully to force the Straits, to capture Constantinople, and to open the way for the shipment of supplies and munitions via the Black Sea to the Russian front.

The Straits have endured as an important control point on the world's high seas, and they're still in the possession of Turkey—although it is now a relatively small power allied with the West. Guarantees are in place that preserve the Straits' status as an international waterway. Rocketry, air power, and nuclear weapons all have reduced the geopolitical and security significance of this traditional gateway, yet Turkey's NATO membership is still deemed important, in no small part due to its control of the Straits.

See also: Dardanelles.

BRANDENBURG-PRUSSIA
See North European Plain

BRAZILIAN HIGHLANDS
Even though Brazil occupies a territory larger than the lower forty-eight United States and is about the size of Europe shorn of the Scandinavian peninsula and Finland, only a very small part of its vast area can be described as a plain. Rising sometimes gradually, sometimes steeply from a narrow coastal strip along the east coast is an ancient plateau surface covered with a variety of types of savanna (Portuguese *campo*). The Brazilian highlands, or *planaltos,* are geologically composed of a basement of crystalline rocks covered in places by stratified sandstones and limestones interlaced with sheets of diabase. In the tropical climate of Brazil, old crystalline rocks like granite and gneiss weather deeply to produce a deep mantle of fine-grained soil and form residual low, rounded hills. Sandstone is a relatively resistant rock type in a humid climate, and it forms characteristic tabular landforms known as *chapadas* or, on a smaller scale near the coast, *tabuleiros.* Younger volcanic flows on the **Paraná Plateau** yield rich coffee lands as well as resistant ledges over which rivers spectacularly fall, as at Iguaçu Falls near the Paraguay border. The planated surface of the Brazilian uplands is evidence of weathering and erosion over long geological periods, and it has been determined that the remaining interfluve ridges topped with inselbergs are relics of the time before the southern hemisphere's supercontinent of Gondwana, including South America, Africa, Australia, and Antarctica, broke up and began to separate.

Though in northeastern Brazil the rise to the Highlands from the coast is gentle, south of Salvador in Bahía the eastern border of the plateau presents a steep, wall-like slope in the Great Escarpment (also known along most of its length by the collective name of Serra do Mar due to its appearing like a mountain from the sea). This rugged backdrop to Brazil's southeastern coastal region has presented a major obstacle to transportation, effectively impeding the flow of Brazil's migrants onto its vast lands until quite recently. Between 18°S and 30°S, the Great Escarpment is crossed by only two well-developed rivers—the Doce and the Paraíba. Otherwise, the crest is scarcely notched along its towering front.

In the southeast lie several ranges of mountains composed of crystalline rocks of a type more resistant than granite and gneiss. These stand above the upland surface in the form of hills with rounded outlines, somewhat resembling the Great Smoky Mountains in the southern Appalachians of the United States. The highest elevation in Brazil, the Pico da Bandeira, reaches 9,462 feet (2,884 meters) above sea level just northeast of Rio de Janeiro.

The major rivers that drain the extensive plateaus include the São Francisco, which drains north and east, with its outlet just south of the bulge of Brazil's northeastern coast line, and the Paraná-Paraguai system flowing to the south and east. Though most of the major rivers and their tributaries rise near the eastern seaboard, they flow in lengthy, circuitous courses away from population centers, impeding access between the littoral and the upland.

From the days of the *bandeirantes,* early adventurers who fanned out from São Paulo advancing Portuguese claims on the extensive plateau lands beyond the **Tordesillas Line;** to the restless seekers after gold and diamonds who flocked into Minas Gerais in the eighteenth century; to more recent waves of settlers seeking new commodities (coffee, cattle, or oranges), the plateau has absorbed the people and energies of Brazil. The relocation

of the capital in 1960 from Rio to the new federal district of Brasília, located far out in the *sertão,* or backcountry, was a symbol of Brazil's intent to pursue a forward settlement policy. Although the country's leaders are generally credited with success in their efforts to extend the line of occupation and congratulated for the innovativeness of the new urban design (the layout of the new capital city is in the form of a bird), many now see big-city problems for Brasília's million-plus population. In addition, the financial problems of inflation and foreign debt continue to plague this tropical giant.

Further Reading: John Dickenson, *Brazil,* London: Longman, 1982.

BRENNER PASS
See Alpine Passes

BRITTANY
See Armorican Massif

BURGUNDY GATEWAY
Formerly a kingdom, a duchy, and a county, the historic region of Burgundy (in French, Bourgogne), located in east-central France, is now administered politically by a number of *départements.* Its traditional core has been the Saône River above Lyon, and it has been a transportation crossroads since the Bronze Age due to the watershed nature of the region. The origin and growth of Burgundy were due to its geographical situation as a meeting ground between France and Germany, between Celts and Romans, and especially to its control of the strategic Burgundy Gateway (also known as the Belfort Gap) to the east.

The Rhône-Saône rivers provide a broad corridor between the **Massif Central** and the Alps, penetrating deep into the interior of France. Transport routes branch out in two directions from Dijon, the traditional capital of Burgundy, where powerful dukes once resided in elegant marble palaces.

To the northwest, routes cross a low plateau and connect with the upper Seine and the **Paris Basin.** (Today the Burgundy Canal connects the Saône with the headwaters of the Seine River.) To the east can be found the historically important strategic passageway and migration corridor of the Burgundy Gateway. The fortified town of Belfort in eastern France commands the low, rolling corridor about 15 miles (24 kilometers) wide between the Vosges (north) and the Jura (south). Crossing the gap to the east, the traveler reaches the upper Rhine near Basel, Switzerland. The Gateway stands astride the connection between Germany and France, as well as between two of the major rivers of western Europe, the Rhine and the Rhône.

It is believed that the earliest Celtic populations in Europe originated in the highlands of Switzerland and upper Austria. These people must have passed through the Burgundy Gateway as they traveled west to reach France. The Celts in the Burgundy region became Romanized after Julius Caesar conquered Gaul in 52 B.C. Later, Germanic tribes known as the Burgundians migrated southwest into this region after they were defeated by the Huns. A characteristic bon vivant attitude reflected in their famous wines (e.g., Beaujolais, Chablis, Mâconnais) and their fine beef dishes (beef stew is eaten for breakfast) has been attributed to the hybrid vigor produced by the fusion of Gallo-Roman and Germanic bloodlines.

Beginning in the sixth century A.D., Burgundy was a kingdom within the Frankish empire and was part of the middle kingdom of Charlemagne's son Lothair, before it was divided in the late ninth century. In 933 the Second Kingdom of Burgundy reunited a region that included western Switzerland and the Rhône Valley. Around the same time, a smaller duchy of Burgundy, roughly corresponding to the modern region, was created by Emperor Charles II and absorbed into the Holy Roman Empire (1034). The golden age of Burgundy occurred after 1364, when Philip the Bold began the Valois-Bourgogne line, leading to the eventual enlargement of the territory to include Belgium, the Netherlands, and Luxembourg as well as areas in France outside the traditional Rhône-Saône axis. By the fifteenth century, Burgundian dukes controlled French politics to such an extent that their alliance with the English was an important factor in the Hundred Years War (1337–1453); however, undermined by costly wars, they were defeated eventually by the Swiss. Most of the Burgundian holdings outside France then passed to the Habsburgs, while the French duchy itself was incorporated into the crown lands by Louis XI.

The town of Belfort, commanding the routes between France and Germany, was heavily fortified by French military engineer Sébastien Le Prestre de Vauban when it passed from Austrian to French possession in 1648. In the Franco-Prussian War (1870–1871) the town withstood a 108-day siege, surrendering only on order from the French government. The events were later commemorated by a statue, the *Lion of Belfort.* Belfort and its surrounding territory was the only part of Alsace that remained with France after the war. The area was successfully defended by France in World War I, and the Germans were able to conquer it in World War II only by swinging around the **Maginot Line** and seizing the town from the rear.

Today's Burgundy is smaller than its once grandiose geographical dimensions, occupying an area that approximates the historical core area of the original duchy in the Saône basin. The region evokes images of fertile plains, golden vineyards, and wooded mountains, as well as a vital stock of red-faced people of mixed Celtic, German, and Latin origins. The Belfort Gap is no longer a strategic passageway, as the region today is an industrial zone with concentrations of metallurgical and textile plants. International rail lines and the Rhône-Rhine Canal cross the historic gap. The broad Rhône-Saône corridor still provides the primary accessway from the western Mediterranean to northern France and to the German Rhineland.

Further Reading: William Davenport, "Living the Good Life in Burgundy," *National Geographic,* June 1978, pp. 794–817.

CAMPANIA (ITALIAN)

Overlooking Naples and its surrounding district is the baleful, smoking mountain of Vesuvius, which erupted in A.D. 79, destroying the Roman cities of Pompeii and Herculaneum. Vesuvius is not the only volcano in the region, as there is also Roccamonfina, now extinct, and the volcanic wreck of the Phlegraean Fields, rich in mythological associations. But volcanoes can be creators as well as destroyers: Due to the high concentration of nutrient bases in weathered ash and lava, especially phosphorus and potassium, volcanic soils are rich and easily worked. The Italian Campania is one of the largest and most fertile growing regions of level terrain in Mediterranean Europe.

The region takes its name from the Roman appellation for the fertile plain spreading out northward from Naples: the Campania Felix, or rich land. The Campania today is an autonomous political district within the Italian state, comprising lands on the western slope of the **Pyrenees** in south-central Italy and extending from the mouth of the Garigliano River south as far as the Gulf of Policastro. Much of the landscape is hilly or mountainous and is either unsettled or else is intensively used as pasture land. But the natural focus of the region has always been the thickly populated and intensively cultivated plains along the coast. Tourists come away from this much-visited land impressed by its rich cultural associations but dismayed by the poverty and wretched living conditions in the teeming city of Naples.

Many layers of civilization can be discerned in the landscape of the Italian Campania. The fertile agricultural land attracted an Etruscan population, which was conquered in the late sixth century B.C. by the Samnites. The city of Naples also originated about this time, when Greek refugees moved to the region from nearby Cumae around 600 B.C. and established a colony at the head of a deep embayment, calling it Neapolis (New City). By the end of the fourth century B.C. the Romans had taken over, but Naples was not to be the chief city under Roman rule. The Roman emperors used the Campania mainly as a resort and getaway during the dog days of late summer, when Rome was hot and unhealthy and regular sea breezes could be counted on to cool things off in this pastoral retreat.

The ancient writers Strabo, Pliny, and Polybius all praised the natural riches of the Campania. It was the chief granary for peninsular Italy during Roman times. Three crops of grain could be taken year after year, with perhaps a vegetable crop as well. Unlike much of the Mezzogiorno (southern Italy and Sicily), the Campania was not traditionally a land of large farms, or latifundia: Small proprietors and renters worked its land, not from dispersed farms but from crowded towns, resulting in a nucleated settlement pattern that remains a distinctive aspect of the region today.

Although large expanses of good agricultural land could be found in northern Italy (Cisalpine Gaul), a good seafront was lacking there. The Bay of Naples comprises a large embayment 20 miles (32 kilometers) across, between the sheltering promontories of Sorrento Peninsula to the southeast (and its sentinel island, Capri) and the volcanic mass of the Campi Flegrei to the west, ending in the islands of Procida and Ischia. The northern end of the Bay of Naples was blessed with a number of excellent harbors, many of which are the flooded craters of ancient volcanoes. Under the lee of Cape Miseno, the ancient port of the same name (Misenum) was one such submerged crater, destined to be the primary station of the Roman imperial fleet. In the furthest recess of the bay, the sheltered site of Naples was a health-and-holiday retreat for the Romans and not their chief mercantile town, a distinction owned by the town of Puteoli (Pozzuoli) at the western edge of the Posilipo ridge just southwest of Naples, in a more open situation. Suitably improved by Roman engineers with extensive harbor works and a breakwater,

A rutted road in Pompeii in the Italian Campania *(photo by Jesse Walker).*

Puteoli was the major seaport of western Italy until emperor Claudius I built a new harbor at Ostia, at the mouth of the Tiber. The ancients believed that the opening to Hades lay at Lake Avernus, another inundated crater in the Campania, surrounded by bleak lava hills. Sulfurous fumes were so thick around the lake that it was believed no bird could fly across it and live. Lake Lucrinus, yet another flooded crater, was an almost landlocked pool where Octavian's fleet could train in security from bad weather and marauding raiders; but the bottleneck entrance of the Portus Iulius constructed there was prone to being sealed with silt and was abandoned by Augustus in favor of the more open but capacious station at Misenum. Not until Byzantine times did Naples with its protected site and access to the interior become the preeminent entrepôt and seaport in the region.

In Roman times industrial activity also took place at various locations around the Campania, notably at Capua, which was

the Mediterranean, the Romans began to envision themselves as the masters of a new world-state.

Further Reading: Leonard Unger, "Rural Settlement in the Campania," *Geographical Review* 43 (1953), pp. 506–524.

CANADIAN SHIELD

This U-shaped region of ancient rocks stretching north from the **Great Lakes** to

The Isle of Capri, a limestone island off Sorrento in Southern Italy, in the Bay of Naples, the seafront of the Italian Campania *(photo by Jesse Walker)*.

originally an Etruscan bridge-town on the Volturno River and later became an important center of glassmaking and the finishing of iron- and copperware. The Capuan forges were a major attraction to Hannibal, who in the Second Punic War took over the district so as to have a first-rate arsenal. During Roman imperial days Capuan bronze found its way as far north as Scotland and Scandinavia. The victory of the Romans over Carthage signaled the gaining of the prize of the Campania with its fertile soils, productive workshops, and excellent seaports. With this window on

the Arctic Ocean comprises the oldest and almost immutable foundation of the North American continent. Composed mostly of metamorphic rocks from the Precambrian era (before the advent of major multicellular life forms), the Canadian Shield covers more than half of Canada and extends into the United States in the Adirondack Mountains of upstate New York, which are often mistakenly considered part of the Appalachians, and in the Superior Uplands of northern Michigan, Wisconsin, and Minnesota. The region is bounded on the west by the Prairie Provinces of Canada, while to the east it extends all the way to the Atlantic coast and includes Greenland (the maritime provinces of Canada represent Appalachian-era rocks).

Also known as the Laurentian Upland, the shield is the largest exposed portion of Archaean bedrock in the world and is geologically comparable to the Scandinavian Shield of northern Europe. Uplifted in an-

The Canadian Shield was a major barrier preventing early settlers from the eastern provinces of Canada from migrating westward, and thus eliminated the kind of frontier—the nearly continuous, westward-moving line of agricultural occupancy—that has been considered an important influence on U.S. history and culture. The obstacle has been due not so much to topography as

The rocky coastline of Lake Superior in the Upper Peninsula of Michigan, part of the Canadian Shield (*photo by Sam Hilliard*).

cient times, this old land surface has been smoothed down by erosion to an area of low relief, with only a few monadnocks and isolated mountains lying above the nearly level plain. Pleistocene glaciation planed the surface even further, gouging out thousands of lakes, disrupting the drainage patterns, and removing much of the soil. The southern part of the region is covered with a thick spruce-fir forest associated with the severe continental climate of the upper midlatitudes, while the Arctic north here is blanketed by tundra, as in northern Russia and northern Scandinavia.

to vegetation and associated soils. Needle-leaved trees contribute little organic matter to the soil, which tends to be acidic. This combines with a lack of nutrients in weathered crystalline rocks and a short growing season to produce a large zone across the top of the Great Lakes lacking in significant agricultural opportunity.

Early French settlers in the lower St. Lawrence Valley were literally hemmed in to the north and south respectively by the Canadian Shield and the Appalachian uplands. The rim of these infertile highlands is visible on the horizon from the floor of the valley and must have been a continual reminder of Quebec's closed agricultural frontier. The core area of Anglo settlement in Canada was a roughly triangular area between Lakes Ontario, Erie, and Huron, particularly the corridor between Toronto and Windsor, in present-day Ontario. Though receiving some Tory sympathizers during the American Revolution, the heavy influx of population arrived here in the early and mid-nineteenth century. More economically dynamic than the French settlement region to the east, expansion of the Anglo zone was restricted by the barren gneiss and granite that lay to the north in what is today Algonquin Provincial Park. The extensive sedimentary formations of the U.S. Midwest and **Great Plains** (which lie on top of the ancient, Precambrian shield) provided a crucial agricultural frontier for the robust young American nation in its midsection, allowing an endless vista of farms, ranches, roads, and towns to stretch westward as far as the foothills of the Rocky Mountains, in sharp contrast to the central parts of Canada. Only in the late nineteenth century, following confederation (1867) and the completion of the transcontinental Canadian Pacific Railway (1885), would the eastern and western parts of Canada be joined across the barren shield.

Further Reading: Charles B. Hunt, *Natural Regions of the United States and Canada,* San Francisco: W. H. Freeman, 1974.

CANARY ISLANDS

A small, colorful bird in the finch family, the canary is native to various groups of islands off northwest Africa and southern Europe, including the Canary Islands. The name of these Spanish lands, however, does not derive from, but rather lends itself to, the bird. The Spanish found a breed of large, fierce dogs on this archipelago of seven major islands some 65 miles (105 kilometers) from the Africa coast (but 680 miles, or 1,094 kilometers, from Cádiz). Canarias, the Spanish name for the isles, derives from the Latin *Canis,* or dog—hence, the place-name actually means Dog Islands. Columbus had so much trouble with the native peoples on Hispaniola and Cuba that he took some of these fighting canines along on his second voyage.

Situated at a strategic shipping crossroads, the Canaries were the last stop on the long oceanic voyage westward from Europe. Columbus stopped here in autumn 1492 to obtain food and provisions (and especially water) before setting a course westward toward the as yet undiscovered Americas. The Canaries' location at a latitude of about 28° N on the edge of the dependable trade wind belt was all-important during the age of sail. Sailing southwest only a short distance, navigators could pick up the easterly trade wind blowing out of the northeast that would carry a ship across the wide Atlantic in about a month, in Columbus's day.

The two largest towns are Las Palmas and Santa Cruz de Tenerife, located, respectively, on the larger islands of Gran Canaria and Tenerife. The islands are mostly mountainous and volcanic in origin. The famous Peak of Tenerife (Pico de Teide) rises to an impressive 12,200 feet (3,719 meters) in elevation and is the highest point on Spanish territory. The coasts are steep and rocky, with only limited level lands available for plantation crops, including historically important sugar cane, cochineal (a natural dye), grapes for wine making, and more recently, bananas and tomatoes. The western islands and the west sides of islands receive more precipitation than the dry eastern or lee slopes. A luxuriant broadleaf evergreen forest of laurel woodlands (*monte verde*) can be found at the lower elevations, while at higher altitudes a pine forest predominates, which features a species of pine (*Pinus canariensis*) that has one of the most restricted geographical distributions of the more than 100 species of the genus *Pinus.* The luxuriance of the original vegetation perhaps resulted in the ancients' felicitous name for the place: Fortunatae Insulae, or Fortunate Islands.

Lying just outside and a little to the south of the **Strait of Gibraltar,** the Canaries were known to the ancient seafaring Greeks, Phoenicians, and Carthaginians. The classical writer Pliny referred to the "Canaria, so called from the multitude of dogs of giant size." Even so famous a traveler as Alexander von Humboldt in 1799 noted in climbing the Pico de Teide that the once dense pine forest had been reduced to a few named landmark conifers acting as guideposts along the way.

Hierro, or Ferro, the westernmost island, was the "first meridian" for ancient Greek geographers, but the influential world map of Ptolemy (second century A.D.) made the nearest of the Canaries to Africa, the island of Fuerteventura, the basis for calculating east-west distance. The Dutch and French later selected the meridian of Ferro as the first meridian. Cardinal Richelieu in 1630 called a congress of scientists to meet and discuss the problem of establishing a base line for measuring longitude. This group recommended the "longitude of Ferro" to Louis XIII, who officially promulgated it in 1634. The English preeminence in matters maritime in the nineteenth century brought the Greenwich line to the fore in consideration of a prime meridian.

Although Arab traders occasionally stopped at the Canaries during the medieval period, the islands were rediscovered by Europeans in 1334. Spanish presence intensified in 1402–1403 with the conquest of Lanzarote, an early goal of Andalusian slaving expeditions, by the Breton Jean de Béthencourt under the auspices of the Castilian monarchy. Using this inauspicious, dry island as a springboard, the Spanish mounted expeditions of conquest to the larger islands populated by large numbers of hostile Guanche natives. The resistance of the fierce Guanches on the three islands of Gran Canaria suitable for commercial production of sugar cane—Gran Canaria, Tenerife, and La Palma—was not finally overcome until 1496.

The technology of sugar making was brought by the Portuguese from the **Madeira Islands.** In the sixteenth century, the wealth of the Canary sugar islands was already proverbial, but by the end of the century, competition with the Caribbean and nearby African coastlands had caused sugar growing to decline in the Canaries. Henceforth, livestock raisers and subsistence farmers would be a larger factor in the clearance of the forest than would the growers of cane. The Fortunate Islands of the ancients were fast becoming skeletal deserts.

The Spanish repelled successive French, Dutch, and British attempts to seize the well-fortified southern coast of Tenerife. In one such attempt, in 1797, the God-like (at least to the English) Admiral Lord Nelson sustained a wound from one of Tenerife's batteries that led to the loss of his right arm. At the military encampment of La Esperanza in the pine forests of Tenerife, Franco first raised the cry of rebellion against the republican government in 1936. With the victory of the Falange three years later, the Caudillo launched a major government program aimed at restoring the forests of the Canaries (as well as of the mainland). Coupled with the decline of subsistence producers and graziers, the ambitious government programs, especially the replanting of the pine forests, were a notable success. Destructive land uses that had followed one another in succession for so many years were now at least partially in check.

See also: Greenwich Meridian.

Further Reading: James J. Parsons, "Human Influences on the Pine and Laurel Forests of the Canary Islands," *Geographical Review* 71(1981), pp. 253–271.

CAPE HORN

At the southernmost point of South America lies a steep, rocky headland (el. 1,391 feet or 424 meters) first discovered and rounded by the Dutch navigator Willem Corneliszoon Schouten in 1616. Cape Horn (in Spanish, Cabo de Hornos) is located on small Horn Island in the Chilean portion of the **Tierra del Fuego** archipelago. Cold, stormy weather prevails in these latitudes, and mariners faced brisk westerly winds, strong currents, and lashing storms when they attempted to round the horn.

The Dutch United East India Company, which was chartered in 1602, prohibited nonmembers from using either the Cape of Good Hope or the **Strait of Magellan** on their way east. This prohibition provoked Isaak Le Mairie, an Amsterdam merchant, and Schouten (of Hoorn, in North Holland), a master mariner who had visited the East Indies three times before, to attempt an alternative crossing. Hoorn, a charming old town on a horn, or spit, in the IJsselmeer (formerly **Zuider Zee**), furnished two ships for the expedition. On 14 June 1615 Schouten and Le Mairie sailed from the Frisian Island of Texel. On 29 January 1616 they passed a "high hilly land, cov-

ered with snow, ending with a sharp point, which we called Cape Horne." The name honors the hometown of the navigator and the principal sponsor of the voyage. Because the Cape was shrouded in fog, its discoverers did not realize that it was an island. This was the most important discovery for oceangoing commerce since Magellan's 1520 crossing of the strait that bears his name.

Due to foul weather and treacherous seas, navigators generally avoided the Cape route in the early years after its discovery. Captain James Cook stated in his journal of the *Endeavour*'s voyage (1769), "The doubling of Cape Horn is thought by some to be a mighty thing, and others to this day prefer the Straits of Magellan." But after Cook's fast passage, the big sailing ships shunned the strait, preferring to fight the high winds of "Cape Stiff" rather than face the dangers of the shorter route.

The mystique of the difficult crossing was used in Coleridge's famous ballad *The Rime of the Ancient Mariner.* The route was a major one in the gold rush from New York to San Francisco, though transisthmian crossings of Central America were also made. After the building of the Panama Canal, the Cape route decreased in importance. Most baseball players today are unaware that they are commemorating this geographic feature when, after completing a successful out, they throw the ball around the infield, calling this "going round the horn." The phrase originally derived from the length and circuitousness of the voyage around Cape Horn.

Further Reading: William DeCosta, "Around the Horn: The Journal of a Voyage to San Francisco," *Missouri Review* 15 (1992), pp. 93–121.

CARCASSONE GATEWAY

See Languedoc

CARPATHIAN MOUNTAINS

The geologically young Carpathians are the largest mountain system in central and eastern Europe. They stretch about 930 miles (1,500 kilometers) in a great arc from Bratislava, Slovakia, across southern Poland and western Ukraine before turning sharply westward in Romania as the Transylvanian Alps to end at the **Iron Gate.** As a terrain unit they link the Alps and the Balkan mountains, but their historical importance has been that they enclosed, and hence partially protected, the fertile corridor of the lower Danube from northern and eastern advances.

Though of the same geological age as the Alps, the Carpathians have been downfaulted and collapsed since the time of their formation, and as a result, upland plateaus, broad valleys, and basins prevail. Nowhere do the mountains present as formidable a barrier as the Alps. The highest elevations are attained on the border between Slovakia and Poland, in the Tatra Mountains (also known as the High Tatras), where Gerlachovka reaches 8,737 feet (2,663 meters) and in the Transylvanian Alps at Moldoveanul (8,343 feet or 2,543 meters). The Tatras, together with the nearby Beskids, compose what are known as the Northern Carpathians. Evidence of past glaciation in the form of cirques, arêtes, and mountain lakes can be found, but no glaciation exists today. The Transylvanian Alps also present some nearly alpine scenery, but their importance has been their enclosure and protection of the fertile plateau of Transylvania. Beginning just north of Bucharest, the Transylvanian Alps are also known as the Carpaţii Meridionali, or Southern Carpathians. Here the mountains have provided an effective refuge for the Danubian plainsmen of Walachia, who have during times of troubles headed for the Transylvanian hills until things settled down. During the decline of the Roman Empire, Roman legionnaires who had been assigned to guard the province of Dacia (approximately the same area as today's Romania) fled before the onslaught of the Visigoths and Huns and took cover in the north. As a result of this series of events, the Romanian language developed as a romance tongue—that is, a language based on Latin.

The Carpathians are crossed by numerous low passes—from west to east, Jablunkov Pass, Lupków Pass, Dukla Pass, Jablonica Pass, and Predeal Pass. At Dukla Pass the Hungarian plain makes its farthest incursion, and only 20 miles (32 kilometers) separate the densely settled regions that flank the mountains. Passes allow two-way traffic, of course, and since prehistoric times, steppe dwellers from southern Russia and central Asia have swept through the Carpathian passes to gain access to the Danube corridor. It is believed that by this route the Magyars drove Slavic peoples from the fertile plains at the great bend of the Danube. The border between Hungary and Romania continues to be a problem to this day, as numerous Hungarians live in Romanian Transylvania. The earlier Roman presence in the region was intended primarily to seal off the Carpathian passes and prevent the incursion of nomadic marauders, whose penetration of the Roman *limes* on a number of occasions had threatened Roman hegemony.

Although the Carpathians are mostly forested and are only thinly populated, they continue to be an important border region. As a watershed they divide the north- and east-flowing rivers like the Vistula and the Dniester from streams that flow south and west into the Danube. Though crossed by railroads and highways today, the mountains still play a significant role in defining and delineating the increasingly fractured map of eastern Europe. The Carpathians are rich in minerals, notably iron, copper, and zinc, as well as timber, but their greatest treasure lies along the foothills of the Romanian Carpathians, near Ploieşti, in the largest petroleum field in Europe outside of Russia.

See also: Hungarian Basin.

Further Reading: Emmanuel de Martonne, "The Carpathians: Physiographic Features Controlling Human Geography," *Geographical Review* 3 (1917), pp. 417–437.

CASTILE

See Meseta (Spanish)

CAUCASUS

This mountain barrier stretching from the **Black Sea** to the Caspian Sea is generally regarded as a natural border between southeastern European Russia and Asia. It thus forms part of the frame rather than the central picture of Western development. Yet a large number of peoples of diverse culture and language have either settled or been driven to this border region, whose complexly folded landscapes mirror the social and cultural divisions of its peoples.

The Caucasian mountain system extends from the mouth of the Kuban River on the Black Sea to the Apsheron Peninsula on the Caspian. It separates the Manych Depression in southern Russia from Turkey and Iran. The Caucasus is traditionally divided into two major regions. The North Caucasus, or Ciscaucasia, rises from the steppes of the Manych Depression to the south until reaching the highest peak in the mountain system (Mt. Elbrus, at 18,481 feet or 5,633 meters). The northwest-southeast-trending mountains here are higher than the Alpine peak Mt. Blanc. The Caucasus Mountains are crossed by several passes,

notably the Daryal Pass, the Georgian Military Road, and the Ossetian Military Road, which connect the North Caucasus with the second major section, Transcaucasia. According to strictly drawn lines, Transcaucasia, or South Caucasia, is on the Asian continent. This region includes Armenia, Georgia, and Azerbaijan, which were republics of the Soviet Union (the Union of Soviet Socialist Republics, or U.S.S.R.) until its demise in 1991. From 1922 to 1936 these three units were known as the Transcaucasian Soviet Federated Socialist Republic, which was one of the original constituent republics of the U.S.S.R.

The leading mineral resource is petroleum, which is found at both ends of the range. The Baku oil field on the Apsheron Peninsula has been especially rich, its exploitation going back to czarist times. No less an individual than Alfred Nobel of Sweden invested in the early twentieth-century boom in Caspian oil.

While the Transcaucasian republics were able to gain their independence following the demise of the Soviet Union, the north Caucasian districts, which lie closer to the Russian core, were not. This includes many small semiautonomous territories and oblasts that remain, often against their wishes, within the Russian polity. This is the case, for instance, with the Chechens of the Grozny area, who have a long history of resisting foreign incursion. Located in the northern foothills of the range and possessing significant petroleum resources, the Chechen lands put up the most active resistance to czarist advances in the nineteenth century. It was only with the surrender of the guerrilla leader Shamil in 1859 that Russia obtained control of the Caucasus. In 1991, the parliament of the Checheno-Ingush autonomous republic declared itself independent of the Soviet Union; but one of the first acts of Boris Yeltsin after the August coup and his takeover of the Russian army was to send troops to the region, to put down the revolt and prevent the fracturing of this republic within the Russian federation.

Known to the ancients as Colchis, the Caucasus was the destination of Jason and the Argonauts in their quest for the Golden Fleece. A high Caucasian peak was the place of exile of the rebel Prometheus, where every day a hungry vulture tore away at his liver, the source of his passions, with no relief, since every night the liver grew back. This borderland has always been contested ground: between the ancient Byzantine and Sassanid (Persian) Empires, and more recently, between the rising Russian peoples and the Ottoman Turks. The people of Christian religion, especially the Georgians and Armenians, accepted the hegemony of the Russian czars as protection against the Turks. In Azerbaijan, Dagestan, and Circassia, the largely Muslim populace resisted the inroads of Russian influence until the mid-nineteenth century. A veritable Babel of tongues exists in the Caucasus, with no less than 40 languages spoken, many with less than 100,000 speakers and in danger of being lost. Despite its sometimes violent history, the Caucasus has been celebrated for its beauty, notably in Pushkin's poem "A Captive of the Caucasus" and in Tolstoy's novels *The Cossacks* and *Hadji Murad*.

CENTRAL AMERICAN VOLCANIC AXIS

The southernmost part of the North American continent, from Chiapas, Mexico to Panama, resembles a funnel steadily narrowing from the northwest to the southeast. A continuous line of young volcanoes runs 800 miles (1,287 kilometers) along the Pacific side of the region.

This volcanic chain is structurally related to the inner arc of volcanic Caribbean islands in the Lesser Antilles, from St. Kitts to Grenada. Together, these sets of volcanic peaks make up the longest and most spectacular mountain range in Middle America (that is, in Mexico, the Caribbean, and the Central American republics from Guatemala to Panama). The conical volcanic peaks rise as high as 13,846 feet (4,210 meters) at their highest point, at Tajumulco in Guatemala.

The central portion of this mountain chain in the Nicaraguan lowlands has experienced crustal fracture in the form of rifting, and the result is a long, narrow depression trending northwest-southeast, occupied by the largest freshwater lakes of Middle America: Lake Managua and Lake Nicaragua. Both drain into the Caribbean through the San Juan River, which forms the political border with Costa Rica and together with the lakes is a historically important isthmian crossing.

As in the Mesa Central of Mexico, here volcanic activity has produced one of the most stunning landscapes in the world, magnificent lake-studded mountain basins encircled by lofty peaks, such as lakes Atitlán and Amatitlán, in the Guatemalan highlands; but geological hazards such as earthquakes are ever present. The volcanic spine spreads out in the Guatemalan highlands and in eastern Honduras, while further south in Nicaragua and somewhat off to the east it cuts a sharp line. Highland basins further south in Costa Rica widen to produce the fertile and well-populated Meseta Central, with elevations between 3,000 and 5,000 feet (914–1,524 meters). South of the Meseta Central rises the Cordillera de Talamanca, with elevations over 12,000 feet (3,658 meters), which is, strictly speaking, a batholith (a granite mass that has cooled beneath the surface and subsequently been uplifted), and therefore is an interruption of the volcanic axis. Vulcanism resumes in Panama, but the peaks diminish as one approaches the Canal Zone. Further south, the low mountain ranges of the **Isthmus of Darién** region are related more closely to the northwest prong of the **Andes** in Colombia. A strict geographic delineation of the axis would then include the region from the **Isthmus of Tehuantepec** in Mexico to the Canal Zone.

Altitude is always an important factor in the Tropics, and nowhere in the Neotropics (the New World Tropics) is this more evident than in Central America, with the possible exception of the northern Andes. A regular sequence of zones of climate and associated vegetation is passed through as one rises in elevation from the hot lower slopes (*tierra caliente*) to the intermediate elevations of temperate climate (*tierra templada*) and then the cooler upper zones of *tierra fría*. Most of the population lives on soils of weathered lava and ash, for in the Tropics weathering is fast and volcanic soils are richer in nutrients than the old, oxidized soils that generally prevail in the low latitudes. Precipitation is heaviest on the eastern or windward side of the volcanic chain, while the Pacific side is dry enough that cotton can replace sugar or bananas as the major cash crop.

Central America has been important in the cultural history of the Americas in two ways: as a land bridge connecting South America to the wide expanse of Mexico and lands northward; and as an obstacle to European colonizers who wanted to travel directly from one ocean to another. The first role ensured the migration of plants, animals, natural foodstuffs, and Indians and their cultures the full length of the Americas, preventing isolation and allowing fruitful interaction of both a social and a ge-netic kind. Europeans from the time of Columbus, who visited the region's Caribbean shores on his fourth voyage (1502), sought to get across the land-mass as quickly as possible. With the exception of the Chiapas and Panama, the region was organized under the captaincy general of Guatemala until independence was attained in 1821.

Transisthmian crossings became increasingly important in the nineteenth century with the rise of the United States as a two-ocean power and the increased role of oceanic shipping. The major transisthmian crossings from north to south include: (1) the Tehuantepec route from Coatzacoalcos on the Caribbean to Salina Cruz on the Pacific; (2) the Comayagua or Honduran Depression route from Puerto Cortés to the Gulf of Fonseca, a major indentation of the coastline on the Pacific side; (3) the Nicaragua route along the San Juan River and the lakes of the rift valley; and (4) the Panama Canal linking Colón to Panama City. Between 1850 and 1900, more than 30 routes were surveyed across the Central American isthmus. Of these the old Panama route was preferred due to its short, 50-mile (80-kilometer) distance between the oceans. After an initial failure by the French, the Panama Canal was built by the United States at great cost and expense of life (yellow fever was endemic to the area). Completed in 1914, the construction of the canal certainly ranks as one of the largest engineering projects in history and is a worthy testimonial to the energies and ambitions of its inspirer, the first American president to contemplate an active role for U.S. foreign policy—Teddy Roosevelt.

Further Reading: Robert C. West and John P. Augelli, *Middle America: Its Lands and Peoples,* 3d ed., Englewood Cliffs, N.J.: Prentice-Hall, 1989.

CENTRAL VALLEY (U.S.)

What has been called the world's richest agricultural valley is an alluvium-filled structural trough stretching more than 400 miles (644 kilometers) from Redding in northern California to the Tehachapi Mountains just outside Los Angeles. The Central Valley occupies a middle ground in a geographical sense because it lies between the coastal ranges and the **Sierra** drier, wider, and more populated than the northern section focused on the Sacramento River. The latter lacks the extensive cotton fields, orange groves, oil fields, and combined Hispanic–Upper Southern stock of the southern section of the valley. Not nearly so flat as often conceived, the terrain of the Central Valley has a pronounced asymmetry, with the alluvial fans of the streams draining the Sierras

Agricultural specialization in the Central Valley of California, Lindsay, about 50 miles southeast of Fresno (*photo by Jesse Walker*).

Nevada, but also in a cultural sense, because it represents a mixture and fusion of elements of urbanized coastal California and the wilderness of the Sierras. John Steinbeck's "Long Valley" today is for the most part an intensively cropped, irrigated land, which boasts an impressive variety of crops, orchards, and vineyards that nearly match in diversity the ethnicities of its people.

The southern two-thirds of the valley, drained by the San Joaquin, Kings, Kaweah, Tule, and Kern Rivers (often referred to as the San Joaquin Valley), is shifting the lowlands toward the west. The San Joaquin features six good-sized cities, from Bakersfield to Stockton, with Fresno the regional capital.

The first Spaniards in the valley found little use for the scattered saltbush at its southern margin or the broad tule marshes beyond, fed by Sierra meltwater. Extensive cattle grazing, organized by Spanish and Mexican missions and ranchos, predominated in the early period, spurred on by the hide and tallow industries, which provided raw materials to New England's burgeoning boot and shoe industry. The great drought of 1862 in conjunction with the arrival of large numbers of Anglos after the midcentury gold rush led to the demise of the rancho system, but Anglo operators of large-scale, technologically innovative bonanza wheat farms were already in evidence by the 1870s, when California became the second wheat state in the nation. Though short-lived, this phase set a pattern of large farms dependent on outside labor that would characterize the San Joaquin part of the valley in the following century.

This largest of agricultural districts in the premier agricultural state in the nation is best known as an intensive specialty crop region. A bewildering variety of fruits, nuts, and vegetables are produced here, often in specialized districts, which has resulted in a finely meshed, microagricultural pattern. Cotton predominates in the southern San Joaquin on the west side of the valley; nut crops are most common on the older red terraces in the eastern valley. Almonds can be found up and down the valley, on small farms as well as large, though the image of a soulless agribusiness has persistently been connected with the valley. Raisin grapes are grown in the sandy soils north and south of Fresno, while table grapes are found in a number of small towns scattered throughout the valley (for example, Reedley, Delano, Lodi). Orange groves today are found in a narrow thermal belt in the south-central San Joaquin, on the east side near the mountains (for example, in Porterville, Exeter, and Woodlake). Many cities are so proud of their agricultural specialty that they advertise themselves as its capital: Patterson, for instance, is the apricot capital of the world, Lindsay, the olive capital, and Mendota, the cantaloupe city. There is a need for continual experimentation and development of new crops and varieties better adapted to the local conditions and the vagaries of the market. Pistachios shot up in production after the traditional supplier, Iran, was cut off in response to the crisis of 1979; but today new products are sought in order to increase earnings.

The Central Valley is not entirely agricultural, nor is it the locale only of success stories. In the far south, oil has been king. As recently as 1986, Kern County was the leading oil-producing county in the United States. Big agriculture here forms links with big railroad and land interests. The extensive land holdings of the Southern Pacific (the government granted this rail company alternate 640-acre [256-hectare] sections along the right-of-way) were sold to Standard Oil, Texaco, Shell, and other petroleum firms. With the advent of cheap, government-subsidized water and deep-well turbine pumping, the oil men found themselves becoming farmers. Superior Oil and Tenneco absorbed the Kern County Land Company and went into agriculture in a big way.

The worst failure brought to light thus far in this massive production system, which today is increasingly on trial, is the befouling of the waters at the Kesterson Wildlife Reserve near Los Banos. The deformity and death of migratory wildfowl in this preserve, which adjoins the gigantic Westlands Water District, signals severe water pollution problems associated with excessive fertilization, depletion of underground aquifers, and the deleterious effects of heavy irrigation of dry soils. The perched water table of the impermeable Corcoran clay causes the ponding of irrigation water, and by capillary action roots accumulate high levels of salts, soluble minerals, and naturally occurring toxic chemicals. Selenium, for instance, increases in concentration as one ascends the food chain (in accordance with the principle of bioaccumulation) until its toxicity is great enough to kill wildlife.

Further Reading: James J. Parsons, "A Geographer Looks at the San Joaquin Valley," *Geographical Review,* Oct. 1986, pp. 371–389.

CHAMPAGNE
See Paris Basin

CHANNEL ISLANDS (BRITISH)
These British dependencies located within the jaws of the bay formed between the Breton and Norman peninsulas long figured in territorial battles between France and England. The islands are strategically positioned at the south end of the **English Channel,** 80 miles (129 kilometers) south of the English coast and only a few miles from France, well within sight of the Cotentin (Norman) coast on clear days.

The four major islands of this group, also known as the Îles Normandes (Norman Isles), are *Jersey, Guernsey, Alderney,* and *Sark,* with 70 of the 75 combined square miles (181–194 square kilometers) and nearly all of the inhabitants accounted for by Jersey and Guernsey. These Gallic bits of Britain are steeped in French culture and tradition: Among their more distinctive features are the antiquated forms of government (Sark is run as a feudal fiefdom complete with manorial seigneur); the old Norman unit of land measure (the *vergée* is slightly less than a half-acre); and a Norman French patois that is rapidly disappearing before the onslaught of English and standard forms of French. Residents deny (with some justification) that the islands are located in the *English* Channel, maintaining that all the islands with the exception of northernmost Alderney are actually in the Gulf of Saint-Malo.

Physically, the islands constitute offshore fragments of the granitic **Armorican Massif,** rising abruptly from the sea in steep, highly indented cliff faces. Most of the area of the two large islands of Jersey and Guernsey comprises a series of surfaces that represent old beach levels, at elevations of approximately 400 feet (122 meters) above sea level. Maritime climatic effects and higher levels of sunshine than those enjoyed by other parts of Britain have benefited local agriculture. The islands are well known today for market gardening of vegetables, especially tomatoes and potatoes, and for flower growing. But their most important contribution to world agriculture has been to stock farming, particularly dairy farming, which depends on their two most famous breeds: the Jersey, a small, tan-colored cow that leads the world in the richness of its butter; and the Guernsey, a larger, brown and white cow also known for its butter production. Strict regulation preventing foreign dairy cows on the islands ensures the purity of these distinctive breeds.

Remains of prehistoric cave dwellers as far back as 110,000 B.P. have been found on Jersey, the nearest large island to the coast. With the rising sea level due to the melting of glaciers, the connection to the mainland was cut off about 10,000 B.P., and evidence of early man disappeared. Not until about 3,000 B.C. did Neolithic boatmen venture out to these islands. Megalithic remains—elaborate stone tombs—have been found on Jersey.

Early Christianization in the sixth century was followed by a period when the islands were assaulted by sea raiders and Vikings. In 933 they were incorporated into the Duchy of Normandy, itself an accession to the domain of the Norse Vikings—hence its name—who were content to settle and be assimilated into French culture rather than continue their marauding ways. With the Norman Conquest (1066), the islands were united with England. Channel Islanders still refer to the English monarch as the Duke of Normandy and point out—correctly—that they conquered England, not the other way around. The French gradually gained control of the mainland territory previously held by the English crown, so that by 1204 the Channel Islands were the only part of Normandy remaining to England.

During the English civil war, Jersey gave refuge to Britain's exiled Charles II. Guernsey—which rarely sees eye to eye with Jersey—declared for parliament, but royalists maintained a garrison overlooking St. Peter Port. Lobbing thousands of rounds on Guernsey's major city, Cornet Castle was the last royalist outpost to fall to parliamentary forces. The graceful, leisurely city of St. Peter Port was the home from 1855 to 1870 of the great French *littérateur* Victor Hugo, who dedicated his novel *Toilers of the Sea* "to the rock of hospitality and liberty, to that portion of old Norman ground inhabited by the noble little nation of the sea; to the island of Guernsey." During World War II, the islands were taken by the Nazis after France fell. They were the only part of British territory to be under German occupation, from 30 June 1940 to 9 May 1945.

Further Reading: Victor Hugo, *The Toilers of the Sea,* New York: Heritage, 1961 (orig. ed. 1866); John Uttley, *A Short History of the Channel Islands,* New York: Praeger, 1966.

CHESAPEAKE BAY

The largest estuary on the east coast of the United States, a superabundant fishery, a place of surpassing beauty, the cradle of American settlement, and a region with a rapidly growing human population are all accurate descriptions of Chesapeake Bay.

Known locally as the Bay, the Chesapeake is the largest arm of the Atlantic along the eastern seaboard. It is separated from Delaware Bay and the Atlantic Ocean by the Delmarva Peninsula, usually referred to as the Eastern Shore, which includes parts of the states of Delaware, Maryland, and Virginia. The bay extends almost 200 miles (322 kilometers) from Havre de Grace at its head (northeast of Baltimore) to the Hampton Roads anchorage, where Norfolk is located. The thirteen-mile-wide entrance to the bay at its southern end lies between Cape Charles (to the north) and Cape Henry (to the south). The width of the bay varies from four to 30 miles (6.4–48 kilometers), but it is sufficiently deep for oceanic vessels and requires dredging only at canal and harbor entrances. At the top and bottom of the bay, canals provide more direct links to the sheltered Intracoastal Waterway.

The Chesapeake resembles a fjord coast in the processes of its formation but not in its final physiognomy. With the melting of the Pleistocene ice sheets around 10,000 B.P., sea levels rose hundreds of feet and drowned the mouths of major streams flowing into the Atlantic Ocean. The bay is the submerged mouth of the lower Susquehanna, and deep-draft vessels trace out the course of this ancient river when they follow the ship channel. The Susquehanna, a major drainage feature in Pennsylvania and New York, flows into the bay at its head and is the most important source of fresh water for the bay.

The rocks of the coastal plain dip to the north and are submerged along the eastern seaboard north of Long Island. In the northern part of the Chesapeake, the coastal plain is only a narrow strip, while to the south the plain broadens considerably. The **Fall Line,** the boundary between the **Appalachian Piedmont** and the coastal plain, crosses Richmond, Virginia, which is located upstream from where the James River flows into the bay. Near the head of the bay at Baltimore, located at the mouth of the Patapso River, the Fall Line is just west of the shore. The rocks of the coastal plain lie like reverse shingles on the uplifted Appalachians and dip to the east as well as the north. As a result, the Eastern Shore consists of low-lying ground—much of it wetlands—and a complex interdigitation of land and water. Before the building of the Bay Bridges, inaccessibility assured the isolation and persistence of traditional ways of life and speech patterns among the proud watermen of the Eastern Shore.

On the western shores of the bay, the strip of coastal plain attracted the first settlers due to the deep penetration of tidewater into the interior. The preferred sites were near the mouths of tidal rivers, creeks, and branches and on the narrow peninsulas of land, known locally as necks, located between the broad river mouths. The best-known of these is perhaps Virginia's Northern Neck, between the Potomac and Rappahannock Rivers.

The first permanent settlement in British North America took place at Jamestown Island in 1607, on the western shore near the mouth of the tidal James River. The extremely high rates of mortality in early Virginia seem to have had more to do with the estuarine location of the initial settlement vis-à-vis water supply than with food shortages or Indian troubles. The early settlers drank river water, the salinity of which varied daily according to the tidal schedule as well as seasonally. Fresher water could be found early in the spring, but by late summer the water became brackish. The most common diseases were gastrointestinal ailments, such as typhoid fever and dysentery, which were the result of the increase of salt water up the estuary in the

summer and the concentration of pathogens in the town's water supply. Mortality rates were as high as 30 percent (for each outbreak).

A year after Jamestown was founded, Captain John Smith explored and mapped the region with considerable accuracy, putting the Indian name Chesapeack (Great Shellfish Bay) on the map for the first time. Fish species, including rockfish, perch, and shad, as well as bountiful shellfish, such as blue crabs, oysters, and clams were especially important in early periods of settlement, when food resources were often undependable. Shellfish became important commercially only in the late nineteenth century, with the development of improved transportation and a growing urban market. The peak of oyster production occurred in the 1880s, when fifteen million bushels of oysters were harvested from the bay, giving rise to the description of the bay by the Baltimore sage, H. L. Mencken, as an "immense protein factory." Today the oyster harvest has declined to such an extent—it is perhaps 5 percent of what it was a century ago—that fewer and fewer watermen can be seen easing their open boats out into the quiet waters of the bay at predawn hours to collect the savory appetizer.

Various tribes of Algonquin-speaking native Americans concentrated in the Virginia tidewater and Eastern Shore. They showed the settlers how to cultivate and smoke the "filthy weed" seen growing in the Jamestown area. Tobacco soon became the primary cash crop destined for European markets. The location of tobacco plantations along tidal rivers and on narrow peninsulas of land accessible to tidewater reinforced a dispersed settlement pattern, to the point of isolation. Tobacco required little processing: It was packed tightly into hogsheads and dispatched directly from landings to foreign markets, thus shortcircuiting processes of urban development. In a situation where "every planter had a river at his door"—in a common locution of the time—roads and bridges were poorly developed, and settlements were only loosely connected to one another.

Tobacco grew fairly well on the somewhat sandy soils of the coastal plain, but the crop is hard on the soil, and continuous cropping leads to depletion of soil nutrients. With declining soil fertility, planters had to clear new ground or migrate to interior places on the Piedmont. This gave rise to a pronounced contrast between yeoman or family farm communities in the western parts of Virginia and Maryland and slave-based plantations in eastern tidewater locations. Maryland had a similar north-south pattern, with important differences between the early-settled southern part of the state, where a plantation economy attached itself to a wide coastal plain, and the northern part, which was settled later and only developed rapidly in the late colonial period with the establishment of Baltimore as an agricultural foodstuff processor. Baltimore did not depend on tobacco but rather on milling, and a steady supply of wheat and other foodstuffs came down the Susquehanna from southeastern Pennsylvania, to be ground into flour or otherwise processed at water power sites on Baltimore's Fall Line.

The bay, with its highly indented coastline and numerous isolated inlets, especially on the Eastern Shore, was a good refuge for buccaneers and privateers during the heyday of piracy in the seventeenth and eighteenth centuries. During the War of 1812, the British reached and burned the city of Washington from the bay in 1814, only to be repulsed at Baltimore, an event celebrated in the U.S. national anthem.

Today there is an appreciation of the delicate estuarine ecosystem of the bay and the need to reduce environmental pressures. The oyster catch has declined precipitously, rockfish or striped bass have been so reduced in numbers that fishing was banned in the mid-1980s, and extensive areas of wetlands that provide flood protection and habitat for wildlife have been destroyed. The blame rests with the growing population on or near the shores of the bay and their escalating demands. The problems of the bay can be attributed to the runoff of agricultural fertilizers leading to increased nutrients in the waters; lack of proper sewage treatment, which adds to the phosphorus load; and chemicals released at the outtakes of numerous industrial establishments.

Further Reading: Carville Earle, "Environment, Disease, and Mortality in Early Virginia," *Journal of Historical Geography* 5 (1979), pp. 365–390; Tom Horton, *Bay Country,* Baltimore: Johns Hopkins University Press, 1987; William W. Warner, *Beautiful Swimmers: Watermen, Crabs, and the Chesapeake Bay,* New York: Penguin, 1977.

COLORADO PLATEAU

The Colorado Plateau covers more than 150,000 square miles (388,500 square kilometers) in the Four Corners area of the southwestern United States, where the boundaries of Arizona, New Mexico, Utah, and Colorado meet at right angles. The region includes most of the area between the southern Rocky Mountains and the **Great Basin** to the west. The Colorado River and its tributaries the Green, Gunnison, Little Colorado, and San Juan have carved magnificent canyons in the broadly upwarped sedimentary rocks that form the plateau, chief among them the Grand Canyon of the Colorado in northwestern Arizona. Weathering and erosion of the relatively soft strata have sculpted the landscape into brilliant colors and fantastic shapes, as at Bryce Canyon and Zion National Parks in Utah and at the Painted Desert in Arizona. Freestanding rock hills with nearly vertical slopes—buttes—have been isolated from the surrounding rock by differential erosion of hard and soft rock layers, and these outcrops seem to be swarming together in breathtaking Monument Valley in Utah. The largest known natural bridge in the

tive American tribes of the Anasazi (Navajo, meaning Ancient Ones) occupied much of the southern part of the plateau as early as 2,200 years before present. Environmental resources were scarce in the desert, but defensible village sites high up the canyon walls, on ledges or on the flat tops of mesas, were available. Around 700 B.P., the ancestors of the Pueblo Indians began to build 20- to

Rainbow Bridge National Monument exemplifies the natural arches, bridges, pedestal rocks, and alcoves that are common erosional features of the Colorado Plateau *(photo by Jesse Walker)*.

world, Rainbow Bridge National Monument in Utah, was formed by similar erosional forces.

The general plateau surface is above 5,000 feet (1,524 meters), with some plateaus and several peaks above 11,000 feet (3,353 meters). Precipitation is scant, usually less than ten inches (25 centimeters) annually, but rises sharply along the saucer-like rim, especially to the southwest.

The Colorado Plateau has the distinction of being both an ancient settlement region and one of the most recently occupied areas, at least by Europeans. Na-

30-room communal cliff dwellings, of which the Pueblo Bonito settlement at Chaco Canyon, New Mexico, is perhaps the most spectacular.

Around A.D. 1100, a major change in the location and structure of the pueblos occurred. Pueblo sites with good agricultural land were abandoned, and larger and more compact villages began to be established. There was a movement to shallow cave and cliff dwellings near dependable water sources, such as springs. Population began to decline, and by around A.D. 1300, most settlements had been abandoned, leaving behind the ruins of Mesa Verde in Colorado and Canyon de Chelly in Arizona. No one knows for sure what happened to the Anasazi, but climatic change, disease, and warfare have been forwarded to explain the sudden disappearance of the ancient ones. At the time the Spanish arrived, many pueblo sites contained large numbers of people, but they were in fact displaced Hohokam in 1540 became the first European to reach the Grand Canyon, reporting that he had seen the Seven Cities of Cibola, which may have been the Zuñi pueblos. Hopi villages were also visited and missionaries and priests dispatched to them; but as they were lacking in gold, Spanish interest in the area soon waned.

Perhaps the first American to reach the Colorado Plateau was James O. Pattie,

Canyon de Chelly, New Mexico, in the Colorado Plateau was the home of cliff-dwelling Indian civilizations including the Anasazi (the ancient ones). Near Casa Blanca (white house) pueblo, desert varnishes (iron and manganese oxides) discolor the sandstone *(photo by Jesse Walker)*.

from the lowlands of the Salt and Gila Rivers in southern Arizona. Also arriving just before the Spanish were the Navajo, who quickly adopted sheep raising as a livelihood, and the war-like Apache to the south.

The first European knowledge of the area was sketchy and vague, if not downright inaccurate. Cabeza de Vaca in his fantastic wanderings in the southwest probably never reached the plateau, but his tales of seven golden cities attracted others. Francisco Vásquez de Coronado who described "the horrid mountains which cage" the Colorado River. In the nineteenth century some of the most colorful episodes in the saga of the West took place here: Mormon settlement from the north, which began at midcentury; the great western surveys of George M. Wheeler, Clarence King, Ferdinand V. Hayden, and John Wesley Powell; the ordeal of establishing and maintaining wagon trails and then rail lines across forbidding terrain; and the creation of Indian reservations at the end of the century.

With the dawn of the twentieth century and mounting concerns about natural resources and the environment, the region assumed even greater significance, given its unusual scenic beauty and the wealth of resources present in its national parks, monuments, and forests. Classic struggles between preservationists and developers have focused on the Colorado Plateau at Echo Park on the Green River in the 1950s; on the battle over the Central Arizona Project water legislation in the 1960s, which threatened to flood parts of the Grand Canyon; and on numerous other instances. A new type of radical environmentalism—monkey-wrenching— was born out of a novel set in this region, Edward Abbey's 1975 *The Monkey Wrench Gang,* which in turn was inspired by the author's intensely personal experience of the region and of the threats to it presented by well-meaning people. It might be said that on the terrain of the ancient Anasazi, humankind has learned the inevitable trade-offs between the needs of an industrial civilization and the yearning for beautiful natural areas.

Further Reading: Edward Abbey, *Desert Solitaire,* New York: McGraw-Hill, 1968; Robert Durrenberger, "The Colorado Plateau," *Annals of the Association of American Geographers* 62 (1972), pp. 211–236.

COMAYAGUA DEPRESSION

The primary interest of the Spanish in Central America in the sixteenth century, especially after Francisco Pizarro conquered the Incas in 1533, was in the safe passage of their cargoes of precious metals across the isthmus in as short a distance as possible. The pattern of Spanish galleons sailing regularly to Europe in convoys and the use of the shortest transisthmian route across Panama was well established by midcentury. Other interoceanic routes attracted attention, including that of the north-south structural depression in western Honduras. This route passed through, approximately at its midpoint, the fertile upland valley that bears the same name as the historic town of Comayagua.

As early as 1529, before Peru was conquered, a report to the Crown by Rodrigo de Castillo and Andrés Cerezeda recommended the route connecting the Gulf of Fonseca in the south to Puerto Caballos (Puerto Cortés) in the north. Six years later, Cerezeda cited the advantages of the Honduran route over that of Panama: The climate was better, the embayed coast had good ports, and the distance from Peru to Havana would be reduced. A midway settlement would facilitate and increase traffic along the passageway, whereas the Panamanian route crossed such a confined, inhospitable area that no settlements existed along the way.

Alonzo de Cáceres conquered the native Indians in part of the Comayagua valley in 1536 and founded the villa of Santa María de Comayagua the following year. Francisco Montejo, the colonial governor, moved the town to its present site in 1539 and began to promote the idea of a transisthmian route through Comayagua that would be an alternative to the Panama passage. He envisaged a mule path, perhaps even a wagon road, connecting Comayagua to the already established town on the other side of the low continental divide at San Pedro, some 25 leagues (65 miles or 105 kilometers) away, and furthermore joining these towns to Pacific and Caribbean ports, respectively. Montejo estimated the distance of the route at 52 leagues (135 miles or 217 kilometers). The southern terminus would be at San Miguel in Guatemala, and this proved a drawback in that administrative confusion and colonial rivalry entered the picture. A lack of Indian labor to construct the road was another problem, but earlier Spanish reports of pueblos along much of the route, especially in the north, suggest the interesting possibility of a preexisting Indian route. The lack of good Atlantic ports in Guatemala and Nicaragua, on either side of Honduras, also recommended the Comayagua route.

Despite the promotion of Montejo and the support given the proposal by the growing town of Comayagua, the efforts to reorient transisthmian traffic came to naught due to jurisdictional conflicts that eventually led to the removal of Montejo and a shift in control of the colony first to Guatemala, then to a royal *audiencia* (a high court that exercised military power and performed various judicial and economic functions). Though some half-hearted attempts to revivify the Honduran routeway followed, the Crown in 1633 removed the Honduran flotilla from its regular trade network and thus ended any possibility of developing a road as an imperial link. A road was eventually built across the continental divide to serve as a local and regional trade artery. The Honduran Interoceanic Railway Company in the mid-nineteenth century planned to build its central section across the Comayagua plain. The old colonial *camino real* passing through Comayagua was replaced in 1970 by the paved Carretera del Norte.

CONTINENTAL DIVIDE

The mountainous backbone of the conjoined American continents stretches some thousand miles from the Brooks Range of Alaska to **Patagonia.** These young mountain systems are uplifted enough that they form a recognizable drainage divide between rivers emptying into the Atlantic and the Pacific Oceans.

The portion of the Rocky Mountains from Colorado to Alberta presents an especially rugged face, with many peaks towering above 14,000 feet (4,267 meters) in elevation. This section of the mountains lies transverse to the major routes of explorers and early settlers, to whom the divide seemed an insurmountable obstacle. Knowledge of the character of the drainage, topography, and pass routes across the mountains came late, and early explorers operated on traditional and mistaken ideas about the landscape of North America.

Among their most ill-founded expectations was that of an interconnected drainage system across the divide, permitting an easy passage from the broad headwaters of one river to the broad headwaters of another stream on the other side. This persistent myth contradicted the hydrologic principle that stream width and capacity actually decrease upstream. In this respect, the myth was essentially a reincarnation of the older, related notion of a "passage to India," by which it was thought that following a large bay or deeply indented coastline would bring a navigator far enough into the interior that he eventually would meet with a drainage flowing the other way. Another related idea that reinforced this misconception was that of a "pyramidal height of land"—a hoped-for topographic simplification that envisaged the western mountains as possessing a zone of greatest elevation and steepness, from which all the major river systems flowed. The source of the Rio Grande, the Colorado, the Missouri, and the Columbia thus might be a single restricted zone at the top of this topographic pyramid. Single-ridge symbolization of the Rockies on early maps was a similar simplification of a complex terrain region. In the absence of more precise information, the mapmaker inevitably distorted the character of the topography and the courses of the drainage. Thus, Western explorers fully expected the headwaters of the Missouri river system to adjoin those of the Columbia at the top of the Continental Divide, permitting an easy crossing of the Rockies.

The third president of the United States, Thomas Jefferson, was in a better position than almost anyone to understand the geographies then prevailing in

full collection of the English and Spanish authors on the subject of Louisiana." Jefferson was especially influenced by the report of the explorer Alexander Mackenzie, who in his *Voyages from Montreal* described a short portage between the Atlantic and Pacific slopes of the Canadian Rockies. As it turns out, the passes across the Rockies north of 49° N are more numerous and present fewer obstacles in

Buffalo grazing under burned forest after a fire in Yellowstone National Park, located on the Continental Divide *(photo by Jesse Walker)*.

the West and to realize the importance of the region and the need for a more accurate survey of its resources. Earlier, as minister to France (1784–1789), he had accumulated an impressive library of maps and documents on American geography. He bought everything he could obtain on this subject, which had fascinated him as a boy growing up in Virginia—the land beyond the mountains. He reported: "While I was in Europe I had purchased everything I could lay my hands on which related to any part of America, and particularly had a pretty

crossing than do those on the present U.S. side of the border.

When Jefferson dispatched Meriwether Lewis and William Clark to chart a route between the Missouri River and the Pacific Ocean, he probably hoped for the increased trade that would follow upon the discovery of a "passage to India," but the results of the epochal expedition would be more in line with the slow but patient accumulation of knowledge of natural history and topography that Jefferson naturally favored. The discovery and mapping of the numerous tributaries of the Missouri; the encounter with the spectacular Yellowstone country, which sits astride the continental divide; the navigation of the raging rivers and canyons on the Pacific slope down into the Oregon country—all these proved more important in the long term than the lack of verification of long-held geographic presuppositions. A passage to India may not have been found, but a garden had been crossed. Successive frontiersmen would have to make similar adjustments between preconceived ideas about Western nature and life and the reality that emerges only in the living.

Further Reading: John Logan Allen, *Lewis and Clark and the Image of the American Northwest,* New York: Dover, 1991 (1975).

COTSWOLD HILLS

Extending about 50 miles (80 kilometers) through Gloucestershire, from Bath to Chipping Campden, the Cotswolds are a low range of limestone hills with picturesque stone villages snuggled in tightly folded valleys. Situated on the western edge of populous southeastern England, which in 1990 had 20 million of the United Kingdom's 57 million people, the region strives to balance the claims of tradition against the demands of modern life, including those of tourists, sightseers, and developers. Rising to 1,083 feet (330 meters) just northwest of Cheltenham (the average elevation is less than 600 feet or 183 meters), the crest of the hills is a drainage divide between the Thames and Severn Rivers.

One of the upland spokes radiating from **Salisbury Plain** in the rim-and-spoke landscape of southern England, the Cotswolds present a nearly vertical escarpment facing west toward the Severn, but elsewhere the terrain is more rolling. The bedrock that underlies the Cotswolds—a type of oolitic limestone or

eggstone—has accumulations of calcium carbonate resembling fish eggs, and this stone is the material used in the distinctive yellow and gray buildings found across the region.

Located on defensible uplands at the head of major rivers like the Thames, the region was a major focus of Roman occupation in southern Britain. The regional capital, Cirencester, was the second largest Roman town in Britain after Londinium (London). Surveyed Roman roads, running straight as an arrow, still exist, though under modern surfaces, like the stretch of the **Fosse Way** extending northward from Cirencester. In Roman times all Cotswold roads led to Cirencester, and the town is yet today the hub of the regional road network.

The Romans also brought the region's signature breed of sheep, the Cotswold Lion, to clothe the legions, and this large, curly-fleeced breed was to prove to be one of the most enduring influences of the Latins. It is no accident that this scenic region has the effect of harkening back to the Middle Ages. During the thirteenth and fourteenth centuries wool was the chief export of England and a staple of the national economy, and the Cotswold Lion, a sheep whose mane hung to the ground, was the finest of English fleeces. Large flocks of sheep grazed the broad open hills, especially in the northern part of the region. The name Cotswold probably derives from this pastoral use of the land: The word is a fusion of *cotes,* or sheep shelters, and *wold,* or unforested hill (the German *Wald*).

The southern Cotswolds, with its quaint villages tucked into narrow valleys known as combes, had a larger percentage of its land in woodland. This area was traditionally more of a cloth-making center, at least once England turned to cloth making as the mainstay of the economy.

The production and export of cloth became so important that in the early seventeenth century James I banned the export of wool. The decline in wool production has continued up to the present, so that today no Cotswold sheep can be seen on the hills west of Oxford, unless they're part of a museum farm.

During the English civil war several important battles were fought in the Cotswolds between the Puritan-Parliamentarians led by Oliver Cromwell and the royalist troops. Today, there are regular reenactments of civil war battles here, just as there are reprises of the American Civil War between the North and South.

Cloth making on a handicraft basis was supplanted in the nineteenth century by new, mechanized forms of production pioneered by the workshops and factories of the **Pennine Hills** in northern England. By the late nineteenth century the Industrial Revolution had brought about a cultural reaction in the form of the arts-and-crafts movement. Many of its practitioners, including William Morris, the poet, designer, and inventor of the Morris chair, moved to the Cotswolds in search of a more harmonious environment.

Though it is difficult to set a precise boundary around a natural region like the Cotswolds, the government has established a preservation zone, known as a beauty region, in which development and maintenance of buildings must be in accordance with traditional styles and materials. Ironically, the high price of the Cotswold stone has made rebuilding and repair prohibitively expensive for some locals; due to the fossiliferous nature of the rock, there can be no blasting in the quarries.

Further Reading: Edith Brill, *Portrait of the Cotswolds,* London: Robert Hale, 1964; James Cerruti, "The Cotswolds, 'Noicest Parrt o'

England'," *National Geographic,* June 1974, pp. 846–869.

CUMBERLAND GAP

This V-shaped notch carved by an ancient stream following a fault through the Cumberland Mountains provided a natural passage for early settlers crossing the rugged Appalachians from the eastern seaboard. At an elevation of 1,700 feet (518 meters), the Cumberland Gap is a wind gap because no present stream drains the saddle position it occupies. The verdant, steep-sided terrain is best viewed from a place called the Pinnacle, positioned 1,300 feet (396 meters) above the valley of the Powell River and 800 feet (244 meters) above the dry notch. Located where the states of Virginia, Kentucky, and Tennessee come together, the natural pass was used by westering pioneers traveling up the Shenandoah Valley from Harpers Ferry along the Wilderness Road. Along with the forks region of the Ohio (Pittsburgh and vicinity) and the valley of eastern Tennessee (located farther south), the gap was a primary focal point for transmontane routes, with several roads flaring out in different directions like so many lengths of rope from a binding knot.

Discovered in 1750 by Thomas Walker, a Virginia doctor turned land speculator, the gap was little used until the Revolutionary War. Daniel Boone blazed the Wilderness Road across the mountains in 1775, and large numbers of settlers soon followed his path across the gap into Kentucky, which after 1776 was a Virginia county. The most difficult section of the road was the crossing of the Holston and Powell Rivers and their intervening ridges just before reaching the Cumberland Gap. The Wilderness Road was a preferred routeway in the early period because the northern approaches into the Ohio country were blocked by unfriendly Indians. It is estimated that 300,000 westward-moving settlers passed this way en route to the bluegrass region, the Nashville Basin, and points westward. Some people rested from their wanderings here amid this distinctive hill country with its narrow valleys, known as hollows, and its residual ridges, called knobs. Though not an obviously promising agricultural landscape, the land was well watered and provided abundant game, and the valley bottoms offered enough arable land, at a time when most agricultural plots amounted to little more than large patches by today's standards.

The Cumberland Gap should not be confused, as it has been by numerous schoolchildren and some teachers, with the Cumberland or National Road, which passed westward from Cumberland, Maryland, into the Midwest. This route, which was the first nationally subsidized road, was joined to the Potomac corridor first by canal and later by railroad connections, making it a primary east-west commercial artery in the nineteenth century. By contrast, the Cumberland Mountains, located far to the south and west, became a refuge for traditional ways of speech, material culture, and music, happily discovered in the twentieth century by an urban society looking for authentic, simplifying experiences.

Further Reading: John Fetterman, "The People of Cumberland Gap," *National Geographic*, Nov. 1971, pp. 591–621.

CURZON LINE

Poland is often cited as an example of a country with a homogeneous population and a compact shape. The ideal of the nation-state, that the boundaries of the people or *nation* should correspond to the political borders of the country or *state,* is nearly attained here. Elsewhere, this condition of what might be called the ethnic state, which in political parlance is the principle of self-determination (the right of a people to govern themselves), is rare except in isolated situations or on islands (such as Iceland), or in textbooks of political theory. Most countries today, with a few exceptions, are multicultural (multinational, defining a *nation* as above), or their peoples are divided among a number of sovereign political entities (as in Ireland today, and Germany after World War II).

The story of Poland's evolution as a political entity and of its changing boundaries, however, has been a long and difficult one. Though attaining greatness in the early modern period, especially in the sixteenth century, when an independent Poland incorporated Ukraine, dominated the Baltic region, and even threatened Moscow, the country suffered a series of partitions in the late eighteenth century (1772, 1793, and 1795), in consequence of which Poland disappeared from the map of Europe. Ground like grain between the stones of its larger Slavic neighbor to the east and strong Germanic states to the west, Poland's territory in the nineteenth century was parceled out among Russia, Prussia, and Austria.

During the course of World War I it was clear that the idealistic principles of self-determination endorsed by U.S. president Woodrow Wilson would require the restoration of Poland after the war, but along which boundaries? The eastern boundary with Russia was especially problematic because no single physical feature, such as a river or mountain crest, or combination of features divided Polish from Russian territory. The Treaty of Versailles (1919) guaranteed the independence of Poland and restored Prussian Poland to Polish rule, but it did not try to resettle large numbers of ethnic people including Germans and Jews living in Poland to other countries (in contrast to the aftermath of World War II). Polish access to the sea was assured by creating an elongated strip in northern Poland along the Vistula River, known as the **Polish Corridor,** extending to the free city of Danzig (Gdańsk), with German areas on either side in Pomerania and East Prussia.

At the Paris Peace Conference, British Prime Minister Lloyd George proposed a Polish-Russian border that would have awarded to Russia large parts of former eastern provinces of Poland inhabited mostly by Belorussians and Ukrainians. This line was later named after the British foreign secretary Lord George Nathaniel Curzon (1859–1925), former viceroy of India (1898–1905), cabinet member of the coalition governments of the Earl of Asquith and of Lloyd George, and senior British statesman in foreign affairs.

The Curzon Line approximates the present eastern border of Poland (1997) except in its northern section near the Baltic Sea. The line is anchored in the center on the western Bug River, an important tributary of the Vistula, draining the Pripet Marsh border zone. North of Brest on the Bug River, a series of line segments extends the border past Grodno to the Baltic Sea. South of Brest the border follows the Bug River almost to Sokol, then west and south past Przemysl to the **Carpathian Mountains.** In 1919 Poland refused this offer, insisting on the 1772 borders, which led to the Polish-Russian War of 1919–1920.

In the course of this war Lord Curzon proposed the Curzon Line for a settlement, but Polish victory obviated the need. During World War II the line served in part as the basis for the Soviet-German partition (1939), and it was later revived for postwar settlement of the Polish-Soviet boundary at the Yalta conference. The Potsdam conference slightly modified the line in favor of Poland. In 1951 further alterations resulted in Polish-Soviet territorial exchange in Sokal and Ustrzyki Dolne.

D

DACIA
See Walachian Plain

DANISH STRAITS
The southern part of Scandinavia is interrupted by a series of narrow water bodies connecting the North and Baltic Seas. Denmark was the preeminent power during the early history of this region, and it controlled the territory on both sides of these straits, although today the water bodies are international boundaries.

The *Skagerrak* is an arm of the North Sea lying between the north end of Denmark's **Jutland** peninsula and southern Norway. One hundred fifty miles (241 kilometers) long and 80–90 miles (129–145 kilometers) wide, it is continued to the southeast by the somewhat narrower *Kattegat,* which lies between Denmark and Sweden and possesses (to the English ear, anyway) a similarly uneuphonious collection of consonants. The Kattegat in turn connects in the south to the historically most important strait in the region, the *Øresund* (the Sound), a two-and-a-half-mile-wide (four kilometers) constriction between the Danish island of Sjælland (Zealand) and the present-day Swedish province of Skåne. In addition, two other straits, *Store Baelt* and *Lille Baelt* (Great and Little Belt), connect the Kattegat to the Baltic on either side of the Danish island of Fyn.

The Øresund is the deepest channel (minimum depth, 23 feet, or 7 meters) connecting the Kattegat with the Baltic, so it was chosen as the primary means of entering or leaving the important resource and trade area to the east. The average width between Copenhagen and Malmö is 17 miles (27.4 kilometers), but between Helsingør and Hälsingborg only two and a half miles (four kilometers) separate present-day Denmark and Sweden.

It was here in 1429 that Erik of Pomerania, ruler of unified Norway, Sweden, and Denmark, decided to introduce a levy on all ships passing through the strait. He required that every merchant ship returning from the Baltic to west European ports pay an English gold noble (hence the name Øresund—*øre* being the Danish word for gold).

To enforce this collection, fortified towers were erected on opposite sides of the sound: Kärnan Tower (part of now vanished Hälsingborg Castle) guarded the eastern end of the strait, while Krogen—later Kronborg Castle—was built at the western end, at Helsingør. The finely preserved Krogen Castle at Helsingør (Elsinore) is famous as the setting of Shakespeare's *Hamlet.* The average range of cannons was less than a mile during this period, so guns had to be elevated on bastions to extend their coverage. In addition to the fortresses, a Danish fleet assisted every ship in stopping at the poor anchorage at Helsingør. The sound is a dangerous waterway for those who don't know where the deep-water channel is located (about one mile, or one and a half kilometers, off the Danish coast), so it was customary for foreign merchant ships to signal for a Danish pilot to guide them through. Though sometimes resisted, here caused spoiling, so the primary means of preservation was salting while the fish were still fresh, which was possible due to the nearness of shore. Salt was a dear commodity, only available from distant places in western Europe, and not until Lübeck merchants developed extensive salt deposits at Lüneburg, about 45 miles (72 kilometers) away, did salt fish become such an important part of the

The Little Mermaid statue (depicting the character from the Hans Christian Andersen story) overlooking the harbor at Copenhagen, Denmark *(photo by Jesse Walker)*.

sound dues were regularly paid for the next 400 years. At the time, they were the primary source of revenue for the Danish crown.

One of the most important trade goods passing through the straits was fish. Scandinavia had a number of excellent fisheries, such as the Lofoten Islands along the north coast of Norway, which provided dried fish, but the sound was the best continuous source of salt herring. Huge shoals of herring arrived in Øresund in late summer, which could not be dried because the warmer temperatures

Skåne fair, held annually beginning on 15 August. This fair was one of the most important fairs in western Europe at the time, and its vitality goes a long way toward explaining the importance of the Danish levy on traffic in Øresund.

The imposition of the levy by Erik of Pomerania partly led to the breakup of the Union and the eventual independence of Sweden. The Danish king's increased territorial ambitions, coupled with other attempts to increase his revenues by additional taxation, aroused the ire of German Hanseatic traders, who blockaded Swedish ports and prevented the export of valuable iron and copper from the Bergslagen area. A coalition of miners, merchants, and farmers was formed in rebellion against Denmark in 1438. Although Sweden continued to be officially part of the Union until 1523, it was practically independent throughout much of the fifteenth century.

A period of struggle began then between Sweden and Denmark for control of the southern end of present Sweden, especially the rich province of Skåne. Decisive clashes took place in the Thirty Years War (1618–1648) and in the Danish-Swedish War (1657–1660). The latter—actually involving two separate encounters—was to prove crucial, as a Swedish victory gave the eastern bank of the Øresund to Sweden, and since then, the provinces of Skåne as well as Blekinge and Halland have been part of Sweden. Denmark continued, however, to exact the sound dues. Not until the mid-nineteenth century did increasing protests against the tolls on the grounds that they violated the principle of the freedom of the seas (made most insistently by the United States) lead to their withdrawal (in 1857), thus ending a long and colorful chapter in history.

Further Reading: Calvin J. Floyd, "The Sound Dues," *American-Scandinavian Review* (Winter 1962), pp. 386–396.

DANUBE RIVER

See Iron Gate

DANZIG

See Polish Corridor

DARDANELLES

Connecting the northern end of the Aegean Sea to the Sea of Marmara and the **Bosporus,** this strait 37 miles (60 kilometers) long, which separates Gallipoli Peninsula (part of Turkey in Europe) from Asia Minor, has been an extremely important commercial passageway and strategic chokepoint since the dawn of history. The strait in ancient times was called Hellespontus, and it is still often referred to as the Hellespont. Its modern name is derived from that of the ancient Greek town Dardanus, on the Asiatic shore. Four miles (6.4 kilometers) wide at its broadest, the southwest-northeast running Dardanelle strait (in Turkish, Çanakkale Boğazi) narrows to less than a mile near its entrance on the Aegean, where a series of forts command the passageway.

Even before recorded history, the strait played a role: According to legend, the heroic Leander swam across the strait to visit his beloved Hero, a priestess in the Temple of Venus at Sestos, on the European side. To commemorate this event but also to magnify his own growing reputation, the English Romantic poet Byron swam across the Hellespont on 8 March 1810 with a companion, accomplishing the feat in 70 minutes.

The strategic key to navigation between the Black Sea lands and the Mediterranean, the Dardanelles has given those who control it a tremendous strategic and commercial benefit. Ancient Troy prospered near the western entrance to the strait. In his attempt to conquer Greece, the Persian ruler Xerxes in 481 B.C. crossed the passageway by constructing a bridge of boats, an action that Aeschylus considered typical of an oriental despot's hubris. Alexander the Great crossed the strait in the other direction, also with a bridge of boats, in his expeditions of conquest in 334 B.C. (As a result, the name Hellespontus is sometimes mistakenly defined as Greek Bridge, when it actually means Sea of Helle, in reference to another legendary story involving the death in the straits of a priestess named Helle.)

Part of the Eastern Roman or Byzantine Empire from the fifth to the fourteenth centuries, the Dardanelles fell to the Ottoman Turks after the capture of the port of Gallipoli (Gelibolu) in 1354 and has remained in Turkish hands ever since. Sultan Mohammed II, conqueror of Constantinople (1453), first fortified the strait in 1462.

With the rise of Russian power in the eighteenth and nineteenth centuries and to prevent Russia from controlling the Dardanelles strait. As early as 1808, Napoleon had written: "If Russia had an outlet on the Dardanelles, she would be at the gates of Toulon, Naples, and Corfu." In 1841 the British succeeded in obtaining an agreement among the European powers that prohibited all but Turkish warships from using the strait, and this was later confirmed by the Congress

A Turkish fortified island in the Dardanelles *(photo by Jesse Walker).*

the decline of Ottoman influence, the Turkish straits (the Dardanelles–Sea of Marmara–Bosporus route) took on increasing geopolitical significance. The Turks were forced by imperial Russia to sign the Treaty of Kuchuk Kainarji (1774), which allowed passage of Russian ships into the Mediterranean. By the end of the nineteenth century, the Turks had been forced to allow free navigation to all the major commercial powers of the West, even though for centuries only Turkish ships had been permitted in these straits.

A primary objective of Great Power diplomacy in the nineteenth century was of Paris (1856) after the Crimean War. The agreement remained in effect until World War I, when an Anglo-French fleet in 1914 attempted and failed to force the strait and capture the major Turkish city of Constantinople, which was allied with Germany. This led to the disastrous Gallipoli campaign of the next year, which degenerated into the kind of trench warfare more familiar on the Western Front, with large numbers of casualties, especially among the Australian and New Zealand Army Corps (ANZAC). Winston Churchill, then first lord of the admiralty, had favored the idea of forcing the strait, and in the political fallout from this disaster, Churchill lost his admiralty seat and was demoted to a subordinate position in the wartime government. By secret treaty entered into between Britain, France, and Russia, Russia was to gain control of the strait at the conclusion of the war, but this arrangement was nullified by the seizure of power by the Bolsheviks, who entered into a separate peace agreement with Germany.

The leader of the Turkish forces in the defeat of the Allies was General Mustafa Kemal (Ataturk), who in the 1920s forged independence for the reduced territorial state of modern Turkey, which still possesses the Dardanelles but now must guarantee its status as an international waterway. The rise of rocketry and airpower have reduced the geopolitical significance of the strait, although throughout the cold war the Soviet Union depended on access to the warm-water Mediterranean via this gateway.

See also: Bosporus.

Further Reading: Alan Moorehead, *Gallipoli,* New York: Harper and Brothers, 1956.

DARIÉN, ISTHMUS OF

The sparsely populated eastern part of Panama, between the Gulf of Darien on the Caribbean side and the Gulf of San Miguel on the Pacific side, is the historic region of Darién. The name once referred to the entire **Isthmus of Panama** but today describes only the southeastern Panamanian region, which more nearly resembles adjacent parts of northwestern South America (i.e., Colombia) in landforms, climate, and vegetation. Along the Caribbean coast the Serrania de San Blas, which only rises to 3,200 feet (975 meters), extends a northern prong of the Andes, while on the Pacific side the Serrania de Baudó of Colombia crosses the border of Panama and continues westward as low hills beyond the Gulf of San Miguel. Between these low ranges lies a structural depression drained most prominently by the Chucunaque River and its tributaries. Heavy precipitation amounting to 80–120 inches (203–305 centimeters) per year supports a dense rain forest that has been home to dispersed groups of Indians and small riverine settlements of black natives.

First reached by the Spanish in 1501, the region was seen by Columbus on his last voyage two years later. The first European settlement here was attempted by Vasco Núñez de Balboa in 1510. From his base in Darién, Balboa traveled across the low continental divide to discover and name the Pacific Ocean in 1513. The Spanish colonists abandoned the region in 1519, when they left to found Panama City on the Pacific side of the isthmus at a more suitable crossing point.

In the celebrated poem "On First Looking into Chapman's Homer," John Keats misconstrued historical facts when he referred to Cortez, rather than Balboa, observing the Pacific Ocean, "Silent, upon a peak in Darien." Criticism of Keats's error has been tempered by the recognition of the lyrical poem's genius in evoking the romantic excitement of travel and discovery.

With its abandonment by the Spanish settlers, the lush rain forest was left to the Kuna Indians, who practiced a kind of shifting cultivation, subsisting by combining starchy root crops like cassava with protein from fishing and hunting. In their dugout canoes the Indians skillfully navigated the rivers, which were the primary means of access in this otherwise inaccessible land. Beginning in 1600 the Spanish established a few small forts to secure the scattered settlements of placer-miners and the riverine route to the Cana gold mine.

The Kuna, who were a friendly tribe, were eager to make alliances with other Europeans who accidentally or deliberately washed up on their shores. More often than not, the European arrivals were buccanneers or pirates. One of the most unlikely allies of the Kuna was a Scots colony that attempted to settle the area in 1698–1701.

The Scots colonization scheme, backed by a large capital subscription at home and promoted by some of the biggest entrepreneurs in Edinburgh, including William Patterson—a founder of the Bank of England—attracted several thousand Scottish settlers. The contrast between the idealistic expectations of the Scots and the realities of tropical geography could not have been greater. Almost as soon as they disembarked at their appropriately named settlement of Caledonia on the Gulf of Darien, about halfway between Portobelo and Cartagena, the colonists encountered major problems: Tropical diseases struck; food stores were rapidly drawn down; and the Spanish very visibly, though slowly and clumsily, had begun to gather a countering force.

The Scots Company, the primary mover behind the settlement project, had hoped to establish a lucrative plantation economy similar to that in Jamaica and to found a trading emporium for transisthmian exchange that would tap into trade as far away as the Spice Islands. About the only thing that went right for the colonists was the friendliness of the Kuna Indians. Diseases decimated their ranks to such an extent that hoes and shovels were used more often to dig graves than to cultivate crops. News that the first group of settlers had given up and returned to Scotland tragically reached Edinburgh ten days after a second fleet with 1,300 colonists was dispatched. The details of this fiasco need not concern us here, as the story has been recounted elsewhere. But the loss of thousands of lives (many on return voyages) was hardly compensated for by the following Act of Union, which resulted in the creation of the United Kingdom (the Scottish Parliament, which had passed a law bringing the sponsoring company into existence, was abolished). That act specified that 400,000 British pounds sterling be paid to Scotland, a part of which amount was to go to the investors of the bankrupt Scots Company.

Thus have European aspirations and ideals—both noble dreams and base greed—often foundered on the rocks of the fundamental geography of the tropics. Soils are never so fertile, climates never so salubrious, markets and transport never so available as in the fevered and biased imaginations of the inhabitants of distant, higher latitudes, especially if some gain is being calculated.

The Spanish never resettled Darién, though they did enlist the support of Colombian Blacks and the Chocó Indians with their feared blowguns as mercenaries against the Kuna. With the abandonment of the Spanish forts in 1783, the region was left to the Kuna Indians, who today occupy the eastern San Blas region (not strictly in Darién province) as well as isolated upper basins of the Río Tuira and the Río Chucunaque, which drain westward into the Gulf of San Miguel. The more numerous Chocó Indians took over land abandoned by the Kuna along the middle and lower courses of the westward-draining streams on the Pacific side. Black-populated towns occupying sites along the primary riverways of the region are peopled by descendants of escaped slaves from the Colombian mines, former mercenaries, and more recent immigrants from the Canal Zone.

A stretch in Darién is the only section of the Pan-American Highway that remains unbuilt. The Darien Gap Highway, built during the 1970s (and officially opened in 1980), opened up this previously inaccessible region to mestizos from other parts of Panama, who were especially interested in the region for commercial cattle raising. The felling of the rain forest, introduction of exotic pasture grasses, and the inevitable loss of wildlife and plant diversity are only a few of the negative environmental impacts associated with the conversion of the original forest to a savanna-like grazing landscape. With the establishment of "culture parks" that foster conservation, and the use of resources by indigenous peoples to preserve their cultures both in semiautonomous *comarcas* or homelands and in Darién National Park on the Colombian border, it is hoped that negative environmental impacts can be minimized and that the Indians can live on the land in a sustainable way.

Further Reading: Peter H. Herlihy, "Opening Panama's Darién Gap," *Journal of Cultural Geography* 9 (1989), pp. 41–59; John Prebble, *The Darien Disaster,* Edinburgh: Mainstream, 1978 (orig. Martin Secker and Warburg, 1968); Timothy Severin, *The Golden Antilles,* New York: Knopf, 1970.

DELAWARE RIVER

Rising in the Catskill Mountains of southeastern New York, the Delaware River flows about 280 miles (450 kilometers) to its outlet on the funnel-shaped embayment of the same name, which separates the southwestern coast of New Jersey from eastern Delaware. In its upper reaches the river's east and west branches join at Hancock, before flowing southeast along the New York–Pennsylvania border to Port Jervis. Then the river takes a more southern direction along the boundary between New Jersey and Pennsylvania.

The Delaware River cuts through Kittatinny Mountain near Stroudsburg, Pennsylvania, forming the scenic Delaware Water Gap, a rock-faced ravine some 1,600 feet (488 meters) deep that has attracted tourists and health seekers since the early nineteenth century.

At Trenton, New Jersey, the river reaches the **Fall Line,** the boundary between the elevated crystalline rocks of the **Appalachian Piedmont** to the west and the younger sands and clays (i.e., unconsolidated sediments) of the Coastal Plain to the east. One can be quite precise about this boundary—down to the street level. The border between Triassic rocks and Cretaceous sands in Trenton lies somewhere around Calhoun Street, crossing the river below the old Calhoun Street Bridge. Below Trenton the river abruptly turns to the southwest, following the strike of the rock formations.

From this point to its mouth the river follows an industrial corridor that includes Trenton, Philadelphia, Camden (opposite Philadelphia), and Wilmington (Delaware). Though the falls of this tidal river were once used to turn water wheels to grind grist and saw logs, the industrial growth of the towns of the lower Delaware owes more to its productive agricultural hinterlands, tapped by innovative forms of transportation, than to water power development. In fact, the latter was considered a shortcoming of the region that some believe led to the handicraft tradition of, say, Philadelphia (the Delaware at Philadelphia drops only three feet per mile). Schooners and shallops and other colonial vessels could not pass upriver past Trenton, which was the head of navigation. The need to break bulk at a transshipment point was probably more important than water power potential in the early industrial history of these towns.

The estuarine bay and the river provided access deep into the interior of the country, allowing Philadelphia to tap the fertile, undulating expanse of the Piedmont to its west. Some sloping farmland might have been an advantage before the advent of mechanized agricultural equipment requiring level land, as it possessed better drainage and a different complement of soils. The rolling, sometimes hilly lands of the Pennsylvania Piedmont, being interspersed with exceptionally fertile limestone basins like the Lancaster Plain, made excellent farmland.

The Dutch navigator Henry Hudson discovered Delaware Bay in 1609. The following year, his compatriot Sir Samuel Argall named the river and bay for Baron De La Warr (1577–1618), the first colonial governor of Virginia. When the Quaker William Penn received his charter for land along the Delaware River in 1681 from Charles II (the grant was to reward Penn's father, Admiral Penn, for his capture of Jamaica in 1655), several town sites farther downriver had been preempted by the Swedes and the Dutch at Wilmington (founded as Fort Christina by the Swedes in 1638) and New Castle (originally Fort Casimir, established by the Dutch in 1651).

Penn's choice of town sites thus was limited by preexisting settlement in the valley. He eventually selected a site for his planned town (at least in its layout) farther upriver, which meant farther from the Atlantic outlet. He laid out two square miles of regular, cardinally oriented streets on a sandy peninsula between the Delaware and Schuylkill Rivers on land that previously had been occupied by Swedish settlers who lacked a good claim.

The Quaker's grant unfortunately overlapped with Maryland's northern boundary, and an acrimonious dispute began between the Calverts and the Penns, which was not settled until some gentlemanly preliminary agreements led to the careful survey of the **Mason-Dixon Line.** The vigorous commercial settlement of Philadelphia and its hinterland combined with the large-scale immigration of, for the first time in British North America, non-Anglo settlers, including Germans (i.e., Pennsylvania Dutch) and Scotch-Irish, the latter important on a violent Indian frontier in the presence of Quaker pacifists. Philadelphia became the premier city of British North America, an object of admiration in Europe, the second largest English-speaking city in the world behind London, and a natural choice for a meeting site when the time came to sign a declaration of independence and to draw up a framework for government.

Canals and railroads extended the reach of the City of Brotherly Love in the nineteenth century, though it faced sharp competition from Baltimore and New York, not to mention nearby, second-tier cities like Wilmington and Trenton. By the end of the century the Delaware valley was an industrial heartland, a concentration of manufacturing perhaps only exceeded in the United States by the steel belt of the **Great Lakes.** Names like Roebling, Baldwin, Du Pont, and Disston made steel, locomotives, gunpowder, and saws respectively. Industrially lighter in weight, many brand-name consumer goods that Americans would come to take for granted were produced along the banks of the Delaware: Campbell's Soup (Camden); Lenox China (Trenton); Fels Naphtha soap (Philadelphia). Philadelphia also produced Tasty Kake, Jack Frost Sugar, Stetson hats, and A. J. Reach baseballs and sporting gear—for seventy-three years, the only maker of official American League baseballs.

Most of this has gone by the wayside and is today the subject of considerable nostalgia. Philadelphia continues to be an important ocean port, receiving and shipping large tonnages. The Chesapeake and Delaware Canal today joins the Delaware River below Wilmington to the head of the **Chesapeake Bay,** forming a link in the Intracoastal Waterway. Large industrial cities along the lower Delaware discharge increasing amounts of waste water and pollution into the bay, which has already become more saline due to the draw-off of large amounts of water near the river's headwaters to New York City via the Delaware Aqueduct. Environmental damage is perhaps inevitable, as it seems to have been in the similar case of the nearby Chesapeake Bay, which is an even larger body of water.

Further Reading: Bruce Stutz, *Natural Lives, Modern Times: People and Places of the Delaware River,* New York: Crown, 1992.

DNIEPER RIVER

One of Europe's longest rivers, the Dnieper (in Russian, Dnepr) rises in the **Valdai Hills** northwest of Moscow. It flows south past Smolensk (Russia) and Mahilyow (Belarus) before entering Ukraine. Passing the old city of Kiev, the river flows southeast past the modern industrial cities of Dnipropetrovsk and Zaporizhzhya (site of the huge Dneproges hydroelectric dam), then turns southwest past Nikopol and Kherson before emptying into the **Black Sea.**

Known to the ancients as the Borysthenes, the river was settled by East Slavs as early as the fifth century. The stretch of the middle Dnieper was the focus of the first self-consciously Russian state in the ninth century. Swedish traders known as Varangians lay behind this early political organization. From Novgorod, an impor-

tant early trading town on the Volkhov River, a group of Swedish Vikings—traders rather than raiders—pioneered a commercial artery between Scandinavia and Constantinople ("from the Varangians to the Greeks"), making use of the navigable waterways of western Russia, especially the Dnieper. Furs, honey, wax, and slaves from the north were exchanged in the Byzantine capital for luxury goods such as silks and wine. Although the extent of cultural as opposed to political and economic influence of the Northmen has been debated, there is little doubt that the Varangians, or the Rus, as they also were called, provided a catalyst for early Russian prosperity and political unification.

They also almost certainly gave Russia its name. The Finnish call the Swedes *Ruotsi,* and the prefix of Swedish place-names like the region Roslagen preserves the old identification of the Rus with the Scandinavians. The issue is clouded, though, because the name Rus does not survive in contemporary Scandinavian languages. Curiously, debate about the putative Slavic versus Scandinavian origins of the name Rus considers as a crucial piece of evidence words used to name the strategically important Dnieper rapids below Kiev.

The dynastic state of Kievan Rus was as troubled by the problem of succession as were later Russian governments, including that of the Communists. Vladimir I (reigned 980–1015) introduced Christianity when he adopted (ca. 989) Greek Orthodoxy from the Byzantines. One wonders how deep the Christianity could have been, given that rulers routinely murdered their siblings en masse to gain unchallenged authority. During the reign of Vladimir's son, Yaroslav the Wise, the Kievan state reached its zenith. Its territory embraced much of northwest Russia as far as the Baltic states; most of Ukraine (with the exception of the lower Dnieper, which was controlled by the Pechenegs); the lower Volga; and the **Caucasus.** Aspiring to rival Constantinople, the rulers of Kiev erected new walls and a citadel (the famous Golden Gate), as well as many ornate churches, among them the magnificent St. Sophia cathedral, which was modeled on Hagia Sophia in Constantinople.

DOVER, STRAIT OF

Only 21 miles (34 kilometers) separate England and France between Dover and Cape Gris-Nez, near Calais. This vital water passageway, known to the French as Pas de Calais, connects the **English Channel** (in French, La Manche) at its eastern end with the North Sea. It has been a key commercial and strategic corridor for the maritime powers of western Europe. The

Dover Castle, a site that goes back to Roman times *(photo by Jesse Walker)*.

Dynastic disputes weakened subsequent rulers and undermined the political control of the centralized state. The Mongol invasions of 1237–1240 brought the 350-year rule of Kievan Rus to an end. Slavic power became more dispersed and shifted to northern principalities such as Vladimir-Suzdal, which became the primary link between the earlier, Kievan state and the later, Muscovite one.

Further Reading: A. D. Stokes, "Kievan Russia," pp. 49–77, in Robert Auty and Dimitri Obolensky, *An Introduction to Russian History,* Companion to Russian Studies 1, Cambridge: Cambridge University Press, 1976.

Narrow Seas, as the strait was once called, have been both an avenue from the continent and a defensive moat, albeit one occasionally breached. The strait formed some 8,000 years ago as a result of rising sea levels (due to the melting of Pleistocene ice sheets), which cut across a chalk ridge extending from Kent to Picardy.

The Romans established a port on the English side, beneath a chalk ridge at Dover, and the Roman town is still in evidence at the Roman lighthouse. The Latins referred to the strait as Dubris Portus, or "water entrance," adopting the Celtic *dubr* (water) for the name of one of their main British ports. A number of important naval battles between England and France were fought here in the late Middle Ages, one of which led to the defeat of French forces by Hubert de Burgh, in the thirteenth century. In a turning point of the war between England and Spain, the Spanish Armada was first checked by the English fleet at Calais in 1588, then decisively defeated just to the east, at Gravelines.

Napoleon gathered a large army at Boulogne in 1804–1805, preparing to invade England, but his anticipated naval support never arrived (a large segment of the French fleet was destroyed by Nelson at **Cape Trafalgar**). The French emperor's ambitions were nonetheless clear: In spring 1804 he gave instructions to his top admiral, Latouche-Tréville: "Let us be masters of the Straits for six hours, and we shall be masters of the world." Adolf Hitler likewise hesitated before crossing the strait with German forces. The Battle of Britain was a sustained aerial bombardment that was meant to destroy the morale and materiel of the British nation; but failing on both scores, Hitler was unable to make his cross-channel invasion.

The 31-mile-long (50-kilometer) English Channel Tunnel, or "the Chunnel" (as it is called by the British), which connects England and France across the Dover Strait, had been contemplated since the time of Napoleon but was completed only recently, in 1994, much to the dismay of traditionalist Frenchmen and Englishmen alike. A 150-foot-deep course through soft-as-soap chalk marls that lie on both sides joins Folkestone, England to Coquelles, France (near Calais), allowing travelers to be carried by high-speed trains across a divide that appeared at the end of the Ice Age.

DROUGHT POLYGON (BRAZILIAN)

Occupying most of northeastern Brazil apart from a thin, well-watered coastal strip, this parched land of limited potential has shaped the destiny not only of the Nordeste but also of Brazil as a whole. Approximately 750 miles (1,207 kilometers) wide and 1,000 miles (1,609 kilometers) long, this region extending between eastern Maranhão and Pernambuco is a semiarid interior adjacent to early settled coastal areas. It includes the states of Ceará, Rio Grande do Norte, Paraíba, Pernambuco, Alagoas, Sergipe, and parts of Piauí and Bahía. (The large number of small states in northeastern Brazil is evidence of its early settlement, as in New England in the United States.) Though never possessing a large population within its fluid boundaries, the region was the source of repeated pulses of migration to other newly settled regions.

Most of the highly irregular and seasonal rainfall comes to the *sertão,* or backland, from January to early May—the summer season in this region south of the equator, although the natives call it winter because the arrival of rainclouds brings cooler temperatures. When drought strikes, which occurs about once every ten years, the people say "The Lord granted us no winter last summer." When the dry years double up, the backwoodsman and his family cannot eke out even a primitive subsistence. A nomadic or migratory behavior is the result; sometimes the migrant returns to his beloved *sertão,* but more often he forms the base population for the teeming southern cities or other interior backlands, such as in Minas Gerais or Mato Grosso or Amazonia.

The occupation of interior northeastern Brazil has been influenced by a distinctive type of vegetation, the *caatinga,* that characterizes the area. Based on a Tupi Indian word that means white forest, the *caatinga* is a scrub forest that appears pale and lifeless but is well adapted to drought with its waxy leaves and stems and its defensive thorns. Clearing of this thorny brushland for pasture has led to the development of a distinctive vaquero culture, in which young boys "put on the leathers" at an early age and learn the traditional ways of the cowboy.

The settlement of the *sertão* was a result of the westward push of people of modest means from the sugar towns along the northeast coast. A pastoral economy gradually evolved in the interior that had little contact with coastal areas. The main centers of early occupation were in the state of Ceará inland from Fortaleza and along the lower and middle course of the São Francisco River in the state of Bahía. With the decline of the sugar plantations in the eighteenth century and the discovery of gold and later diamonds in Minas Gerais (the state's name means general mines), many plantation owners moved along the valley of the São Francisco to its headwaters in the newly opened mining regions. It has been estimated that 500,000 people, both landowners and slaves, left the northeastern sugar lands before the middle of the eighteenth century. Pastoralists in the northeast, attracted by vacant or cheap land, began to occupy a more settled agricultural ring around the northeastern coastal strip. This pattern of internal migration and rearrangement of land use occurred again, with the exodus of coastal dwellers to the newly opened coffee fields of Maranhão in the late eighteenth century.

In the nineteenth century, the continuing decline of sugar and the spread of coffee onto plateau lands in the south caused even more northeasterners to migrate, a trend that was deepened by a series of droughts. An extremely severe drought in 1877–1879 spread so much disaster and ruin (the population of Ceará was reduced by one-half) that the government finally began to survey the resources of the region and to formulate water management schemes, including the creation of reservoirs and canals. That the area is still prone to periodic drought is well illustrated by the hardship endured in this traditional land of the cowboy during the early 1970s, when the winter rains once again failed to interrupt the summer.

Further Reading: Friedrich W. Freise, "The Drought Region of Northeastern Brazil," *Geographical Review* 28 (1938), pp. 363–378; John Wilson, "Drought Bedevils Brazil's Sertao," *National Geographic,* Nov. 1972, pp. 704–723.

E

EAST PRUSSIA
See Polish Corridor

ENGLISH CHANNEL
This arm of the Atlantic between the southern coast of England and northwestern France has been both an avenue to the British Isles and a natural defense. Two historic Channel crossings, separated by a thousand years, have crucially determined the fate of England and the West.

The English Channel (the French call it La Manche, or The Sleeve) is 350 miles (563 kilometers) long from its western entrance at Land's End, at the western extremity of Cornwall, to the **Strait of Dover,** where it connects with the North Sea. To the west (down channel) it is considerably wider, reaching about 150 miles (241 kilometers) between the inner coast of Lyme Bay and the inner coast of the Gulf of Saint-Malo, while at its eastern end (up channel) the Dover crossing is only 21 miles, or 34 kilometers. The French channel coast is characterized by large bays on either side of the Cotentin Peninsula of Normandy (the Gulf of Saint-Malo to the west and the Bay of the Seine to the east), and the long, relatively unindented curve of the Picardy coast as far as Calais, just opposite Dover. The southern coast of England is naturally divided at the Isle of Wight, one of the major islands in the Channel. West of

Wight the coast is older, steeper, and lacking the shingle beaches favored by holiday visitors in the southeast. East of Wight the rocks are relatively soft, and numerous old ports once were located at lagoonal inlets and at the mouths of rivers. Marine transgression has eroded parts of the cliffs, marooning former mainland towns offshore. In a number of other places, heavy silting, combined with the British practice of "inning" (closing in shallow bays and protecting them from the sea), has reclaimed land from the sea. The eastern part of the English coast is continuous around the chalk ridge of Dover with the forelands and the Thames estuary, which are also geologically young. The geologically ancient coastline of the west country contrasts with the Sussex and Kent coastline in the east, which is the result of rising sea levels that cut off a land bridge connecting England to the continent as recently as 7,500 B.P. The first humans to reach Britain literally walked from France.

Recorded history begins rather abruptly in England with the arrival of Julius Caesar's invasion forces in 55–54 B.C. Although Caesar was successful in overpowering the Celtic tribes that inhabited England, especially the Belgae in the southeast, who had recently arrived from the continent, the Romans did not choose to stay. Emperor Augustus laid down a conservative policy on projects of expansion, and it was not until Claudius's reign in A.D. 43 that the Romans returned to England. By this time they had a thoroughly Romanized Gaul behind them rather than the unruly crowd Caesar had to worry about, as well as an accurate idea of the geography of Britain. Importantly, Rome looked to its distant, northwestern province for surplus foodstuffs and for the tin needed to make bronze implements and arms (Britain was often referred to by the Romans as the Tin Islands.) The Romans stayed for four centuries.

Germanic tribes—the Saxons and the Jutes—arrived from North Sea coastlands first to raid, then to settle the Channel coastlands after the withdrawal of the Roman legions. The Jutes concentrated in the east, in what was to become Kent. The Saxons took over the wealthier villa lands of West Sussex (Sussex is an elided form of South Saxon), from the north facing escarpment of the Downs to the coast. As a result of a later colonization to the west, the Saxons occupied the Hampshire coast, protected by the Isle of Wight, and penetrated to the fertile, interior **Salisbury Plain,** where they established the Wessex (West Saxon) Kingdom that was to furnish the first great English king, Alfred, who united the various Germanic tribes against the invading Danes beginning in the ninth century.

The Norman Conquest of 1066 is one of the most important events in British and European history not only because it was the last time England's channel defense was breached, as Churchill valiantly reminded his people during World War II's Battle of Britain, but also because it established the kind of strong, centralizing monarchy with a regular system of law and taxation that could allow the countervailing institution of parliament.

The Channel crossing of William the Bastard (later the Conqueror), Duke of Normandy, and the subsequent Battle of Hastings are so extensively discussed in the historical literature that I will confine myself only to certain aspects of these epic events, especially the geographic ones. From the region around Bayeux on the Norman coast William assembled 8,000 men, 2,000 horses, and 450 ships—an extremely large force for the time—in preparation for his assault on England. Though William never declared his intentions, they may be judged easily enough by his actions. William clearly hoped to establish a defensible beachhead along the Hastings coastline, from which he could send out later raiding and conquering parties in widening circles, in the classic Viking style. The Fairlight ridge, a clay-and-sandstone extension of the Weald upland, runs southeast from Battle (a present-day village named after the famous battle but nonexistent in 1066), tracing an oblique angle to the coastline, which it reaches just east of old Hastings. On either side of the ridge, streams drain toward the coast, which is reached in broad, level tidal lagoons. Thus, William took not only a coastal port but secured a small but defensible upland—the Hastings Peninsula—that could be counted on to provide food for his men and feed for his horses and the livestock he would seize from the surrounding area on marauding raids. The only means of access to the peninsula was along a narrow trackway connecting the Weald forests with the coast across the swampy divide between the two major drainages. This geographical background allows us to see why William waited two weeks after his decisive victory at Hastings before proceeding further. Even at the end of the two weeks, rather than advance on London, partly because of the heavily wooded and swampy Weald route, he traveled eastward to Dover and thence toward the Thames along the high ground of the North Downs. In this way, William avoided another pitched battle with the Saxons, choosing instead to circle London and await the results of political negotiations, which allowed him to enter London and take England peacefully.

The increasing commercial importance of England in the later Middle Ages, combined with the French threat, led to major developments along the Channel coast. The most important story up-channel was the formation of the Cinque Ports, an association of maritime towns in Sussex and Kent. Required to provide ships and men for protection against invasion at a time when the threat from France was strong and when England had no permanent navy, the towns were relieved of taxation and enjoyed other privileges. (The name Cinque Ports, or Five Ports in Old French, referred to the five original members of the association—Hastings, Romney, Hythe, Dover, and Sandwich.) The other major development of the later Middle Ages was the rise of the western ports. Towns like Plymouth, Dartmouth, Poole, and Southampton were founded, or grew from slight beginnings, in response to English control of the Bordeaux region of southwestern France—which resulted from Henry II's marriage to Eleanor of Aquitaine—and to the increasing importance of long-distance trading routes. Renewed emphasis on shipping in the fifteenth century eventually led to voyages of exploration on lines of access extending from the West Country ports.

The defeat of the Spanish Armada in 1588 is an oft-told tale. Suffice it to say that the celebrated defeat of the most powerful European nation at that time took place in the English Channel, even though the English had hoped for an encounter in Iberian waters. With people watching from the cliffs, the English fleet chased the armada up-channel from Plymouth, where it was first unexpectedly sighted, to just east of Calais, at Gravelines, where it was decisively routed, after which it retired to the North Sea, never to be seen again. The Channel had not previously been much of a defensive guarantee, as France had repeatedly raided ports during its long wars with the English. But with the creation of the royal navy by the Tudors, the defeat of the Spanish, and the increasing political and economic influence of England as it entered its imperial phase, the Channel became a defensive moat, successfully crossed by neither Napoleon nor Hitler, though each had amassed large forces on the other side of the Channel in preparation for an assault. (For treatment of the most important Channel crossing in recent history, the June 1944 D-Day invasion of the Normandy coast, see **Armorican Massif.**)

Shakespeare rather anachronistically made his dying John of Gaunt exclaim, with reference to the island nature of England:

> This precious stone set in the
>   silver sea,
> Which serves it in the office
>   of a wall
> Or as a moat defensive to a house,
>   . . .
> England, bound in with the
>   triumphant sea,
> Whose rocky shore beats back the
>   envious siege
> Of watery Neptune. . . .
>   (*King Richard II,* II, i, 40–66)

But Gaunt's message is not an optimistic one: He declaims against the "inky blots and rotten parchment bonds" that signify the dying days of what scholars have called the "bastard feudalism" of the fourteenth and fifteenth centuries. Shakespeare was flattering his Tudor sovereign, Elizabeth, for setting the ship of England on a more secure course, and this idea was never far from Shakespeare's mind in his history plays. The Channel would henceforth be England's primary line of defense; but this fact, of inestimable importance, had hardly been established in Shakespeare's day.

Further Reading: James A. Williamson, *The English Channel: A History,* London: Collins, 1959.

FALL LINE

This irregular line of waterfalls and rapids along the eastern side of the Appalachians exerted an important influence on the pattern of American settlement and development.

If we approach the subject from a technical point of view (admittedly, a scenic one is more attractive), a waterfall is a *knickpoint:* a discontinuity in the longitudinal profile of a river viewed from its side—from its source to its mouth. Such a sharp change in a river's slope reflects geological structure and differential erosion. In the eastern United States the older, crystalline rocks of the **Appalachian Piedmont** literally fall down onto the younger sedimentaries of the coastal plain. Though a fall line is sometimes considered a generic feature—occurring wherever the lithic structure dictates a marked break in a river's gradient—the proper name usually refers to this particular irregular line of falls and cascades, which acted as a spatial anchor in the location of many early cities of the eastern United States. (However, the Canadian province of Quebec also has a Fall Line at the southern edge of the **Canadian Shield**.)

The rivers of the slightly elevated Piedmont plateau thus reach the nearly flat coastal plain along a line of falls. Since this line of falls marks the head of naviga-tion for ships as well as a ready source of waterpower for grinding grist and sawing logs (and later, for making textiles), it provided ideal sites for establishing towns. The Fall Line is oriented southwest to northeast, like the Appalachians. From north to south, early established towns along the falls include some of the major cities of the eastern seaboard: Trenton, New Jersey; Philadelphia, Pennsylvania; Baltimore, Maryland; Georgetown, the initial site of the nation's capitol; Richmond, Virginia; Raleigh, North Carolina; and Augusta, Macon, and Columbus, Georgia. Note that the Fall Line cities in the South draw away from the coast. These towns were generally the most important interior Southern cities. Atlanta is not a Fall Line city—though nearly so—as it is situated within the Piedmont. Its development was all in the nineteenth century and related to the building of railroads (its original name was Terminus). The Fall Line as a boundary between the crystalline portions of the Appalachians and the coastal plain peters out in Alabama.

The rocks of the coastal plain not only dip toward the east, lying like reverse shingles on the Appalachians, but are also inclined toward the north. The result is the submergence of the coastal plain in the embayed midsection of the eastern seaboard. Excellent protected harbors from the mouth of the Hudson to North Carolina's Neuse River include such cradles of American settlement as the Delaware and **Chesapeake Bays.** The submergence of this portion of the east coast was aided by the melting of the **Würm (Wisconsinan)** stage of Pleistocene glaciation, beginning about 18,000 years ago. Chesapeake and Delaware Bays, cultural hearths of American settlement, are the drowned river mouths respectively of the Susquehanna and **Delaware Rivers.** The Fall Line cuts across this embayed section of the mid-Atlantic coastline. Baltimore, for instance, derives a number of advantages from its terrain and location: Its site affords a protected harbor on the Chesapeake Bay; harnessable water power lies at its back door; and the infant city had the Patapso River valley as an immediate agricultural hinterland, indispensable in the early days before Pennsylvania goods began to arrive via the Susquehanna and Midwestern produce via the Baltimore & Ohio Railroad.

In New England north of the Hudson, the coastal plain and the Fall Line are almost totally submerged. Only parts of Cape Cod and some islands possess the characteristic sandy-textured soils of the "sea sand region," as early inhabitants called the coastal plain, although the nutrient-rich shallow offshore banks, which have played such an important part in New England's history, once were elevated parts of the coastal plain.

FLANDERS

Extending along the North Sea west of the Scheldt River almost all the way to Calais is the historic region of Flanders (in Flemish, Vlaanderen; in French, Flandre). Today divided between Belgium and France, this coastal strip was a prosperous county in the Middle Ages, thanks to textile making and long-distance trade. West

European trade and finance got their start in the bourses of Flemish towns like Ghent and Bruges. The liberty-loving weavers of Flanders often fought among themselves, thereby assisting outside powers in subduing them—first the Burgundians, later the Spanish and Austrians. Belgium did not gain its independence until 1830, when the nation was created as a buffer between France and Germany. The inhabitants of Belgian Flanders speak a Low German dialect akin to Dutch. The strategic location of Flanders has made it a major battleground since the Middle Ages.

The Flemish Plain is a low, flat, and damp country abutting on the south the heights of Artois and the Brabant plateau. The boundary of the medieval county varied considerably, including at one time French Artois and Picardy. Belgian Flanders today includes the provinces of East and West Flanders, while French Flanders, lying mostly in the Département du Nord, includes the industrial city of Lille and the seaport of Dunkirk.

In few places have the people been able to overcome the obstacles of nature so well as in Flanders. The northernmost parts of Belgium, in what might be described as outer Flanders, consist of a coastal plain that has been invaded by the sea as recently as the fourth century A.D. No historical records mention this submergence because the region was then experiencing an interregnum between Roman and Frankish occupation. During historic times the sea has continued to pull away from the land, and with the help of river siltation, has caused the great port of Bruges to be abandoned by its burghers in favor of Antwerp. Much of the land in this northern strip, which is no more than ten miles (16 kilometers) across at its widest, has been drained and protected from the sea by arduous reclamation work that compares favorably with the better known efforts of the Dutch. This outer belt has the most fertile soils in Flanders and is notably an agricultural landscape. Traditional crops include wheat and flax, the latter providing raw material for the manufacture of linens. Towns are uncommon in northern Flanders, except along the coast where they function as seaports or along the border with inner or southern Flanders, of which Ghent is the premier example. Ghent is today a local capital and market town, but in the thirteenth century the town was the commercial hub of northwest Europe.

Inner or southern Flanders has soils of low fertility—unstable sands in places, and elsewhere sticky, impermeable clays. Only the stubborn persistence of the Flemish peasant has managed to produce an agricultural surplus from such ungrateful soils. The farmers of Flanders have always been innovators. It was Flanders, not England, that pioneered the introduction of new root crops like turnips and new rotations that ushered in the agricultural revolution of the eighteenth century, a revolution that was a necessary precursor of the more famous industrial revolution of the following century. The Flemish textile industry was always in the vanguard of new techniques and forms of organization. The cloth industry initially made use of locally produced flax and wool for making linens and woolens, but dependence on English wool was so great by the fourteenth century that the cutting off of English exports due to the alliance of Flanders with France against Edward III threw the Flemish cloth industry into disarray. Flanders pioneered the protoindustrial organization known as the putting-out system, by which a merchant provided materials and sometimes equipment (but not a work site) to rural out-

workers, which proved a resilient and enduring form of industrial production well into the nineteenth century.

It has been the fate of the Belgian Gate—the low-lying lands of central and northern Belgium—to swing both ways before the advance of invading armies. In the twentieth century both world wars resulted in important battles on Flemish terrain. During World War I, fighting was heavy in west Flanders and French Flanders. In the well-known poem "In Flanders Fields," the Canadian poet and physician John McCrae memorialized the slaughtered dead:

In Flanders fields, the poppies blow,
Between the crosses, row on row.

The Nazi invasion of the Low Countries on 10 May 1940 initiated the Battle of Flanders, which ended with the defeat of the Belgian army and the evacuation of the British at Dunkirk.

Further Reading: Raoul Blanchard, "Flanders," *Geographical Review* 4 (1917), pp. 417–433; David Nicholas, *Town and Countryside: Social, Economic, and Political Tensions in Fourteenth-Century Flanders,* Bruges: De Tempel, 1971.

FLORIDA, STRAITS OF

Following Columbus's epoch-making voyages of discovery in the Caribbean, the Spanish installed governors on the larger islands and explored the limits of their new maritime empire. It was perhaps inevitable that the Spanish would soon run into the lengthy peninsula of Florida, which juts out conspicuously from the mainland of the northern Gulf Coast.

In 1513 Juan Ponce de León, former governor of Puerto Rico (whose subjects had rebelled against him the year before), was rumored to be searching for a spring whose waters would restore youth. Instead, he found and explored both coasts of Florida. There were two reasons for the name he gave the peninsula: his observation of a flowery land, and the reaching of the peninsula only six days after the Easter of Flowers. The navigating officer for this voyage was the capable Alaminos, who was to make the first navigational map of the Caribbean for the Spanish. He recognized that the usual homeward voyage across the Caribbean via the Windward Passage between Cuba and Hispaniola—Columbus's route—could be improved considerably by navigating the passage between Florida and Cuba. He had observed the broad highway of warm water streaming out of the Gulf of Mexico toward the northeast as he navigated the Straits of Florida. This favorable current for a homeward voyage, now known as the Gulf Stream, has at its southern end the Florida Current, which crosses the 90-mile-wide (145-kilometers) straits between Cuba and Florida. Alaminos communicated this information to the Spanish authorities, and the Iberians lost no time in following up on it. Hernán Cortés sailed across the Straits of Florida on a homeward-bound passage in July 1519, reaching Spain via the **Azores** within two months.

The straits thus became the preferred route for the Spanish when making their return trips to Europe. Through this broad gateway traveled the protected flotillas of Spanish galleons, laden with treasure from Peru, on their once-yearly trip back to Spain. Though often described as the West Indian Gibraltar, the Straits of Florida are not so much a narrow point of constriction as a broad corridor joining the Gulf of Mexico and the Atlantic.

Havana, Cuba, became the most important settlement in the Caribbean, eclipsing Santo Domingo (which remained the administrative capital), be-

cause it was of vital importance along the route of the treasure fleet. In early summer, before the hurricane season, ships converged here from Portobelo, Cartagena, Vera Cruz, and other ports of the **Spanish Main.** The Bahama Channel along the north coast of Cuba, with its treacherous coral banks, was as much to be feared as the fairly easy passage across the Straits of Florida.

After the English settled in the late 1600s along the Atlantic coast in the Carolinas and Georgia, numerous pirates and privateers found in these protected waters—and numerous other places in the Caribbean—secure bases for their marauding expeditions aimed at hijacking Spanish treasure. The Spanish either built or had planned a series of forts along the Atlantic Coast as far north as the **Chesapeake Bay** as a means to protect the treasure fleets. It is in this context that one can appreciate the significance of the fact that the oldest permanent settlement in what is now U.S. territory is at St. Augustine (Florida), in the northern part of the state along the Atlantic Ocean, 35 miles (56 kilometers) southeast of Jacksonville. Founded by Pedro Menéndez de Avilés in 1565, the town was the site of the great stone fort of San Marcos, which was begun in 1672 and completed in 1756.

Thus Cuba and Florida achieved their strategic significance during the colonial Spanish period. It was not at a single point such as at Gibraltar but along a line stretching from Cuba to the deeper waters of the Atlantic and back again from Cuba to the ports of the Spanish Main (for ships bringing treasure to Havana could be picked off as easily as ships carrying it away) that the route of the Spanish treasure fleet was vulnerable to attack.

In the seventeenth century, threats to Spanish hegemony in the Caribbean increased, partly as a result of the colonization and enrichment of the tiny islands of the Lesser Antilles by northwest Europeans (the Spanish had ignored these islands until then, due to their lack of gold). The British settled Saint Kitts and Nevis (1625 and 1628), at the northern end of the volcanic arc, and just outside the arc to the south, the limestone island of Barbados (1626). These sugar-producing islands would prove much more valuable in the long run than if they had contained precious metals.

The Spanish convoy system worked remarkably well. Although individual merchant ships were sometimes isolated and seized, over the course of two centuries the treasure fleets were only taken in entirety on three occasions (in 1628, 1656, and 1657). Far more treasure lies along the bottom of the Straits of Florida or the Yucatán Channel (separating Cuba and Mexico) as a result of cataclysms of nature—be they hurricanes or treacherous currents—than of depredations by romantic pirates, buccaneers, and freebooters—the heroes of childhood adventure stories.

Further Reading: Clarence H. Haring, *The Spanish Empire in America,* New York: Oxford University Press, 1947.

FOSSE WAY

By A.D. 47, the lowlands of south and east England had been secured by the Romans, who either directly garrisoned the region or permitted local control by friendly kings. A defensible frontier was established approximately along a diagonal line from Severn to Trent, which is yet today considered an important cultural and political boundary. A fortified line, or *limes,* connected a series of forts whose names ending in a modified form of *castra* belie the original purpose of many present-day towns as garrisons. The Roman road running along the frontier linked the

towns of Axmouth, Ilchester, Bath, Cirencester, Leicester, and Lincoln. The accompanying ditches gave the name to this feature, the Latin word *fossa* meaning something sunken or buried.

Contemporary scholarship considers the limits of Roman control shortly after conquest more as a broad frontier zone with lateral communication than as a linear feature resembling the boundary of a modern nation-state or the physical barrier of **Hadrian's Wall,** built three-quarters of a century later. Roman castra can be found north and south of the supposed frontier line, so the limits of Roman control are best viewed as a diffuse zone, with the Fosse Way linking the various lines of military control radiating across country in all directions from the southeast.

The anachronistic idea of a neat sea-to-sea perimeter may be a limitation on our understanding of the important processes of Romanization of southern England. There is evidence of a preexisting road system centered on Cirencester, the terminus or head of the original section of the Fosse Way. The Romans extended a road to the southwest to reach a new harbor at Topsham. The roads radiated in various directions from Cirencester, allowing troops to move forward or rearward as well as laterally in this key zone. There is no need to postulate a linear Roman road running straight across the country from the start.

Further Reading: Ivan D. Margary, *Roman Roads in Britain,* London: Baker, 1967; Peter Salway, *Roman Britain,* vol. 1A, *Oxford History of England,* Oxford: Clarendon Press, 1981.

FRONT RANGE

The southern section of North America's highest mountain range presents an abrupt, elevated front, rising to about 14,000 feet (4,267 meters). A major barrier to travel, the mountains can only be crossed through high passes, all above 9,000 feet (2,743 meters), some at 11,000 feet (3,353 meters). As a result, the major emigrant roads followed routes to the north and south of the mountains, while only one railroad, the Denver and Rio Grande, forged a route across the heart of the range ("through the Rockies, not around them" was the railroad's slogan).

brian basement rocks of a crystalline kind (anticline) and the subsequent stripping away of overlying, hence younger sedimentaries, which accumulated in eroded form in the apron of the **Great Plains.** At the end of this process, which began about 65 million years ago, the high country of Colorado was a rolling plain with some slightly higher, rounded summits and only locally carved, narrow gorges.

Rocky Mountain National Park, part of the Front Range, near Estes Park, Colorado. This view from Trail Ridge Road shows the effects of glaciation (note especially the bowl-shaped cirque at upper left) *(photo by Sam Hilliard).*

While the Rocky Mountains extend all the way from the Brooks Range of Alaska to the Sangre de Cristo Mountains in New Mexico, the most elevated part of the range is this 300-mile (483-kilometer) section from east-central Wyoming near Casper to the Pikes Peak region of Colorado. Rising steeply to the west of the piedmont cities of Colorado Springs, Denver, Boulder, and Cheyenne, this range was not formed by upthrust faulting, as were the Canadian Rockies, but rather by the bowing upward of Precam-

Not until the onset of Pleistocene glaciation some two million years ago did the landscape begin to resemble its present, sharpened form. Alpine glaciers filled all the high-country valleys, gouging out nearly vertical headwalls at the tops of the mountains (cirques) and widening and deepening the main valleys to produce characteristic U-shaped profiles. The ice eroded headward from both sides of drainage divides to fashion knife-edge ridges (arêtes). The spectacular scenery of the Front Range, with its peaks, cliffs, waterfalls, and lakes, is thus more a legacy of the glacial epoch than of earlier mountain-building periods.

Abundant furs, skins, and hides were the initial attractions of the region to Europeans. An era of trapping and trading began almost as soon as Lewis and Clark returned from their expedition (1804–1806). This colorful era of the Mountain Men, with larger-than-life characters like Jim Bridger and Jedediah Smith, lasted until about midcentury, by which time several prominent companies (Missouri Fur Company, Pacific Fur Company, American Fur Company, Rocky Mountain Fur Company) had already experienced early prosperity and subsequent decline as a result of a drastic reduction in the number of beavers, the preferred game, as well as a declining consumer demand for beaver hats, which had passed out of fashion.

The discovery of gold in Colorado in summer 1858 ushered in a rambunctious pioneer phase of placer mining of alluvial gravels. The site of the original discovery was on Cherry Creek near its junction with the South Platte, perhaps a dozen miles east of the mountains—in a word, present-day Denver. Miners quickly exhausted surface deposits, and literally tracing the course of the gold upstream, they moved their operations up into the hills. Now the serious business of the underground mining of hard quartz rock could begin, and towns such as Blackhawk, Central City, Nevadaville, and many others less renowned grew up overnight—and often just as rapidly declined.

Denver was the most successful of the piedmont towns benefiting from their location at the eastern edge of the Rocky Mountains. The piedmont region had a semiarid climate but with access to water from the high country. Denver became a transportation center, although this development was not necessarily mandated by its physical geography. In the perspective of transport analysis, route knotting tends to occur at physiographic boundaries such as the transition between mountains and plains due to changes in the modes of conveyance and in rates. Where only a limited number of routes cross a mountain range, a small number of centers develop to handle the traffic (another example would be the north Italian city of Bologna, on the northern border of the **Apennines**). The Mile-High City does not guard any strategic defile across the mountains, as there are no low passes behind it. Rather, the city grew when a deserted mining town reestablished itself as a distribution center for an emerging commercial hinterland. The town that formerly outfitted settlers and provisioned travelers transformed itself after World War II into a major metropolis, to whose traditional list of industries—mining, food processing, transport, and banking—can be added new jobs in aerospace, publishing, federal government services, and tourism.

Further Reading: T. S. Lovering and E. N. Goddard, *Geology and Ore Deposits of the Front Range, Colorado,* U.S. Geological Survey Professional Papers, no. 223, Washington, DC: Government Printing Office (GPO), 1951.

FULDA GAP

This opening through the **Hercynian Uplands** of central Germany connects the northern plains with the Rhineland. The Fulda River rises on the Wasserkuppe, flowing north past Fulda, Hersfeld, and Kassel as far as Münden, where it joins the Werra River. The Werra in turn flows into the Weser, one of the major south-north-flowing German rivers. It is at the southern end, where the corridor joins the Rhine-Main valleys, that important urban, economic, and cultural developments have been promoted.

The older, medieval city of Mainz is located on the east bank of the Rhine, where the Main tributary opens up onto the plateau lands to the east. Just upstream on the Main, the industrial and financial center of Frankfurt grew rapidly in the modern period on the basis of its being a transport hub. It had natural connections up and down the Rhine and Main valleys, and through tectonic depressions to the north it was also accessible to the Fulda Valley.

Fulda provided eastward penetration for cultural expansion. During the early Middle Ages, it was the main avenue for the spread of Christianity in central Europe. St. Boniface established a Benedictine abbey in A.D. 744 at Fulda, which became the major center of German missionary activity. A preeminent cultural center at this time, the Fulda monastery, library, and *scriptoria* produced some of the greatest works of Carolingian art in the form of illuminated manuscripts. The Fulda abbots were princes of the Holy Roman Empire and controlled a large territory until the abbey was secularized in 1803. The scene of annual conferences of German Roman Catholic bishops, Fulda is the site of the crypt containing the tomb of St. Boniface (at the cathedral).

Since World War II, Frankfurt-am-Main has been the headquarters for the U.S. Army and a major American business center in Germany. It was believed that the most likely spot where the opening shots of a hypothetical World War III would occur if Russia and the Warsaw Pact countries attacked would be in the Fulda Gap. The corridor not only is located along the boundary between the northern plains and the central uplands, with access to the Rhine-Main area, but also approaches the border of the former East Germany (the town of Fulda lies just within the political border of what was West Germany). An advance regiment of the U.S. Army (11th Armored Cavalry Regiment) was stationed at Fulda. With the collapse of communism and the end of the cold war, the Fulda forces found themselves in the center of a reunited Germany, with no frontier to defend. As the United States reduced its military presence in Europe, the Fulda regiment departed in the early 1990s.

See also: Iron Curtain.

GALÁPAGOS ISLANDS

Some 650 miles (1,045 kilometers) west of Ecuador is the isolated Pacific island group of the Galápagos (the Spanish word for tortoises). This island chain is best known for its barren, almost unearthly volcanic landscapes; the bewildering but well-adapted fauna; and a brief visit made by a nineteenth-century naturalist, who discovered here key evidence for the theory of evolution.

Officially administered as the Archipiélago de Colón by Ecuador, the group includes 13 major islands and numerous smaller islands, islets, and rocks. Most are circular in shape due to their being the tops of volcanic mountains, with the exception of Isabela (Albemarle Island), which consists of several coalescing volcanic fields stretching to the north and west from the main, southern mass. Largely desolate piles of lava, the upper slopes of the mountainous interiors have dense, jungly vegetation due to their interception of the moist trade winds and the resulting mountain rainfall. The cool Humboldt Current traveling from far to the south sets to the west in northern Peru and Ecuador, deflected by the westward trend of the coast, and the effect is a more moderate temperature regime than one would expect, considering the islands' location at the equator. But it is the queer wildlife of the islands, much of it found nowhere else in the world, that has been the chief attraction of these islands: giant land tortoises weighing as much as 500 pounds (227 kilograms) and living as long as 300 years; clownish-looking birds accurately described as Blue-Footed Boobies; marine as well as land iguanas; flightless cormorants; and 13 distinct species of finches, each microadapted with its own specialized tool for a beak—the latter being the centerpiece of Darwin's case for evolution, although he didn't know it at the time of his famous visit.

The island group, originally known as the Encantadas, or Enchanted Islands, was discovered in 1535 by the Spanish navigator Tomás de Berlanga. In the following century English buccaneers stopped here to obtain larders for their long sea voyages: Giant tortoises stacked in the holds of ships could survive for as long as 18 months without food or water and be turned into a delectable stew called sea pie. The greatest depredations of these gentle giants (the Galápagos animals are without fear) occurred in the nineteenth century at the hands of American and British whalers and oilers, who slaughtered the tortoise for food and rendered its blubber into fuel for illumination. It has been estimated that the buccaneers, whalers, merchantmen, and fur sealers destroyed two to three hundred thousand of these reptiles in just two centuries. As late as the 1930s tortoise fat was being rendered into oil that was shipped back to the mainland in 50-gallon (189-liter) drums. Under protection today, the giant tortoises have new threats due to altered habitats and the introduction of exotic predators like pigs and rats, which eat their eggs, and several populations are threatened with extinction.

The 26-year-old Charles Darwin visited the islands in 1835 on the voyage of the HMS *Beagle,* a survey expedition run along the lines of Captain Cook's South Seas voyages a half century before. Its primary purpose was to explore and map the coastline of South America. Though officially employed only as a companion to the ship's melancholic Captain Robert FitzRoy, the young student of natural history who had just graduated from Cambridge busily collected specimens of the exotic flora and fauna of the islands during his brief stay (he stayed only five weeks, which is amazing when one considers the importance of the results). The variations in species from island to island was complicated by the fact that each of the islands has two names, an English name and a Spanish one. The former, it is assumed, was assigned by the English buccaneers. For example, the island first encountered by Darwin's party was San Cristóbal, at the eastern end of the chain, which also goes by the name of— what could be more English?—Chatham Island.

More importantly for Darwin, the plant and animal populations varied from island to island in noticeable ways. The vice-governor of the island, a Mr. Lawson, told Darwin that he could tell which island a tortoise came from if one was brought to him. Darwin did not at first pay sufficient attention to this crucial piece of evidence, as he tells us that he mingled specimens from two of the is-

lands before he realized the importance of separating them. Variations of biological offspring and the effects of geographical isolation—two of the linchpins of organic evolution—were already firm in Darwin's mind in 1839, when his observations on the Beagle voyage were published, twenty years before the appearance of *The Origin of Species* (1859).

> I never dreamed that islands, about fifty or sixty miles apart, and most of them in sight of each other, formed of precisely the same rocks, placed under a quite similar climate, rising to a nearly equal height, would have been differently tenanted. . . . It is the fate of most voyagers, no sooner to discover what is most interesting in any locality, than they are hurried from it; but I ought, perhaps, to be thankful that I obtained sufficient materials to establish this most remarkable fact in the distribution of organic beings. (Charles Darwin, *Journal of Researches,* 1839)

Not yet a theory of evolution, to be sure, but the underpinnings of one, and the sure recognition of the importance of geographical distribution. But we, too, must hurry from our discovery.

The Galápagos frequently have been visited by scientific expeditions since Darwin's time. During World War II the United States took over the islands to serve as a naval air base to protect the **Panama Canal** and returned them to Ecuador in 1946. A Darwin Research Station now exists on Santa Cruz island along with a large tortoise reserve. Most of the territory of the islands composes Ecuador's most popular national park. Where only 200 tourists visited the islands in 1969, today 60,000 tourists arrive yearly. They come not to see barren specks of spent volcanoes but to witness the natural theater of evolution and to have fun. Visitors "do" the Galápagos by traveling from island to island aboard cruise ships, landing at the larger islands from inflatable rubber rafts called *pangas* (Spanish slang for boats). In the town of Puerto Ayora on Santa Cruz, souvenir merchandise and token mementos of the trip are sold. It might be noted that the Sandal-Footed T-Shirt Merchant is a species far from extinction.

> *Further Reading:* Charles R. Darwin, *Journal of Researches into the Natural History and Geology of the Countries Visited during the Voyage of H.M.S. Beagle round the World, under the Command of Capt. Fitz Roy, R.N.* London: John Murray, 1839; Jonathan Weiner, *The Beak of the Finch: A Story of Evolution in Our Time,* New York: Knopf, 1994 (reprinted by Vintage, 1995).

GALLIPOLI PENINSULA
See Dardanelles

GASCONY
See Aquitaine Basin

GAUL
In the first millennium B.C., the Iron Age Celts were the dominant population in Europe north of the Alps, from the Atlantic Ocean to the **Black Sea.** Though early Hallstatt (560 B.C.) and La Tène sites (400 B.C.) are dispersed throughout central Europe, the cultural hearth for the Celts appears to have been in upper Austria, southwestern Germany, and the Swiss plateau. This ancient people, whose descendants today can be found on the hilly and isolated parts of northwestern Europe (the so-called Celtic Fringe), migrated south and east down the Danube, followed the Rhine valley to the north, and passed easily westward through the **Burgundy Gateway** into France. Fortified hill sites known to the Romans as *oppida*

were perhaps the most distinctive feature of their dwelling places, and this gave rise to their name, as *cel* meant hill or rise in their native tongue. The great age of the expansion and dominance of the Celts, or Gauls, as the Romans preferred to call them, occurred in the period marked by the decline of classical Greece and the beginnings of Roman expansion, roughly between 450–250 B.C. During this period, Celtic invaders advanced on Rome and even sacked the temple of Delphi in Greece.

By the third century the Romans had conquered the Celts who had invaded northern Italy, and this region became known as Gallia Cisalpina or Cisalpine Gaul (this side of the Alps). This in turn was subdivided into Cispadane Gaul (this side of the Po) and Transpadane Gaul (the other side of the Po). By 100 B.C. the Romans had acquired the southern part of the Celtic domain beyond the Alps, in Transalpine Gaul. One of the first accessions to Rome outside peninsular Italy, Provencia (hence, modern Provence) included a 100-mile-wide (161 kilometers) strip along the sea from the eastern Pyrenees extending northeastward and up the Rhône River nearly to Lyon. Julius Caesar's initial success came from his conquest of Gaul in the Gallic Wars (58 B.C.–51 B.C.), about which he wrote in his *Commentaries,* which is considered the best source of information about Celtic Gaul. He immortalized the ethnic and geographic divisions of Transalpine Gaul in the famous first sentence, learned by countless Latin students, "All Gaul is divided into three parts." Aquitania included the lands in southwestern France as far north as the Garonne River; Belgica constituted the tribes living in the area of northeastern France, extending into Belgium; and Gaul proper referred to modern central France. The population of Gaul proper in the Loire and

Seine valleys was of Celtic origin, and so, it is believed, were the Belgica tribes; but the Aquitani are a somewhat mysterious Iberian people, who might have been the ancestors of the Basques. Rome reformed these provinces on a number of occasions during its imperial phase, at one point establishing Gallia Narbonensis (Narbonese Gaul) in old Provence, with its capital at the **Languedoc** city of Narbonne. During

awe ever since ancient times. One of the fabled labors of Hercules was to venture out into the Atlantic in search of the mythical islands of Hesperides, but his path was blocked by a ponderous mountain enclosing the Mediterranean. He cleft the mountain and tore it asunder, opening a passage to the Atlantic that had massive promontories on each side, upon which he placed the Pillars of Hercules.

Rock of Gibraltar, one of the two Pillars of Hercules *(photo by Jesse Walker)*.

Rome's later days the prefecture of Gaul was one of the four divisions of the Roman Empire.

GDAŃSK
See Polish Corridor

GIBRALTAR, STRAIT OF
Gibraltar is at once a town, a garrison, a rock of impregnable reputation, a colony (the only one in Europe), and a key strategic location.

The opening that connects the **Mediterranean Sea** to the Atlantic has been viewed with commingled envy and

Tradition has it that these legendary pillars are actually the massive Jurassic limestone block of Gibraltar Rock, at the southern end of Spain, and about 12 miles (19 kilometers) away, in Morocco, Mt. Acho on Point Almina, at the end of the peninsula where Ceuta is located. The real-life Pillars of Hercules lie at the eastern end of a strait about 36 miles (58 kilometers) long. The western entrance is generally wider, with 27 miles (43 kilometers) separating **Cape Trafalgar** from Moroccan Tangier. The narrowest point of the strait is about eight miles (13 kilometers) off Cape Marroquí.

The Pillars of Hercules have long been part of the Spanish heraldic arms and were incorporated into the design of the Spanish Milled Dollar that circulated as legal tender during colonial and early national times in the United States and was the basis of the American dollar. The motto "Ne Plus Ultra," or "Nothing Beyond," which appeared on the Spanish coins, referred to the end of the known

evidence of early man has been found in Gibraltar caves, including the first Neanderthal finds, discovered here in 1848.

Known to the ancients as Calpe, Gibraltar Rock has been occupied in turn by the Phoenicians, Carthaginians, Romans, and Visigoths. The Rock takes its name from the conquering forces of the Moor Tariq, who inaugurated Moorish control of Iberia in A.D. 711. Gibraltar is

A Barbary ape—the only species of monkey in Europe—on Gibraltar Rock *(photo by Jesse Walker)*.

world. It is an ironic title because so many of these coins circulated in the new Spanish Empire in Latin America, which clearly lay beyond the ancient gates.

The Rock of Gibraltar rises to 1,396 feet (426 meters), with steep precipices on the eastern side but more gentle slopes on the western side, descending to the city and port nestled in Gibraltar Bay. The porous limestone of the Rock is honeycombed with caverns and passageways, many excavated during the Great Siege of 1779–1783, when the British defended the bastion against combined Spanish and French forces. Some of the best fossil

an Anglicized corruption of Jebel-al-Tariq (Mountain of Tariq). It was Tariq who first fortified the rock, which resembles an enormous crouching lion with its head pointed northward across a narrow, sandy peninsula (Neutral Ground) that connects it to Spanish territory.

British possession dates from 1704, when, during the lengthy War of Spanish Succession, Admiral George Rooke seized the Spanish garrison with an Anglo-Dutch fleet. The Treaty of Utrecht of 1713 ceded the fortress to the British, but only after its heroic resistance against the Great Siege (1779–1783) did Gibraltar become a legitimate colony, accepted by the other great powers.

In the nineteenth century, Gibraltar was the key to the Mediterranean. The defeat of Napoleon hinged on British control of this chokepoint, and the climactic defeat of the French navy occurred just west of the entrance to the Mediterranean. During the heyday of the British Empire, this position standing astride the boundary between Africa and Europe and controlling access to the Mediterranean was perhaps the finest pearl in a string of key maritime points stretching from Gibraltar to Singapore.

Following post–World War II decolonization and Britain's decision in the late 1960s to withdraw from positions east of Suez, Gibraltar lost much of its strategic importance. Nevertheless, Britain continues to hold onto this small tract of land—the only colony in Europe—despite recurrent attempts by the Spanish to claim what they consider rightfully theirs. Gibraltar has more value for Britain today as an important naval position on the Atlantic than for its Mediterranean influence. It is certainly more important than the distant Falkland Islands, for which Britain was willing to fight a war in 1982. Moreover, the residents of the town of Gibraltar naturally favor the familiar English culture and educational system and feel threatened by a Spanish takeover.

Further Reading: Joel Cook, *The Mediterranean and Its Borderlands,* 2 vols., Philadelphia: John C. Winston, 1910.

GRAND BANKS

The coastal plain of the eastern United States, a series of southwest-northeast-trending layers of young deposits, lying like reverse shingles on the older Appalachian rocks of the interior, not only inclines in the direction of the sea but

dips to the north. The result is that the coastal plain and continental shelf are almost wholly inundated north of Cape Cod, forming submerged platforms known as banks. There are three main groups of banks, all of which have been excellent fishing grounds in the past: Georges Bank, east of Nantucket, ends at a submarine valley opposite the mouth of the Bay of Fundy; several smaller shallows and islands off Nova Scotia—Browns, La Have, Cape Sable, and Banquereau—collectively known as the Scotian Banks; and the Grand Banks south and east off Newfoundland. The Georges and Scotian Banks are separated from the Grand Banks by the Laurentian Channel, which extends up the Gulf of St. Lawrence and the St. Lawrence River as far as Quebec.

The Grand Banks is about 300 miles (480 kilometers) long and about 400 miles (640 kilometers) wide, with depths from 20 to 100 fathoms (one fathom is equal to 6 feet or 1.8 meters). Its shallowness allows sufficient light to penetrate to support a prolific growth of phytoplankton, which is the explanation for the large schools of fish found in the waters of the banks. In addition, the mingling of the cold Labrador Current, which flows over most of the banks, with the warmer Gulf Stream sweeping along the eastern edge leads to nutrient-rich waters, as well as notorious fog fields. (Add the danger of icebergs to the treachery of these waters.) The nurseries of phytoplankton and various small fish then are fed upon by cod, haddock, halibut, and other fish. Lobsters are also found there.

The Grand Banks have been the world's most important international fishing ground almost since their first exploitation by westward-venturing seamen from England's West Country and the Breton and Iberian coasts in the fifteenth century. The voyage of discovery of the English explorer John Cabot (1497–1498) touched off widespread interest in the North Atlantic cod fishery, which subsequently has received regular visits by fishermen from the British Isles and France, Scandinavia, and Iberia, as well as North America—once settlement was established on this side of the waters. The banks initially attracted poor fishermen, such as the Basques from northern Spain, but soon the English and French claimed the fishery exclusively as an appurtenance of their adjacent New World empires. Visiting French and English ships were in a rough balance until the eighteenth century. Then the Treaty of Utrecht (1713) gave Newfoundland wholly to Great Britain, allowing the French to catch their fish and dry them only along certain stretches of beach. At the conclusion of the French and Indian War (Seven Years War) in 1763, Canada, Nova Scotia, and Cape Breton were added to the British Empire, France retaining only the tiny islands of St. Pierre and the Miquelons, presumably for staging a fishing expedition. It has been suggested by some wag that the British viewed Newfoundland—not a part of Canada until 1949—as a great English ship moored near the banks for the convenience of English fishermen. With the establishment of British dominance, the banks fishery entered its heyday in the late eighteenth and early nineteenth centuries.

New England benefited from fishing the banks, as a series of neat and prosperous fishing towns sprang up along the coast. The area around Massachusetts Bay, including Boston, Salem, Cape Ann, Gloucester, and Marblehead, was advantaged not only by the provision of foodstuffs by its fishermen but their support of ancillary mercantile and manufacturing jobs (e.g., shipbuilding, salt making, finance, and insurance).

Historically the cod fishery comprised two branches: those ships that threw their catch into the hold and salted them (green cod), whence they were often immediately transported to Europe, reflecting the fishermen's desire to be the first in with the new catch; and those ships that landed and dried their take along the beaches on staging equipment, such as wooden frames known as fish flakes, the latter the basis for most Newfoundland settlements. There was a tendency through time for migratory fishing with ships returning each season to Europe to give way to permanent fishing villages. American "bankers" would often make three or four trips to the fishing grounds each season. The snug harbor of Gloucester, to cite an example, had no less than 35 bankers attached to its fair town, and on a given summer day in the early nineteenth century at least one of these ships would likely clear port. To give another, more sensual example, in the fields south of Marblehead in the autumn millions of cod were spread to dry on frames, giving off an irrepressible odor.

Today the banks provide, alas, a classic example of overfishing and consequent loss of livelihood and economic base. This has been experienced most sharply by the small Newfoundland fishing villages that dot its south coast. Blame has been assigned to the large factory ships arriving from countries that did not traditionally visit the banks, such as Russia and Japan. However, the causes of the decline are probably more complex, involving the activities of many more countries. In 1977 Canada extended its offshore jurisdiction to include most of the area, with the result that the banks' days as the premier international fishing ground appear to be over. Oil drilling began on the banks in the late

1970s but slowed after the loss of the Ocean Ranger rig on 15 February 1982. No other primary livelihood has replaced fishing as a mainstay of the economy in Newfoundland, and unless tourism takes up the slack, the oldest British colony in the New World will continue to experience economic hard times.

Further Reading: Ralph H. Brown, *Mirror for Americans: Likeness of the Eastern Seaboard,*

ally exceed 5,000 feet (1,524 meters), but altitudes range from below sea level at Death Valley, California, on the southwestern margin of the region, to more than 13,000 feet (3,962 meters) above sea level.

The topography is complexly faulted, with evidence of uplift in several geological periods. The ridges represent a series of parallel fault block mountains, each 50–75 miles (81–121 kilometers) long

An abandoned mining camp in silver country near Hamilton, Nevada, in the Great Basin *(photo by Jesse Walker).*

1810, American Geographical Society Special Publication, no. 27, New York: American Geographical Society, 1943; H. A. Innis, *The Cod Fisheries: The History of an International Economy (The Relations of Canada and the United States),* New Haven: Yale University Press (Toronto: Ryerson Press), 1940.

GREAT BASIN

Situated between the western edge of the Rocky Mountains and the **Sierra Nevada,** this austere land of rough, jagged mountains alternating with dry basins has been a transit region for most Americans in their experience of the West, although not for all. Centered on the state of Nevada but extending into adjacent states, the Great Basin consists of linear, north-south mountain ranges separated by valleys with internal drainage. The relief between the valleys and adjoining ridges does not usu-

and 10–25 miles (16–40 kilometers) wide, with steep escarpments on the western side where faulting has occurred, and more gradual slopes to the east due to the tilting of the blocks. Conspicuous aprons of gravel lie along the fronts, the results of weathering and erosion from the still rising ridge. In the central parts of the basins are intermittent dry alluvial valleys and playas (dry lake beds)—such as the Great Salt Lake and its nearby freshwater cousin, Utah Lake, both relics of glacial Lake Bonneville, which was once twice as large as Lake Erie.

A vivid portrait of the region's topography can be found in John McPhee's paean to geology, *Basin and Range:*

> Each range here is like a warship standing on its own, and the Great

Basin is an ocean of loose sediment with these mountain ranges standing in it as if they were members of a fleet without precedent, assembled at Guam to assault Japan.

The terrain is unlike that of the Appalachian Ridge and Valley province, not only in that it is the result of different geological forces—tensional rather

cuted flock of latter-day saints out of the Midwest and across the West, looked down from a high terrace at the mouth of a canyon in the Wasatch Front and exclaimed, "This is the place." His benediction of the Salt Lake valley was important because it was not simply an opinion but a theocratic pronouncement, a consecration of a new Zion, and it would set in train a half century of

A view into the valley from the Wasatch Mountains in Utah *(Corel Corporation).*

than compressional forces—but also because its wide valleys are interconnected across low divides, allowing transport lines to cross the region with comparative ease. Wagon roads, telegraph lines, railroads, and interstate highways all have crossed the states of Utah and Nevada without too much difficulty. The Humboldt River of northern Nevada is one of the few rivers that flows east to west, and its valley was selected by western migrants who followed the California Trail from the Wyoming Basin and thus avoided the harsh desert west of Great Salt Lake.

The eastern edge of this desolate wasteland received an influx of that curiously American Protestant group, the Mormons, beginning at midcentury. It was reported on 24 July 1847 that Brigham Young, after leading his perse-

Mormon colonization. Brigham Young did not utter the precise words attributed to him (he actually said "This is the right place"). A more important error in the legend of the siting of Salt Lake City at the eastern edge of the Great Basin is the mistaken impression it gives that the leader of the Mormons stumbled on the area without preparation. In fact, Young carefully considered a number of alternative destinations in the period of trouble following the murder of Joseph Smith in Illinois in 1844, including Texas, Oregon, California, and the Great Basin. He decided in favor of the last only after diligent study of J. C. Fremont's recent report of the region.

The core of the Mormon culture region extends up and down the Wasatch Front, from Brigham City in the north to

Provo, on the banks of Utah Lake, in the south, with Salt Lake City approximately at a midpoint. The Mormons laid out their towns and agricultural villages in regular gridirons, with large, spacious blocks resembling the settlements of New England—not a spurious cultural association, given that the Mormons originated in the Yankee-transplant region of upstate New York. In 1849 Young petitioned Congress to accept the state of Deseret (a word from the Book of Mormon, meaning honeybee, chosen to symbolize the industriousness of the ideal society), whose territory embraced a large section of the newly acquired Far West, as far south as the Gila River and as far west as the crest of the Sierra Nevadas. A frontage on the Pacific in the vicinity of present-day Los Angeles was also requested. Congress declined the Deseret proposal, substituting instead Utah Territory, half as big and with a more humble name derived from the local Indians. By the end of the century, Mormons had colonized a domain extending up and down the Wasatch as far south as the Virgin River in southern Utah, whose drainage is part of the Colorado's, and as far north as the upper Snake River valley in southern Idaho. Outliers of Mormon settlement exist in Arizona (Mesa was established as a Mormon farm village in 1878) and even into Mexico. Expansion was less vigorous to the north due to Young's persistent southern bias, which denigrated the agricultural potential of northern lands in favor of the desolate south; but distant outliers of Mormon colonization can be found even as far north as the province of Alberta, Canada.

The western part of the Great Basin was for the most part left to Gentiles (non-Mormons). A series of ephemeral mining booms spread a thin layer of semipermanent occupants across Nevada's landscape, in sharp contrast to the social clustering of Utah. The Basin and Range is a mineral-rich region, with especially important commercial deposits of silver, copper, and salts. While searching for placer gold in the wake of the midcentury California boom, prospectors discovered extensive silver deposits in 1859 at the Comstock Lode, in Virginia City.

Conventional underground mining of silver veins in fissures at the Comstock resulted in a mining boom. Elsewhere, miners searched through surface deposits, literally turning over rocks in search of geological concentration of silver by erosion and enrichment. The 1870s were the heyday of these isolated and scattered mining camps in Nevada, and by the turn of the century they had become ghost towns. Evaporative salts also were important resources extracted from the arid region. Borax was first produced in large quantities from Death Valley about 1882, when the well-advertised 20-mule teams hauled deposits from the valley to the railroad—a ten-day trip. The search for mineral and other forms of wealth inevitably spread to the Mormon oasis. Huge open-pit mining of low-grade but concentratable copper is still under way at Bingham Canyon near Salt Lake City.

Fortuitously, the capital city of the Mormon religion was located a short distance from the intersection of the first two transcontinental trunk lines, the Central Pacific and the Union Pacific. Benefiting economically from this position, Salt Lake City gradually became an important mercantile, processing, and service center. As a result, although its population is still predominantly Mormon, many tangible expressions of Gentile intrusions can be found in the cultural landscape: At one end of the main retail shopping district is Hotel Utah, and opposite it, the Mormon Square, with the temple and the Tabernacle. Four blocks away stands Hotel Newhouse, built with profits from the silver mines of southwestern Utah, with a U.S. post office facing it.

Further Reading: John McPhee, *Basin and Range,* New York: Farrar, Straus, and Giroux, 1981; D. W. Meinig, "The Mormon Culture Region: Strategies and Patterns in the

Draining from Canada and the north, the Columbia River is forced to veer to the west, then south around extensive lava beds, finally swinging to the west again near where it is joined by its main tributary, the Snake. The river has formed a narrow, entrenched valley, which lies well below the basaltic tablelands that are most developed south and east of the river's great bend. The region is hardly uniform in

An extensive lava plateau east of the great bend of the Columbia River near Spokane, Washington *(photo by Sam Hilliard).*

Geography of the American West, 1847–1964," *Annals of the Association of American Geographers* 55 (1965), pp. 191–220.

GREAT COLUMBIA PLAIN

This mountain-girdled plain, most of which is situated in the eastern part of the state of Washington, is one of the most colorful and distinctive of American regions, yet its peculiar character has been so eroded by the forces of national economic change and transport innovation, starting with the railroad, that its name is hardly known to most Americans.

character and is certainly not a level plain. It includes dry coulees that once received glacial meltwaters in a short-cut across the meandering river; a mosaic of scoured rock and deep soils known as the channeled scablands; and to the east, the rolling hills of the Palouse, which have produced rich yields of wheat for more than a century. The Yakima country, to the west of the river, is located in the dry lee of the Cascades. With the aid of irrigation, it has developed California-style specialty agriculture, with emphasis on fruits and nuts.

Another valley that drains into the Columbia just below the mouth of the

Snake—the Walla Walla—was the most important point of initial attachment of European culture, not only as a result of the broad fertile plain along the river and its major tributary, the Touchet, but also due to its strategic access to trails debouching from the Rockies, most notably the Oregon Trail. Following Lewis and Clark's epochal trip across the Rocky Mountains and down the Snake–Columbia River system to the sea, a brief period of fur trading and missionary expeditions gave way to colonization. The Willamette River valley attracted the majority of settlers at midcentury, but by the 1870s an increasingly large number of agriculturists—both farmers and pastoralists—took up land in fertile river valleys, along terrace strips, and around the margins of the drier interior parts of the great Columbia plain. With the recognition that farmers could harvest bountiful crops year after year in the semiarid climate (there is almost no rain from May to October), pioneers streamed into the region. They were especially drawn to the fertile, loess-derived soils of the rolling Palouse. The fertility of the soil in such dry conditions was a puzzle to early soil scientists like E. W. Hilgard until they realized that weathered volcanic soils were rich in nutrient bases, that windblown loess, or silt, improved the texture and natural fertility of the soils, and that the amount of rainfall was less important than its timing. The lack of timber for fencing, fuel, and construction was a problem for early settlers until the arrival of the railroad, but the cultivation of these lands, formerly deemed barren deserts, proceeded apace. A saying of the day was borne out: "Wherever bunchgrass grows, wheat will grow." The harvests in certain years were so large that the crop couldn't be carried away by the additional cars assigned by the railroads until the next season, so grain was piled up on railroad platforms and in makeshift warehouses. Walla Walla wheat, marketed in sacks as in California, unlike in the Midwest, where bulk shipment was more common, became a staple on the world market in the 1880s. On these immense steps descending from the Rockies, whose reputation during the trapping era was for good horses and a lack of furs, farmers began to reap a previously undreamed-of golden harvest.

Ironically, the region's distinctiveness was undermined by the same forces that had created it. The building of the great transcontinentals, especially the Great Northern, and the extension of Midwestern lines like the Chicago, Milwaukee, and St. Paul, drew the Columbia plain into the trade orbit of the Puget Sound cities of Seattle and Tacoma, reorienting commerce away from its prior outlet downriver to Portland. In the late 1880s, a short-lived movement flared up, seeking the creation of a separate state of Columbia together with the panhandle of Idaho; but with the admission into statehood of Washington in 1889, the political geography at the state level became permanently fixed.

Spokane grew rapidly in the 1880s, becoming the capital of the Great Columbia Plain, with Walla Walla and Yakima much smaller in size and serving tiny hinterlands. After 1890 the "Minneapolis of the West," as boosters referred to Spokane, grew more slowly. The region was increasingly tied into a national system of cities with interlocking and overlapping financial spheres. References to Spokane's "Inland Empire" became less frequent, the name only surviving among a diminishing number of old-timers.

Further Reading: D. W. Meinig, *The Great Columbia Plain: A Historical Geography, 1805–1910,* Seattle, Wash.: University of Washington Press, 1968; Edward L. Ullman,

"Rivers as Regional Bonds: The Columbia-Snake Example," *Geographical Review* 41 (1951), pp. 210–225.

GREAT LAKES

The largest body of fresh water in the world, the Great Lakes of central North America, with the exception of Lake Michigan, form the international border between the U.S. Midwest and Canada.

The lakes were gouged out by fingers of the Pleistocene ice sheet, which some of them resemble in shape (e.g., Michigan), although there is evidence also of preexisting drainage. As a result of glacial action, all of the lake bottoms, with the exception of Lake Erie, extend below sea level. Curiously, the Great Lakes have small watersheds relative to their size: Most of the large rivers of the interior—the Missis-

A U.S. postal-issue three-cent stamp, 1955, commemorating the one hundredth anniversary of the opening of the Soo (Sault Sainte Marie) Locks, showing the Great Lakes and two steamers *(courtesy of the American Numismatic Association).*

This huge inland sea with an area only slightly less than the United Kingdom invites superlatives. The distance from Duluth, at the western end of Lake Superior, to the eastern outlet of Lake Ontario near Kingston is 1,160 miles (1,867 kilometers). Lake Superior is the largest lake in the world in surface area, although it is second to Russia's Lake Baikal in volume.

The names of the Great Lakes can be remembered with the aid of the acronym HOMES: H (Huron); O (Ontario); M (Michigan); E (Erie); and S (Superior). This mnemonic device does not, however, relieve the student of the need to consult a map to locate the lakes.

sippi, the Ohio, the Wisconsin, and Illinois—do not empty into the lakes, which they approach, but instead flow southward away from the lakes, whose outlet is the Saint Lawrence River. The need to obtain water for drinking and other uses from the lakes rather than from flowing streams accentuates the seriousness of recent water pollution problems, for example, the infection by parasitic microorganisms of drinking water in Milwaukee in spring 1993 as well as the discharge of polluted water from steel and paper mills and the ever-present fertilizers that run off Corn-Belt farms.

The lakes are connected to one another by straits, short rivers, or artificial canals. Examples of each are, respectively, the Strait of Mackinac between Lakes Huron and Michigan; the St. Marys River between Superior and Huron; and the Welland Canal, a bypass for the Niagara River and Falls, between the two lower lakes of Erie and Ontario. In addition, the Soo Canal, which was opened in 1855, provides a sufficiently wide berth to allow giant ore freighters to pass from Superior to the lower lakes. At Chicago, the Illinois Waterway connects the short Chicago River to the Illinois River, draining south to the Mississippi River and the Gulf of Mexico. At the other end, the St. Lawrence Seaway, completed in 1959, allows oceangoing ships to pass the difficult Thousand Island stretch of the upper Saint Lawrence between Montreal and Kingston, converting the lakes into an international waterway.

French traders were the first to explore the Great Lakes. Étienne Brulé visited Lake Huron around 1612. Brulé and French explorer Robert de la Salle explored Lake Huron and Lake Ontario in 1614. Superior—or Supérieur, in French, meaning elevated (not biggest or better in any way)—was not visited until 1661, by Pierre Radisson, a French explorer and fur trader, and later in 1679 by Sieur Duluth, who was heading an expedition to conquer the Indians and put an end to the Ojibwa-Sioux War. The French built forts at strategic sites—Niagara, Detroit (the French word for narrows), and the Strait of Mackinac—to afford protection against the Indians, to counter the eventual challenge of the English, and to serve as trading posts. The French empire in North America, as extensive as it was, was fragile, and little colonization extended west and south of the Saint Lawrence corridor. This pattern contrasts with that of settlement by the English, which was not only territorially extensive but was also intensified by the growth of commercial agriculture and towns. Defeated in the French and Indian War (known in Europe as the Seven Years War) between 1756–1763, the French lost this vast interior, eventually selling their remaining interests in North America in 1803, in what came to be known as the Louisiana Purchase.

With the completion of the Erie Canal in 1825, western farmers had an eastern outlet for their surplus agricultural production, while eastern manufacturers now had a way to transport their goods to paying customers in the burgeoning Midwest. New York City, long rivaling Boston and Philadelphia for preeminence, tapped the hinterlands of the Midwest opened up by the Erie Canal and became the nation's premier city, earning its state the epithet "Empire State." Steamboats could make the trip from Buffalo, on Lake Erie at the western end of the canal, to Chicago, at the south end of Lake Michigan, in a few days rather than the weeks that an overland trip required.

Most of the settlement of the Great Lakes was concentrated on the southern shores. Of the six great cities of the lakes (Chicago, Milwaukee, Detroit, Cleveland, Buffalo, and Toronto), only Toronto is located on a northern shore. In the past, iron ore went down the lakes, at least once the Mesabi Range of northern Minnesota was opened after 1890, and coal from the northern Appalachians was brought up lake; at intermediate points, the steel industry developed, in an arc of cities from Green Bay to Cleveland to Hamilton (an industrial outlier of Toronto). With recent restrictions on the use of high-sulfur eastern coals and increased mining of near-surface Western deposits, coal now moves both ways, with Western fuels loading at Duluth and moving down the lakes from there.

A commercial wheat frontier in the mid-nineteenth century (Illinois was the leading wheat-producing state in the United States in 1850) was transformed by the end of the century into a steel belt with an associated, intensified agricultural economy focused on livestock raising and dairying. The story of this remarkably successful changeover can be broadly sketched as follows. It might be said that the Midwest possessed both forward and backward linkages between agriculture and manufacturing, and that this was the crucial feature of the region's dynamic growth. A forward linkage would be represented by a farmer's production requiring processing at a mill, while a backward linkage would be exemplified by the reapers and threshers, later tractors and synthetic fertilizers, that farmers would need to purchase from industrial concerns in order to be more efficient and profitable. With the agrarian and urban interests hitched together like a team and its wagon, the Midwestern economy moved forward. Its people continued to display their own brand of common sense and humor that undoubtedly had to do with their farm background or at least a realization of its importance. As the literary wit Christopher Morley once noted, "The Midwest has its feet set in corn and manure."

However, all the linkages in the world would have been for naught without the entrepreneurial skills, sheer willpower, and just plain cussedness of the likes of Cyrus McCormick, Philip Armour, John D. Rockefeller, and Henry Ford, who pioneered the industrialization of the Great Lakes region. The recent change from steel belt to rust belt since the 1970s and the region's subsequent recovery to a position where its economy is based more on services and diversified manufacturing are part of ongoing processes in the region's economic development.

Further Reading: William Cronon, *Nature's Metropolis: Chicago and the Great West,* New York: Norton, 1991; U.S. Environmental Protection Agency and Environment Canada, *The Great Lakes: An Environmental Atlas and Resource Book,* Chicago and Toronto, 1987.

GREAT PLAINS

Sloping eastward from the foot of the Rocky Mountains at about 5,500 feet (1,676 meters) are young, nearly level rock formations that contain the sediments eroded from the mountains and washed eastward as far as the central lowlands. Lying in both the United States and Canada, the semiarid Great Plains province has for its approximate eastern boundary the 2,000-foot (610-meter) contour, the 20-inch (51-centimeter) isohyet of precipitation, and the **Hundredth Meridian.**

The undulating terrain of the plains is interrupted by the domal uplift of the Black Hills, an outlier of the Rockies, in western South Dakota; the nearby volcanic neck of Devil's Tower, Wyoming, standing about 1,000 feet (305 meters) above the plains; the Badlands (in French, Mauvaises Terres) of the Dakotas; and the Sand Hills of central Nebraska. In the United States, the eastern border of the plains marks the transition between short- and long-grass prairie. Farther north in Canada, the prairie border veers to the west, reflecting the greater effectiveness of precipitation there due to lower evaporation. Nonetheless, only the southern third of Canada's Prairie Provinces—Alberta, Saskatchewan, and Manitoba—are covered with grass, while to the north are forested wildernesses. In the U.S. plains, trees grow only in moister areas or along watercourses. At the southern end of the plains, the Edwards

Plateau of Texas—a thick layer of Cretaceous limestone—forms the conspicuous rise of the Balcones Escarpment along its southern and eastern boundary, overlooking the Gulf coastal plain.

The Great Plains are not as monotonous as the traveler thinks who follows the interstate routes along the floodplain of a major river like the Platte in Nebraska. Some areas do fit the conventional mate than they were used to as in anticipation of the western extension of rail lines to provide access to the interior grasslands. The uncertainty of the slavery-extension issue, which was fought out in violence in the Nebraska Territory in the 1850s, and the ensuing civil war slowed settlement, but by the late 1860s and 1870s immigration into the central portions of the plains was brisk. In his classic work *The Great*

An abandoned house on the Great Plains near Sligo, northeastern Colorado *(photo by Jesse Walker)*.

image: The Staked Plain, or Llano Estacado, in southeastern New Mexico and the Texas Panhandle is a nearly flat, featureless plain, one of the most level parts of the United States. The name is supposed to indicate that stakes had to be driven into the ground to mark trails across the prairie or to water.

Early nineteenth-century explorers like Zebulon Pike and Stephen Long described the plains as a desert. The label "Great American Desert" remained on maps until about midcentury, by which time settlers waited along the western border of Iowa or Missouri, not so much in fear of a drier cli-

Plains, Texas historian Walter Prescott Webb described what he believed were three necessary adaptations settlers to the plains environment needed: (1) the six-shooter, (2) barbed wire, and (3) the windmill. The list is revealing: Not only were all these innovations manufactured goods from the East, but none were institutional or social adaptations. One is tempted to substitute another list of requisite adaptations: (1) Deere's all-steel plow; (2) the Timber Culture Act (1873), which allowed the actual settler an additional quarter-section of land if trees were planted; and (3) the Indian Peace Policy, which combined paternalism with suppression, amounting to a reservation policy.

The open-range cattle kingdom gave way after 1886 to settled agriculture. By the early years of the twentieth century, the major agricultural regions of the plains had begun to take shape: the spring-wheat belt of the Dakotas and Montana, extending into the Prairie Provinces of Canada; the winter-wheat belt of the southern plains, centered on Kansas but extending south to the Texas Panhandle; and in between the two wheat belts, in eastern Nebraska and northern Kansas, a midwestern-style corn belt with an emphasis on both crops and livestock. Additionally, cotton spread from its core in the American southeast across the red soils of central Oklahoma and out onto the fertile sandy loams of the Texas high plains as far as Lubbock. A peripheral cattle- and sheep-raising region lay to the west, in south-central Montana, Wyoming, the western parts of the Dakotas, and on its eastern perimeter, the Nebraska Sand Hills.

Though the towns of the Plains—from Edmonton, Alberta, to Lubbock, Texas—periodically receive fresh pulses of economic life, much of the remaining area has lost rural population almost continuously since the peak year of about 1920. The Dust Bowl, which affected the southern plains most severely, cannot be blamed entirely for this: The choice to move away from drudgery and isolation, from grasshoppers and variable farm prices, has proven a more enduring reason for the depopulation of the rural portions of the Great Plains. Many who visit or settle in the region, as well as many of those who have left it, respond more to the accounts of the region's fine novelists—the heartfelt tale of the Hansa family in O. E. Rölvaag's *Giants in the Earth* or Willa Cather's elegiac portrait of the immigrant woman in *My Ántonia*—than to the cheery chants and chamber-of-commerce optimism that have long dominated the voices of the plains.

Further Reading: James L. Malin, *History and Ecology: Studies of the Grassland,* ed. Robert P. Swierenga, Lincoln, Nebr.: University of Nebraska Press, 1981; Walter Prescott Webb, *The Great Plains,* Boston: Ginn, 1931; David J. Wishart, "Settling the Great Plains, 1850–1930: Prospects and Problems," pp. 255–278, in Robert D. Mitchell and Paul A. Groves, eds., *North America: The Historical Geography of a Changing Continent,* Totowa, N.J.: Rowman and Littlefield, 1987.

GREAT SALT LAKE
See Great Basin

GREENWICH MERIDIAN
It was the accomplishment of the ancient Greeks to recognize that the precise location of a place required a set of intersecting grid lines, which they chose to call latitude and longitude. Just as the Cartesian coordinates X and Y only make sense if measured with respect to an X and a Y axis, so the geographical interpretation of latitude and longitude requires base lines of origin. The equator (0°) is a natural, nonarbitrary line (actually, a circle) that divides the world into two equal halves equidistant between the poles.

The problem then becomes one of deciding on a north-south line of longitude, or meridian, to serve as a baseline for the measurement of distances east and west. There is no nonarbitrary line, so the question becomes which to select as the prime meridian. Since time is a function of longitude, this problem became increasingly compelling in the late nineteenth century in Europe and the United States. The building of railroads and the introduction of rapid-speed telegraphy effectively shrank geographic space and brought previously disparate regions into near proximity with one another. High on the agenda of the first International Geographical Congress, held in Antwerp in 1871, was the need to adopt a universal prime meridian so as to standardize time and to facilitate the efforts then being undertaken to map the world. Previously, each of the major countries in chauvinistic style had selected for a prime meridian its major city or, in some cases, cities. Depending on one's national origin, the prime meridian passed through Paris; St. Petersburg; Copenhagen; Madrid, Toledo, or Cádiz; Washington, D.C., or Philadelphia; or the British Royal Observatory located in suburban London.

At the recommendation of the Third International Geographical Congress (Venice, 1881), a meeting was held to discuss the issues related to time and the selection of a prime meridian. Representatives from twenty-five countries convened in Washington in October 1884 at the International Meridian Conference and passed a series of resolutions. The most significant recommendation was for the adoption of "the meridian passing through the center of the transit instrument at the Observatory of Greenwich as the initial meridian for longitude." The division of the world into 24 time zones of 15° of longitude was also a result of this international conference. It is significant that the meetings were held in the United States. The construction of a continent-spanning railroad system with stations often using many different and potentially conflicting local times (Pittsburgh at one time used six different local times for its schedules) meant that standardization of time in the United States was most urgent. In fact, a railroad association had anticipated the work of the conference, when in April 1883, a Time Convention of Railway Superintendents and Managers met at St. Louis, Missouri, and rec-

ommended a system of national standard times based on one-hour zones resembling those that now exist. Almost a year before the International Meridian Conference convened, the railroads already had agreed to all of the essential matters concerning standardized time and had put the system into general effect on 78,158 miles (125,780 kilometers) of rail lines.

In the second century A.D. the Greek scholar Ptolemy, who is best known to geographers for his systematic compilation of the latitude and longitude of individual places into a map of the known world of his time, placed his zero meridian through the Fortunate Islands, just west of Gibraltar. If these islands were one of the island groups in the eastern Atlantic not too distant from Europe and North Africa, such as the **Madeira** or **Canary Islands,** as is commonly believed, then Ptolemy's prime meridian does not deviate much from the Greenwich Prime Meridian currently used on world maps.

Regardless of all efforts to establish a standard, however, your own true solar time—as defined by the angle of the sun's rays to the horizon—is not likely to be the same as the time recorded on your wristwatch or clock unless you are located precisely in the middle of a time zone.

Further Reading: Lloyd A. Brown, *The Story of Maps,* New York: Dover, 1977 (1949).

GUERNSEY
See Channel Islands

GUIANA HIGHLANDS
The uplifted plateau and mountain region lying between the Brazilian portion of the **Amazon Basin** and the Orinoco River valley in the west, and between the Amazon and the coastal plain of the three adjoining countries in the east, is referred to as the Guiana Highlands. The western

limit of this physiographic region follows the headwaters of the Orinoco River; the upper Río Negro, an important left-bank tributary of the Amazon; and the Río Casiquiare, a short connecting link between the Orinoco and the Negro. The Guiana Highlands are a geologically ancient tableland covered with dense *selvas* (rain forests) and surmounted by occasional mountain ranges, from which tumble some of the world's highest and most spectacular waterfalls. The three small countries that used to be known to the world as the "three Guianas" are, from west to east, Guyana (former British Guiana), Suriname (former Dutch Guiana), and French Guiana.

The Guiana Highlands comprise an assemblage of terrain units similar to the **Brazilian Highlands** south of the Amazon. Atop a basement of ancient crystalline rocks lie stratified sandstones and limestones and sheets of diabase. In the continuously hot and humid equatorial climate, crystalline rocks weather deeply to form characteristic fine-grained soils, but sedimentary rocks and diabase are relatively resistant to weathering and erosion and form conspicuous ridges and cliffs. Stumps of ancient crystalline mountains that have resisted the process of denudation in the rainy Tropics occasionally top the ancient plateau. The Tumac-Humac Range (about 3,000 feet or 914 meters in elevation) represents an almost continuous line of low mountains with rounded tops and steep sides. Conveniently, this range is also the political boundary between Brazil and the states of Suriname and French Guiana. Sandstone plateaus are more evident to the west, where the highest elevation in the whole region is attained at Mt. Roraima (9,432 feet or 2,875 meters), a flat-topped but steep-sided range on the borders of Brazil, Venezuela, and Guyana.

The rivers that rise on the sandstone plateau of western Guyana fall over steep cliffs in magnificent waterfalls. For example, Kaieteur Falls drops 741 feet (226 meters) down a sandstone rim, making it one of the highest waterfalls in the world. Angel Falls, the highest falls in the world at 979 feet (298 meters), is located within the highlands region in southeastern Venezuela. The rivers draining in the direction of the Atlantic drop sharply from the crystalline uplands onto the narrow coastal plain, resulting in the heads of navigation being relatively close to the coasts, which has confined the population of the Guianas. The people of the three countries comprise a mixed stock of Europeans (the smallest numbers), Africans who are the descendants of slaves, and South and East Asians, whose forebears were brought there in the nineteenth century as laborers.

The coast was sighted by Columbus on his third voyage, in 1498, and was surveyed by other Spanish explorers between 1499 and 1500. The Spanish sought the mythical golden land of El Dorado here, but they found no easy access to the interior, nor did they locate any stores of accumulated treasure they could seize. The Elizabethan poet-adventurer-courtier Sir Walter Raleigh, who is better known for organizing the "Lost Colony" expeditions to Roanoke Island, North Carolina (1587), sailed 300 miles (483 kilometers) up the Orinoco River and into the interior of the Guianas in 1595, bringing back specimens of gold. The accession of James I (1603) led to Raleigh's downfall and imprisonment in the Tower. He was released in 1616 to make another voyage up the Orinoco in search of the fabled El Dorado, again with his friend, the adventurer-scholar Laurence Kemys. Though told not to harass the Spanish, Kemys seized a Spanish town. On returning home to England, Raleigh was once again imprisoned. This time, unable to escape his fate, he was executed.

One of the puzzles about the Guianas is how and why this region—located in the midst of Latin America—was colonized by northwest European states. The answer seems to lie in their isolation from the main routes and centers of the Spanish and Portuguese. The Guianas lay near the northeastern coast of South America, in a vaguely demarcated region between the Spanish and Portuguese empires. The Iberians were not blocked so much by the terrain as by the dense forests. Unlike the north Europeans, who were used to advancing on forest frontiers (as they did in North America), the Spanish and Portuguese tended to shun densely forested areas, at least if they were far removed from their main population centers.

The Dutch were the first Europeans to succeed in occupying the coastal plain, as their reclamation skills were useful in draining and diking the marshlands. The English and French soon followed suit, so that by the mid-seventeenth century the major settlements and a plantation form of economy had been established. Curiously, the settlement near the mouth of the Suriname River, Paramaribo, was originally the work of the English. In 1667 the Dutch, believing they could develop these settlements as prosperous sugar lands, accepted this English colony in exchange for their toehold on Manhattan Island, at the mouth of the Hudson River, which did not seem to offer any short-term financial gain. The English got the best of the bargain, having traded a malarial strip of ground in the Tropics for the lion's share of what would one day be New York City.

The Guianas changed hands several times, most notably during the Napoleonic era, before a series of treaties between 1812 and 1817 fixed their boundaries. The British and Dutch colonies gained independence during the post–World War II period of decolonization, but French Guiana remains an overseas department of the French state. The popular novel by W. H. Hudson, *Green Mansions* (1904), in which the beautiful Rima wanders spirit-like across the forested mountains in her quest for her people, is set in the Guianas.

H

HADRIAN'S WALL

In 122 the emperor Hadrian (ruled 117–138) visited Britain, having just completed a tour of the German frontier. A defensive system—a road linking turf and timber forts—had been in place in the Rhineland since the time of Domitian, and was especially well developed on the Taunus and Westerwald uplands. While in Germany, Hadrian initiated an artificial barrier, a timber palisade, which was apparently the first bulwark of its type in Roman history.

Although we cannot know the precise purpose of the stone wall Hadrian commanded his legionnaires to build across northern England, nor its original design (numerous additions were made over the centuries), the wall is the best-preserved evidence of the Roman defense perimeter.

Most of Hadrian's Wall—sometimes referred to as the Roman Wall, though it was not the only one—was built between 122 and 127. It stretches some 73 miles (117 kilometers) from Wallsend on the Tyne River to Bowness at the head of Solway Firth. Solway being a deep indentation of the coast in the manner of a fjord, the wall is at the narrowest part of the island south of the Cheviot.

The Romans took advantage of the terrain in their construction of the wall, which today lies just south of the Scottish border. The valleys of the Tyne, Irthing, and Eden Rivers form an almost continuous trough from sea to sea, with Hadrian's Wall running along its northern rim. A preexisting military road, the Stanegate, lay at the bottom of the valley within the defensive line of the wall. The northern edge of the Tyne-Solway Gap generally presents commanding heights viewed northward. At the center rose the heights of the basalt cliffs known as the Whin Sill.

Based on what remains of the wall and on what can be inferred from similar Roman sites, scholars believe that the original plan was to build a small lookout ahead of the main garrisons rather than a major barrier against attack. The Romans added a number of different elements in the construction: After a continuous base was laid, a stone wall 16 feet (4.9 meters) high to the rampart walk was constructed in the east, where stone for building was plentiful. In the west, a lower but wider turf wall was built—originally 20 Roman feet (6.1 meters) wide, compared to half this width in the east, with a height of about 12 feet (3.6 meters). Since the dimensions of preserved parts of the original "curtain," or continuous wall, are less than this by a factor of about one-half, it can be inferred either that the constructed wall was smaller than when in design or that later depredations and modifications reduced its scale. Small forts known as mile-castles were erected at intervals of one Roman mile. There were two turrets between each pair of mile-castles.

An impressive system of rearward earthworks known as the Vallum was a later modification of the original wall, but today the two are considered integral. The Vallum was a continuous ditch 20 feet (6.1 meters) wide and ten deep, flanked by mounds 20 feet high. With the

the Cumbrian coast for another 50 miles (80 kilometers) with a series of forts and minor works but without the curtain wall.

An eminent scholar of Roman Britain noted that the "scale, complexity, and modifications [of Hadrian's Wall] are symbolic of the vast and restless imagination of Hadrian himself" (Salway, 1981). An orphan who had been raised in the

Hadrian's Wall remains the best-preserved evidence of the Roman defense perimeter and still stretches 73 miles (117 kilometers) across northern England *(Corbis-Bettmann)*.

mounds set back from the ditch, this huge work cut a swath almost 120 feet (37 meters) wide, from sea to sea. The purpose of the Vallum has been a subject of controversy among scholars, but it may have been a screening area to prevent unauthorized access to the military zone or an overnight camping ground for units in transit along the wall.

North of the wall were a number of advance forts, which were especially prominent in the west, at Birrens, Netherby, and Newcastle. These forts were the most important modifications to the wall, being literally incorporated into it in order to accommodate military garrisons during construction. The towns of Newcastle and Carlisle thus began as castra, or forts, along the Roman wall. The largest fort on the wall was Stanwix, part of modern Carlisle, where the western route to Scotland crossed Hadrian's line. At its western end, the frontier continued along

provinces, Hadrian spent much of his reign touring the provincial areas, seeing that order and stability were maintained. Unlike his predecessor Trajan, he was not a seeker of military glory by conquest but a worshiper at the aesthetic altar, devoted as he was to Greek culture. Though facing acute trouble in the perennially troubled East, he attempted to achieve a more harmonious unity in his polity by bounding the imperium at its northern end. Extended by Severus around A.D. 200, the wall that bears the name of Hadrian stood for almost three hundred years as the limit of the Roman conquest, and still stands today in places, bearing mute testimony to a great emperor and a greater Rome.

See also: Antonine Wall.

Further Reading: I. A. Richmond, *Roman Britain*, 2d ed., Harmondsworth, Middlesex, England: Penguin, 1963 (orig. ed. 1955); Peter Salway, *Roman Britain*, vol. 1A, *Oxford History of England*, Oxford: Clarendon Press, 1981.

HARZ MOUNTAINS

This oval-shaped range of hill lands located south of Brunswick (Braunschweig) straddles a region that was once the border between East and West Germany. Lying between the Elbe River (to the east) and the Leine River (to the west), the Harz Mountains are the most northerly units of the **Hercynian Uplands,** and they lend their name to this latter belt of rounded massives and small hill districts, which stretches across the midsection of Europe. Although the Harz are one of the smaller Hercynian regions, extending only about 60 miles (96 kilometers) in a northwest-southeast direction, they are rugged in places and were until recently densely forested. The highest peak, the Brocken (el. 3,747 feet or 1,142 meters), lies in the Upper Harz, to the northwest, a region of extensive moors and wastelands and heavy rainfall (64 inches, or 163 centimeters fall annually on the Brocken). The Lower Harz is a shale plateau with a milder climate, lower elevations, and good agricultural potential. Bounded by fault scarps, the Harz is an uplifted former plain, exhibiting overthrust folding toward the northwest and metamorphosis of thick beds of sandstones and shales. Pleistocene glaciation once covered part of the area, and windborne loess blankets the northern slopes.

The forests of central Germany once aroused pagan superstitions and fears, being considered sacred ground. As a rule, the plains and valleys were settled first; only later did early Germanic peoples care to occupy the heavily forested uplands. This was true of the Harz Mountains, as plainsmen from Hannover and lower Saxony to the north were awed by the sight of the forest in the vicinity of the residual granite mass of the Brocken, imagining that it was an abode of witches. The persistence of these beliefs is indicated by the celebration of Walpurgis Night on the windswept Brocken, where a meeting of witches is said to take place each year on 30 April.

Goslar, the main town of the Upper Harz, is located at the mouth of a valley leading into the mountains. It was one of the most important towns in medieval Germany due to the nearby silver mines, which financed the Salian kings. The historic Harz mining industry, which focused on nonferrous ores, especially silver and copper, has been in decline since the eighteenth century, and today the region derives more economic benefit from visitors and vacationers, who, no longer fearing witches, are attracted by the cool woods in the summer and the snow in winter.

HELGOLAND

History sometimes comes in small packages. The fortunes of the tiny island of Helgoland (Eng. Heligoland) have risen and fallen in response to what has happened in the surrounding European great powers. A flyspeck of sandstone only 150 acres (60 hectares) in size, Helgoland is yet strategically located with respect to the Rhine, Elbe, and Weser Rivers. The rocky island directly faces the mouth of the Elbe and the port of Hamburg. With the rise of German naval power in the late nineteenth century, its possession by the British was an object of concern for the Germans, who initiated a series of talks to obtain it.

Though the island's most prominent place in history was as a result of the unwinding of these events in the late nineteenth century, European powers had contested its ownership before. Belonging to the German state of Holstein from 1402–1714, Helgoland was taken by the Danes in the latter year. During the Napoleonic Era it passed to England, becoming a formal British possession in 1814. In the late 1880s Germany and England entered into private negotiations between the ministers of the aged Queen Victoria and the German counterparts serving the Wilhelmine government. (The ruling families of Great Britain and Germany were related, as Queen Victoria had married Prince Albert of Saxony.)

Ever since the English had seized Helgoland from the Danes, they had found it valueless. The British colonial minister Joseph Chamberlain was more interested in South Africa and wanted to swap Helgoland for Germany's colonies in southwest Africa (Namibia), which could then be added to Cape Colony. In contrast, Germany's interests in its African colonies, with the possible exception of German East Africa (Tanzania), were half-hearted, and few German settlers had arrived from Europe. The colonies' greatest benefit to Germany, in the view of that master of *realpolitik,* Otto von Bismarck, was as an obstacle to the spread of the British Empire or as a trading token to be exchanged for other valuable real estate. And Helgoland's value to the Germans was incalculable: If the island were taken by an enemy such as France and used as a coaling station, the German navy would be effectively bottled up.

Nonetheless, in 1890 German adventurers like Carl Peters were exploring the contested interior of central Africa, where English empire-builders like Cecil Rhodes and colonial secretary Joseph Chamberlain hoped to establish a link joining British-controlled territories in Egypt and the Sudan to Cape Colony, in a north-south, Cape-to-Cairo axis, suitable for the building of a transcontinental railroad. Hence, the British Prime Minister Lord Salisbury was very pleased when in May 1890 his offer to exchange Hel-

goland for a British protectorate over Zanzibar, plus assurances of the lion's share of territory west of Lake Nyasa (Malawi) and key access points in the interior, was met with approval by the kaiser without any counterdemands. In fact, the subdued Germans were jubilant. The kaiser had told his negotiator, Count Hatzfeld, that Helgoland must be acquired at whatever cost in Africa. The Kiel Canal, constructed across the base of the peninsula of **Jutland** to reduce travel times between the North and Baltic Seas, was useless without strategic control of Helgoland, which could do for Germany what **Gibraltar** and Malta did for Britain in the **Mediterranean.** The doddering Queen Victoria, who had been on the throne more than 50 years, was at first displeased when she heard of the transaction (she was reported to have grumbled that "giving up what one has is always a bad thing"), but was reconciled when told she had received 100,000 square miles of Africa in exchange for less than one square mile in Europe.

So the island passed to Germany in 1890. Its fortifications were razed after 1918 but reconstructed following 1935. The island was something of a seaside resort before World War II, when it was used as a German naval base and received heavy aerial bombardment. After evacuating its population (mostly fishermen), a British occupation force in 1947 blew up the fortifications and part of the island in an explosion that was considered at the time the largest nonatomic blast ever. West Germany took possession of the island in 1952. A few thousand people occupy the island today, with an economy dependent on tourism and scientific activity—mainly research in ornithology. This minuscule island has truly been a mirror to the changing balance of power in western Europe.

HELLESPONT

See Dardanelles

HERCYNIAN UPLANDS

Hill lands dominate the midsection of Europe, stretching eastward in a broad, irregular belt from western France to the rimlands that encircle Czech Bohemia. Lying between Alpine-era mountains to the south and plains to the north, this fragmented zone known as the Hercynian Uplands consists of numerous small hill districts and more extensive regions of rounded massives, with intervening basins and lowland corridors. The major upland units include the **Armorican Massif** in western France, consisting of the Norman and Breton Peninsulas; the **Massif Central** in south-central France; the **Ardennes** of Belgium, Luxembourg, and northeastern France; the Vosges of France and the **Black Forest** (Schwarzwald) of Germany, lying on opposite sides of the **Rhine Graben;** the **Harz Mountains** in north-central Germany; the Thuringian Forest in eastern Germany; the Bohemian Massif, on the border between Germany and the Czech Republic; and the **Sudetes,** between the Czech lands and Poland. The Hercynian Uplands have a number of important outliers that belong with the region by virtue of similar geological structure and surficial form: the **Pennine Hills** of northern England, the central plateau or **Meseta** of Spain, and the **Ural Mountains** of Russia.

The compactness of many of these landform units, along with their separateness and individuality, has contributed to the compartmentalization of European terrain into a geographic pattern that resembles a crazy quilt. Distinct units of this upland belt only gradually received the imprint of humans, and protected by relative isolation, natural regions were slowly transformed into cultural regions. The compartmentalized terrain, coupled with a climate that guaranteed enough precipitation for rain-fed agriculture, is of prime importance in distinguishing Europe from the rest of the world. Try to imagine Europe in the midst of an expansive plain in Asia, or in an arid or semi-arid region in Africa, and you will find it difficult. Of course, the individual terrain units of the Hercynian Uplands were only *relatively* isolated, as they were connected by numerous low corridors and passes over short distances. The result was that accessibility was insured between regions, producing a well-connected system of regional settlements, even as important cultural and economic differentiation took place.

The Hercynian or Central Uplands were the result of an orogeny of relatively ancient date—but not as old as that forming the Fennoscandian shield of Scandinavia. Subsequent to their formation, the crystallines that are the core of the Hercynian region were eroded away to a peneplain (almost a plain), subsided, and were covered with sediments in a shallow sea. Then, with the thrusting upward of the relatively young Alps, this central region was rejuvenated, that is, uplifted, and reshaped to its present configuration. Complexly faulted and folded formations make up this jumbled landscape, which some have described as a "chaos of physiography." High tablelands and hilly massives of irregular sizes and shapes sometimes bear pieces of the overlying sedimentary layers that once covered them and were generally carried away by erosion during uplift; elsewhere, there is evidence of recent and powerful volcanic activity. Between parallel faults a massive block of the earth's crust has foundered in the Rhine Graben (*Graben,* the German term for a geographic depression, has become the name for this landform type around the world).

The phrase "chaos of physiography" is an equally apt description of the fragmentary nature of the German political state until relatively recent times. To be sure, the political fragmentation of German lands had other causes besides geography, such as the different course of development of church and state in central Europe; but compartmentalized terrain also undoubtedly contributed to one of the most important and persistent features of Europe's political map.

HINDENBURG LINE

Paul von Hindenburg (1847–1934) today is widely characterized as the feckless and senile president of the declining Weimar Republic between 1925 and 1934, a hollow figurehead who acceded to and oversaw Adolf Hitler's takeover of the German government. Yet this German field marshal and statesman, whose full name was Paul Ludwig Hans Anton von Beneckendorff und von Hindenburg, had an illustrious career, beginning with the Austro-Prussian and Franco-Prussian Wars (1866 and 1870–1871, respectively). He derived his greatest prestige from a series of World War I victories, when he was commander of the German forces in the East, then field marshal general, and eventually commander of all the German armies. His initial victories in the East (e.g., in the Battle of Tannenburg, in August 1914) led to his assuming control for the overall war effort, including virtually dictatorial control with General Ludendorff over German civilian life and the national economy.

Germany's western line of defense in World War I came to be named after Hindenburg when, in spring 1917, General Ludendorff prepared a shorter, more defensible position about 20 miles (32 kilometers) behind the winding, overextended Arras-to-Soissons line in northeastern France. Ludendorff's plan, approved by Hindenburg, called for German soldiers to withdraw gradually, so as not to attract attention, to the so-called Hindenburg Line, or Siegfried Line, which followed a line in northeastern France from Lens in the Pas de Calais southeast through Saint-Quentin to the cathedral city of Reims. Taking a leaf from the annals of military history dating back to the Roman defense of the frontier, the Germans constructed their defense in depth—in a zone rather than a line—with two successive positions behind a lightly held outpost line. As the German troops retreated from the Arras-to-Soissons line, they followed a scorched-earth policy, leveling forests, destroying roads, razing towns, and poisoning water sources. Later in the war, when they attempted a western surge across the same terrain, they encountered obvious difficulties.

Heavy fighting occurred along the Hindenburg Line throughout 1917. With Romania crushed and Russia withdrawing from the war at the end of the year, after the Bolshevik coup, Germany's position seemed to improve. But the U.S. declaration of war on 6 April 1918 and the arrival that autumn of the American Expeditionary Force under General John Joseph ("Black Jack") Pershing brought fresh recruits and new ideas to the line. By the end of September, U.S. troops had made a breakthrough in the Meuse-Argonne offensive, permitting British and Belgian troops to cross the Hindenburg Line on 5 October. Germany's defeat and surrender then was little more than a month away.

After the war, Hindenburg managed to avoid being indicted as a war criminal by a special German court at Leipzig. When the Weimar Republic's President Ebert died unexpectedly in 1925, a conservative group of nationalists and Prussian Junkers persuaded the aging veteran to run for office. Hindenburg served a full term as president and was reelected in 1932, defeating Adolf Hitler at the polls. He gave in to his advisers and appointed Hitler chancellor in January 1933, but continued to serve as president until his death the following year.

Further Reading: John Wheeler-Bennett, *The Wooden Titan: Hindenburg in Twenty Years of German History, 1914–1934,* New York: Morrow, 1936.

HUNDREDTH MERIDIAN

The boundary between the humid eastern United States and the drier West, a line running approximately north-south through the central **Great Plains,** has been the focus of a long-running historiographic debate. The concern has not been so much the precise measure of the 20-inch (51-centimeter) isohyet of precipitation or any other climatological measure of aridity as the actual and perceived effects of this agricultural limitation on the occupancy of the region, and whether or not settlers properly adjusted to the new environment.

John Wesley Powell, veteran of the American Civil War and former Illinois schoolteacher, made a splendid career exploring and analyzing the West, eventually serving as the first director of the U.S. Geological Survey. In his *Report on the Lands of the Arid Region of the United States* (1878) Powell planted the idea of government-subsidized irrigation, which would bear fruit in 1902 with the passage of the Reclamation Act and the creation of the U.S. Bureau of Reclamation. Powell described the limitations of agriculture where less than 20 inches (51 centimeters) of precipitation fall each year. Irriga-

tion on a communal or public basis would be necessary in future in the sub-humid West. The government should abandon the 160-acre (64-hectare) homestead as the prototype of its land policy, grant larger pasturage-farms of four square miles or 2,560 acres (1,024 hectares), and establish land use categories for the different kinds and qualities of Western lands. Unpopular in the independent-minded and optimistic West, Powell was branded a socialist, a Georgite Single-Taxer, or worse yet, an Easterner. The novelist and historian Wallace Stegner lauded Powell for his early awareness of the need for reforms, most of which would not be adopted until the 1930s, noting that "the myth-bound West . . . insisted on running into the future like a streetcar on a gravel road."

University of Texas professor Walter Prescott Webb followed an essentially Turnerian line of argument in his classic 1931 work *The Great Plains.* However, he ended up at a different place than the popular University of Wisconsin (later, Harvard) professor Frederick Jackson Turner, who along with his students had done so much to reorient American history from the search for European antecedents of colonial society to the study of the westward-moving frontier and its influence on American behavior. Webb, who was most decidedly a Westerner, considered the 98th meridian the crucial boundary in delineating the semiarid Great Plains. West of what Webb described as an institutional fault, settlers accommodated themselves to the Western environment by the adoption of three necessary innovations: (1) barbed wire, (2) the windmill, and (3) the six-shooter. Webb gave precedence to ranching over crop cultivation because pastoralism was better adapted to arid conditions. Webb's thesis was popular because it echoed

Westerners' experiences; but its publication, coinciding as it did with depressed economic conditions (which had begun to take a toll on the farm belt as early as the 1920s) and the swirling clouds of the Dust Bowl and all its human wastage, made his optimistic scenario controversial. It was soon recognized that the 98th meridian was inaccurate as the eastern delimitation of the semiarid region. The line

John Wesley Powell *Beyond the Hundredth Meridian* (1954). In a more direct assault on Webb's thesis, Wishart (1987) stated that the advancement of the frontier didn't stall on the southern Plains for several decades after 1860 because pioneers were waiting for the adoption of certain innovations but because they were blocked by hostile Kiowa and Comanche tribes until about 1875.

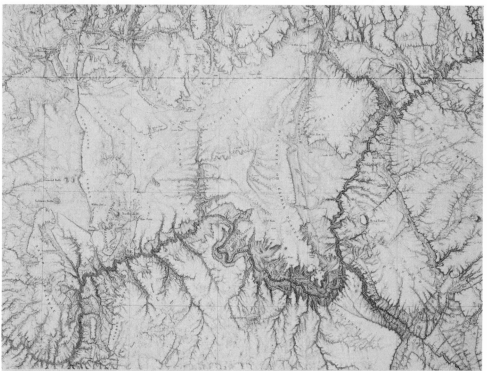

This U.S. Geographical Survey of the area west of the Hundredth Meridian, done in 1873, was probably one of John Wesley Powell's first projects after he became director of the survey *(Library of Congress/Corbis)*.

would have to curve to the west as one traveled north, due to the greater effectiveness of precipitation in cooler areas, with less evaporation (hence, the displacement of the wheat belt to the west in Canada). Moreover, the 98th meridian crossed fertile, relatively well-watered places like Hutchinson, in east-central Kansas. Gradually, the 100th meridian gained favor as the closest approximation to the boundary in question, and thus Wallace Stegner titled his biography of

Another native son of the region, James Malin, took up his pen from the University of Kansas at Lawrence, a town that many consider to this day a civilized and enlightened oasis on the Plains. In a comparatively sophisticated analysis of climatic variability (at least for a historian), Malin suggested that the wheat farmer wasn't so far out of bounds, at least for the relatively moist years in the late nineteenth century when arable agriculture attached itself to the region, and given the misunderstandings of climate and environment that were common at that time. For instance, settlers mistakenly thought that "rain follows the plow," and even the U.S. government believed that planting trees would affect the climate (the Timber Culture Act of 1873). However, neither the land nor its cultivators were as pitiful as Powell and Webb would have us believe, Malin implied. Because Malin's books were self-published, which gave them the appearance of hastily thrown together pamphlets, they had a limited influence; but their author had a keen mind, and even his critics had to admit that he made some excellent points. His ideas have a freshness about them that speak to today's generation more than do Turner's and Webb's. Perhaps this is because Malin was writing more recently than were the other two; but whatever the reason, in Malin's books one finds signs of the continued vitality of the Progressive–New Deal era's concern for the land, which predated today's environmentalism.

Further Reading: James L. Malin, *Grassland Historical Studies: Natural Resources Utilization in a Background of Science and Technology,* vol. 1, *Geology and Geography,* Lawrence, Kans. (self-published), 1950; John Wesley Powell, *Report on the Lands of the Arid Region of the United States,* U.S. House of Representatives, Executive Document 73, 45th Congress, 2nd Session, Washington, D.C.: U. S. Government Printing Office, 3 April 1978; Walter Prescott Webb, *The Great Plains,* Boston: Ginn, 1931; Donald Worster, *Rivers of Empire: Water, Aridity, and the Growth of the American West,* New York: Pantheon, 1985.

HUNGARIAN BASIN

Some 125 miles (201 kilometers) downstream from Vienna, the Danube emerges from a gorge near Esztergom and turns sharply to the south, bisecting Hungary. The extensive interior lowlands of the Hungarian or Pannonian Basin are nearly surrounded by mountains of the Alpine orogeny: the **Carpathian Mountains** to the north and east, the Dinaric Range to the south, and the Austrian Alps on the west. The basin straddles the middle segment of the Danube and extends into the adjoining countries of Yugoslavia, Romania, Ukraine, Slovakia, the Czech Republic, and Austria.

The plain has not been isolated by its mountain rim. Not only does the Danube provide access upstream to German lands and downstream to the Balkans, but numerous easy passes connect the region to other parts of Europe. Greece and the Aegean are accessible via the **Vardar-Morava Corridor** crossing the Balkans. In the northwestern corner of the basin, the Moravian Gate opens to the **North European Plain** along a route followed in ancient times by the Amber Road, which connected Scandinavia to the **Mediterranean Sea.** Several passes across the Carpathians have been the preferred routes of steppe nomads, who crossed from Iran and Turkistan through Ukraine into the Hungarian lowlands. Representatives of almost every cultural and linguistic group of Europe and adjacent parts of Asia have crossed into this region either as invaders or refugees, making its recorded history turbulent, with almost ceaseless conflict between Roman and barbarian, German and Hun, Turk and Christian, Magyar and Slav. The region truly has been a meeting ground of eastern and western cultures.

Two-thirds of landlocked Hungary lies at an elevation below 650 feet (198 meters). Even the mountains seem to be miniature in scale, for the highest, the Kékes, in the northern Mátra ranges, rise only 3,330 feet (1,006 meters). The country most associated with the basin—Hungary—has two distinct regions: the low ridges and hills west of the Danube, mostly of limestone but with occasional volcanics, constituting about one-third of the territory, and the extensive level lands of the Great Alföld (meaning plain, in Hungarian), stretching east of the Danube into adjoining parts of Romania and Yugoslavia, amounting to two-thirds of the country's land surface. The semicircle of hills to the west and northwest bears comparison with the lower Austrian hill lands, which it borders. Major features in this western region include Little Alföld (to the north) and the Trans-Danubian Hill Lands (to the south), separated by the northeast-southwest-trending Lake Balaton, the largest lake in Hungary and in Europe, and the parallel Bakony Forests.

The relationship between terrain and historical development is best illustrated by the extensive plains of eastern and central Hungary, which are the heart of the basin. The Alföld is a relatively young geological depression covered with flat sediments. Sweeping winds have caused the accumulation of sand dunes in some places and the creation of small lake blowouts in others. A wide stretch of fertile loess extends down the center of this region and along the two major rivers—the Danube and the Tisza—which flood on a regular basis, contributing to the fertility of the soil. It is sometimes said that here the steppe, or grassland, of the east meets the timbered portions of western Europe. Actually, the Alföld was originally wooded, but Magyars or Hungarians, who migrated to the area from east of the **Ural Mountains,** decided to abandon their nomadic ways and settle the fertile lands of the middle Danube. Having made this decision, they not only had to fend off other invaders but also had to clear the forest.

The Alföld is on a primary invasion route to Europe and has been the scene of numerous battles in history. Mongol invaders swept across the plains in the thirteenth century, settling there for a time, and then moving on after no more than a year. More significantly, Ottoman Turks under Suleiman the Magnificent overran the country in 1526 and established themselves for a century and a half in Buda Castle, on the right bank of the Danube, overlooking the low, eastern plains. The open plains, or *puszta,* were invitingly accessible to horsemen, and thus invaders from the east created an island of non-Indo-European peoples amid the vast plains of eastern Europe.

Surrounded by peoples of Germanic and Slavic ancestry, the Magyars resisted numerous invasions throughout their history, maintaining a distinctive culture. The wide-open spaces in which they made their home might also have been conducive to a melancholy introspection that seems characteristic of Hungarians: The nation has the highest suicide rate in the world. (An apparently dominant note of melancholy can be found also in many other steppe cultures around the world, perhaps most notably that of southern Russia and of the vast American grasslands.) Magyars colonized only the central portions of the Alföld, leaving large stretches of open steppe devoted to extensive cattle raising, with little arable agriculture. After the Turks retreated in the eighteenth century, large colonization schemes took place under Hungarian and Austrian landlords who owned large domains. Political rule passed to the Habsburgs of Austria, who settled a multitude of Germans and Slavs in the region, thereby destroying the homogeneity of the Magyar population and creating the difficult modern problem of minorities. Grasslands still covered much of the plains until the late nineteenth century, when extensive irrigation and drainage projects converted parts of the Alföld into fertile farms producing cereals, vegetables, feed crops, and livestock.

Although Hungary achieved a status nominally equal to that of Austria in the Dual Monarchy of the late nineteenth century, it was only with the conclusion of World War II that the country attained its independence and became a republic (in the interwar years Hungary's political status was unclear, as a monarchy prevailed but the throne was vacant). Soon after the conclusion of World War II, Hungary fell under the tutelage of the Soviet communists, who had established more or less direct control of the country by 1949. Since about 1990 Hungary has been independent of Soviet control and holds free elections for its representative government bodies.

Subject to long periods of foreign domination partly because of its accessibility to both European and Asian invaders, Hungary nonetheless has shown great resilience and ability to survive. Perhaps its problematic accessibility has also been the key to its survival, as no one invader has succeeded in achieving complete and permanent mastery over the region.

Further Reading: Bart McDowell, "Hungary," *National Geographic,* April 1971, pp. 443–483; Janos Thuroczy, *Chronicle of the Hungarians,* Bloomington, Ind.: Indiana University Press, Research Institute for Inner Asian Studies, 1991.

HY-BRAZIL

The late medieval geographical imagination sprinkled numerous islands across the north Atlantic: **Antillia, Saint Brendan's Islands,** Buss Island, Demonias Island, and Hy-Brazil being the most prominent. Widespread and persistent belief in the existence of these phantom islands, nurtured by their frequent ap-

pearance on maps, influenced the early explorers in their search for riches—and resupply points on their way to riches.

The island of Brazil, which bears no direct relation to the present-day country, is one of the more elusive of these legendary islands. Not only does it appear in two different geographic positions—off western Ireland and as part of the eastern Atlantic archipelagoes; more vexing yet, the island sometimes can be found in two places on the same map! Like the other phantasmal island of the Atlantic, Hy-Brazil's cartographic position shifted westward as geographical knowledge increased and the map of tradition took on the more recognizable form of today's maps.

The mythical island of Brazil first appeared on the 1325 map of Angellinus Dalorto of Genoa, where it is shown as a perfectly round circle off the west coast of Ireland. The island's position and shape persisted throughout the late Middle Ages and Renaissance with little change. In the Catalan map of 1375, however, the island appears to have been confused with Terceira in the **Azores** (so called because it was the third island discovered by the Portuguese). After this, maps can be found with two (or more) islands labeled Brazil or Brazur on the same map. Most commonly, the island is placed off the coast of southwest Ireland or in the vicinity of the Azores. The puzzle can be solved if we take into account the linguistic basis of the name, for it turns out that the two different positions are indeed two different places in two different traditions.

The name Jnsola de Bracil, for Terceira, originates in the word *brazil,* commonly used in the Middle Ages to mean red dyewood. References to an island where red dyewood could be obtained go back as far as A.D. 982, to Hudûd al-'Alam (*A Persian*

Geography: Regions of the World). A commercial treaty of 1193 between two Italian city-states mentioned *grana de brasill* (grain of brazil). We know that the most valuable resource initially in the Azores, as in the other islands in the eastern Atlantic (and later, in the initial settlement of Brazil), was red dyewood, in great demand in the flourishing Mediterranean cloth trade. References to Bracir or Brazil are not so much to a specific island as to forests capable of producing this valuable

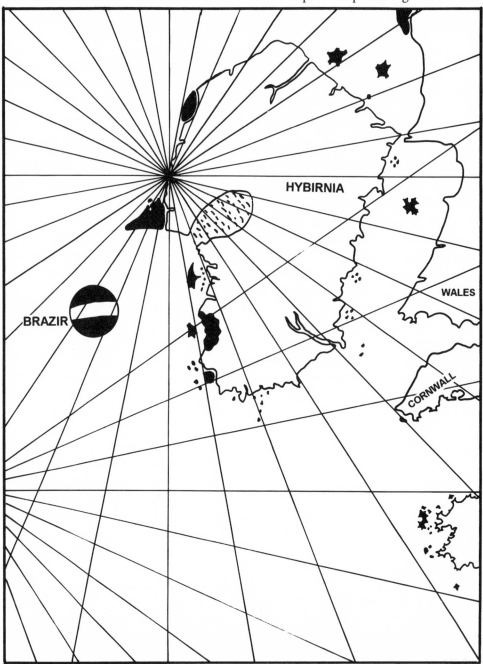

The island of Hy-Brazil (Brazir); detail of Pizigani Brothers map, 1367, adapted by the author. The straight lines are rhumb lines used for navigation *(drawing by Laura Penn).*

export. Hence the possibilities of the multiple use of the name on a single map: an indication of the harvesting of dyewood in the forests of several different islands.

By way of contrast, Breasil, Hy-Brazil, O'Brassil, and O'Brazil are Celtic in origin, derived from the ancient Gaelic word *breas* (noble, prince, or fortunate). In the Celtic imagination Hy-Brazil was a sunken island of enchantment, which reappeared once every seven years. The spell of enchantment could only be broken by fire, just as the sun evaporated the dense fogs off the coast of Ireland only occasionally to reveal outlying islands. It has been suggested that since Hy-Brazil lies very close to the Irish coast, roughly along the 100-fathom (600-feet) line, the late medieval conception may not have been a myth but a folk memory of the time when lower sea levels exposed more land to the west of the present sea margin. The perfectly circular shape of the Irish offshore island, without the scalloping characteristic of the cartographic portrayal of islands at the time, plus the island's bisection by a river suggests symbolic and religious associations (the biblical Book of Revelation's river of life flowing through God's light). The island does seem less realistically portrayed than other islands and coastlines on these early maps. Or is the circle interrupted by a horizontal band a result of the well-known arctic mirage, or perhaps other optical phenomena? Tired, lonely, and hungry, ancient Irish mariners might have commonly observed strange sights on the horizon, especially at dawn and dusk, when sunlight plays tricks with the observer.

The depiction of the island of Brazil was not confined to the late medieval and Renaissance periods. The Irish offshore island persisted on nautical charts well into the nineteenth century, cartographically losing its island status in 1830 when it became Brazil Rock. Not until 1865 did the island disappear from the charts. At its other location on early maps, however, a remnant of the old label survives to this day: One of the volcanic peaks on Terceira is named Monte Brazil.

Further Reading: Donald S. Johnson, *Phantom Islands of the Atlantic: The Legends of Seven Lands that Never Were,* New York: Walker and Co., 1994.

IRON CURTAIN

After losing the British general election in 1945, Sir Winston Churchill became the leader of the opposition in parliament. The loss of the premiership by the popular wartime leader was a surprise to some, but it can be explained by the British populace's desire for Labour-backed social reform and improved material well-being after years of sacrifice. In spring 1946, taking leave of parliament, Churchill accepted an invitation to deliver an address at Westminster College in Fulton, Missouri. The former prime minister traveled with U.S. president Harry Truman in a private train to the president's home state. The talk Churchill gave on 5 March proved his most famous and influential postwar speech.

Much of the talk was devoted to the need for international cooperation and support of the recently formed United Nations (U.N.). Churchill urged the United States to assume new responsibilities in world affairs in accordance with its new position in the world. After paying compliments to the Russians, whom he thanked for their support during the recently concluded war, Churchill proposed to recount certain facts to his audience. There followed a detailed geographic description of Soviet domination in eastern Europe. He enunciated some of the most memorable lines of political discourse for

that generation, at least until Kennedy's inaugural address in 1960: "From Stettin in the Baltic to Trieste in the Adriatic, an iron curtain has descended across the Continent. Behind that line lie all the capitals of the ancient states of Central and Eastern Europe." He then enumerated the great cities. One can almost hear the drumbeats of Churchill's bass voice as he names them: "Warsaw, Berlin, Prague, Vienna, Budapest, Belgrade, Bucharest, and Sofia, all these famous cities and the populations around them lie in what I must call the Soviet sphere."

Churchill continued, noting that only Athens, with all her "immortal glories," was free to conduct an election supervised by British, American, and French observers. Elsewhere, totalitarian governments and police states were being installed by tiny local Communist parties augmented by the Soviets. Only Czechoslovakia and Germany lay in some doubt. Churchill boldly warned of the danger that these new developments posed to a pacified Europe and to the special relationship between Britain and the United States. Churchill concluded his speech by pointing out that it was in the U.S. interest to oppose Soviet expansionism, and he called on the recently formed U.N. to assume its new responsibilities to promote peace.

Churchill had used the words "iron curtain" before, as early as 12 May 1945, in a telegram to President Truman, in which he referred to a Lübeck–Trieste–Corfu line of domination. Only ten days earlier German foreign minister Count Schwerin Krosigk had described, in a speech printed in the *The Times,* an "iron curtain" of destruction moving across Germany. This speech, in turn, might have been an echo of a phrase used earlier in the year by Dr. Goebbels, Hitler's minister of propaganda, who referred to an *eisener Anhalt* (German for iron curtain).

Churchill's Fulton speech, made at the outset of the cold war, proved a remarkably accurate prophecy of the extent of Soviet control of eastern Europe in the latter half of the twentieth century. He cannot be faulted for considering lower Austria unfree, because Vienna at the time of the speech was indeed in a Soviet zone of military occupation and only later obtained its independence.

Churchill was reelected prime minister in 1951, but he resigned in 1955. His style no longer fit the times, as Great Britain was withdrawing from the international arena. Having granted independence to India in 1947, Britain was preparing to divest itself of its other colonies. Soon it would initiate a wave of nation-making that would grant self-government to people around the world, from Ghana to Belize and from Zanzibar to Fiji. Churchill won the Nobel Prize for literature in 1953 for his historical writing and oratory. In 1963 he was made an honorary citizen of the United States, the only other person who had received this distinction being Lafayette.

IRON GATE

The **Carpathians** are a crescent-shaped arc of mountains that dominate the topography of eastern Europe. Beginning opposite Vienna on the Danube, they stretch eastward across Slovakia, continue southeast through Romania, then double back to the Danube, where they form a western extension known as the Transylvanian Alps. Between the Transylvanian prong of the Carpathians and the Stara Planina Range (Balkan Mountains), the Danube has cut a winding, rocky gorge two miles (3.2 kilometers) long and 550 feet (168 meters) wide. The location of the Iron Gate is readily evident on a political map of Europe, because the border between Serbian Yugoslavia and Romania makes a small, neat loop just east of Belgrade, turning to the north before resuming its southeastern course.

Situated between the towns of Turnu Severin and Orsova, where the river narrows and swiftly flows through a gap in the mountains, the Iron Gate has historically been of strategic significance in controlling the lower Danube. It is a key access point between two broad plains along the lower course of eastern Europe's major river: the **Hungarian Basin** and the **Walachian Plain.** The narrow passageway presents problems of navigability, with swift currents and dangerous shoals. Moreover, anyone attaining the high ground above the river can exact tolls or prevent access. In the numerous battles between Hungarians, Serbs, Walachians (Romanians), and Turks, control of the Iron Gate was often a primary strategy. In the Hungarians' successful attempt to turn back the Turks (if only temporarily) between 1440 and 1444 under the reign of Ladislas, the Battle of the Iron Gates (1442) was fought and won by the Magyars.

Because of the difficulty passing through this restriction and its possible control by one's enemies, the region's main roads avoided this natural opening in the mountains. A number of Carpathian pass routes reached the Danube from the north just above the Iron Gate, thereby circumventing the strategic chokepoint. Likewise, major routes through the Balkans from the south followed the **Vardar-Morava Corridor,** which also opened to the Danube above the Iron Gate. Even the route linking the Walachian and Hungarian plains did not make use of this obvious water gap. Instead, it cut across the Porta Orientalis, a far easier gateway through the Transylvanian Alps, just north of the Iron Gate.

The Danube was made navigable here when the channel was cleared of rocky obstructions in the 1860s. The Sip Canal (opened in 1896) allows river traffic to move easily past the gorge. One of the largest hydroelectric dams in Europe was completed in 1971 on the site of the Iron Gate. This joint Yugoslav-Romanian project impounds water and permits its controlled issue along the lower course of the flood-prone Danube.

JABLONICA PASS

Although the major mountains of eastern Europe, the **Carpathians,** are part of the young Alpine orogeny, they do not stand as high nor present as great an obstacle in crossing as do the Alps proper. In the eastern Carpathians near the borders of Hungary, Ukraine, and Romania, the low mountain ranges present easy pass routes, which historically have facilitated the migration and conquest of peoples who have crossed this sparsely settled borderland en route to densely settled lands on either side.

The Jablonica Pass, located about 30 miles (48 kilometers) southwest of Kolomyya (Ukraine), joins the upper course of the Prut River, which drains east and south to the **Black Sea,** to the deep incursions of the **Hungarian Basin** into the western flank of the mountains along the Tisza River. Also known as the Tatar Pass or Pereval Yablonitsky (in Russian), the pass crosses the divide between the Chernagora and Gorgany ranges, both of which rise above 6,000 feet (1,829 meters).

The route was taken by the Tatars (Mongols) in their conquest of Hungary in 1241. It was the scene of heavy fighting between Austrians and Russians from October 1914 to February 1917. The Soviet Union used the Tatar Pass in its attack on Hungary in 1944. The pass today is crossed by a major rail line that links Ukraine to the Danubian plain.

JERSEY

See Channel Islands

JUTLAND

Home of the ancient Jutes, a Germanic tribe who settled the southeastern coast of England (e.g., Kent) after the departure of the Romans, this roughly 250-mile-long (402-kilometer) peninsula between the North and Baltic Seas is an extension of the **North European Plain.** Divided at its base between Germany and Denmark, Jutland (in Danish, Jylland) has traditionally been a rural and isolated periphery, remote from the cosmopolitan island populations to its east, including Copenhagen on the island of Zealand (Sjælland) and Odense on Funen (Fyn). Only a few scattered cities and villages serve the local population and connect the region to the outside world. A rich, pre-Viking culture can be found here, and Viking sites include the ancient trading town of Hedeby, the great burial mounds of the earliest Danish sovereigns at Jelling (near Vejle), and the Danevirke, a boundary wall at the region's traditional southern limit.

The northern and western parts of Jutland comprise extensive dune lands, lagoons, and sterile outwash plains.

Much reclamation work has been done, draining the marshes and marling the heath, in imitation of the Dutch, though here diked marshlands are known as *kog*s rather than polders. The push to convert the heathlands was especially strong in the late nineteenth century, after the loss of North Slesvig in 1864. Under the auspices of the redoubtable Danish Heath Society (Det danske Hedelselskab)

untenanted compared to the sheltered southern and eastern coasts. All the major towns of southern Jutland are on the east coast, most of them tucked at the head of winding, shallow-sided, wooded fjords. These include, from south to north, the towns of Schleswig and Flensburg in Germany; and Kolding, Horsens, and Randers in Denmark. Sonderborg, at the narrowest point of the Alsfjord, commands

Rolling farmland and farmstead on the Jutland Peninsula *(Bob Krist/Corbis)*.

formed in 1866, outwash plains and adjacent poorer moraines were converted to farms and estates to the extent that the original heath only survives today in scattered patches, which are now carefully preserved as reminders of the original landscape. The Limfjord, which crosses the entire peninsula at its northern end, provided the Vikings with an ideal situation, since they could strike out from its protected recesses to the east or west, and its shorelands made excellent farmland.

The low-lying lands, facing stiff winds off the North Sea, are stark and relatively

access to the island of Als. The only major town of the west coast, Esbjerg, didn't exist until 1868, when the Danish Parliament passed a bill to make a sandy cliff into a dock, and subsequently to establish a deep-water haven for the export, especially to England, of high-quality Danish agricultural produce—butter, cheese, eggs, and poultry products. Denmark may have lost Norway, which it ruled from 1397 to 1814; given way before Sweden in the Baltic; and even sold to the United States its Virgin Islands (1917), but as a small country it is almost without parallel in successfully intensifying land use and parlaying skills and education into industry—that is, in truly *developing* its land and people, rather than depending on the exploitation of others' resources in an imperial mode.

After 1864 the former Danish province of Slesvig (in German, Schleswig) in southern Jutland was forcibly annexed by German Prussia. This gave rise to the famous "Schleswig-Holstein problem" that exercised the minds of many Victorian gentlemen. Denmark's creation of the port of Esbjerg on the west coast was stimulated by its loss of Slesvig. In 1920 a plebiscite was held and the northern part of Slesvig passed to Denmark along a line running approximately from the island of Sylt on the west to the Flensburg Fjord on the Baltic, while the southern section remained in German control. The two Schleswigs remain officially divided by the international border to this day; however, because the towns never had linguistically segregated quarters and most Danes are bilingual, cultural divisiveness has not prevailed, at least since the inevitable difficulties caused by World War II.

The only major battle between the British and German fleets in World War I occurred some 60 miles (97 kilometers) off the west coast of Jutland. On 31 May 1916, the British Grand Fleet under the command of Admiral Sir John Jellicoe engaged the commander of the German High Seas Fleet, Vice-Admiral Reinhard Scheer. A detachment of battleships and battle cruisers under Vice-Admiral Betty tried to cut off the return of German Vice-Admiral Hipper's battle cruisers to the haven of the Elbe mouth. Although the Battle of Jutland (known in Germany as the Battle of the Skagerrak) turned out to be indecisive, with the Germans gaining a slight tactical advantage (the Germans lost 11 ships and about 2,500 dead; the British 14 ships and about 6,000 dead), the British navy was able to bottle up the German fleet for the rest of the war. The Germans had demonstrated, however, that British power as expressed by the Royal Navy was not invincible, a lesson that populations under British colonial rule around the world did not fail to appreciate. The first and last battle between large fleets of Dreadnoughts had come to a draw off the Jutland coast. An era was closing: The iron rule of colonial force based on steam and steel was slowly giving way before the widespread demand for independent political rule, although this process would be delayed until after World War II. Jutlanders, of course, stood apart from this process, continuing along the same nonimperial, autonomous path of economic development they had always pursued.

Further Reading: Brian Fullerton and Alan F. Williams, *Scandinavia,* 2d ed., London: Chatto and Windus, 1975.

KATTEGAT
See Danish Straits

KLONDIKE
In the wake of a severe economic depression, the August 1896 discovery of rich placer gold deposits in this district of the upper Yukon near the Canadian-Alaskan border understandably led to a massive stampede of fortune seekers. The Klondike rush was not the result of an accidental discovery, in the way that the fortuitous discovery of gold on the American River during the course of the construction of a sawmill had led to the California gold rush at midcentury, but the result of a series of sustained prospecting forays and minor rushes beginning with the Cassiar Rush in British Columbia in the mid-1870s.

The Klondike River is a short, eastern tributary of the Yukon, located just within Canada's Yukon Territory. It was along Rabbit Creek (later renamed Bonanza Creek), a tributary of the Klondike, that valuable coarse gold deposits were first discovered. As soon as ships reached San Francisco and Seattle with news of the strike, a major population migration to the north country was on. The city of Dawson sprang up overnight at the junction of the Klondike and Yukon Rivers, with perhaps a population of 30,000 by 1898, if anyone had taken the time to count. Meanwhile the country was buzzing with talk of trying to reach the remote interior of icy Alaska.

Travelers to Dawson and the creeks could choose among a variety of routes, but most frequently they followed the inner passage along the west coast of Alaska, threading the channel between the numerous offshore islands and the highly indented fjord coastline as far as Skagway or Dyea. These towns were the jumping-off points for crossing the coastal mountains to the headwaters of the Yukon. Although the Skagway trail across White Pass is better known due to the notoriety of Skagway's corrupt bosses, the trail leading out of nearby Dyea across Chilkoot Pass has left a more indelible imprint on the American imagination. The last leg of the ascent to the summit involves a three-quarter-mile climb from the last staging point (known as the Scales) up the 1,500 icy steps of the Golden Stairs. The image is that of a string of men climbing in zigzag fashion, looking like a column of ants. If we realize that only a 50-pound weight could be taken to the top at one time, and that the average outfit of one ton would require 40 such trips up and down the mountain, the awesomeness of the ascent can be fully appreciated. It took each man on the average three months to pack his outfit the 27 miles (43 kilometers) from Dyea to Lake Lindeman. Once trekkers reached the lakes in the headwaters of the Yukon, they paused to fell trees and construct a boat or barge (and a mongrel assortment of other kinds of vessels) that would take them down the Yukon to Dawson.

Several other routes to the gold fields besides this well-known route existed, including the Copper River Trail and the Teslin Trail, which followed the Stikine River and Teslin Lake, as well as the all-Canadian trail emanating from Edmonton; but these routes proved even more arduous than the Skagway and Dyea routes, as did the attempts to proceed straight up the Yukon from its mouth by steamboat, an obvious if lengthy route, which led to near disaster when many were caught below Ft. Yukon in the winter of 1897 when the river froze. With thousands of people suddenly stranded in the desolate northlands, Canadian authorities began to require all travelers to carry a year's supply of provisions, which only made the packing more difficult along the already demanding trails. Within a few years thou-

sands had been disappointed in their expectations of making a great fortune, and some drifted down the Yukon to discover rich placer deposits in other places, notably at Nome on the southern coast of the Seward Peninsula, just opposite the mouth of the Yukon—which led to a secondary rush.

Although the Klondike gold rush lasted an astonishingly short time (gold production declined after 1900), the colorful stories of the hardships of those days live on. Numerous literary adventurers took off for the gold fields, including Jack London and Hamlin Garlin, and their stories stamped a vivid impression of gold miners and their adventures on the American imagination. Movies, books, songs, and even an ice cream treat (the Klondike Bar) remind us of these colorful, turn-of-the-century events.

Further Reading: Pierre Berton, *The Klondike Fever: The Life and Death of the Last Great Gold Rush,* New York: Carroll and Graf, 1958; William Bronson, *The Last Grand Adventure,* New York: McGraw-Hill, 1977.

LAKE DISTRICT (ENGLISH)

This beautiful region of lakes and mountains located in three counties of northwestern England—northern Lancashire, western Westmorland, and southern Cumberland—is the beloved landscape of poets, artists, and vacationers.

Including the Cumbrian Mountains and parts of the Furness peninsula, the district, which is approximately 30 miles (48 kilometers) in diameter, comprises a dome of ancient slates and volcanic rocks. Streams radiating from the central, elevated portions were deepened by Pleistocene glaciers and dammed in places to form characteristic ribbon lakes that fan out in various directions from the highlands.

Among the most celebrated lakes are Windermere, Grasmere, Ullswater, Derwent Water, West Water, and Coniston Water. The largest of the 16 lakes, Windermere, is only about ten miles (16 kilometers) long and one mile (1.6 kilometers) wide, so the beauty of the lakes can often be taken in with a single view. A colorful vocabulary describes the features of the region. Mountains streams are called becks, wet uplands fells. Small glacial lakes are known as tarns, while isolated peaks have the unlovely appellation of stickles.

The mountains are of modest elevation, reaching only to 3,162 feet (964 meters) at Scafell Pike, but they present a majestic appearance due to the variation of slope—its oversteepening at the head of valleys and overall smoothness elsewhere. Combined with the mirroring effect of the lakes, it is not surprising that the region has a reputation as a vacation spot.

The Lake District is better known for its vistas than its history; yet its association with the English Romantic writers marks it as a natural landscape that has been humanized as much by the written word as by the fence, field, and road. The prehistoric stone circle at Castlerigg, near Keswick, testifies to occupation by Bronze Age peoples. Romans and Norsemen deforested many of the region's valleys. Numerous ancient ruins of castles and churches are in evidence. The district's chief claim to fame in royal matters is that Catherine Parr, the sixth and last queen of Henry VIII, was a Westmorland girl, born at Kendal.

The arrival of a gaunt young man with a Yorkshire accent at Dove Cottage at Grasmere in 1799 accompanied by his dutiful younger sister was to bring great changes to the district's identity. William Wordsworth tramped across the rocky uplands from lake to lake, describing his impressions in a new style of verse that placed a higher evaluation on the natural world than had previously existed. This new Romantic style owed much to recent German intellectual developments that would culminate with Goethe. The mantle of romanticism was taken up by Robert Southey and Samuel Taylor Coleridge, who soon joined Wordsworth, the three thereafter being referred to as the Lake Poets. The praise of specific spots in the district was now being sung and remembered by readers of English

LANGUEDOC

The historic province of Languedoc, located in southern France west of the Rhône Delta, is at once a major center of wine production, the site of an important gateway connecting the Atlantic and Mediterranean coasts, a well-known traditional peasant region, and the locale of the most widespread heretical movement in the Middle Ages.

Windermere sits in the middle of the Lake District in northern England, a region closely associated with this country's Romantic poets *(Corel Corporation)*.

literature. At Ullswater, for instance, Wordsworth "wandered lonely as a cloud" before gaining a sudden, transcendent inspiration upon sight of a bank of golden daffodils along the lake's margin. Shelley, Keats, Tennyson, and Ruskin all resided at least temporarily in the district and were influenced by Wordsworth and his followers. Since 1951 the Lake District has been designated a national park, and developments such as above-ground utility lines that would destroy the aesthetic value of the region are strictly forbidden.

The region is bounded on the north by the **Massif Central,** on the east by the Rhône River, and on the south by the foothills of the eastern **Pyrenees.** The vaguely defined medieval province of Languedoc spilled over to the west into the **Aquitaine Basin** and into Provence east of the Rhône. This sun-drenched land covered with vineyards is the epitome of southern France. The vineyards produce 40 percent of all of France's wine and most of its cheap table wine. The historic capital was at Toulouse on its western edge, but its heartland was the coastal plain around Montpellier. The name today refers to Lower Languedoc, the warm alluvial plain along the Mediterranean.

This region's name derives from the distinctive medieval French dialect, *langue d'oc* (literally, "language of yes"), spoken here. North of a linguistic boundary running approximately from Bordeaux to Grenoble, another dialect, *langue d'oïl* (also meaning "language of yes") was spoken. The northern tongue eventually became standard Parisian French due to the importance of the capital city and its university, so that today the French affirmative is *oui,* a modified form of *oïl. Langue d'oc* includes the Provençal speech popularized by the troubadours in the south of France.

The through-route of the Languedoc plain attracted Phocaeans from Greece as early as 600 B.C., who brought the grapevine and the olive tree to the region. This same group established the important Greek colony of Massilia (now Marseilles) around this time. Rome made Narbonne the capital of a key province of the empire known as Gallia Narbonensis (Narbonese Gaul). The time from the Frankish conquest (completed by the eighth century) to Languedoc's incorporation into the French royal domain (1271) was a golden age in which the Counts of Toulouse ruled the independent province, fostering high levels of intellectual excellence. A distinctive blend of elements from Greek, Roman, Islamic, and German cultures has been identified as contributing to this era's signal achievements.

In the thirteenth century, the region was the center of the Cathars or Albigenses (so called from their stronghold at Albi). This group of alleged heretics presented a major challenge to the supremacy of the Roman papacy, developing its own doctrines and rituals, holding councils, and establishing dioceses. Widespread support garnered from powerful individuals in local communities led to the perceived need for the brutal suppression of what was considered a dangerous heresy. A crusade was launched with the full backing of the king of France and the pope, not to far-off Palestine, but to southern France, to stamp out these heretical activities. Two hundred Albigenses were burned alive at the stake at the mountain citadel of Montségur, and in Béziers some 20,000 men, women, and children were butchered in 1209. By 1229 the region's independence and its culture had been destroyed.

Standing astride the Carcassonne Gateway between the Pyrenees and the Massif Central is the splendid medieval fortress town of Carcassonne. One of the architectural marvels of Europe, the old city sits atop a hill overlooking the Aude River valley. Fortifications built during the Roman imperial period were subsequently extended and improved, so that by the time of Philip III the site was reputedly impregnable. Edward the Black Prince drew up short at its walls in 1355.

The old Protestant city of Nîmes (yes, the region was a center of that heresy, too) is best known for its magnificent Roman ruins, including an arena seating up to 24,000, which is still in use, and the well-preserved temple of Maison Carée (square house), considered one of the finest examples of Roman architecture. But Nîmes is also a commercial center and railway hub, with important textile and clothing industries. The city invented the kind of jeans worn today by the youth of the world (and not just the youth), denim being a corruption of *de Nîmes* (from Nîmes).

LATIUM

The central Italian province of Latium (in Italian, Lazio) extends from the western slope of the **Apennines** to the Tyrrhenian Sea. Drained at its northern end by the lower course of the Tiber River, this historic region includes rocky mountains, volcanic hills, crater lakes, fertile alluvial plains, notoriously unhealthy coastlands, and the site of ancient Rome.

Situated along the Tiber some 15 miles (24 kilometers) from its mouth, the Eternal City was set amid a jumble of low bluffs (the celebrated Seven Hills of Rome) and intersecting valleys. Unlike other early Greek and Italian towns, Rome was not sited on a defensible high point or acropolis, although its interior location gave it a measure of additional security. Rome was, however, a natural center of trade and communication along the course of Italy's most navigable stream. Downstream cargoes of timber and stone helped build the largest city in the ancient world, whose population of one million was not reached again by any city until London surpassed it in the first decade of the nineteenth century. Seagoing vessels of light draft brought grain and other commodities upstream from the coast. Due to the submergence of the coast, no excellent natural harbors existed, and as a result Rome never became as important a commercial entrepôt as might be expected. The actual site is at a river island at the lowest point along the Tiber that would support bridge abutments. More important than its natural site was the central situation of Latium within the Italian lands, at an approximate midpoint on the elongated boot of the peninsula. Rome became the natural focus of an extensive road system fanning outward from the imperial center.

The Greek geographer and historian Strabo (ca. 63 B.C.–ca. A.D. 22) described Latium as a naturally productive land. Though noting its rocky wastes and unhealthy marshlands, Strabo drew a flattering portrait of the Roman homelands at about the time the **Mediterranean** was becoming a Roman lake. As early as the third century B.C. Latin tribes had conquered the neighboring Etruscans (located north of the Tiber) as well as other Italic tribes then living in Latium. In ancient times Latium constituted only a comparatively small area east and south of the Tiber as far as the Alban Hills. Only when the region became part of Italy in 1870—it had previously been part of the Papal States—did it attain its present boundaries.

The low-lying area around Rome (Campagna di Roma) was a favorite retreat of early Roman citizens. By late imperial days, the region was abandoned, and relict aqueducts and old monuments were the only evidence of its former occupancy. One of the few positive contributions of Mussolini's Fascist government (1922–1943) was the reclamation of the Roman Campagna and the beginning of its resettlement. Mussolini's systematic works of *bonificazione* also extended to the marshy coastal strip of the Pontine Marshes in southern Latium. The Roman-built Appian Way follows this low route, along which the Emperors Trajan and Theodoric began land reclamation works, which the Fascists completed in the 1930s.

Further Reading: Max Cary, *The Geographic Background of Greek and Roman History,* Oxford: Clarendon Press, 1949, pp. 128–133.

LEEWARD ISLANDS

The northern group of islands in the Lesser Antilles extends southeast from Puerto Rico to the butterfly-shaped island of French Guadeloupe. Volcanic in origin, the islands are carpeted by lush, subtropical vegetation, thanks to abundant precipitation. Their Edenic beauty has attracted large numbers of tourists to their shores. At the northern end, Great Britain and the United States each possess a group of the *Virgin Islands,* named by Columbus on his second voyage (1493), after the legendary Saint Ursula and her eleven thousand virgin companions. Former British colonies that are now independent include *St. Kitts and Nevis, Antigua and Barbuda,* and *Montserrat.* Reflecting the seventeenth-century struggle among the rising north European powers, the Dutch retain *Sint Eustatius (Saint Eustatius), Saba,* and the southern section of *Sint Maarten (Saint Martin).*

The name Leewards has been a source of confusion for history readers and atlas perusers. A recognized authority on the geography of the region notes: "There is no rational basis for the trade-wind nomenclature applied to these islands. The Leewards are not to the west, or leeward, of the windwards, but to the north." Further complicating matters, the Dutch call Saba and nearby Dutch possessions the Bovenwindse (Windwards). However, the islands that the English know as the Windwards were an administrative grouping within the British Empire: The larger islands were Crown Colonies, with the executive authority vested in a governor representing the power and person of the British monarch, and the smaller islands had administrators.

The Spanish were the first to establish a sphere of interest in these waters. The *Lesser Antilles,* with their resistant Carib tribes and lack of precious metals, however, did not attract Spanish colonists. In the early seventeenth century the rising European powers of France, the Netherlands, and Britain began to settle the smaller islands in the southeastern part of the Caribbean basin, partly to establish a geopolitical foothold, partly to create an export platform for subtropical crops.

The oldest island and by far the most productive is the sugar island of St. Kitts (Saint Christopher), where settlement dates from 1624 when Sir Thomas Warner and 20 "gentlemen adventurers" founded the first British settlement in the Caribbean. Though the settlement's growth was slow at first (partly because of the initial choice to grow tobacco), before too long it was sending colonists to Nevis, Montserrat, and Antigua. In 1625 Warner was named governor of these islands, and he continued to rule until his death in 1649.

The Dutch are traditionally credited with having introduced sugar cultivation and associated expertise to the West Indies. Between 1630 and 1654, the Dutch West Indies Company occupied the Pernambuco region of northeast Brazil, and from there an agricultural system based on sugar spread to the Caribbean. The Dutch contributed more than just the plant: They also introduced processing technology, such as the three-roller mill and copper furnace pots, and financial procedures such as credit extension.

By 1647, large planters on St. Kitts were growing sugar on the ash aprons at the base of the higher peaks. An essentially colonial economy based on the monocropping of sugar evolved in the Leeward Islands. In the late eighteenth century, St. Kitts surpassed *Barbados* as the leading sugar producer in the region. It has been said that in 1776—as the American colonists gathered arms against the motherland—the richest colony in the British Empire was St. Kitts. Sugar prices later fell, but the islands enjoyed one final period of prosperity in the early nineteenth century, before slavery was abolished in the British colonies (1833). This undermined the labor system on the islands and was deeply resented by local sugar producers.

The Leeward Islands had been united under a common legislature early in the eighteenth century, and after a brief interruption, they were again united under a common council in 1871. After World War II they obtained self-rule—the first stage in gaining complete independence—and formed a division of the West Indies Federation (1958–1962). Britain wanted a single federal entity to emerge from this nation-building process; but in the heady days of the early 1960s, this was not a practicable goal. The West Indian group broke apart, partly due to resentment against the Barbadian premiership but more fundamentally because the large islands of *Jamaica* and *Trinidad* possessed strong leaders and well-developed party systems and therefore opted for independence for themselves. After 1962, when these large islands obtained full sovereignty, the West Indian Federation fell apart. The peripheral islands that never joined the federation, including the *Bahamas,* the *Cayman Islands, Turks and Caicos,* and *Bermuda,* remained colonies of the now greatly reduced British authority.

See also: Atlantic Ocean, Legendary Islands of. *Further Reading:* Richard Dunn, *Sugar and Slaves: The Rise of the Planter Class in the English West Indies, 1624–1713,* New York: Norton, 1973; Elisabeth Wallace, *The British Caribbean: From the Decline of Colonialism to the End of Federation,* Toronto: University of Toronto Press, 1977.

LESBOS
See Aegean Islands

LOMBARDY
See Po Plain

LORRAINE BASIN
French Lorraine and German Saarland are complementary borderland regions whose economic and political fates have been intertwined in modern times.

The Lorraine Basin is the eastward continuation of the **Paris Basin**'s cuesta-form landscape, with alternating hard and soft sedimentary rocks. The plateau is cut by rivers flowing from south to north in the valleys of the Moselle and Meuse, and by east-facing scarps that parallel these two rivers (Côte de Moselle, Côte de Meuse). The best agricultural soils are at the base of the escarpments, where vineyards predominate, while the limestone uplands are heavily wooded. The sedimentary basin passes eastward into the heavily timbered crystalline Vosges as far as the crestline in Alsace. Here the Vosges Mountains, part of the **Hercynian Uplands,** form a natural frontier with Germany, although the political border passes to the east along the Rhine River.

Lorraine boasts a rich agriculture and fine wines, but its main economic specialization in the nineteenth and twentieth centuries has been in iron and steel. The northern part of the province contains the largest European iron-ore deposit west of Russia. At shallow depths, four billion tons of ore are to be found, though it is of low grade (25–50 percent iron) and rather phosphoric. A small area between Metz and Thionville featured metallurgical works as early as 1800. Though limestone for flux can be found in the neighborhood, coal cannot. Here is where the Saarland comes into the picture. Located northeast of Lorraine across (today's) German border, the Saar Basin has a rich coal deposit that nicely complements Lorraine's iron ore. From the beginning of the Common Market (1958) up to today's European Union, coal and ore have passed freely and virtually tariff-free across the international border. Coal and steel pacts even predated the formation of the European Economic Community.

In the past it was different: The iron district of Lorraine along with Alsace was annexed to German territory after 1871 and did not return to French control until 1918. It was during this period that new techniques of steelmaking (the Thomas and Gilchrist methods) permitted the production of high-grade steel from phosphoric iron ore. A vast industrial region stretching from Luxembourg and the German border region down to Nancy (the capital of Lorraine) in the south developed rapidly in the late nineteenth century under the goad of German capital and organization. After World War I not only was Lorraine returned to France but the Saarland also was assigned to France under the administration of the League of Nations. A plebiscite loosely attached the Saarland to Germany in 1935, and in 1940, Hitler annexed the territory along with Lorraine, calling the new province Westmark. Reoccupied by France in 1945, Saarland remained in political limbo during the postwar period until 1957, when it became a state of the Federal Republic of Germany.

In sum, control of the industrial borderlands of the Saar-Lorraine has been perpetually and hotly disputed until the postwar era. Germany twice seized and lost the iron ore deposits of the Lorraine, while France twice tried (unsuccessfully) to pry the coal-rich Saarland from German control. It is sad to contemplate how much blood was shed during the two world wars in an attempt to monopolize these regions, when today the most innovative steelmaking does not even make use of the low quality coal of the Saar (**Ruhr** coking coal is now brought by barge to the Lorraine by the Moselle Canal), nor does it require interior locations. Iron ore and coal are now brought together at tidewater locations, as at Europort (Rotterdam), to take advantage of the lower transport costs of oceanic shipping.

Further Reading: David Burtenshaw, *Saar-Lorraine,* London: Oxford University Press, 1976; John Martin, "Location Factors in Lorraine Iron and Steel Industry," *Institute of British Geographers, Transactions and Papers,* no. 23 (1957), pp. 191–212.

MACEDONIA

See Vardar-Morava Corridor

MADEIRA ISLANDS

Known to the Romans as the Purple Islands (Insulae Purpurariae), the Madeiras lie about 350 miles (560 kilometers) off Morocco but over 600 miles (960 kilometers) from Lisbon. Located in subtropical latitudes in the east Atlantic, within easy reach of Iberia, this archipelago, like its neighbor to the south, the **Canary Islands,** served as an important stepping-stone and way station for the trans-Atlantic voyages of discovery and as an experimental laboratory for the transplantation of European agricultural systems to the Americas.

The volcanic archipelago comprises two inhabited islands, *Madeira* and *Porto Santo,* and two uninhabited island groups, *Desertas* and *Selvagens,* the latter only 120 miles (193 kilometers) north of the Canaries. The islands' landscapes present scenes of striking beauty, especially on the large island of Madeira: a mountainous spine rising above 6,000 feet (1,829 meters), yawning green ravines, and volcanic spurs reaching the coast in sheer basaltic cliffs. The moderate temperatures of their Mediterranean-type climate are interrupted by occasional hot, dry east winds blowing off the Sahara. The islands' production of sugarcane,

Madeira wines, and fruit have been the mainstay of an essentially colonial economy, although tourism and resort development have been more important moneymakers of late.

The explorers João Goncalves Zarco and Tristão Vaz Teixeira rediscovered the Madeiras (1418–1420), sailing under orders from Prince Henry the Navigator, the Portuguese patron of exploration who initiated voyages of discovery that led to the foundation of an overseas empire and Portugal's rise to international prominence in the sixteenth century. Settlement immediately followed, as Prince Henry encouraged colonization. Funchal, the main city, was founded on the south coast of Madeira Island in 1421. By the mid-fifteenth century, terraced slopes of sugarcane began to appear behind the broad harbor. This was the first demonstration outside Europe of the viability of tropical or subtropical plantation agriculture and its characteristic mode of organizing work and selecting crops, which would prove so important later in transforming the New World.

Unlike the Canaries with their fiercely resistant Guanches, the Madeiras had no inhabitants when first encountered by Portuguese *marinheiros* and bore no mark of human occupation. The feudal captaincy of Porto Santo was given to Bartholomeu Perestrello, future son-in-law of Christopher Columbus. In one of the earliest well-documented cases of ecological damage to an island ecosystem, Perestrello let loose a single female rabbit and her offspring born on the voyage, leading to an overpopulation of rabbits, who ate everything in sight, including the crops the settlers had planted for food. The colonists had to move to the larger island of Madeira, and though Porto Santo

task of clearing land, agricultural settlers set fires, one of which reportedly burned for seven years. Even discounting this story with its biblical span of years, the propensity to clear land by burning seems to have been characteristic of the Lusitanians. (Might this be a precursor to the burning of the Amazon rain forest in northern Brazil today?) Porto Santo proved too dry for sugarcane, as its lower

The compass rose at Prince Henry the Navigator's school at Sagres on Cape St. Vincent, Portugal. Explorers João Goncalves Zarco and Tristão Vaz Teixeira rediscovered the Madeiras while sailing under orders from Prince Henry, a patron of exploration *(photo by Jesse Walker)*.

was later resettled, reports of abundant rabbit populations continued.

The luxuriance of the vegetation and the size of the trees impressed the early settlers, coming as they did from the denuded slopes of the Mediterranean basin. The name they gave to the island—*Madeira*—means wood, and woodcutting and export were important early industries. In an era before the development of modern synthetic dyes, the natural dyes that could be extracted from certain trees were especially valuable. To speed up the

elevations don't interrupt the passing winds enough to produce condensation and precipitation.

Early experiments in cultivating cane were successful enough that in 1452 the Portuguese crown authorized the first water-driven sugar mill. Production of sugar increased from 6,000 arrobas (an arroba equals 11 to 12 kilograms) in 1455 to 15,000 arrobas in 1472, and reached 140,000 arrobas per year in the first decades of the next century. Ships carried Madeira sugar to England, France, **Flan-**

ders, Rome, Genoa, Venice, and even as far as Constantinople. A population of about 800 in 1455 increased to 15,000–20,000 by the end of the century, of which about 10 percent were slaves.

A necessary first step in the creation of a sugar estate was to conduct water from the mountains via an ingenious system of conduits and tunnels known as *levadas*. The importance of these improvements and the pride the people felt in having constructed them is captured by the traditional Madeirense saying, "Pharaoh had his pyramids; the Madeirense, their man-made water courses." A tremendous amount of labor was needed to cultivate, harvest, and mill the sugarcane, as well as to build and maintain the *levadas*. Though some early slaves may have been Berbers or Moors exiled from the Spanish Canaries, by the end of the fifteenth century Portugal had begun to involve itself in Africa's Atlantic coast slave trade.

The British occupied the islands for a short time during the Napoleonic wars, in 1801, and again from 1807–1814. Due to a long-standing alliance between England and Portugal, the English were allowed to distribute the local wine in all of Britain's territories, where it became extremely popular. Today the Madeiras, like the Azores, are an autonomous region of the Portuguese republic.

Further Reading: Alfred W. Crosby, Jr., *Ecological Imperialism: The Biological Expansion of Europe, 900–1900,* Cambridge: Cambridge University Press, 1986; Francis M. Rogers, *Atlantic Islanders of the Azores and Madeiras,* North Quincy, Mass.: Christopher, 1979.

MAGELLAN, STRAIT OF

This shortcut across the southern tip of South America was first discovered by Ferdinand Magellan in 1520 during the course of a voyage meant to find a route to the Moluccas that could be controlled by Spain. The channel is about 350 miles (563 kilometers) long, connecting Cabo Vírgenes (Cape Virgins) on the Atlantic to Cabo Pilar (Cape Pillar) on Desolation Island in the Pacific. The eastern part of the strait, from two and one-half to 15 miles (4–24 kilometers) wide, is known in Spanish as Estrecho de Magallanes. It consists of a series of dangerous narrows separated by sheltering bays. In contrast, the western part of the strait forms a straight line across a trench at the southern end of the Andes Mountains, providing spectacular scenes of fjord landscapes. Separating mainland South America from Tierra del Fuego, this water corridor was an important route during the age of the sail, especially before the Panama Canal was built, since it provided an inland waterway protected from the buffeting of winds and heavy storms off Cape Horn. Except for a few miles at its eastern end in Argentina, the strait is entirely within Chilean territory.

On 21 October 1520 a fleet sailing under the command of Ferdinand Magellan, a Portuguese navigator with Spanish sponsorship, raised a prominent peninsula of elevated white clay banks. By the current Catholic calendar it was the feast day of St. Ursula and the Eleven Thousand Virgins, named after a seagoing Breton princess and her martyred companions, and Magellan promptly named the headland that guards the strait's eastern entrance Cape of the Eleven Thousand Virgins, or Cape Virgins for short (Cabo Vírgenes). The full name qualifies as one of the most unusual and colorful place-names anywhere, though the Caribbean Virgin Islands have the same derivation.

The entrance to the strait was not obvious. The men thought it was closed on all sides, as they perhaps expected the opening to be so broad as to afford a view of its opposite end, as at **Gibraltar**. According to a firsthand account, Magellan said he had seen depicted on a Portuguese *carta* (this could be either a map or globe) a strait at the southern end of the landmass. Though the account names "Martin de Boemia" as the cartographer, it probably was not Behaim's famous 1492 globe (which Columbus probably saw before his 1492 voyage) that Magellan was

or navigation aids and in the absence of good anchorages, ranks as one of the greatest sailing accomplishments of all time. The length of the strait is equivalent to the entire length of the **English Channel** from Bishop Rock to **Dover Strait,** or to that of the Panama Canal from its entrance to Barranquila. A month after entering the strait, on 28 November 1520, three ships passed Cabo Pilar and sailed out into a

An aerial view of Punta Arenas, the southernmost city in the world, on the Strait of Magellan *(UPI/Corbis-Bettmann).*

referring to but a map of South America made by the German geographer Johannes Schöner (1477–1547), which showed a strait in the **La Plata** region or farther south.

Magellan's passageway across the strait was a high point in one of the great voyages of discovery, during which the globe would be circumnavigated for the first time in history. Although Magellan did not have a particularly difficult crossing compared to later voyages, his navigation of a 350-mile (563-kilometer) channel with dangerous tidal races, without charts

boisterous sea that Magellan knew was part of a larger ocean. Seven years earlier, Balboa had gazed southward from a peak in **Darién** and called this body of water the Sea of the South (Mare del Sur), but Magellan's smooth crossing led him to rename it the Pacific Ocean. Balboa's earlier name for the largest ocean in the world is recalled when the southern parts of the Pacific are referred to today as the South Seas, though strictly speaking the Spanish name meant South Sea. Magellan and most of his crew did not live to complete this trip around the world, as they got entangled in local political intrigue in the Philippines, and Magellan himself was murdered. A remnant of the original expedition under the command of Moscoso reached Sanlúcar on 6 September 1522, having conclusively established that the world was round, a large western ocean existed, and the Americas were indeed a new world, separate from Asia.

See also: Atlantic Ocean, Legendary Islands of; Leeward Islands.

Further Reading: Samuel Eliot Morison, *The European Discovery of America: The Southern Voyages, A.D. 1492–1616,* New York: Oxford University Press, 1974, pp. 380–401.

MAGINOT LINE

In January 1923, due to Germany's default in the payment of war reparations, French and Belgian forces invaded and occupied the key German industrial heartland of the **Ruhr.** Over the course of the next two years Germany met or rescheduled its financial obligations, and the Treaty of Locarno (5–16 October 1925) seemingly guaranteed the peace of Europe. Nevertheless, the nervous French feverishly began to build what they hoped would be an impregnable line of defense along their eastern border against any future German aggression.

The Maginot Line, named after André Maginot (1877–1932), the French minister of war who oversaw its construction, was mostly built between 1930 and 1934. It extended some 200 miles (322 kilometers) from the Swiss border at Epinal to the Belgian border. From that point to the North Sea, the line was weak and still incomplete when World War II began in 1939. While the main line in eastern France included concrete, steel-turreted structures surmounting a maze of trenches and underground forts, the Belgian flank consisted of outmoded, pre–World War I defenses.

The false sense of security behind the Maginot Line was especially evident during the "phony war" period, between the onset of war following Germany's invasion of Poland (September 1939) and the outbreak of conflict in the West the next year (June 1940). The collapse of France between 5 and 25 June was the result of the inactivity of French troops waiting behind the apparently secure Somme, Aisne, and Maginot Lines. German forces invaded the Low Countries in blitzkrieg style, adopting tactics of rapid movement to outflank the generally fixed position of the French army. The Germans easily broke through the Somme and entered France, which soon capitulated.

Fixed security lines like **Hadrian's Wall** and the Great Wall of China create an unfounded sense of security, and it is the lesson of history, as evidenced by these examples, that no landscape is impregnable and any such emplacement can be outflanked by a flexible deployment of forces.

Further Reading: Vivian Rowe, *The Great Wall of France: The Triumph of the Maginot Line,* London: Putnam, 1959.

MÄLAREN BASIN

The central parts of Sweden comprise a relatively level lowland of glacial origin. Cultivated lands occupy the better soils, and forests the poorer. This fertile agricultural landscape is set in the midst of the three great lakes of Sweden: to the south Lake Vättern, an elongated fracture oriented north-south; to the west Lake Vänern, practically an inland sea; and to the north, Lake Mälaren, a long, east-west fjord communicating to the Baltic through a narrow bottleneck, the site of Stockholm. Sinuous glacial ridges, or eskers, partition the landscape and serve as natural sites for highways and towns. The shores of Lake Mälaren also are partly determined by esker topography: The lake is narrow where esker ridges cross it and widens out between the ridges. Many rivers or water channels link the lakes: A famous internal route, the Göta canal, passes through central Sweden, linking Göteborg (Gothenburg) on the west coast to Norrköping at a fjord head on the eastern shore, south of Stockholm. The southern boundary of the lake region is clearly indicated on the ground by a range of morainic heights, beyond which lie the cooler, more elevated, and generally poorer glacial driftlands of the southern Swedish upland.

Sweden's capital city of Stockholm was founded about 1250 as a fortress on the island of Staden, in the bottleneck between Lake Mälaren and the Baltic. At that time, Lake Mälaren was an elongated fjord or arm of the sea extending 70 miles (113 kilometers) inland. Due to isostatic recovery of the Scandinavian landmass since the end of the Pleistocene (rocks rebounding from the prior weight of glacial ice), central Sweden is rising about one and one-half feet (0.46 meters) percentury. This amount of uplift would not be noticeable in the lifetime of a human being; but since the time of the Vikings (around A.D. 1000), the land around Lake Mälaren is 13 feet (4 meters) higher than it previous was, with the result that the previous strait is now only a channel (the Strömmen) that flows out to sea like a river (except during periods of drought or east winds), and is thus no longer an arm of the sea.

By 1280, Stockholm was a major port. Lübeck merchants of the Hansa exchanged salt, clothing, and consumer goods from western European centers for iron from the Bergslagen, a prosperous mining area located on the forested northern rim of Sweden's great lakes. Stockholm became the official port for the iron trade, and all production issuing from the prestigious Bergslagen had to be weighed and assessed on the island in the stream. At the same time, the fertile clay margins of Lake Mälaren and its western extension, Lake Hjälmaren, served as an agricultural breadbasket for the increasing population of central Sweden, and this region could be considered (along with the earlier settlement zone to the north, Uppland) the core area of the Swedish nation. By the seventeenth century Stockholm had outgrown its original site and had begun to spread to mainland locations—to Norrmalm, Östermalm, and Södermalm—but the central island still houses the main political and ecclesiastical buildings: the palace, parliament, law courts, and cathedral.

Stockholm earned the appellation Venice of the North from the sea's penetration far into its interior and from the importance of its sea-based commerce. The city became the capital of Sweden after the dissolution of the Kalmar Union in 1533. Largely on the basis of Stockholm's prosperity, Sweden became the dominant imperial power in the Baltic region in the seventeenth century, when the country reached its zenith as a world power.

Sweden's influence in the Baltic Sea region began to wane in the nineteenth century, with the rise of Prussia and Russia (it lost control of Finland in 1809). Although the main port functions have moved to Göteborg, Stockholm remains an elegant city, managing to grow gracefully within its natural framework of water channels, bare rock, and glacial ridges. Suburban development, the growth of outlying industrial towns, and the provision of recreation have been accomplished without destroying the attractiveness of the lake basin.

Further Reading: Roy Millward, *Scandinavian Lands,* London: Macmillan, 1964; W. William-

Olsson, "Stockholm: Its Structure and Development," *Geographical Review* 30 (1940): 420–438.

MARATHON, PLAIN OF

This plain in eastern Attica, about 24 miles (39 kilometers) northeast of Athens, was the site of a much celebrated Greek victory in the early years of the Persian Wars (500–449 B.C.).

The Persian Empire at the beginning of the wars included all of western Asia, as well as Egypt, which recently had been conquered. Under Darius I several small Greek towns on the west coast of Asia Minor, including Miletus at the mouth of the Meander River, rebelled against the oppressive rule of the barbarians (literally, those who spoke a different language and hence said "bar-bar . . ."). After squashing these rebellious Ionian cities, which had been aided by Athens, the Persians landed a fleet across the Aegean to punish the Athenians and to add Greece (and places farther west) to their empire. The city-state of Athens was just beginning to come into its own as a great metropolis and had recently established important democratic institutions. Its golden era of philosophy, art, and architecture, however, still lay in the future.

A first Persian expedition was successful in either subduing or pacifying the northern regions of Thrace and Macedonia, but a storm prevented the Persians from advancing to the south. A second expedition was launched (490 B.C.). The Persians encamped on a strip of coastal plain that borders the Bay of Marathon, an inlet of the Aegean Sea. The Marathon Plain extends five miles (8.0 kilometers) in length and two miles (3.2 kilometers) in width, ending in a marsh on the north. To the south is the present town of Marathon, and it was near this site that the famous battle of 490 B.C. took place.

The 10,000 Athenian hoplites (heavily armed infantry), aided by 1,000 soldiers from Plataea, were overwhelmingly outnumbered by their Persian foes, who supposed themselves superior. Commanded by the Athenian general Miltiades, a brilliant strategist, the Greeks routed the Persian army, killing some 6,000 Persians, while losing only 200 men themselves. A tumulus in the southwestern portion of the plain (now in ruins) contains the remains of the Athenian dead.

The Marathon race, an event in the Olympic games since 1896, commemorates the distance traversed by a runner dispatched to Athens with news of the victory. The standard distance of the race—26 miles, 385 yards (4,537 kilometers)—was first set in 1908. A less well-known feat of endurance was the 150 miles (241 kilometers) covered in two days by a courier sent from Athens to Sparta with a request for military assistance. Sparta responded, but its soldiers did not arrive at Marathon until the day after the battle.

The victory at Marathon has often been considered a critical turning point in Greek and thereby Western history because it ushered in a period of resurgent Athenian democracy. The politically astute Aristotle commented that the victory at Marathon gave the Athenian people political confidence. The 192 figures in the cavalcade of the Parthenon frieze have been ingeniously interpreted as a representation of those who died at Marathon. Though not narrowly determined by physical environment, the battle at Marathon and its artistic portrayal have been significant shapers of the Western tradition. In the words of the oracle of Apollo at Delphi, fifth-century Athens was an "eagle in the clouds for all time."

See also: Thermopylae; Salamis Island.

MASON-DIXON LINE

The survey boundary between Pennsylvania and Maryland is often considered the division between Northern and Southern states. During the antebellum period, an extension of this line west along the Ohio River was the border between slave-holding and non-slave-holding states.

The historical background to what may have been the most thorough, professional land survey ever done in the American colonies was a lengthy and fiercely contested border dispute between William Penn, Quaker proprietor of Pennsylvania, and the Lords Calvert, who were the proprietors of Maryland. The southern colony, with most of its population concentrated on the western shore of the **Chesapeake Bay,** had been granted to the first Lord Baltimore in 1632, while Penn's colony, at the head of the Delaware Bay and in lands farther west, stemmed from a grant in 1681. At a time when royal grants of land in unknown and unsurveyed parts of the world were often magnificent and sometimes fanciful (colonial Virginia claimed a diagonal block of land extending west of the Appalachians as far as Wisconsin), it is not surprising that the abutting colonies of Pennsylvania and Maryland would have boundary disputes. The Maryland charter specified that the northern boundary of its grant was "that part of the Bay of Delaware on the North, which lieth under the Fortieth Degree of North Latitude, where New England is terminated." Obviously drawn before any Middle Colonies were conceived, Maryland's northern border, if interpreted as 40 degrees of latitude, would have been in the present city of Philadelphia, which the Penns would not tolerate. In addition to settling how far "under" the fortieth parallel the boundary was to run, there was a need to delineate the north-south running boundary between Maryland and Delaware on the Eastern Shore of the Chesapeake. Delaware was originally granted to Penn as an addition to his lands and only later did it separate from Pennsylvania to become an independent colony. (By the way, Penn received all this land not because he was a good Quaker, but because his father, Admiral William Penn, captured Jamaica from the Spanish in 1655.)

To survey the disputed line, the English astronomers Charles Mason and Jeremiah Dixon were brought in at the recommendation of the Astronomer Royal at Greenwich, who praised their integrity and lack of bias as well as their abilities in mathematics and instrumentation. The two men had worked together previously as a team sent out by the Royal Society to the Cape of Good Hope to observe the transit of Venus across the sun. Arriving in Philadelphia in November 1763, Mason and Dixon brought with them two transits, two reflecting telescopes (to see posts at a distance), and a newly improved zenith sector for observing the elevation of stars. Thomas and Richard Penn, the sons of William who were most active in this affair, and Lord Baltimore agreed that "under the fortieth parallel" would mean a line 15 miles (25 kilometers) south of the southernmost limit of Philadelphia. Using the zenith sector to make some 60 observations of stars over a period of three weeks, the surveyors determined the precise latitude of the southern limit of Philadelphia. Since the point 15 miles (24 kilometers) due south of Philadelphia was in New Jersey, the surveyors moved westward about 30 miles (48 kilometers) along the same line of latitude to the farm of John Harland on the Brandywine River. After checking to see how well their instruments had withstood the journey by horse and cart (they had been couched in a feather bed to protect them), Mason and Dixon ran a line due south "to a plantation belonging to Mr. Alexander Bryan." This was to be the starting point of the survey, and the commissioners for the Penns and Lord Baltimore concurred. Before running the east-west line, Mason and Dixon ran the north-south line between Maryland and the counties of Delaware during the period from June to September 1764. After a winter layover, they proceeded to their zero milestone in the spring of 1765 and began to run the line that would immortalize their names.

A detailed account of the survey work need not detain us, but some highlights might be emphasized. The job was an arduous one, performed in frontier conditions. A team of axmen went ahead of the surveyors, clearing a rough path about 30 feet (9.1 meters) wide for the observations and measurements. There were encounters with "border ruffians" and threatening Indians. The work was meticulous, done by men who were performing as astronomers as much as land surveyors. Lines were surveyed and resurveyed, with much checking done, as the line would surely be used as a baseline in subsequent surveys.

Mason and Dixon crossed the Susquehanna and continued their line west to Blue Mountain (the Pennsylvanian name for the **Blue Ridge**) and beyond, eventually reaching the westernmost point indicated by Pennsylvania's charter, which turned out to be five degrees of longitude west of the starting point. Colonial officials prevailed upon the surveyors to extend their West Line the following year in 1767 as far as a point about 15 miles (24 kilometers) southwest of Uniontown and 45 miles (72 kilometers) due south of Pittsburgh.

The final report of the surveyors, including a detailed map, was every bit as professional as their fieldwork. Their work done, Mason and Dixon sailed home to England in September 1768. Little was heard about Jeremiah Dixon, who died in 1779. Charles Mason participated in other projects for the Royal Society, but his health and finances suffered a setback in the 1780s. Something must have attracted him to Philadelphia again, for he returned there in 1786. He died a few weeks later and was buried in an unmarked grave in Christ Church Burying Ground.

Further Reading: John Noble Wilford, *The Mapmakers: The Story of the Great Pioneers in Cartography from Antiquity to the Space Age,* New York: Vintage, 1981.

MASSIF CENTRAL

In this large plateau region in the south-central part of France are the headwaters of most, though not all, of the country's rivers. The Massif Central is the source of the longest river in France, the Loire, and the most celebrated, the Seine, though the south-running Rhône heads up in the Alps, and the major river of the southwest, the Garonne, has its beginning in the **Pyrenees Mountains.** A pattern of light settlement in this diverse hill land suggests the region's major role: It has blocked population advance and channeled migration around it. To the east, the Rhône-Saône trough provides a broad corridor between the Massif Central and the Alps, permitting access either to the **Paris Basin** or through the **Burgundy Gateway** to Germany. A passageway that flanks the region to the southwest is the Carcassonne Gateway, which stands astride a corridor between the foothills of the Pyrenees and a southern extension of the Massif Central. This lowland route provided access from the **Mediterranean** to the fertile **Aquitaine Basin** in southwestern France.

Covering almost one-sixth of the surface of France, the Massif Central is the most rugged and geologically diverse region in the country. The core of the upland is the Auvergne district, around Clermont-Ferrand. Underlain by ancient granitic rocks, more recent volcanic activity has produced basaltic lava flows as well as volcanic cones known as *puys* that dot the landscape. Old volcanic cones in the western Auvergne provide the highest elevations in the region—at Mont Dore (6,186 feet or 1,885 meters) and Plomb du Cantal (6,094 feet or 1,857 meters). The upland surface of the Massif Central is tilted downward to the north and west, with higher elevations to the southeast in the Cévennes, where a steep escarpment overlooks the Rhône valley. The Limousin Plateau in the west is an ancient crystalline surface about 3,000 feet (914 meters) in elevation. Without the complex faulting or volcanic activity evident in other parts of the region, Limousin presents a flat-to-undulating terrain that is the most geologically stable part of the Massif. A southern abutment of the region is formed by the Causses, a limestone plateau deeply dissected by the Dordogne, Lot, and Tarn rivers.

Civilization has forked around this upland region since the time of the Romans. It is reported that Julius Caesar, the conqueror of **Gaul**, attacked but failed to defeat the Celtic leader Vercingétorix near Clermont in 52 B.C. The stocky, dour peasants of Auvergne have persisted for centuries in its lush landscape, amid extinct volcanic cones and dense pine and chestnut forests. A large migration to the cities occurred beginning in the nineteenth century, especially to Paris where they form distinctive enclaves and practice traditional occupations (it is said that Auvergnats own or manage 60 percent of Parisian cafés). The outflow of people has left the Massif Central the least populated region in France. Limousin, with only 114 people per square mile, has the lowest population density in mainland France. Though some mineral deposits like coal and kaolin clay exist, and there are a few industrial centers, such as Clermont-Ferrand (the Michelin tire business, dating from the nineteenth century, is headquartered here), the region continues to be primarily a periphery, albeit an attractive one. Robert Louis Stevenson traveled through the scenic hill country of the Cévennes, recording his observations in his famous *Travels with a Donkey* (1878). Best known today for its mineral waters and restorative spa, Vichy, located in the northern Auvergne, was the site of the client state set up by the Germans during World War II. Never recognized by the Allies and not totally satisfying to the Germans either, the Vichy government could not prevent the worst Nazi atrocity committed on French soil. On 10 June 1944 a German SS division smoke-bombed a church at Oradour-sur-Glane, near Limoges, killing 642 villagers who had gathered there for refuge, most of them women and children.

Further Reading: Hugh D. Clout, *The Massif Central,* Oxford: Oxford University Press, 1973.

MEDITERRANEAN SEA

The world's largest inland sea occupies a deep trench between Europe and Africa. About six and a half million years ago, this sea was dry land. The Tethys Sea, which preceded the Mediterranean, came into existence as a result of the Alpine orogeny (ca. 44 million years B.P.). At present, the Atlantic Ocean spills over an underwater ledge connecting Spain and Morocco at the **Strait of Gibraltar.** The distinctive assemblage of plants and animals in the Mediterranean basin owes as much to this bottlenecking at Gibraltar as to the effects of insular location.

The tectonically active Mediterranean comprises several major divisions: the Aegean Sea east of Greece; the Adriatic Sea between Italy and the Dalmatian Coast; the Tyrrhenian and Ionian Seas in the mid-Mediterranean (separated by the **Strait of Messina**); and the Ligurian Sea

have likewise provided obvious control points, whether for military or trading purposes, but these water gateways have more difficult currents than those that prevail at Gibraltar. The Messina chokepoint between Sicily and mainland Italy is notorious for tricky currents produced by the narrowing of the waters.

Ancient civilizations flourished on the margins of the Mediterranean Sea and its

Seawall, agricultural terraces, and beach in the Cinque Terre (five towns) region on the West Italian coast south of Genoa *(photo by Jesse Walker).*

in the northwestern part of the basin along the French-Italian border.

The Mediterranean Sea is more saline than the Atlantic, and as a result, its water is heavier. This sets up a circulation pattern in which lighter Atlantic waters enter the sea at the surface near Gibraltar, while heavier, saline waters flow out of the basin at depth. The eastward-flowing (surface) current at Gibraltar has been less of a factor in history than the possibility of strategic control of the constriction. Connections to the **Black Sea** through the **Dardanelles** and the **Bosporus** straits

islands. The eastern Mediterranean, in particular, was the focus of early maritime civilizations, which were the most advanced cultures of their time, at least in the Western world. Phoenicia, Minoan Crete, Mycenae, and ancient Greece represented significant advances on the older, land-based civilizations of Mesopotamia and Egypt. The new maritime societies depended more on trading; their cultures and populations were more cosmopolitan, and their peoples were eager to adopt innovations and to expand into new areas of settlement.

Between 750 B.C. and 550 B.C. the seafaring Greeks extended their influence into the western part of the Mediterranean basin, planting colonies in Sicily, southern Italy, and as far west as the coastlands of France and Spain. The Mediterranean had a number of physical advantages that benefited the mariner as he traveled westward. The shoreline is highly indented, especially along the northern margin of the

Nostrum (Our Sea). Later Byzantine, Arab, and Norman attempts at political dominance fell short of the earlier Roman success, and visions of a reunited Europe on the model of the Roman Empire have exerted a not always salutary effect on the imaginations of European leaders. With the discovery and colonization of the Americas, major trade lanes, which had crossed the Mediterranean connecting the

A view of Genoa near the head of the Ligurian Sea, an arm of the Mediterranean, showing how the houses rise from the port *(photo by Jesse Walker).*

basin, which provided numerous sheltered beaches for harbors. The clear, sunny weather during the summer sailing season, from March to November, is almost ideal. Tides and major currents are virtually absent; yet moderate sea and land breezes can be relied on. Lacking compass and charts, sailors employed point-to-point navigation, which was made relatively easy by the high relief of the coastline and excellent visibility, at least from June to November.

During the period of the Roman Empire, nearly the entire basin was controlled by the Latins, who called it Mare

Orient to the lands of Europe, were reoriented toward the Atlantic. The opening of the Suez Canal (1869) and the discovery and exploitation of Middle East oil in the twentieth century have made the Mediterranean again into an important trade artery, though lacking the dominance it once enjoyed. The region's importance as a trade link and as a route for attack on Europe led to major campaigns to control its coasts and islands during both world wars.

Further Reading: David Attenborough, *The First Eden: The Mediterranean World and Man,* London: Collins/BBC Books, 1987.

MESETA (SPANISH)

The great heart of interior Spain consists of extensive plateaus and high plains surrounded and occasionally interrupted by long narrow mountain ranges. Though a somewhat barren landscape, it is yet the core area of the modern nation-state.

At an average elevation of 2,000 feet (610 meters), the Meseta (Spanish for tableland) covers almost three-fourths of the country. It extends from the Cantabrians in the north as far as the Sierra Morena in the south, beyond which is the historic province of **Andalusia.** The Meseta is an immense, uplifted fault block of ancient rocks, exposed toward the west but covered by younger sedimentary formations, notably limestone, in the east. The rocks have either been worn down to a peneplain (almost a plain) or deposited in horizontal levels in the first place, so that broad expanses of nearly level terrain are the norm. The major divisions of the region include Old Castile, a province drained by the Duero (Douro) in the northwest; New Castile, drained by the Tagus to the southeast, including the modern capital, Madrid; the Central Sierras, forming a horizontal divide between Old and New Castile; and the western border area of Estremadura.

The barrenness of the terrain in interior Spain has almost certainly been aggravated by centuries of improvident land use, particularly the historic emphasis on sheep grazing. The basin was originally clothed with a mixed Mediterranean forest including oak, but the woods were long ago removed to feed the foundries and to extend the limits of arable and pasture land. Patches of forest exist at higher elevations in the sierras, but even here much of it is a result of replanting that the Spanish government has undertaken since the late nineteenth century.

In the Middle Ages, Castilian rulers strongly encouraged pastoralism based on sheepherding. The long, fine, white wools of the Merino sheep had become the primary Spanish export, replacing coarse English wool in the textile centers of northern Italy and the Low Countries. (The famous breed originated in central Spain and was later brought to Argentina, Vermont, and elsewhere.) In 1273, Castilian sheepmasters formed the association of the Mesta to control movement of sheep across the interior parts of Spain. From the Middle Ages until the coming of the railroad, the sheep followed well-defined tracks, known as *canadas,* between high, cool summer pastures in the sierras and winter pastures in the lowlands. These traditional routeways extended all the way from the Cantabrians to Andalusia. Though not unique to Spain, seasonal movement of sheep was most pronounced in Iberia, with Castile reporting 3,450,000 sheep at what might have been its peak in the 1520s. It might be remembered that Don Quixote, a chivalrous but somewhat myopic knight, not only tilted at windmills but also attacked the Mesta's sheep, believing them to be an army of infidels.

Full blame for the barrenness of central Spain cannot be placed on the Merino sheep, however. The dissolution of the Mesta in 1836 resulted in increased peasant cultivation of former woodlands and pastures, and after only a few good years of harvest, the thin Mediterranean soils were depleted of their nutrients and yields declined. The impoverished look of the rural landscape in interior Spain may have had as much to do with the relatively recent extension of arable lands as to the overgrazing of the great flocks of sheep that existed during Castile's Golden Age.

Located in the northern part of the Meseta, the historic provinces of Old

Castile and León are sometimes referred to as the shell of central Spain. In the Middle Ages they alternately conquered one another until 1188, when Castile established hegemony over León under Alfonso VIII, followed by the union of the two crowns by Ferdinand III in 1230. Subsequently, a united front was established against the Moors, who were slowly driven southward. By the mid-thirteenth century, Castile's *Reconquista* extended as far as Andalusia, and consequently Castile became identified with all of Spain, which it proceeded to unify. The creation of modern Spain was completed by 1512, when Castile annexed part of Navarre after previously uniting with Aragon.

Today Old Castile gives the appearance not only of a land out of the distant past, but of a land long passed by. Yet its capital, Burgos, has some fine examples of decorative display, for example the elaborate Gothic cathedral containing the tomb of the national hero, Rodrigo Díaz de Vivar—better known as El Cid—who gained fame fighting the Moors. Salamanca boasts the oldest university in Spain (est. 1218), one of the first in western Europe.

The Central Sierras of Guadarrama and Gredos are a southwest-northeast trending range separating Old and New Castile. Presenting a steep face toward Old Castile, the massif, consisting of ancient granites and schists of the Meseta platform, slopes more gradually to the southeast in the direction of Madrid, the capital of Spain, which lies at the foot of the Guadarrama. With power and riches so concentrated in this great capital, no other Spanish city has been able to achieve greater population or influence. Madrid (and New Castile generally) illustrates the importance of relative isolation and centrality in the formation of modern European nation-states. Philip II chose it

as his capital and built a massive granite palace nearby, the Escorial, not because it had access to natural resources or navigable waterways, but because it lies in the center of Spain and could not easily be conquered from the coast. Unlike Italy, most of whose regions and cities are vulnerable to maritime attack, Spain benefited from the Meseta's valuable interior location in the subcontinental landmass of the Iberian Peninsula. Madrid's central position also allowed it to strategically control and eventually to unify outlying provinces. During Spain's golden age, Madrid was the most important city in Europe, and in the reign of Philip IV the city had more than 100,000 inhabitants.

Toledo, lying just south of Madrid, was eclipsed in modern times by the latter city, but its roles as an Islamic center of learning and as a bridge between the Gothic north and the Moorish south permanently safeguard this city's cultural importance.

The heart of Spain may appear barren, but this very austerity has shaped the Spanish national character, with its combination of rugged virtue, courage, and (some would say) brutality, best displayed during the *Reconquista* and the settlement of Latin America. No region of New Castile so well illustrates the difficulty of the terrain as the barren limestone tableland of La Mancha basin, located to the southeast. The legendary primitiveness of its inhabitants and poverty of its land did not prevent Cervantes from making it the home of his celebrated hero Don Quixote.

To the west, on the border with Portugal, is Estremadura. Its southern part, Badajoz, was once a rich granary for the Romans, and it remains an important agricultural region today. Here the Romans also located their Lusitanian capital, Emerita Augusta (now Merida). The northern region of Cáceres, which has a granite bedrock and poor soils, is best known as the homeland of many important American conquistadores, many of whom later returned to embellish their native province and hometowns.

Further Reading: R. Aitken, "Routes of Transhumance on the Spanish Meseta," *Geographical Journal* 106 (1945), pp. 59–62.

MESSINA, STRAIT OF

This narrow waterway between Sicily and peninsular Italy, joining the Tyrrhenian and Ionian Seas, has historically been a key control point in the mid-**Mediterranean.** From the Punic Wars to the invasion of Sicily in World War II, the Strait of Messina (anc. Fretum Siculum) has been an important strategic and military corridor as well as a focus of trade. Across the strait from the mainland lies Sicily, the largest island in the Mediterranean Basin and a stepping-stone between Africa and Europe. (Sicily has been well described as a football being kicked by the Italian boot between Europe and Africa). The strait thus guards not only a crucial position between the eastern and western parts of the Basin but also lies astride a vital north-south axis.

The relatively shallow waters (around 300 feet, or 91 meters, at the narrowest point) combine with the constricted passageway (from two to ten miles, or 3.2 to 16.1 kilometers, wide) to produce the tricky currents so dreaded by ancient mariners. Flanked by crystalline masses on either side, the strait occupies a fault zone that is prone to earthquakes, the most serious in recent times having occurred in 1908, when the town of Messina (on the Sicilian side) was totally destroyed. The much-feared monsters Scilla and Charybdis of classical mythology occupied this site, with the rock of Scilla on the Calabrian coast, and the

Charybdis whirlpool, on the Sicilian side, believed to be the Garafola current off the Messina harbor.

The northern entrance to the strait is guarded by the Lipari Islands, including the active volcanic island of Stromboli, whose intermittent flashes, visible from the strait, have earned it the sobriquet "Lighthouse of the Mediterranean." The Greeks named one of the islands in this group Vulcano, a name today reserved for the generic feature, because they believed the forge of the mythological smithy Vulcan was located beneath the island's volcanic cone. In Greek mythology, Aeolus ruled the winds from these islands, which are thus also called the Aeolian Islands. Ulysses came here in his wanderings. The Greeks settled the islands, and the Romans—though leery of them—used them as a place of exile.

The northern entrance to the strait is almost entirely concealed. This is the result of an overlap between a promontory of the coast of Sicily at the Cape of Faro (Punta del Faro) in northeastern Sicily and on the opposite shore just to the south the rocky "corn" of Scilla Rock, which extends the coastline of the Italian toe. Legend has it that Hannibal, while escaping from the Romans, had difficulty finding the entrance to the strait, so he sacrificed his native pilot Pelorus, only to round, a moment too late, the Cape of Faro. The cape was called Promontorium Pelorum after the unfortunate pilot, and Hannibal reputedly erected a monument in his honor at the site.

The port of Messina has benefited from its location alongside the strait. The town was founded by the Greeks around 730 B.C. It was originally named *Zancle,* or Sickle, due to its natural sickle-shaped harbor. Later, colonists from the **Peloponnesian** district of Messenia renamed it after their homelands. The town of Reggio de Calabria just opposite Messina derives its name from the Greek word meaning torn apart or split, referring to the break between the island of Sicily and mainland Italy. Destroyed by the Carthaginians in 397 B.C., Messina subsequently was involved in the wars between Carthage and Syracuse before Rome stepped in, backing the mercenary Mamertines (men of Mars) and triggering the first of the Punic Wars. Messina became the Roman free city of Messana in 241 B.C.

With the collapse of the Roman Empire, Messina fell to the Byzantine emperor (A.D. 535), was later taken by the Saracens (A.D. 831), and finally, was liberated by the Normans (A.D. 1061). Under a strong, centralized government imposed by the Normans, similar to that established in England after the Conquest, Messina shared in the general prosperity of Sicily at the time. Messina became an important entrepôt between the East and West, a center of learning and a meeting-place of Islamic and Christian cultures, Arab and European traditions. Politically under the influence subsequently of the Crusaders, the Angevin kingdom, the Aragonese, and after 1735, the Spanish Bourbon ruler of the Kingdom of the Two Sicilies (i.e., Naples and Sicily), Messina eventually became part of unified Italy in 1860. The crossing of the strait in August 1860 by Garibaldi—a sort of peasant George Washington—in advance of his march northward is a much-celebrated event in modern Italian history, and its depiction bears comparison with the famous crossing of the Delaware by Washington.

The Sicilian campaign in World War II ended with the taking of Messina by the Allies on 17 August 1943. Despite the great antiquity of the city, most of its structures are of recent vintage. To the damage of the earthquakes of 1783 and 1908, which was almost total, must be added the effects of intensive bombing during World War II. Nevertheless, the city has been fully restored, with great attention being given to traditional architectural styles—perhaps most notably exemplified by its Norman-style Romanesque cathedral (rebuilt after 1908).

Further Reading: Joel Cook, *The Mediterranean and Its Borderlands,* vol. 1, Philadelphia: John C. Winston, 1910, pp. 525–545.

MEXICAN PLATEAU

This tilted block that lies a mile or more above sea level is one of the largest landform units in Middle America and one of the most significant in terms of human settlement. Elevations are greatest to the south, where the plateau's surface rises above 8,000 feet (2,438 meters), but as one travels north from Mexico City, near the plateau's northern edge, elevations descend to less than 4,000 feet (1,219 meters) at El Paso on the Mexican-U.S. border. The northern section of the upland, sometimes called Mesa del Norte, is arid and best suited to ranching, whereas south of about San Luis Potosí (22°N) there is a gradual blending into a higher and more humid environment. The southern rim of this Mesa Central is formed by high, widely spaced volcanic peaks, including Citlaltépetl, the highest elevation in Mexico at 18,700 feet (5,700 meters), Popocatépetl, and Ixtacihuatl. The northern plateau has few permanent streams, and on the eastern side desert basins (*bolsones*) flanked by alluvial gravels and rock pediments form plains between the ranges. The plateau is fringed by two mountain ranges, the **Sierra Madre Oriental** (to the east) and the **Sierra Madre Occidental** (to the west). Although the Tropic of Cancer passes through the center of Mexico, altitude rather than latitude is the primary determinant of the various Mexican climates, with recognizable vertical zones of tierra caliente, templada, and fria associated with hot, temperate, and cool temperature regimes.

The Mesa Central is the heart of Mexico. Comprising eroded remnants of ancient volcanoes and intervening flat-floored basins, this region has attracted advanced cultures of Mexican Indians as

on the west side of Lake Texcoco around 1250, and according to legend built their capital, Tenochtitlán, at a place directed to them by their god Huitzilopochtli, where they found a cactus on which sat an eagle eating a snake. An eagle-and-snake design can be found on the various issues of Mexican coinage.

The marshy site of the Aztec capital may not seem to have been propitious, yet wild-

A cone-shaped granary on a farmstead near Mazapil (Zacatecas state) on the eastern edge of the Mexican Plateau *(photo by Robert C. West)*.

well as the conquering Spaniards, who rightly viewed it as the strategic center of Mexican life. Since prehistoric days the basins have been the most culturally significant of the plateau's landforms. Although the Mayans preferred the coastal lowlands and the **Yucatán Peninsula**, the transitional Toltecs and the Indians encountered by the Spanish, the Aztecs, favored the southern parts of the Mexican plateau, especially the oval-shaped valley (actually, basin) of the Valley of Mexico, which includes the site of present-day Mexico City. The Aztecs settled an island

fowl from the lakes and rich, silty soils on the adjacent volcanic slopes and basin flats benefited the region. The preconquest population of the Aztec capital has been estimated at 300,000. In 1521 Hernán Cortés conquered the Aztec empire, leveled the old city, and constructed the colonial Spanish town of Mexico City, with its plazas, parks, and broad avenues. On the site of the main Aztec temple, Cortés built in 1525 the first Christian church in North America, later replaced by a cathedral.

The broad, shallow lakes of the Mesa Central's basins have been growing smaller since the Pleistocene epoch, the glacial period in the Tropics being associated with pluvials, or wet periods. To accommodate urban expansion, artificial drainage of the lakes has been undertaken, especially since the nineteenth century, so that, for instance, all five of the original lakes of the Valley of Mexico have disappeared. Many of the poorer residential areas of Mexico City are on the dry, windblown flats.

Important basins away from Mexico City include those of Toluca and Puebla, flanking the capital, and farther west, Morelia and Guadalajara. The eastern and central portions of the Mesa Central form the core area of the Mexican nation, being the site of dense concentrations of Indian and mestizo populations, major food-producing areas, prehistoric centers of the Aztec and Tarascan states, and the political and economic capital of both colonial New Spain and modern Mexico.

Further Reading: Carl O. Sauer, "The Personality of Mexico," Geographical Review 31 (1941), pp. 353–364; Robert Wauchope and Robert C. West, "Surface Configuration and Associated Geology of Middle America," in Wauchope and West, eds., Handbook of Middle American Indians, Vol. I: Natural Environment and Early Cultures, Austin: University of Texas Press, 1964, pp. 33–83; Eric R. Wolf, Sons of the Shaking Earth, Chicago: University of Chicago Press, 1959.

MISSISSIPPI RIVER VALLEY

The combined Missouri-Mississippi River extends about 3,759 miles (6,049 kilometers), from the Missouri's headwaters in the Rocky Mountains to the river's outlet south of New Orleans, and ranks as the third longest river in the world, behind the Nile and the Amazon. The river is navigable from South Pass, a dredged channel in the Bird Foot Delta, as far north as the Falls of St. Anthony in Minneapolis. Oceangoing ships can reach Baton Rouge, beyond

which access is restricted to shallow draft barges and towboats. At its northern end the Mississippi is connected to the **Great Lakes**–St. Lawrence Seaway via the Illinois Waterway, while in the south the Intracoastal Waterway, paralleling the Gulf Coast, joins the river at several places in southern Louisiana. The course of the upper river above St. Louis descends a series of falls and rapids. The Army Corps of Engineers, the primary federal agency responsible for flood control and navigation on the river, has constructed a number of locks—essentially, gigantic water staircases—to maintain navigability. Below Cairo, Illinois, the river widens noticeably as it receives its most important eastern tributary, the Ohio. From Cape Girardeau, Missouri, to Natchez, Mississippi, the meandering river has created a broad alluvial plain stretching more than a hundred miles across. Numerous oxbow lakes and meander scars, with place-names like Old River and False River, testify to the broad belt of the shifting river. Sediment is not only deposited along its banks, building natural levees, but on the riverbed, so that the river is elevated above the level of the surrounding plain, as evidenced by the St. Francis, Yazoo, and Tensas Basins.

Since around A.D. 1500, the Mississippi has emptied into the Gulf of Mexico through the Bird Foot or Balize Delta, a landform extended out from the mouth of the river by sedimentation at the low-energy river mouth. The most recently abandoned delta is the Lafourche (pronounced La-FOOSH) Delta in present-day Lafourche and Terrebonne Parishes. The river emptied into the Gulf at this position, west of the current outlet, from about 1200–1700, so there was a two-century period or so when the river had two mouths. Older yet, the St. Bernard Delta east of New Orleans is highly fragmented and eroded because it hasn't received land-building sediments since the time of the Crusades. However, when Jesus walked the hills of Galilee and preached to simple fishermen, the Mississippi River was emptying into the Gulf of Mexico through the St. Bernard Delta.

The Atchafalaya River connects to the Mississippi above Baton Rouge by way of Old River. Since the Atchafalaya route to the Gulf is shorter than the current route

when the Atchafalaya Basin would act as a giant spillway to protect the urban, industrial corridor between Baton Rouge and New Orleans. A nearly disastrous collapse of the Old River Control Structure in a 1973 flood led to the construction of the Auxiliary Structure, completed in 1986, at a cost of $206 million.

The Spanish explorer Hernando de Soto was the first European to see the

A Mississippi River gauge at Vicksburg, Mississippi *(photo by Jesse Walker).*

past Baton Rouge and New Orleans (155 miles or 249 kilometers via the Atchafalaya River; 325 miles or 523 kilometers by the present route), the Mississippi, if allowed to flow freely, eventually would take the shorter Atchafalaya route. In order to prevent the natural rerouting of the Mississippi and maintain the status quo, the Army Corps built the Old River Control Structure (completed in 1962). Congress mandates that no more than 30 percent of the Mississippi flow should pass down the Atchafalaya, except in the event of a Century Flood (probability of one in 100),

river, which he crossed near Memphis in 1541 and named the Río del Espiritu Santu because he discovered it on the Catholic Feast of the Holy Spirit. The river retained this name for another century and a half before the French renamed it after an Algonquin Indian term meaning great stream. The French missionary-explorer team of Father Jacques Marquette and Louis Joliet pioneered the portage route across central Wisconsin linking the Fox River, which drains into Green Bay on the western side of Lake Michigan, to the Wisconsin River, which flows first south then west to the Mississippi. Following this route, Marquette and Joliet discovered the Mississippi River in 1673, descending as far as its confluence with the Arkansas River. In 1682 the French fur trader and explorer Robert de la Salle, starting from the southern end of Lake Michigan where Chicago is today, and crossing the low divide to the Illinois River, traveled the entire length of the

to mean the land west of the river as far as the **Continental Divide,** with the single important exception of the **Isle of Orleans,** containing New Orleans, which is on the left or east bank. The French did not make a serious attempt to settle the region until the founding of New Orleans in 1718, and even then colonization was slow and lackadaisical, compared to the rapid growth of the Anglo populations

A U.S. postal-issue five-cent stamp, 1966, showing the Great River Road, which extends 5,600 miles (9,016 kilometers) from Kenora, Ontario, to New Orleans, Louisiana *(courtesy of the American Numismatic Association).*

river to its mouth and claimed the territory for his monarch, Louis XIV, the Sun King. He could not have known when he named this land that it constituted 42 percent of the area of what would one day be known as the lower 48 states and included all the land from the Rocky Mountains to the Appalachians. Because English traders and settlers had already begun to move west of the mountains and had effective possession of much of the land east of the Mississippi, the French claim to Louisiana came to be interpreted

along the eastern seaboard in the colonies of Virginia and Massachusetts.

Much American history and frontier development took place along the mighty Mississippi: the romance of keelboats and flatboats descending the Western waters with foodstuffs to be used by Southern plantation owners; the rise of steamboats after 1811 permitting movement both ways on the river; the use of the Mississippi as an avenue of penetration by Federal troops during the Civil War, which divided the Confederacy in two; the disastrous effects of that war, with river traffic only attaining its prewar levels in the following century. To get a firsthand account of those times, one could do worse than consult one of America's greatest writers, Mark Twain (Samuel Clemens), who in his *Life on the Mississippi* (1883) drew a marvelous portrait of his early experiences as an apprentice pilot on the river. Since the 1950s, the river has carried—slowly, but cheaply—an increasing amount of heavy cargo. Petroleum products, chemicals, sand and gravel, limestone, and agricultural commodities, especially corn and soybeans, provide the bulk of this traffic. A 220-acre (89-hectare) model of the Mississippi Basin is located at Clinton, Mississippi, where the U.S. Army Corps of Engineers simulates various conditions on the river.

Further Reading: John M. Barry, *Rising Tide: The Great Mississippi Flood of 1927 and How It Changed America,* New York: Simon and Schuster, 1997; Timothy Severin, *Explorers of the Mississippi,* New York: Knopf, 1968.

MOHAWK VALLEY

This fertile corridor cutting across the northern Appalachians is perhaps the preeminent example of a nineteenth-century American region that experienced commercial agricultural development and rapid urban growth on the basis of transport innovation.

The Mohawk River rises in central New York, flows south and then southeast nearly 140 miles (225 kilometers), past Utica and Schenectady, to enter the Hudson River at Cohoes. In the early nineteenth century, the flow of westward migration from the agriculturally restricted zones of the Atlantic Seaboard, especially New England, funneled through the Mohawk Valley, the only breach in the rugged Appalachians of western Pennsylvania and upstate New York. This region

is properly known as the Appalachian Plateau, though northerners are more likely to call it the Alleghenies (and southerners, the Cumberlands), and its topography contrasts with the Ridge and Valley and Piedmont provinces of the Appalachians.

West of Utica, an array of attractive settlements fan out among the glacial lakes and fertile valleys. Among the valleys is the famous Genesee Country, which encompasses the fertile Genesee River, flowing south to north across the western part of the state, as well as the lakes in the district. The Falls provided a good site for milling agricultural produce, and Rochester was a flour-mill city before the arrival of the canal and railroad, or later, the Eastman Kodak and Xerox corporations. The Genesee Road led west from Utica along the southern rim of the valley to Geneva and Canandaigua.

The valley's history presents a classic example of sequential transportation innovation. The Mohawk Trail, the old Indian footpaths traced by the native tribes of the Iroquois Confederacy, gave way to a series of private turnpike roads built during the colonial period. These efforts in turn were supplanted by what has been called the most ambitious and successful state-funded project in U.S. history—the Erie Canal. Built between 1817 and 1825, the canal links the **Great Lakes** at Buffalo to the Hudson River and the New York portal, stimulating by its 90-percent reduction in freight costs (and 50-percent savings in time) not only upstate New York and the growth of New York City, which quickly surpassed Philadelphia as the nation's preeminent metropolis, but also the settlement of the Great Lakes plains. The legendary Erie Canal inspired a wave of canal building across the country, as far west as the states of Wisconsin and Illinois. Not until midcentury did the canal mania subside. The purchase of steam passage at Buffalo allowed a traveler to reach Chicago, at the eastern edge of the fertile prairies, within a single day instead of the week it took by overland route. Midwestern farmers and entrepreneurs found that they had a more efficient and dependable market in the growing eastern seaboard cities linked to them by the Erie Canal than in their southern outlet via New Orleans.

The Erie Canal was first and foremost a state effort. The canal paralleled the Mohawk Valley as far as Seneca. Farther west, it was an entirely artificial waterway cutting into the low southern shoreline of Lake Ontario. The enterprising New York state governor, DeWitt Clinton, proceeded with the ambitious project despite rejection from Washington, where he first went for funding, and the reluctance—though eventual endorsement—of risk-averse English investors.

This piece of Americana, with its mule-drawn canal boats, neat towpaths, and locks constructed of local limestone did not seem assured of success at its start. Nor was the path of the canal dictated by nature alone. The shortest route to the Great Lakes from the Hudson valley was via the Oswego River to the town of the same name on Lake Ontario. Although a feeder canal would later be built along this route, the main stem canal took a longer, western route to reach Lake Erie at a site that its promoter hoped would be named New Amsterdam (a deliberate attempt to flatter his backers) but that has always gone by the name of a small watercourse—Buffalo Creek—at the site of the city. This longer route followed by the Erie Canal avoided British-controlled Lake Ontario and reached the Great Lakes above Niagara Falls. Governor Clinton began his canal at Rome, where flat land permitted easy going. (Classical

place-names are sprinkled across upstate New York, reflecting the high-mindedness and classical education of many transplanted New Englanders.) The first segment of the canal, connecting Utica with the Seneca River, was opened in 1819. Though helped by English capital and expertise, the Americans characteristically adapted seat-of-the-pants solutions as problems arose. New ways of toppling giant trees were devised, and cements were concocted using local materials.

The first railroads generally followed the pattern of earlier, water-based systems of transportation. In New York, the Mohawk & Hudson (1832) was a short portage railroad, bypassing the Cohoes Falls near the Mohawk's confluence with the Hudson. The New York Central railroad would follow a circuitous route, passing through Albany, Syracuse, and Rochester as well as servicing many small towns that grew up along the canal. The route of the New York Central was chosen according to the traffic-serving function: The maximum amount of freight required a long route, linking as many towns as possible. The connection between New York and Buffalo made by the New York & Erie followed a minimization principle: The best route linked the two cites in as direct and short a route as possible to minimize the costs of construction. In 1852 these two rail lines not only actively competed but operated at different gauges.

The Erie Canal today is part of the New York State Barge Canal System, but its canals are too shallow and narrow to handle today's large ships. In 1930 another New York governor, Franklin D. Roosevelt, crossed the state during a reelection campaign in a canal boat. Not wanting to display his handicap (Roosevelt was confined to a wheelchair by polio), he stayed on the boat, while his energetic wife Eleanor mingled with the crowds that had assembled along the canal. The governor promised that, if elected (which he was), he would call for the federal government to widen and deepen the canal. Two years later when he was elected U.S. president, he conveniently forgot his promise, as the national economy was in a depression, and the railroad companies, near bankruptcy, did not want their rivals strengthened.

See also: Appalachian Piedmont; Blue Ridge.
Further Reading: D. W. Meinig, *The Shaping of America: A Geographical Perspective on 500 Years of History,* vol. 2, *Continental America, 1800–1867,* New Haven: Yale University Press, 1993.

MYCENAE
See Peloponnese

NICARAGUAN RIFT

At the middle of the Central American landmass is a crustal fracture or rift that forms the lowlands of Nicaragua. The largest lakes in Central America or Mexico—Lakes Nicaragua and Managua—occupy the central portion of this northwest-southeast-trending depression.

In 1522 the first Spanish explorer in the region, Gil González Dávila, inferred from the freshness of the water in Lake Nicaragua that it drained to the sea, and named the outlet (that is, today's San Juan River) Desaguadero, the Spanish term for a drainage outlet. The following year, the town of Grenada was founded at the north end of the lake. It soon became the focus of trade and transshipment across the region. By combining the San Juan River, which today forms the political boundary between Nicaragua and Costa Rica, whose outlet is on the Caribbean side, the two large lakes, and the narrow Isthmus of Rivas on the Pacific side, an efficient, mostly water-borne transisthmian route was conceived, though this route was little used in colonial times. The Spanish established ports at both ends of the route; but cataracts along the San Juan, in conjunction with hostile Indian tribes (e.g., the Miskitos) spurred on by the British, and conflicts with an assorted group of pirates and privateers—the two were scarcely distinguishable—lessened the importance of this interoceanic transport route.

To the northwest of the Nicaraguan lakes lies an extensive, fertile plain whose soils derive from the ash spewed from nearby volcanoes. This was a densely populated region even before the Spanish conquest, and it became a granary of the Spanish New World empire, sending corn, pork, and poultry down the Desaguadero and receiving African slaves and Spanish manufactured goods upriver.

One can infer that the Nicaraguan rift valley was not used as a primary means of bridging the isthmus from the fact that during the colonial period Peru did not receive Nicaraguan foodstuffs by the most direct route, west to the Pacific port of Realejo and thence by ship to Peru, but instead from the east, down the San Juan to Nombre de Dios (later Portobelo), on the Caribbean side of the **Panama Isthmus,** and then across Panamá to the south. It has been suggested that the hazards of navigation in the Gulf of Papagayos on the Pacific side may account for the disuse of the crossing. (Papagayos are strong offshore winds that combined with turbulent currents to make navigation treacherous.) A more reasonable explanation is that the Spanish never tapped the potential of this crossing because their highly regulated, mercantilist empire did not primarily try to rationalize transport systems any more than it revolutionized production. The Spanish never worried about least-cost transport routes and therefore never developed any.

It took the California gold rush in the mid-nineteenth century and no less a person than Cornelius Vanderbilt, the railroad and shipping magnate, to develop the isthmus's prospects and increase its traffic by signing a contract in 1849 to open a shipping canal across Nicaragua, providing transit between the oceans. The uncomfortable though colorful route combined lake steamers, river boats (large, shallow draft dugout canoes or *bongos*), and horseback, cutting short the long haul around **Cape Horn** to the gold fields. The young San Francisco newspaperman Samuel Langhorne Clemens (Mark Twain) traveled this Nicaraguan route on his way east to regale the big-city folk with his western yarns.

NORDEN

The name Scandinavia, referring to the northernmost lands of Europe, is of relatively recent date. The name first appeared in Pliny's *Natural History*, but it was a misspelling of Scadinavia, the name then assigned to Skåne, the southernmost province of Sweden, which Pliny believed was an island. The term does not appear at all during the medieval and early modern periods, and it was not until the eighteenth century that it began to be commonly used.

The term Scandinavia today has two primary meanings: the double peninsula consisting of Norway and Sweden (a restricted geographic meaning); and places of Scandinavian culture, especially defined in terms of the prevalence of north Germanic tongues, including Denmark, Sweden, Norway, the Faeroe Islands, and Iceland. In the latter sense, Finland is not part of Scandinavia, since its language is

non-Indo-European, although its shared history and geographical proximity often result in it being included in descriptions of the nearby countries. Perhaps because of these complexities and the commonness of multilingualism in the area, natives often use the appellation Norden, or Nordic Europe, to comprehend all of northern Europe.

The origins of the names of the three central countries of Norden shed light on their geographies. Norway's name derives from the Anglo-Saxon Norweg, or Northern Way, referring to the protected coastal route on this country's western side, which is sheltered by numerous small, low, offshore islands (skerries).

Denmark (Danish march) is an ironic but nevertheless geographically revealing name. In the medieval period Denmark controlled both sides of the Øresund, and thereby ruled over the southern parts of present-day Sweden. This frontier region, now Swedish Skåne, originally was referred to as Denmark, meaning the Danish frontier. Somehow the latter name's meaning changed with time to refer to the Danish archipelago and the **Jutland** peninsula rather than the northern frontier.

Sweden's name relates more to its earliest peoples than to relative position. The Svear were a north Germanic tribe occupying the coastal areas of eastern Sweden in and around Uppland. The country's name today is Sverige. An alternative explanation of the origin of Sweden's name is that it is a corruption of *zwerijke* (two realms), referring to the division between the Svear and the Götar, the latter occupying lands to the west (i.e., Götaland), in the direction of present-day Norway. Or perhaps there was a division among the Svear?

By the sixth century A.D., the Svear had conquered the Götar, and these two people merged to become the dominant nationality in the region. Breaking away from the late medieval political pact of the Kalmar Union (1397–1523) was a necessary condition for the rise of a strong Swedish monarchy under the Vasa dynasty. In the seventeenth century, Sweden controlled territory in northern Germany, northern Poland, and the Baltic republics, and in 1660 it

encircling rimlands, all of diverse ages and varying characteristics. These segments of terrain are not, however, airtight compartments lacking exchange and social interaction. Accessibility has been guaranteed by the presence of low hills, Alpine passes, the dense pattern of rivers, deeply indented coastlines, and long peninsulas. All have permitted relatively easy movement among the regions of Europe. The

Medieval Stave Church, a Norwegian national symbol, in western Norway on the road from Oslo to Bergen *(photo by Jesse Walker).*

recovered its southern provinces from Denmark.

See also: Danish Straits.
Further Reading: Birgit and Peter Sawyer, *Medieval Scandinavia: From Conversion to Reformation, circa 800–1500,* Minneapolis: University of Minnesota Press, 1993.

NORMANDY
See Armorican Massif

NORTH EUROPEAN PLAIN
Much of Europe has an intricate topography of hills and mountains, basins and

resulting pattern is a complex patchwork, not of independent cells depending upon themselves alone but an organismic interaction, with trade and migration encouraged by the terrain's moderate relief and its maritime accessibility.

Stretching across northern Europe in a broad belt from west to east, all the way from the North Sea to the Urals, is an extensive plain of nearly level, young sedimentary rocks and recent, unconsolidated sediments laid down by rivers, melting glaciers, and fluctuating coastlines. Sedimentary rocks of varying resistance to erosion dip slightly in the direction of the sea. Exposed to the processes of weathering and erosion, the upturned edges of these rocks form characteristic steep escarpments (scarps) and gentle back slopes (dip slopes) in classic cuesta form. This is best seen in southern England and northern France, which are connected by a chalk (limestone) layer that has been submerged by rising sea levels since the melting of the Pleistocene ice sheets. Although the resulting scarp-and-vale landscape is similar in England and France, the geographic pattern is different: In France the scarps, known as côtes, take the form of partial concentric rings, while in England they adopt a hub-and-spoke pattern centered on **Salisbury Plain,** with ridges emanating outward from this somewhat eccentric center located west of London. The present coastlines of the North and Baltic Seas are only temporary boundaries between land and sea; sea levels have changed in the past, especially during the Pleistocene epoch (between about two million and ten thousand years ago) when the climate fluctuated repeatedly between cold periods of glacial advance (glacials) and intervening warm periods (interglacials). A regular sequence of marine transgression and coastal emergence occurred in response respectively to warming and cooling trends, and the character of the northern plains, especially in the coastal areas at its northern edge, reflects changing sea levels in response to climatic variation.

The European lowlands broaden toward the east, providing a natural corridor for travel and communication all the way from the Baltic and White Seas to the Black and Caspian. Narrow in northern France and western Germany, these plains compose the entire territory of Poland, except in the mountainous

Carpathians along its southern border. History has made Poland pay a price for its flatness. Accessible not just to traders but also to armies, Poland suffered a series of annexations in the late eighteenth century. A great kingdom in medieval times, Poland was parceled out in the nineteenth century among Russia, Germany, and Austria.

The Great Russian Plain is the eastern extension of these lowlands, stretching all the way to the **Urals,** the traditional though somewhat arbitrary division between Europe and Asia. It used to be said to visitors to Cambridge University, as they looked eastward from the low Gog Magog Hills, that no higher ground lay between them and the Urals. Drained by the three great south-flowing rivers of Russia—the **Dnieper,** the Don, and the Volga—Russia has escaped the fate of Poland and has not easily been overrun because of its vastness and its distance from other major power centers. It lies far enough from the European core—a shifting center of population and economic activity, but always far to the west of the Russian homelands—to maintain its independence, using the enormous natural resources at its disposal.

At the other geographic extreme, the lowlands in France form an irregular zone, sweeping around northern France and extending to the southwest in the **Aquitaine Basin,** a region drained by the Garonne and Dordogne Rivers, the numerous watercourses of which so impressed the Romans that they gave the region its name, meaning Land of Many Waters.

Prehistoric settlement and migrations avoided the northern lowlands due to their extensive marshes and the unbridged rivers of its major north-flowing watercourses—the Rhine, the Elbe, and the Vistula. Maritime and river penetration of prehistoric Europe was initially preferred. A few bold venturers must have made the "great sweep" from the east across the plains, but most early arrivals in prehistoric German lands followed the longer but easier transport route of the Danube as far as the headwaters of the Rhine, which could then be followed downriver.

The German borderlands (Ger. Börde), along the margin between the plains and the **Hercynian Uplands,** were the site of much rural settlement in prehistoric times, with towns like Münster, Hannover, Leipzig, and Dresden scattered here and there. In the Middle Ages, these market towns formed a kind of *Hochstrasse,* with a sequence of fairs moving from town to town on a regular schedule. Except for the ports located at or near the mouths of major rivers, the growth of which depended on long-distance trade, there were few cities in the sterile outwash (*Geest*) of the northern part of the German plain. The barren Lüneburger Heide, stretching south from Hamburg almost all the way to Hannover, is the best example of these extensive heath lands.

It is ironic that the core area in the unification of the German states in the late nineteenth century was Brandenburg, a southern extension of the plains in the vicinity of present-day Berlin. The poor soils of this region gave rise to its epithet as the "sandbox of Europe." It was from just such an agriculturally limited environment that the Prussian state expanded its territory first toward the west in the direction of the Rhine, then eastward as far as the present Baltic states.

Farther west, in the low countries of the Netherlands and Belgium, extensive outwash plains, glacial lakes, marshes, and interrupted drainage testify to the youthfulness of the terrain and glacial influences. Much of the land is only suitable for grazing and forestry, as in the sandy Campine on Belgium's eastern border or in the relatively infertile Netherlands province of Friesland, located east of IJsselmeer (Lake Ijssel). Extensive moraine lands in Holland, which are more likely to be below sea level than in Belgium, have been diked to produce reclaimed lands, known as polders. An emphasis on dairying in Holland represents a careful adjustment of land use to terrain, due to the fact that so much land is best left in pasture. Though the intelligence of Hollanders has sometimes been called into question with epithets like "cheese-mongers" (perhaps the origin of the playful but derogatory name "cheeseheads" for the residents of another dairy area, Wisconsin), the wise husbandry of resources practiced by the people of the Netherlands (and Wisconsin) indicates not backwardness but its opposite—a progressive application of knowledge to problems at hand, within the constraints of the environment.

See also: English Channel; Povolzhye.

NORTHEAST PASSAGE

While the Portuguese and Spanish sought southern sea routes to the Orient around South America and Africa, north Europeans naturally looked northward for routes penetrating or circumventing intervening landmasses. The search for a **Northwest Passage,** a navigable shortcut across northern Canada, attracted the most attention, and in hindsight, wasted the most resources. Although a water route of that name does exist, it was not traversed until the 1903–1906 expedition of the Norwegian explorer Roald Amundsen, and the passage is hardly the easily navigable route sought for centuries by dreamers and seamen.

English, Dutch, and Russian explorers, in similar fashion, sought a northeast route by sailing northward along the coasts of Scandinavia and Russia, far out into the Arctic. The English led the way in 1553, when Sir William Willoughby directed an expedition that rounded North Cape and reached as far as Archangel (in Russian, Arkhangelsk). Although blocked by polar ice, they did make contact with Russia, which led to the formation of the Muscovy Company

Barents Sea—represents a relatively open arm of the western Arctic Ocean northeast of Scandinavia. Farther east, the ocean is frozen most of the year and is only navigable without the assistance of icebreakers for a few months of the year, in summer.

Another Dutch navigator, Henry Hudson—better known today for the bay and river he discovered, which were named after him—also made several un-

Frost-weathered rocks in Norwegian Svalbard (Spitsbergen) *(photo by Jesse Walker)*.

of Merchants Adventurers, a trading company organized along lines that a half century later would be followed by the enormously successful British East India Company.

While Sir Martin Frobisher and John Davis probed the east coast of Canada, looking for a passage to India, the Dutch explorer Willem Barents made three voyages to Arctic waters in the 1590s, in search of a northeast passage, reaching as far as Bear Island in 1596–1597. After accidentally discovering Spitsbergen (Norwegian Svalbard), the last Barents expedition rounded Novaya Zemlya, which had been discovered and explored on the two previous voyages, but was caught in the ice. After the Arctic winter, the crew divided into two boats to head for the mainland, but Barents died on the way. The sea that bears the Dutch navigator's name—the

successful eastern voyages in search of the passage. With the decline of Dutch shipping by the 1700s, further exploration was left to the Russians. As early as the sixteenth century, Russian trips to the north coast, such as the Kara Sea Expedition, had revealed the value of the fur resources there. Expansion beyond the **Ural Mountains** into Siberia stimulated interest in the Arctic coast and the routes taken by the great north-flowing Siberian rivers. Vitus Bering, a Danish explorer in the employ of the Russians, was personally chosen by Peter the Great just before the czar's death to conduct an eastern voyage of discovery. Bering explored the eastern part of the interoceanic passageway in several expeditions between 1728 and 1741. The Russian Great Northern Expedition (1733–1743), overseen by Bering, was a large government project undertaken to survey and map the northern coast of Siberia.

It was not, however, until 1878–1879 that the northeast passage was first traversed, when the Swedish explorer Nils A. E. Nordenskjöld successfully accomplished the feat. Icebreakers navigated the route in the early 1900s. The Soviet Union in the 1930s established the Northern Sea Route, a shipping lane that

explore the eastern approaches to the passage (1576–1578). John Davis, an able seaman and navigator, secured merchant backing for several voyages (1585–1587) that reached as far as 63° N, and explored the coast of Baffin Island, but failed to penetrate Frobisher's "mistaken strait" (Hudson Bay). In 1610, the Dutch explorer Henry Hudson, sailing an English ship, reached the large bay named after

A statue of Norwegian explorer Roald Amundsen, the first navigator of the Northwest Passage (later the first to reach the South Pole), in Tromsö in arctic Norway *(photo by Jesse Walker)*.

cut the distance between Russian Atlantic and Pacific ports in half.

Further Reading: Constantine Krypton, *The Northern Sea Route: Its Place in Russian Economic History before 1917,* New York: Research Program on the U.S.S.R., 1953.

NORTHWEST PASSAGE

A water passageway around the northern margin of North America—actually a string of water bodies threading the Arctic Archipelago—really exists, but is hardly the accessible and lucrative "passage to India" that infected the imaginations of west Europeans for so many years.

The English explorer Sir Martin Frobisher is credited with being the first to

him and navigated down its eastern shore as far south as the deep pocket of James Bay, where in November his ship was iced in. In June of the next year, freed of the ice, Hudson appeared to want to head farther westward, but the mutinous crew set him and eight others adrift in a small boat, presumably sending them to their deaths.

The search for a northwest passage in the late sixteenth and early seventeenth centuries was a visionary commercial enterprise involving risk-taking businessmen who were willing to venture capital on the basis of imperfect geographic information. Exploration and capitalism went hand in hand, and to this day the term *venture capital* refers to money put up at the beginning of a company's uncertain career. During the Elizabethan period numerous joint-stock companies amalgamated capital to spread out risk, and Northwest Passage companies intermittently sprang up. In the course of the seventeenth century, the fervor for discovering an accessible waterway across North America gradually died down, as British settlements along the eastern seaboard

Cook's last expedition, the explorer of the South Seas attempted to discover such a passage from the west, steering a course up a large fjord in southern Alaska in the mistaken idea that it was the northwest passage. Cook reached about as far north as the present-day site of Anchorage, on the eastern side of a body of water now named after him (Cook Inlet), before turning back to meet his fate in Hawaii.

The Arctic coast of Canada, where explorers long sought the Northwest Passage, showing a gravel beach, driftwood, and the edge of the tundra *(photo by Jesse Walker)*.

were established, alternative sea routes to the Orient were pioneered by Drake and others, and the looting of Spanish galleons by pirates and privateers became fashionable.

Although one of the stated purposes of the 1670 charter of the Hudson Bay Company was to discover a northwest passage to the Orient, it was not until a century later that the British explorer Samuel Hearne went overland as far as the Coppermine River (1771–1772) and demonstrated that there was no short passage to the west. On Captain James

The stage was now set for the nineteenth-century expeditions, which were motivated more by the quest for scientific information than by commercial gain. The voyages of the Canadian explorer Alexander Mackenzie, the Russian explorations of Kamchatka and Alaska, and the epic expedition of Lewis and Clark all had shown the contours of the massive continental obstacle between the Atlantic and the Pacific. The mythical **Strait of Anian** leading between the oceans, usually placed in temperate waters, could finally be removed from the world map.

The desire to extend the limits of knowledge was the primary basis for British expeditions, which were resumed after hostilities with the French had ended. Arctic expeditions were undertaken as early as 1818 by John Ross and David Buchan, followed by Sir William Edward Parry, F. W. Beechey, Sir George Back, Thomas Simpson, and Sir John Franklin. The last-named expedition (1845–1848) came to a tragic ending when Franklin and his team became icebound and perished in Victoria Strait. This led indirectly to the discovery of much knowledge about the Arctic region and the Northwest Passage by those attempting to discover his fate. In 1850–1854, Sir Robert John LeMesurier McClure penetrated the passage from the west, reaching by an overland expedition Viscount Melville Sound, which had previously been reached from the east by Parry. The existence of a northwest passage finally had been proved, and a long era of searching came to an end.

But it would be another half century before a successful transit of the passage occurred, when the Norwegian explorer Roald Amundsen became the first to make the crossing in his ship *Gjöa* (1903–1906), requiring a number of seasons to do so. The account of the Norwegian's expedition appeared in English as *Amundsen's North West Passage* (1908). Later Amundsen would become the first to reach the South Pole (1911). Interest in the icebound and inaccessible northwest passage slackened until the discovery of oil in northern Alaska in the 1960s, when there was a desire for a short water route to the east coast of the United States. The ice-breaking tanker SS *Manhattan* became the first commercial vessel to navigate the Arctic route in 1969. Questions have been raised about the political sovereignty of the region (the passage is politically part of Canada's Northwest Territories) and adverse environmental impact (petroleum transportation and development threaten the vulnerable tundra ecosystem).

Further Reading: Willy de Roos, *North-West Passage,* Camden, Maine: Maine Publishing, 1979; Bern Keating, *The Northwest Passage: From the Mathew to the Manhattan, 1497–1969,* Chicago: Rand McNally, 1970; George Malcolm Thomson, *The Search for the North-West Passage,* New York: Macmillan, 1975.

OCEAN SEA

Today's oceans—the Atlantic, the Pacific, the Indian, and the Arctic—were until the sixteenth century considered one body of water, with a number of separate seas. The same ocean that washed the west coasts of Europe and Africa also rose and fell against the shorelines of Asia and east Africa. The Indian Ocean, according to this rooted belief dating from the time of the ancient Greeks, was but an arm of an encircling Ocean Sea, in the same way that the **Mediterranean Sea** was. In this view, the three continents of the known world—Europe, Africa, and Asia—were a single large island in the midst of a single massive ocean.

For Homeric Greeks, Oceanus was a river that ran around the disk (or alternatively, the cylinder) of the world. This encircling river, which was sometimes described as a sea, was the source of all the water for the world's rivers, seas, gulfs, and bays. Personified, Oceanus was the Titan son of Gaea, the earth goddess, and Uranus, the unkind ruler.

By the fourth century B.C., Eratosthenes, the father of geography, had not only shown by a number of ingenious though not original proofs that the world was round but had also calculated its circumference to a remarkable degree of accuracy. For classical Greeks and Romans the sphericity of the earth was not in question, nor was it for Europeans in the late Middle Ages who rediscovered or reread classical writers like Aristotle, Ptolemy, Strabo, and Pliny the Elder, all of whom accepted the roundness of the world. What was doubtful was the precise circumference of the earth and the consequent distance across the Ocean Sea between the west coast of Europe and the eastern coast of Asia.

Columbus adopted an overestimation of the length of a degree, so his reckoning of the distance around the earth was too short by about 25 percent. Whether he did this deliberately to increase the likelihood of receiving royal patronage by downplaying the distance and time across the Ocean Sea we probably will never know, but this error, coupled with the lack of the intermediate islands in the Atlantic that Columbus had counted on for rest and resupply, is what turned Columbus's 1492 expedition into such an epochal voyage.

The discovery of the Pacific by Balboa in 1513 and its navigation by Magellan in the course of his 1519–1522 voyage around the world put a decisive end to the notion of the all-encompassing Ocean Sea. Columbus's fourth and final voyage (1502–1504) clearly showed the existence of a large, new landmass of continental scale, but the great navigator (Columbus was a genius at dead reckoning) refused to believe that he had not encountered the outlying islands of East Asia. It is ironic that one of the titles conferred on him after the 1492 voyage testified more to vanishing geographies than to the new worlds opened up by his discoveries. In addition to being named viceroy and governor of any lands or territories he might encounter, he was dubbed Admiral of the Ocean Sea.

See also: Atlantic Ocean, Legendary Islands of; Seven Seas.
Further Reading: Geoffrey J. Martin and Preston E. James, *All Possible Worlds: A History of Geographical Ideas,* 3d ed., New York: Wiley and Sons, 1993.

OFFA'S DYKE

Offa was an early king of Mercia (ruled 757–796) who is best known for his establishment of overlordship over Kent, Sussex, and East Anglia, thereby anticipating the unified kingdom of England. His fame is also due to two quite tangible effects: his introduction of the mintage of pennies, a denomination that would last more than 1,000 years (pennies based on the Roman denarius were originally small silver coins); and his construction of an earthen embankment 170 miles (274 kilometers) long, along the border between England and Wales.

Built sometime between 784 and 796, Offa's Dyke runs from Prestatyn on the coast of north Wales to Chepstow on the Severn estuary in the south. In the words of an ancient historian, Offa "commanded a great dyke to be made from sea to sea between the lands of the Britons and Mercia." The purpose of the original dike is not known. It may have served to demarcate an administrative border or to control trade or the movement of animals, as it did not have the defensive ability of **Hadrian's Wall**, which is located along the northern border of England.

Whatever the rationale for its construction, already by the tenth century laws were being passed, dictating what was and was not allowed when crossing the dike.

Though not marking the English-Welsh political border today, the dike can still be seen in places, especially on open hillsides, as on Llanfair Hill above the market town of Knighton in mid-Wales, whose Welsh name describes its location (Tref y Clawdd, or the Town on the Dike). Much of the dike has been leveled by farmers' furrows or by the erosive forces of wind and rain, but about 80 miles (129 kilometers) of the original earthworks remain. Since 1971 a long-distance hiking path has been opened, following the windings of this medieval relic feature.

Pennies are no longer issued by the British mint since the adoption of decimal coinage in 1971 (100 pence to the pound, rather than 240 as formerly), but Offa's Dyke survives at least in places to bear mute testimony to the ancient king's power and the persisting importance of the cultural division between the Germanic English and the Celtic Welsh.

Further Reading: Roger Thomas, "Offa's Dyke," *British Heritage,* Feb. 1997, pp. 40–45.

OREGON TRAIL
See South Pass

ØRESUND
See Danish Straits

ORLEANS, ISLE OF (U.S.)
Renewed rivalry between the European powers beginning in the 1670s spilled over into conflicts in the middle section of North America. René-Robert Cavelier, Sieur de La Salle, advanced French claims in 1682 when he traveled from the southern end of Lake Michigan, across the Chicago River–Illinois River portage

route pioneered ten years earlier by Marquette and Joliet, and thence down the Mississippi River all the way to the Gulf outlet. Claiming all land drained by the great river for the Sun King (Louis XIV), La Salle named this southern extension of New France *Louisiane,* in honor of his monarch. It would be almost two decades before the French would establish any kind of settlement in the strategic southern part of the region, and almost four decades before any town graced the banks of the Mississippi in present-day Louisiana.

The French language allows for more latitude in its definition of an island than does English. The word *île* in French refers not only to a piece of land surrounded by open water—the usual definition of an island—but also to a distinguishable lowland ringed by wetlands or waterways. It was not only permissible but ennobling to describe an interior place with the word *île,* as the original domain of the Capetian monarchy lay in the inner parts of the **Paris Basin,** in a region known as the *Île-de-France.* Sicily Island, Delacroix Island, the Five Islands of southwestern Louisiana, and the Isle of Orleans are just some of the noninsular islands of Louisiana.

The Isle of Orleans (Fr. Île d'Orléans), the core area of French settlement in Louisiana, refers to the left bank of the Mississippi River from just below Baton Rouge to the mouth of the river, extending as far as the lakes of the Lake Pontchartrain Basin and a series of connecting waterways. This narrow, approximately triangular region was bounded on the west by the Mississippi, on the east by the Gulf of Mexico, and on the north by the historic water passageway representing a shortcut around the circuitous lower course of the Mississippi. The Indians referred to this path as *manchac* (rear entrance), and they had shown the pass route to Pierre Le Moyne, Sieur d'Iberville, French explorer and future governor of Louisiana, as early as 1699, as a way of reducing travel time between Biloxi (the first French settlement in the region) and the upriver country. This historic route, which represented an international boundary between French Louisiana and Spanish West Florida (i.e., the Florida Parishes), comprised a number of distinguishable yet connected segments: Just below Baton Rouge, Bayou Manchac, once an active distributary of the Mississippi, flows eastward before emptying into the lower Amite River. The river in turn flows into a small lake, Lake Maurepas, which connects via Pass Manchac with the much larger Lake Pontchartrain. Proceeding eastward of the lake, through the narrow constriction of the Rigolets, brings us out into the Mississippi Sound, behind the fringing barrier islands Ship and Cat.

On the second-to-last major meander of the Mississippi, where the river approaches closest to Lake Pontchartrain, the city of New Orleans was laid out in 1718. The original design was that of a fortified town with streets in gridiron formation, which was the fashion in Europe at the time; however, certain elements of the plan, such as elevated defenses on Rampart Street, were never built. Sited on a narrow natural levee surrounded by unattractive cypress swamps, marshes, and sandy wastes, the city yet had some natural advantages. It was connected to Lake Pontchartrain (and the Manchac pass route) by Bayou St. John, which debouched into the lake approximately where the University of New Orleans campus is located today. In addition, its location was far enough upriver to lessen the potential damage of a hurricane; and, most importantly, its command of the outlet of a river that drained 41 percent of what would eventually be the United States (excluding Alaska and Hawaii) guaranteed its future as a major entrepôt.

Despite the region's advantages, the French were slow to settle it, and the colony was a continual drain on the burdened French treasury. The allied French and Spanish Bourbon monarchies played a version of hot potato with the undesirable colony (at least from a financial standpoint), and it passed to Spain in 1763, then back to French hands in 1800. Before official notification had been made that the Louisiana colony had passed once again to the French, President Thomas Jefferson dispatched his newly appointed ambassador, Robert Livingston, to France, to purchase the land around New Orleans so that American products coming down the Mississippi could pass freely without being subject to foreign customs and regulations. Earlier, as secretary of state in the 1790s, Jefferson had described the location of the "Island of New Orleans" as "a long, narrow slip of land" between two Mississippi channels, and noted the suitability of the Bayou Manchac–Amite River channel as a boundary with Spanish Florida. The problem presented to Jefferson once he acceded to the presidency in 1801 was whether to seek an alternative American entrepôt, perhaps at English Turn just below New Orleans, thereby creating an American enclave functioning something like British Hong Kong in the Orient; or to purchase the Isle of Orleans including the city of New Orleans; or perhaps to incorporate West Florida, which would give the Americans access to Baton Rouge (although this latter territory the French could not give, as it belonged to Spain). In April 1802, Jefferson instructed Ambassador Livingston to offer to purchase "the island of New Orleans and the Flori-

das." When it was learned later in that same year that the Spanish, still officially in control of the lower Mississippi, had suspended the American privilege of deposit at New Orleans, in violation of the 1795 Treaty of San Lorenzo (Pinckney's Treaty), Jefferson sent his fellow Virginian, James Monroe, to France to assist in deliberations. Livingston made a new proposal to the effect that the United States would purchase Florida as far east as the Perdido River; the Isle of Orleans (the real interest); and extensive, mostly uninhabited territory north of the Arkansas River that was part of the French claim on the basis of La Salle's 1682 exploration, which might be viewed as a buffer between British Canada and the French colony farther south.

Jefferson privately admitted during the months of negotiation that he doubted the French would be willing to part with New Orleans for a cash settlement. But in April 1803 the French foreign minister surprised Livingston with an unexpected offer: the sale of the whole of Louisiana. It will never be known for sure what had caused Napoleon to change his mind, but it is likely that he realized that the English navy could control the Gulf Coast just as effectively as they did the **English Channel**, and moreover Anglo pioneers were advancing across the southern frontier and soon would be able to take the tiny French settlements from the landward side. Napoleon's major ambitions were in Europe, and his plate was certainly full there. The news of the Louisiana Purchase was revealed to Jefferson on 3 July, and he announced it to the American public on 4 July, the twenty-seventh anniversary of the Declaration of Independence.

Though no precise boundaries or maps were attached to the purchase, the Americans interpreted the French claim as inclusive of all lands west of the Mississippi as far as the **Continental Divide.** Only a small portion of the purchased land was located east of the Mississippi, including the Isle of Orleans, which had been the primary focus of Livingston's mission. At the stroke of a pen, the world's largest republic nearly doubled in size—and at a relatively small cost. The price tag for the 875,000 square miles of the Louisiana Purchase was $15 million, or 2.7 cents per acre—perhaps the best real estate deal in history. However, even more important than the cheapness of the land was its sheer vastness, which could be carved up into survey townships and counties for settlement, eventually forming new states that would further enrich and extend the power of the evolving Union.

Further Reading: D. W. Meinig, *The Shaping of America: A Geographical Perspective on 500 Years of History,* vol. 2, *Continental America, 1800–1867,* New Haven: Yale University Press, 1993.

OSLO FJORD

Although it is sometimes said that Norway is all mountains and sea, several important agricultural regions stand out in this scenic fjord land. The Östland, or southeastern district, is comparatively low and open on its eastern side. It stretches across the political border into Sweden without crossing any natural frontier. Though lacking extensive plains, this region comprises a number of elongated, flat-bottomed valleys. The political, commercial, and cultural capital of the country, Oslo has for a natural site a hill slope at the head of the area's most sheltered fjord. An arm of the Skaggerak, the Oslo Fjord extends inland 62 miles (100 kilometers). The shores of the fjord are generally fault guided, with slopes rising steeply to gneiss or lava-topped plateaus. Only at the fjord head and along the lower courses of streams drain-ing into the fjord is there a sufficient amount of level land for town development and agriculture.

The eastern valleys of Norway focus on Oslo, like the spokes of a wheel. Although Oslo is cut off to the north and west by a 20-mile (32-kilometer) stretch of forested hill country, a gap in the hills to the east, the Grorud valley, gives access to the head of Lake Øyeren on the Glåma River, and so to Lake Mjøsa and the Gudbrandsdal and Osterdal routes to Bergen and **Trondheim Fjord.** Just as in the early period Oslo was able to organize the trade of eastern Norway along these traditional routes, so with the building of the railroad network from the late nineteenth century with Oslo as its hub, the capital tapped an increasingly large area, effectively the national territory.

Founded in 1050 by Harold III (Harold Fairhair), Oslo became the national capital in 1299. In the fourteenth century the city flourished as a result of the activities of Hanseatic League merchants, but after Norway formed a union with Denmark (1397) the capital declined in importance. The wooden city was destroyed by a great fire in 1624, then rebuilt by Christian IV as a Renaissance city and renamed Christiania. After gaining independence from Denmark (1814), Norway joined a union with Sweden under one monarch, retaining more political rights than it had enjoyed under Danish rule. A Norwegian cultural renaissance in the late nineteenth century, which included such important modern figures as Edvard Grieg, Henrik Ibsen, and Edvard Munch, preceded the reestablishment of independent Norway in 1905.

Oslo's population in 1814 was only 10,000; by 1990, it had grown to 500,000. The capital city's growth dates from the late nineteenth century, when it eclipsed Bergen as the major Norwegian city. Reassuming the name Oslo in 1925, the city was delivered to the Germans at the start of World War II by Vidkun Quisling's group. Today Oslo is a clean, efficient, and modern city. The islets in the fjord, abundant park land, and surrounding wooded slopes (ideal for ski jumps) are an attractive setting for this important north European city.

See also: Danish Straits.

PALLISER'S TRIANGLE

The southern parts of what are today the Canadian provinces of Alberta, Saskatchewan, and Manitoba (i.e., the Prairie Provinces) were even more isolated in the early and mid-nineteenth century than were the corresponding plains areas of the United States. The Canadian population was growing less rapidly, its economy was less dynamic, and the eastern Canadian hearths along the lower Saint Lawrence (Lower Canada) and the region north and west of Lake Ontario (Upper Canada) were cut off from the fertile Western lands by the granitic wastes of the **Canadian Shield.**

Rupert's Land—as the Western Interior was then called—was at the time a dependency of the Hudson Bay Company, whose primary concern was to gain access to fur resources rather than to promote commercial agriculture. It is true that Lord Selkirk had established an agricultural colony along the Red River to tap the deep, rich soils of the former glacial lake bed as early as 1812–1815. The Red River Settlement might contribute provisions and serve as a place of retirement for traders and officials of the company. But the Assiniboia district grew very slowly, with most of the immigrants being French Canadian, and gave little indication of its future metropolitan status (as Winnipeg). Mixed-blood Indians, or métis, formed the majority of the traders and trappers employed by the Hudson Bay Company as well as of free traders who operated independently of the large organization. Seminomadic, these Northwesterners tended to look with disfavor on the settled agriculturists of the slowly growing Red River colony.

So things stood when Captain John Palliser was dispatched by Her Majesty's government to explore the unsettled interior of western Canada, with an eye toward surveying its resources and exploring passes in the western cordillera that might permit the construction of a road connecting British west-coast possessions (e.g., Fort Vancouver) to the territory administered by the Hudson Bay Company. Palliser had no special expertise as he set off on his well-publicized expedition (Darwin was even consulted about its advisability), except that he was a gentleman with an Irish estate who had done some buffalo hunting for sport on the Upper Missouri a few years before, about which he had written a popular book. The success and influence of the British North American Exploring Expedition (1857–1860) and its report, published in a parliamentary blue book, was largely the result of the outstanding specialists Palliser gathered around him: the amiable French botanist Eugene Bourgeau; the medical doctor James Hector from

Edinburgh University, who conducted extensive geological observations; the fastidious Lieutenant Thomas Blakiston of the Royal Artillery, who made important observations on magnetic declination (the deviation between true north and magnetic north) with sensitive equipment, but who chose to retire from the exploring party due to disagreements over its command; and John Sullivan,

The expedition had three major purposes: (1) to explore westward from Lake Superior as far as the Red River settlements in order to determine the possibility of a road linking forts at the upper end of the Great Lakes (e.g., Fort William) to the southern end of Lake Winnipeg; (2) to survey the 300,000 square miles (777,000 square kilometers) that stretched west from Red River

The stark landscape of Palliser's Triangle, shown here in southern Saskatchewan *(photo by Jesse Walker)*.

who took charge of the astronomical work of the expedition.

The most famous finding of Palliser's expedition—which deserves to rank with that of the American surveys undertaken by Zebulon Pike and by Stephen H. Long—was that the southern part of the Canadian plains along the South Saskatchewan and its tributaries the Bow and the Red Deer was barren of trees, and therefore less suitable for agriculture than the mixed parklands of aspen groves and prairie meadows growing along the North Saskatchewan in a fertile belt as wide as a hundred miles in places.

to the Rocky Mountains as far north as the North Saskatchewan and south to the U.S. border (49° latitude), which was just then being surveyed by a joint boundary commission; and (3) to explore the various passes through the western mountains. One of the most remarkable feats of the Palliser expedition was its peacefulness: No wars or skirmishes resulted when hostile tribes were encountered, although there were some narrow escapes when the party crossed into Blackfoot country with Cree guides, as these two tribes were traditionally antagonistic and could coexist only by maintaining a neutral ground between them.

Using the palisaded forts of the Hudson Bay Company as provisioning points and resting places, Palliser and his men made numerous trips, crossing and recrossing the Canadian plains; they hunted buffalo, elk, grizzly bear, and Canadian geese for sustenance; noted characteristic plains phenomena, such as chinooks, which cooled the air temperature as much as 30°F in a matter of minutes; observed a "black unctuous mud" (petroleum) near Edmonton, for which they saw little use but which a century later would revive the region's economy; made step-like rises as they proceeded westward, observing knolls and buttes as detached outliers of the next higher level; penetrated the Rockies through a number of passes, including the Kicking Horse Pass, which 27 years later would be the site of the Canadian Pacific Railway; and discovered the beautiful Waterton Lakes region (named after a British naturalist) near the border, which today forms part of the international Glacier-Waterton National Park.

Palliser's reservation about the potential of the approximately triangular-shaped southwestern portion of the Canadian prairies was in the end a cautious statement about the inaccessibility and dangers of a remote region rather than a scientific description of soil quality. As a conscientious servant of his government's Colonial Office, Palliser wisely advised against an overhasty expansion into a region whose agriculture was limited by rainfall. The western interior of Canada was only a small part of the British Empire, which was expanding during this time to include, by the end of the century, one-fourth of the world's land area. Palliser's caution was seconded at about the same time by another Canadian explorer, H. Y. Hind, who con-cluded that the Canadian prairies were an extension of the Great American Desert and that lands suitable for agriculture were confined to a fertile belt bounding the prairies to the north and east.

The excellent reputation enjoyed by Palliser can be detected in the statement made some twenty years later by the leader of a survey party charged with laying out a route across western Canada. The railway engineer Sandford Fleming said that he always took Palliser's report along on survey trips as he found it useful. The doctor-cum-geologist of the expedition, James Hector, later explored the Southern Alps of New Zealand and eventually became Sir James Hector, the first head of the Geological Survey. Although there is no monument to Palliser in the little church at Kilrossanty, County Waterford, where he is buried, scores of rivers, mountains, and lakes in western Canada named after Palliser, Blakiston, Bourgeau, and Sullivan testify to the enduring importance of Palliser's British North American Exploring Expedition.

Further Reading: Irene M. Spry, *The Palliser Expedition: The Dramatic Story of Western Canadian Exploration, 1857–1860,* Saskatoon, Sask.: Fifth House, 1995 (1963).

PAMPA (ARGENTINE)

This extensive, nearly treeless grassland of east-central Argentina fans out from the banks of the **Río de la Plata** and the urban center of Buenos Aires. Though this region is the most populous part of the country and the nation's heartland, the seemingly boundless monotony of billowy grasses did not initially attract the Spanish colonists, whose focus was on the **Andes** and the exploitation of the native peoples of the highlands. Permanent settlement of the Plata shore came from Asunción. Founded in 1580, Buenos Aires derived its importance at the time from its strategic location: It guarded Spanish interests at the mouth of the Río de la Plata. With the Portuguese establishment of Colonia on the opposite bank of the river, the entranceway became an important outpost in the Spanish and Portuguese struggle for control of the Plata estuary.

By the middle of the nineteenth century a primarily pastoral economy had developed in the region, based on the grazing of animals inherited from colonial times on the vast, unfenced range. The stage was set for the dramatic transformation of the pampa landscape, especially in its humid eastern portions. Between 1853 and 1914 a number of changes occurred, all relating to the intensification of land use and increasing commercialization of agriculture: the arrival of the first railroad in 1857; the division of *estancias* into smaller tenant units; the adoption of new crops of commercial value, such as wheat and alfalfa; and the immigration of large numbers of Europeans, especially those of Italian and Spanish mainland descent, who were struggling to make a profit rather than to sustain a traditional land-based patrimony. Curiously, the change—from extensive range livestock to intensive crop cultivation—was spearheaded by independent tenant farmers, brought in by the large landowners to grow alfalfa as feed for the owners' animals, who at the same time raised wheat for commercial sale. The owners didn't object to the extra activity because they received a portion of the proceeds in sharecropping fashion.

Soon settlers crossed the Río Salado, which had marked the boundary between largely unoccupied drier portions of the pampa to the west and the humid, intensively cropped ring of land around Buenos Aires. The Indians were eliminated from the Argentine scene in the wars of 1879–1883. Subsequently, large numbers of immigrants descended on this temperate grassland, whose course of development closely followed that of the North American **Great Plains.**

Today, concentric rings of nearly uniform agricultural type and land use are found around Buenos Aires, with diminishing intensity of land use the farther one is from the market. There are four major zones: (1) livestock raising without cultivation of crops in the most distant zone, corresponding approximately with the drier parts of the pampa; (2) wheat and alfalfa cultivation in a broad crescent for 600 miles around the humid pampa; (3) maize (corn) in an approximately 150-mile ring around the interior port of Rosario (corn is not fed to animals, but exported); and (4) intensive truck, dairy, and fruit growing near Buenos Aires (this began with World War I, when European sources of canned milk and butter were cut off). Deviations from theoretical Von Thünen patterns (named after the nineteenth-century German geographer who first described the patterns of land use around a market) in the Argentine case are the results of a number of factors: multiple ports (La Plata, Mar del Plata, and Bahía Blanca all serve the region, in addition to Buenos Aires); the railroad grid fanning out from Buenos Aires, creating different market access; and the physical variation of the soils, some in wet conditions, others having received more of the fertile windblown loess.

Major towns are located along navigable waterways at the margin of the pampa (Córdoba to the northwest on the edge of the Andean piedmont; Bahía Blanca on an indentation of the coastline near the Río Colorado, which is considered the region's southern boundary). Smaller towns like Pergamino, Junin, and Tandil function like smaller versions of the U.S.

towns of Kansas City and Omaha, located as they are on the boundary between long- and short-grass prairie and corresponding land uses, and able to gather tributary economic activity across the zone of transition. One is, however, inevitably drawn toward the metropolis of the plain just as surely as Chicago is a magnet that attracts the inhabitants of the Midwest. The city brought the settler to the plain, sold him his agricultural machinery and equipment, and received him to its brimming suburbs in the more recent period. For surely Buenos Aires and the pampa are South American equivalents to Chicago and the Midwest.

Further Reading: Preston E. James, *Latin America,* New York: Lee and Shepard, 1942, especially pp. 324–359.

PANAMA CANAL

The discovery of gold in the foothills of California's **Sierra Nevada** (1848) and the lure of the newly opened Oregon Country created the need in the mid-nineteenth century for a shortcut for passenger traffic across the conjoined American continents. Long used by the Spanish as a cart road during colonial times, the *camino real* that crossed at the narrowest point of the Central American land bridge linked Panama City on the Pacific Ocean to Portobelo on the Caribbean. An alternative route using the Río Chagres plus some short overland hauls was pioneered at an early date by the Spanish, and this route became the preferred one during the rainy season, when the overland route was sodden. The route of the Panama Railroad, built between 1848 and 1855, wisely followed the drier route along the Río Chagres.

The Spanish never abandoned the idea of a transisthmian canal, but upon attaining independence in 1821, first as part of Gran Colombia (Colombia, Venezuela, Ecuador, and Panama), and later, shorn of Venezuela and Ecuador, as part of Colombia, the Panamanian people lacked the capital and the expertise to undertake such a major project. The increased traffic across the isthmus at midcentury once again brought world attention to this shortest of shortcuts across the American land bridge and the possible construction of an interoceanic canal. Between 1850 and 1900, U.S. and European engineers surveyed more than 30 possible crossings of the land bridge, all the way from the **Isthmus of Tehuantepec** at the waist of Mexico to the Atrato River and its lower tributaries in northwest Colombia. The old Panama crossing was preferred, primarily because it provided a short, 50-mile (81-kilometer) stretch between the oceans. Great Britain, France, and the United States all showed interest in developing the waterway, but it was the French who first essayed it during the 1880s. Although it was under the direction of the brilliant engineer Ferdinand de Lesseps, who had just completed the Suez Canal (1869), the French project never came to fruition due to a number of factors: disease, poor planning, and inadequate financing. Construction halted altogether due to bankruptcy in 1889. A decade later, when the United States gained new territories in the Caribbean and Pacific after the Spanish-American War (1899), U.S. interest in a transisthmian canal increased. Although the Congress initially favored the route following the **Nicaraguan Rift**, the rough rider President Theodore Roosevelt, who was the first president to pursue an active foreign policy, made the construction of the canal the linchpin of his global policy and convinced Congress to go along with him. Built between 1904 and 1914 by the United States, the Panama Canal shaved 7,000 miles (11,265 kilometers) off the distance by ship between east and west coasts, dramatically cutting the costs of oceanic shipping as well as providing a strategic path for U.S. naval vessels bound between the oceans.

The story of the actual construction of the 51-mile (82-kilometer) seaway is a tropical saga and a tale often told: the battles with yellow fever and malaria; the monumental earth-moving required to make the Gaillard Cut at the highest point along the route (at Gold Hill, with an elevation of 643 feet or 196 meters); and the construction of enormous locks and reservoirs. The route followed that of the railroad, which in turn followed the old Spanish rainy season route along the Chagres.

Something remains to be said about the canal's dimensions, its geographical layout, and its limitations. The canal is of the lock-and-lake type. Traffic moves in both directions, as all locks are double. Efforts to increase the canal's capacity in 1939 by building an additional lock came to naught when war preparations intervened. Ships entering from the Atlantic side at the Caribbean port of Colón on Limón Bay travel south and east along the route before reaching the Pacific side at Balboa, a suburb of Panama City. Ironically, the Pacific terminus is 27 miles (43 kilometers) east of the Atlantic entrance; due to the sinuous winding of Panama's coastline, the sun rises in Panama City over the Pacific Ocean.

U.S. president Jimmy Carter signed a treaty in 1977 granting the Canal Zone (a 10-mile- or 16-kilometer-wide strip of land), previously under U.S. jurisdiction, to Panama. The plans are that at the end of 1999 the operation of the canal itself will pass to the Panamanians.

The usefulness and strategic position of the canal has been somewhat diminished by recent developments. Giant superships carrying petroleum and other bulk products cannot fit through the canal's locks, nor can many of the navy's new ships. The canal's continuing strategic importance to the United States is, however, evidenced by U.S. armed intervention in Panama in the 1980s. Recent proposals for an all-sea-level route, a railroad portage across the isthmus, and a "dry canal" among others—whether constructed in Panama or elsewhere—demonstrate the continued importance of the Central American obstacle and the need for an isthmian passage.

Further Reading: Frederic J. Haskin, *The Panama Canal,* Garden City, N.Y.: Doubleday, Page and Co., 1913; David McCullough, *The Path between the Seas: The Creation of the Panama Canal, 1870–1914,* New York: Simon and Schuster, 1977.

PANAMA, ISTHMUS OF

The land bridge connecting the two continents of the Americas reaches its narrowest point in the middle section of present-day Panama. The Spanish early discovered that the easiest way to transport valuable goods—especially silver from Potosí (Bolivia) and gold from Quito (Peru)—was to ship them in galleons to Panama City, established in 1519 by Pedro Arias Dávila as the major transshipment port on the Pacific side of the constriction. An approximately 40-mile (64-kilometer) transisthmian route encompassing tropical forests, mountains, and meandering rivers separated the Pacific terminus from Portobelo, which was established in 1596 on the Caribbean side (earlier, Nombre de Dios just down the coast had been the outlet, but its location was less suitable). The *camino real* linking these two ports was more of a mule path than a road, as it was not permanently paved until the eighteenth century. Nevertheless, it was used enough that the

Spanish sought an alternative to the difficult *camino real* during the 1527–1533 period, creating a combined river-overland route that made use of the winding Río Chagres, the outlet of which is on the Caribbean side, plus short overland stretches. This mostly water-based route avoided the depredations of the *cimarrones* (escaped African slaves), who preyed on slow-moving pack trains, aided and abetted by the British. Besides, the new route could be used in the rainy season, when the *camino real* became a quagmire.

Pirates, privateers, and officially sanctioned foreign ships posed constant threats to the fleet of Spanish galleons that plied their way between the New World and Spain under protective convoy. Adversaries also attacked the major ports. The first English circumnavigator, Sir Francis Drake, raided Nombre de Dios, the first Caribbean terminus of the transisthmian route, in 1572, and sacked and burned the port in 1596—thus providing the occasion for moving the settlement up the coast to Portobelo. The Welsh buccaneer immortalized by the rum label—Henry Morgan—raided Panamá on the Pacific side in 1671 and caused the Spanish to move the port about two leagues (ca. 4.4 miles or 7.1 kilometers) west of the old settlement.

Despite the use of the easier Chagres route in the wet season and the improved port locations, English depredations and the rise of Anglo supremacy in seaborne commerce took its toll on the Panama route, and a weakened Spanish empire abandoned the isthmian passage and the convoy system in 1748, directing all ships around **Cape Horn**. Transisthmian traffic was reduced to a trickle and did not revive until the middle of the next century, with the need to transport settlers and miners to the California gold fields and to the newly opened Oregon country. A railroad was completed across the isthmus in 1855, following the rainy-season route along the Río Chagres, which was also to be the route taken by the **Panama Canal** constructed in 1904–1914.

Further Reading: Clarence Haring, *Trade and Navigation between Spain and the Indies,* Gloucester, Mass.: Peter Smith, 1964; Gerstle Mack, *The Land Divided: A History of the Panama Canal and Other Isthmian Canal Projects,* New York: Octagon, 1974.

PANNONIAN BASIN
See Hungarian Basin

PARANÁ PLATEAU
One of the most extensive areas of lava flows in the world is located in south and south-central Brazil. Diabase-derived soils here have contributed to the development of a distinctive coffee landscape, which has been important not only to São Paulo but to Brazil as a whole. The upper course of the south-flowing Paraná River and its tributaries dissect a broad plateau composed of dark-colored diabase interbedded with layers of sandstone. The interior plateau extends from the southernmost Brazilian state of Rio Grande do Sul as far north as Minas Gerais and Mato Grosso, and includes adjacent parts of the countries of Paraguay and Uruguay.

But it is in São Paulo state that the plateau has featured so largely in Brazilian development. São Paulo was originally the only important town located away from the coast up on the highlands, but it was not a major focus of settlement until the late nineteenth century. Then the rise of the European and North American market for coffee, combined with the spread of coffee onto suitable lands of the Paraná Plateau, suddenly transformed the area.

Excellent coffee lands can be found in the vicinity of São Paulo. A deep, porous soil containing considerable humus derives from the weathering of diabase. The soil has a dark, purple-red color, hence the name *terra roxa* (from Portuguese *roxa* or purple—pronounced ROH-sha). The *terra roxa* has enough porosity to allow the penetration of the roots of the coffee trees deep into the ground. For cotton, however—one of the alternative crops in the region—the chemical composition is inferior, as the plant tends to form leaves and branches instead of fiber.

Something else was needed besides excellent soils and a market to precipitate the late-nineteenth-century coffee boom. The São Paulo region received large numbers of Europeans beginning about 1885. Italians, Portuguese, Spaniards, and Japanese (after World War I) poured into the agricultural hinterlands of São Paulo. This wave of immigration was also directed to temperate portions of South America, that is Argentina and Chile, and to the United States. Between 1827 and 1936, São Paulo received 2,901,204 new arrivals, with only 53,517 coming before 1886. Many of the immigrants were *colonos* or tenants, working on large coffee estates, and as a result they did not benefit from the large profits made from coffee growing or the rapid runup in land values. Wages were relatively high, though, and a diligent worker could soon earn enough money to buy a piece of land or move into the city.

Fazendas, or large farms, spread out from Campinas—an early coffee district—in the period following 1885. Owners quickly discovered the value of *terra roxa* in the planting of their trees. The areas of diabase soils were originally wooded, so owners learned to avoid the open savannas and plant on the wooded ridges. The area around Ribeirão Prêto to the north of Campinas and São Carlos to the northwest were regions of early coffee concentration associated with *terra roxa.* São Paulo state has only narrow zones of *terra roxa,* so planters had to spread out onto less suitable sandstone soils. Coffee crossed the border into northwest Paraná state shortly before 1930, where large amounts of diabase soils could be found. Coffee cultivation has also extended to the north into Minas Gerais and Mato Grosso states, due to the frost problems encountered periodically in the south.

Coffee had already begun to decline before 1930, due to overproduction and recurrent frosts, when the collapse of prices during the Great Depression caused a major crisis. A pound of coffee valued at 24.8 cents in March 1929 was only worth 7.6 cents in October 1931. The resulting financial crisis led to a political revolution, and President Getúlio Vargas came to power in October 1930, bringing to an end the first Brazilian republic (1889–1930) that had been associated with the rise of coffee in São Paulo state.

Much has changed since 1930: Large holdings have yielded to smaller rural properties in many places; a more diversified agriculture of cotton, sugarcane, oranges, and new tropical fruits as well as coffee has developed; and large-scale industrialization has turned São Paulo into the leading industrial city in Latin America. But coffee continues to be an important agricultural product for Brazil, as the country regularly provides about half of the world export market, with most of this production originating on the Paraná Plateau.

PARIS BASIN

Paris is situated near the center of a lowland of sedimentary rocks that takes the form of a bowl-shaped basin. The geological structure appears at the surface as a series of concentric rings of hill lands, with the steep, outward-facing slopes forming escarpments and the gentle interior slopes merging imperceptibly into broad, fertile valleys. The general configuration of the sedimentary layers resembles a nested set of saucers, with the smallest, central saucer occupying the inner ring, known as the Île-de-France. This cuesta-form landscape (see Introduction) has acted in conjunction with other natural and cultural factors to decisively influence the siting, growth, and development of Paris and the surrounding region.

The French capital has derived benefits from both its natural site and its relative position. Located at a river-ford site on the banks of the Seine River some 110 miles (177 kilometers) from the **English Channel,** the city was originally at a critical junction of natural routes between the **Aquitaine Basin** and north-central Europe. In another direction, to the southeast, the headwaters of the Seine join the Rhône-Saône Corridor and thereby link the region to the **Mediterranean Sea.** Gaul, or Celtic France, represented the first major expansion of the Roman Empire outside the Mediterranean Basin. Julius Caesar conquered the Gallic fishing village known as Lutetia, or Lutetia Parisiorum, which was located on the Île de la Cité (where Notre Dame cathedral now stands), because he needed the fording site as well as control of the lower Seine.

A great world city like Paris cannot be reduced to its physical geography, yet at the same time it is hard to imagine a city prospering as much as Paris did unless its surrounding countryside had fertile soils. The accession of Hugh Capet in 987 began the identification of the Paris region with the royal domain, initially the Île-de-France, and the story of the subsequent growth of Paris coincides with the rising fortunes of the Capetian monarchy.

Expansion from the Gallo-Roman nucleus of the Île de la Cité occurred first on the left or south bank of the Seine, in the old Latin Quarter, which has been the haunt of students and faculty since the chartering of the University of Paris (the Sorbonne) in 1200. The northern or right bank community, larger and more recently developed, has been the focus of business and entertainment and the museum area of the city. The landscape of the right bank is dominated by Montmartre (named for the martyrdom of St. Denis, the legendary first Bishop of Paris) topped by the impressive onion dome of the Sacre Coeur cathedral. Approximately concentric rings of urban development, beginning with the *faubourgs,* or old suburbs, outside the Grands Boulevards, to distant metropolitan construction today, extend the range of the City of Light throughout much of the inner ring of the basin.

The east-facing escarpments have resisted erosion more than those in the west and thus are more conspicuous. Famous examples include the Île-de-France escarpment east of Reims and Épernay, which bears the vineyard of the Champagne, the Côte de Meuse along the western valley of the Meuse River, and the Côte de Moselle, draining the western Moselle. These arcs of low, asymmetrical hills are especially conspicuous east of Paris. They form a defensible natural wall around the city that has been especially important in France's wars with Germany.

The series of natural defense lines made the Île-de-France a natural core area for the formation of the French nation-state. Invaders from the north and east have had to fight their way up steep, forested slopes in the face of French fortifications to reach the capital city. The city of Verdun, which lies at the foot of one of these escarpments, was the scene of bitter fighting in World War I, when, during a six-month period in 1916, 600,000 French and 600,000 Germans died trying to secure the slope. Prussian and Austrian armies invading after the French Revolution, trying to overthrow the new regime, met an obstacle of a different kind, as the troops crossed the vineyards located on the east-facing escarpment slopes. The soldiers could not resist gorging themselves on the grapes, and did so to the point where they developed diarrhea and could not advance on Paris.

The basin is a traditional grain-growing area in France and one of the major agricultural regions in western Europe. The wide valleys and terraces of the Seine River and its major tributaries, the Marne and the Oise (whose confluences with the Seine are just above and below Paris, respectively), provide first-rate soils on level valley bottom locations. The Paris region became an important center of agriculture because of a number of interrelated factors. The soils are derived from the weathering of the sedimentary rocks—sandstone, limestone, and marine clays—that underlie the basin. Such sedimentary rocks provide parent materials for soil formation far superior to those provided by, say, the crystalline rocks found in nearby Brittany and Normandy (in the **Armorican Massif**). Additionally, a reworked glacial deposit known as *limon,* found to the north and west of Paris, adds to the fertility of the soil.

The relatively dry climate of the Paris Basin has helped make this region a traditional grain belt. Moisture-laden air blowing off the Atlantic is blocked by the plateau lands of Normandy and Brittany, and as a result the Paris Basin lies in a dry, leeward position. The atypical dry climate (at least by west European standards) is a necessary requirement for the cultivation of wheat. The climate is both warm enough and dry enough to grow the type of grain preferred by the French for breadmaking, whereas farther east in Europe, in Germany and the Slavic lands, rye is the grain of choice because it is more suited to the cooler, wetter conditions that prevail there.

Why have so many French farmers over the years continued to produce sugar beets at uncompetitive prices? It's an old story: When the English threw up a blockade of the continent during the Napoleonic Wars, the French needed a substitute for sugar that had previously been supplied from the West Indies. It was only natural that farmers from the most productive agricultural region of France, the Paris Basin, would respond by growing sugar beets, which benefited from a new chemical technology that converted the crop into a sugar that was indistinguishable from that provided by cane. Although sugar beets are still grown in the region, much of the countryside is now given over to intensive dairy, poultry, and horticulture.

Further Reading: Maurice Druon, *The History of Paris from Caesar to Saint Louis,* New York: Charles Scribner's Sons, 1964; Lucien Gallois, "The Origin and Growth of Paris," *Geographical Review* 13 (1923), pp. 345–367.

PATAGONIA

Windswept and arid, Patagonia is an elongated plateau situated at the southern end of South America. Like other dry peripheral locations, the place derives its significance partly from the adjoining cultural heartlands. The plateau of Patagonia stretches through Argentina east of the **Andes** and south to **Cape Horn** (although the region south of the **Strait of Magellan** is usually referred to as **Tierra del Fuego**). The terrain of the tapering landmass between 38° and 55° south latitude—roughly equivalent to the territory in North America between the **Chesa-**

peake **Bay** and Labrador—comprises two major types of surface elements: elevated plateaus of nearly level sedimentary or, in some cases, igneous rocks (e.g., lava flows), and hill lands underlain by resistant crystalline rocks that stand above the plateaus. The dry upland tableland reaches elevations of 5,000 feet (1,524 meters) above sea level. It has been cut into by a number of deep canyons that cross the plateaus from west to east. The availability of water and the natural windbreaks provided by the steeply cliffed canyons have made these valleys excellent sites for ranches as well as safe routes of travel across the Patagonian desert.

Aridity and high winds define this nearly thousand-mile-long slab of Argentina south of the Río Colorado. Precipitation is minimal, with only 5.3 inches (13.5 centimeters) at Santa Cruz and 4.9 inches (12.4 centimeters) at Colonia Sarmiento. Most is received in the winter months in contrast to places farther north. The arid strip of Patagonia is the only example in the world of a desert east coast in latitudes poleward of 40°. This aridity is partly the result of a rainshadow produced by the Andes, whose blocking effect on the westerly winds causes dry conditions on the lee or eastern side, but it also is due to a cold current—the Falkland Islands Current—that chills the air blowing onshore, producing heavy sea fogs, like the *garuas* of Peru, especially in the far south. Seasonal temperature variation is moderate in Patagonia; as the landmass narrows to the south, distance to the sea decreases, and marine effects take over. Accessibility to the plateau from the east is not easy because there are few protected bays, the coastland is cliffed, and large tidal ranges prevail. Only on the western border of the region is there a significant amount of rainfall. Glacial lakes and humid conditions can be found in the eastern foothills

of the Andes due to the presence of transverse (east to west) valleys that allow the passage of humid westerly breezes. Along this sub-Andean corridor lies a chain of lakes that has provided a natural pathway for settlement to advance onto the forbidding tableland.

First visited by Magellan in 1520, Patagonia was long avoided due to the presence of better watered lands nearby on the Argentine **Pampa.** Nor did the recalcitrance of native peoples aid colonization. With the exception of Carmen de Patagones, an east-coast city that was an early source of salt for Buenos Aires, most of the land was left to nomadic tribes of Puelche and Tehuelche, who hunted the swift guanaco and rhea (a kind of ostrich) with their characteristic weapon, the bola (two stones tied together with a thong). Charles Darwin visited the region in the 1830s on the famous voyage of the HMS *Beagle*. The primary mission of the five-year voyage was to survey and map the complex coastline of Patagonia and Tierra del Fuego—an essentially geological purpose—though the voyage's most famous result was the slowly growing idea of organic evolution in the mind of the young naturalist, whose official position on the voyage was traveling companion to the captain.

In a series of aggressive military campaigns against the native peoples of the area between 1879 and 1883, reminiscent of the nearly contemporaneous Indian wars on the North American **Great Plains,** the Patagonian region was readied for European settlement and colonization. Among the pioneers were people from Wales, Scotland, and England, as well as migrants from elsewhere in Argentina. Occupancy proceeded primarily from two directions: northward along the relatively humid eastern foothills of the Andes from Punta Arenas on the Strait of Magellan, and southward from the humid pampa at

Bahía Blanca. Settlers also fanned out from the east coast. Land use was primarily pastoral, with sheep ranches being the predominant form of economic activity. Though intensification of land use has occurred recently in river oases, and there is some patchy oil and gas development, this windy plateau continues to be defined as a pastoral periphery to the urban and industrial northern core of the country.

separated by mountains; by the presence of numerous islands, peninsulas, and intervening gulfs; and by the availability of only small pockets of arable land along narrow coastal strips or in protected interior valleys. Ancient Greeks eventually dispersed throughout nearly the entire **Mediterranean Sea** basin during the eighth to sixth centuries B.C., and Athens, Greece's most famous city-state, had an imperial phase;

The theater at Epidauros, in Peloponnesus, held 14,000 spectators in 55 lines of seats, still in use today. Note the wedgelike seating arrangement, still employed by theaters today *(photo by Jesse Walker)*.

Further Reading: Bruce Chatwin, *In Patagonia,* London: Jonathan Cape, 1977; G. Williams, "Welsh Settlers and Native Americans in Patagonia," *Journal of Latin American Studies* 11 (1979), pp. 41–66.

PELOPONNESE

The intimate relationship between Greece's terrain and its historical development is a staple of historical interpretation that is as valid for the southern part of Greece as it is for the rest of the Hellenic world. Isolation and independence were fostered in classical city-states by widely scattered populations

but the grandeur that was Greece was not of an imperial kind, and reflected, at least in part, its small-scale, highly compartmentalized terrain.

The Peloponnese (former Morea) is a mountainous peninsula at the southern end of Greece, attached to central Greece at the narrow Isthmus of Corinth and separated by the Gulfs of Patras and Corinth and the Saronic Gulf. On the east it is bounded by the Aegean Sea and on the south and west by the Ionian Sea. A deeply indented coastline, especially in the south and east, results from the extension of a number of finger-like peninsulas jutting out into the sea, ending in rocky capes. The interior from which these fingers project is the upland basin of Arcadia. With patches of oak forest at altitudes of 2,000 to 2,600 feet (610–792 meters), this region contains a number of verdant valleys, which earned it a reputation as a place of harmony and rustic happiness, as described in Sir Philip Sidney's prose romance *Arcadia* (published posthumously in 1590). Today any large, conglomerated urban area might be referred to as a megalopolis (e.g., the Boston to Washington corridor; the London region); yet there is an actual city of that name located in southern Arcadia, dating from ancient times.

To the north and east of Arcadia are the plains of Corinth and Argos, where most of the population is clustered. At the head of the Gulf of Patras in the northern Peloponnese is the ancient region of Achaea, homeland of early Greek peoples who predated the classical Greeks. Achaea is best known in history for a defensive league its cities formed with Athens against Sparta. To the west is found the ancient country of Elis, whose prestige for centuries was enhanced by the enactment of the Olympic Games at the town of Olympia from 776 B.C. onward (Olympia was also the site of one of the **Seven Wonders of the Ancient World,** a giant statue of Zeus).

At the southern end of the peninsula, in the protected valley of the Eurotas River, is the Laconian district, with its chief city-state Sparta, known for its military discipline and its rivalry with Athens. Although Sparta was able to conquer the nearby district of Messenia, one of the most fertile parts of Greece, Messenians migrated to Sicily, giving their name to an important city and straits (see **Messina, Strait of**).

A great stone fortress built on the brow of a low hill at Mycenae, about 12 miles (19 kilometers) from the Gulf of Argolis in the northeastern Peloponnese, dates from about 1600 B.C. Part royal residence, part graveyard, this impressive site has been described as the palace of Agamemnon, suggesting that the site might be the place of origin of Homeric-age Greeks, though this is not known for sure. The Mycenaean culture of mainland Greece, which lasted until about 1100 B.C., must have had contact with earlier Cretan civilization. Though more austere than the palace of Knossos on Crete, the Mycenaean ruins unearthed by Heinrich Schliemann in the nineteenth century possess many similarities in material culture: wall paintings, massive stone gates, and beaten-gold face masks. Tablets of Linear B script (an early form of Greek) have been found throughout the Peloponnese. One tablet from Pylos, a well-preserved Mycenaean palace site in Messenia, even describes the same gods and goddesses as those known in classical Greece.

There were a number of intervening peoples and migrations between the Mycenaeans and the historic Greeks. The Achaeans began to rule the region by about 1250 B.C. They were in turn displaced by the Dorians, arriving from the northwestern mountain districts of Epirus and Macedonia between 1150 and 950 B.C. Between the eighth and fifth centuries B.C. the classical Greek city-states of Sparta, Argolis, and Elis flourished on the Peloponnese.

The Peloponnesian War (431–404 B.C.) was the decisive struggle between maritime Athens and the land-based empire of Sparta, ending in Athens's defeat. Bringing to a close the Golden Era of Periclean Greece, the war was eloquently chronicled in Thucydides's classic *History of the Peloponnesian War.* Writing in a naturalistic style and consciously avoiding the kind of supernatural devices employed by his predecessor Herodotus, Thucydides paid careful attention to the role of the physical environment in influencing the outcome of military battles (effects of storms, concealing terrain, covering darkness, drought).

An eclipse of the moon contributed to what Thucydides considered the turning point of the war, the defeat of the Athenian navy at Syracuse in 413 B.C., the nineteenth year of conflict. The Athenian fleet had planned to leave Sicily after a long, unsuccessful campaign and set the date at the time of the full moon. The night before, an eclipse occurred, and the superstitious sailors refused to sail until the traditional "thrice nine days" had elapsed. This bottled up the Athenian fleet and permitted Syracuse to bring up enough reinforcements so that they eventually destroyed the escaping fleet and killed most of the Athenians, including the commander Nicaias (whom Thucydides describes as having been addicted to divination) and the celebrated Greek leader Demosthenes. Most of the fighting of the war did not occur on the Peloponnesian peninsula (an important battle did take place at Pylos) but at strategic outlying locations, such as Sicily, Thrace, and the **Dardanelles**, suggesting the scope and influence of the two greatest Greek city-states.

Athens was not entirely ruined by its defeat in the Peloponnesian War. Nonetheless, within a half century of the end of the war, the Macedonian influence pervaded the Greek lands. Philip II's conquest of Greece in 338 B.C. paved the way for his son, Alexander the Great, who spread Greek culture throughout the known Western world and across Asia as far as India. Rome incorporated the Peloponnese in 146 B.C., with the region comprising the largest part of the province of Achaea. With the collapse of Roman rule, the Peloponnese, like much of the rest of Greece, underwent a long period of foreign invasions, the detailed chronicle of which would be as complex as it would be tedious. The homeland of Socrates and Plato fell subsequently to rule by the Byzantine Greeks, Bulgars, Pechenegs (a Russian steppe folk), Latin Crusaders, the French noble family of Villehardouin, the Angevin dynasty, Navarrese adventurers, Venetians (who controlled some port cities), and eventually the Ottoman Turks. After the Greek war of independence against the Turks from 1821 to 1829, the Peloponnese became part of free Greece.

The Corinthian Canal was completed across the isthmus in 1893 and now saves 150 miles (241 kilometers) on the voyage from Corfu to Piraeus, Athens's port. With the Peloponnese no longer peninsulated, it is interesting to speculate how the Peloponnesian War and the fate of Greece might have differed if this project—long contemplated—had been undertaken in ancient times. Would the canal have had any significant influence on the course of the war and subsequent history, or was it in the nature of things that Athenian democracy would enter a period of decline? Thucydides might have worded it just so.

See also: Aegean Islands.

Further Reading: Peveril Meigs, "Some Geographical Factors in the Peloponnesian War," *Geographical Review* 51 (1961), pp. 370–380; Robert B. Strassler, ed., *The Landmark Thucydides: A Comprehensive Guide to the Peloponnesian War,* New York: Free Press, 1996.

PENNINE HILLS

This southern extension of the upland part of Britain into the Midlands seems an unlikely place for an early flowering of the Industrial Revolution: Peaceful valleys, with sheep grazing the lower slopes, above which loom desolate wastelands of heather and peat, belie the profound economic and social transformation that began on the fringes of these hill lands (sometimes mistakenly called a mountain chain). Yet it was here, some two centuries ago, that the coordination of a dispersed labor force and the application of mechanized power—in a word, industrialization—first took hold.

The "backbone of England" extends 140 miles (225 kilometers) from north to south, from the Cheviot Hills on the Scottish Border to the Peak District of Derbyshire. The geological structure consists of a faulted arch of Millstone Grit underlain by carboniferous limestone, which is exposed in Derbyshire and West Yorkshire. These discontinuous hills (*pen* is a Celtic word meaning headland or hill, and is commonly a part of place-names in northern Britain) are grouped naturally into three sections, with convenient separations provided by transverse, glaciated valleys.

The north Pennines are bounded on the north by the Tyne Gap, an important east-west crosspoint between Newcastle and Carlisle, guarded in ancient times by **Hadrian's Wall** on its northern side. The basis of this division is a rigid crustal block, the Alston Block, which terminates on the west in a sharp escarpment overlooking the Eden valley. To the east, streams of moderate gradient have opened up the limestone-walled Yorkshire dales. Karst (limestone-dissolution topography) is common in this section, including swallow holes, dry valleys, underground caverns, and distinctive limestone pavements that are crossed by thousands of hikers each year who follow the Pennine Way footpath. The generally rounded hills of the Pennines attain their greatest heights

in this section, with elevations at Cross Fell of 2,930 feet (893 meters), at Mickle Fell of 2,591 feet (790 meters), and at Pen-y-ghent of 2,278 feet (694 meters).

South of the Aire Valley and the Aire Gap lie the central Pennines, which are lower lying than the northern section. Here settlement approaches the top of the uplands. Roads and rails link the small towns and their valleys to the industrial districts of Yorkshire on one side and Lancashire on the other. The Industrial Revolution might be considered to have begun when part-time farmers who worked a sideline activity of domestic textile weaving on the uplands moved down into the towns nestled in the creased Pennine hills. There they found full-time employment that provided higher wages than they were used to receiving. The mechanized workshops that began to appear owed their efficiency and reduced costs of production as much to the coordination of labor as to the application of mechanized power, though the latter became especially important with the invention of the rotary-based steam engine. The first mills were located on the streams that tumbled off the Pennines, but later establishments anchored themselves on the coal deposits that are plentiful on the margins of the hills. The sharp contrast between the scenery of sooty industrial valleys and wild moorlands is still visible today.

In the south Pennines, Millstone Grit forms an eroded central plateau, with resistant limestone hills facing inward in characteristic cuesta fashion (see Introduction). Veins of lead ore lace the limestone in the south Pennines as in the northern section. The mines have been abandoned for generations, but derelict landscapes of rusting machinery, tramways in grass, and underground tunnels have exerted a powerful influence on the imaginations of poets like W. H. Auden, who as a child wandered among limestone hills and abandoned lead mines. Auden created verse with a distinctive landscape (Auden Country) reminiscent of the Pennines that was to have a notable influence on the interwar generation of British writers.

Further Reading: W. H. Auden, "In Praise of Limestone," *Collected Shorter Poems, 1927–1957,* New York: Random House, 1966, pp. 238–241; A. Wainwright, *A Pennine Journey: The Story of a Long Walk in 1938,* London: Penguin, 1986.

PLATA, RÍO DE LA

In addition to the ancient crystalline shields of the **Brazilian** and **Guiana Highlands** and the younger, folded mountains of the **Andes,** the landforms of South America encompass extensive sedimentary basins of younger age. Three rivers whose names begin with the letter P—Paraguay, Paraná, and (La) Plata—form a major river system that dominates the drainage of the southern part of the continent just as the **Amazon Basin** does the north. The Río de la Plata is the lower part of this important river corridor, which not only provides access to the interior but has been the primary route by which commercial production reaches its market. To give an idea of the length of these rivers, the Paraná River, the segment of the river above La Plata, is about 2,000 miles (3,219 kilometers) long and drains a sizable portion of southern Brazil, while the next section of the river upstream, the Paraguay, is about 1,300 miles (2,092 kilometers) long. A look at a map shows that the Río de la Plata is really an enlarged river mouth similar to the lower course of the Saint Lawrence below Quebec City. This estuary formed by the confluence of the Paraná and Uruguay Rivers is 170 miles (274 kilometers) long and separates southwestern Uruguay from the

Buenos Aires province of Argentina. A funnel-shaped indentation of the coastline, the Plata is about 120 miles (193 kilometers) wide at its mouth on the Atlantic Ocean, narrowing to about 20 miles (32 kilometers) near its head. Its northwestern end receives enough discharge from upstream that it contains fresh water. Sand bars and shoals reduce navigability, but dredged channels permit navigation by oceangoing vessels.

The first European to visit the estuary was Amerigo Vespucci in 1501. He was followed by Juan Díaz de Solís in 1516 and Ferdinand Magellan in 1520. We don't know for sure who gave the river its name, but since *plata* is silver in Spanish, Río de la Plata means River of Silver, which is curious since there is no silver nearby. The Spanish in the early period considered the estuary an eastern guarding post of the Spanish Empire, and routes did connect it to Andean silver sources, which may have given rise to its name. (The origins of Argentina's name, based on the Latin word for silver, are similarly murky.) The English name for the Río de la Plata, the River Plate, just confuses things more. Continuing this foray into the meaning of names, in 1520 when Magellan sailed up the Plata, he reportedly uttered in Latin, "Mont vide eu" ("A mount I saw") at the site of Uruguay's present-day capital, Montevideo.

The region of Buenos Aires and the Plata estuary attain their greatest significance due to the accessibility of the agricultural district of the Argentine **Pampa.** After the first settlement at Buenos Aires in 1536 was abandoned, colonists coming downstream from Asunción in 1580 soon reestablished the town. Generally low, marshy ground along the southern shore of the Plata gave way to relatively deep water at the town site, where boats could gain a dry landing spot at the base of the barranca. A tributary stream, the Riachuelo, provided an anchorage for the shallow-draft boats of the sixteenth century along a shore more conspicuous for exposed mud flats.

Until 1778 Buenos Aires was not even officially a port, as Spain wanted to restrict overseas trade to the colonies to the Panamá route. Its chief purpose during this early period was to provide a place where ships, after a long voyage from Spain, could obtain fresh water and provisions before making the long and difficult trip upriver to Paraguay. The establishment of a Portuguese settlement at Colonia on the opposite shore of the Plata in 1680 alerted the Spanish to the need for a major outpost guarding the estuarine entrance to their empire. But it was not until the nineteenth century, with the creation of new international markets in agricultural commodities and the establishment of a dense road-and-rail network serving the humid Pampas, that the town would attain substantial levels of growth.

Military action took place here during the early days of World War II. In the Battle of the River Plate on 14 December 1939, British warships drove the small German battleship *Admiral Graf Spee* into the river's mouth, where it was scuttled.

PO PLAIN

Continuously occupied since Roman times, the towns of the North Italian plain have kept alive the classical spirit of humanism and civic culture through long periods of darkness, while undergoing in the modern period exceptional rates of industrialization and economic growth.

The Po River valley, known to Italians as Padania, or the Valle Padana, represents a gigantic apron of glacial outwash laid down at the margin of Alpine foothills. The southern part of the valley, derived from the fluvial deposition of Po tributaries coming out of the **Apennines,** is less extensive. From Turin in the western valley to the marshy outlet on the Adriatic south of Venice, the approximately triangular tract of land is the result of the deposition of sediments as the grade of the Po and its major tributaries originating in the Alps flattens, where the rivers reach the structural depression of the plain. The central and flattest portions of the valley were an arm of the Adriatic Sea (there also once were connections through the Ligurian Alps to the Tyrrhenian Sea) as recently as the Pliocene epoch, some five million years ago. Thus, the region as a whole consists of a series of terraces, with coarser debris upstream and finer materials down valley, in addition to the restricted floodplain and the morainic arc of hills marginal to the Alps.

The cities of the plain are generally located away from the river, on elevated terraces at some remove from the flood-prone and miasmic bottoms. The site of the major city in the heart of the Po valley, Milano (in Latin, Mediolanium, or Middle of the Plain), is well north of the river on fertile lands between the left-bank tributaries of the Adda and Ticino Rivers, with access both to the port of Genoa and the **Alpine Passes.** Below Piacenza, the Po has such a flat slope that it meanders lazily through marshlands, with cities spaced along it at regular intervals, partly because of careful Roman planning of the urban network with respect to access to mountains on either side of the valley. Two clusters of cities can be distinguished at approximately equal distance from the river: cities of the elevated terraces away from the river (Mantua to the north, Ferrara to the south); and cities at the foothills of the flanking mountains (Brescia and Verona to the north, and Parma, Reggio nell'Emilia, Modena, and Bologna to the south). To the north of the river, the siting of cities astride the main routes to the Alpine Passes is noteworthy, as in the case of Verona, which has access to the Brenner Pass, to which it owes its great medieval past.

The lower course of the Po, which divides the province of Veneto to the north from Emilia to the south, is a vast deltaic surface augmented by the Adige. The river reaches the sea 35 miles (56 kilometers) south of Venice along an inhos-

ern Europe. Intensive specialty crop agriculture results in a kind of polyculture, but with a Mediterranean character: Wheat and flax growing combine with transhumance of sheep; rice growing is practiced in the damp bottomlands; mulberry trees in the east provide the raw material for the silk industry of the towns, notably Milan; olive woods on exposed slopes in Veneto generate every

Agricultural landscape of the Po Plain *(photo by Jesse Walker)*.

pitable coast, where mud and sand have been pushed laterally to the south by currents, thereby building up long coastal spits (*lidos*) enclosing lagoons that sometimes have access to the sea via gaps, or *porti*. South of the Po outlet on the Adriatic, Ravenna is the site of a once bustling Roman and Byzantine port famous for its mosaics. The town lies at some distance from the coast today due to siltation. It is one of the few examples of a town in the region that is relatively down-at-the-heels compared to ancient times.

The Po valley is the broadest extent of fertile land in all Italy, perhaps in south-

Italian's favorite condiment. The land is so intensively cultivated and has been remade for so long that a common saying is that the Po plain "is not the mother but the daughter of its inhabitants." Due to the dry summers characteristic of southern Europe, irrigation has been necessary, especially on the elevated terraces along a line of springs known as *fontanili*, which surge through the alluvial fans at the base of the mountains. The rich agricultural landscape of the Lombardy region is perhaps best characterized by its long irrigation canals, lined by tall, graceful poplar trees that share its name. The lower valley with its numerous fens has been extensively reclaimed, with diking especially prominent below Piacenza.

Very few towns of the northern plains cannot trace their ancestry back to Roman colonies of the first and second centuries B.C. Many of the settlements took advantage of the routes connecting the margins of the plain to accessible mountain passes. Some cities guarded bridge crossings, as did Piacenza and Cremona, the oldest settlements in what the Romans called Cisalpine Gaul, which guarded the bridges where the Via Emilia and Via Postaumia crossed the Po. North of the river, many of the towns, such as Verona and Turin, controlled the routes through the treacherous Alps.

The Padane towns have achieved economic success and political prominence since ancient times and have been the scene of many important historical events. The Ticino joins the Po where the Carthaginian general Hannibal triumphed over the Romans in 218 B.C. Turin was the most important Roman town in the western valley, but the earliest occupation of the Romans was at Piacenza and Cremona, both uncharacteristically located on the river. Originally a Celtic settlement, Milan was by the fourth century almost as important as Rome. The eloquent church father St. Ambrose was this city's bishop from 374–379, and his work (e.g., he founded what today is the oldest functioning public library in Europe) helped make Milan the most important religious center in northern Italy and the capital of the western Roman Empire.

Renaissance princes were able to tap the trade across the Alps while at the same time improving their agricultural hinterlands. Lombard bankers taught financial science to Europe, and it is no coincidence that the name of the street running through the heart of the City of London's financial district bears the name of this Italian region. Napoleon referred to the Po valley as "the most fertile plain in the world" and made its conquest the object of his first European campaigns. In the nineteenth century, large areas were transformed by intensive cultivation of rice and maize. Piedmont remained backward until the mid-nineteenth century, when the reforming Conte di Cavour (1810–1861) extended new irrigation lines to boost agricultural productivity, while at the same time engineering the eventual unification of the Italian states in 1861.

Further Reading: C. J. Robertson, "Agricultural Regions of the North Italian Plain," *Geographical Review* 28 (1938), pp. 573–596.

POITOU GATEWAY

A relatively narrow strip of limestone about 40 miles (64 kilometers) wide provides a natural pathway between the two major agricultural lowlands in France—the **Aquitaine Basin** and the **Paris Basin**. Located in west-central France between the crystalline hills of the **Armorican Massif** (Brittany and Normandy) and the **Massif Central**, the strategic gateway has been passed through by soldiers, raiders, traders, and travelers from time immemorial. The sill of Poitiers, as it is known to geologists, has long been an invasion route and was the site of a number of important battles.

The former province of Poitou was the home of the Gallic Pictavi (or Pictones) tribes until it was conquered by the Romans. Christianization occurred in the fourth century A.D. with the arrival to the capital city of Poitiers of its first bishop, St. Hilary. The region fell to the Visigoths in the fifth century before being overrun by the Franks in 507. The first Battle of Poitiers (732) was won by the Frankish leader Charles Martel, the grandfather of Charlemagne, against the advancing Arabs, whose progress was checked at this point. (Despite its name, the battle actually was fought somewhere between Tours and Poitiers.) Poitiers will be remembered forever as the place marking the northernmost advance of Islam in western Europe. Only fourteen years earlier the Muslims had been repulsed in the east at Constantinople, and soon the Saracens, as they were called in Europe, would be confined to the Iberian Peninsula.

The level plains of Poitou became attached to Aquitaine in the Middle Ages, and the region was fought over during the course of off-and-on skirmishes between the English and the French that lasted the better part of four centuries. Passing to England in the twelfth century with the marriage of Eleanor of Aquitaine to Henry II, Poitiers became the center of a glamorous court life focused on the brilliant Eleanor. The French recovered Poitou (1204), only to have it taken again by Edward the Black Prince at the second Battle of Poitiers on 19 September 1356, during an early engagement in the Hundred Years War (1337–1453). After this long period of periodic warfare, which lasted for more than a century but engaged armies for far less, France emerged victorious, and Charles VII incorporated Poitou into the royal domain as a province, which it remained until broken up into the present French *départements* in 1790. Part of it, the Vendée, was the scene of important antirevolutionary activity between 1793 and 1796.

POLISH CORRIDOR

Though potentially referring to a general situation—the open access provided by the broadening wedge of the **North European Plain** as one travels east—to students of the twentieth-century interwar years, the Polish Corridor has a more particular and portentous meaning: This thin strip of Polish territory separating German lands on each side became the subject of Nazi posturing, and its crossing led to the beginning of World War II.

Poland had no political existence in the nineteenth century, having suffered a series of partitions at the end of the previous century. After World War I newly independent Poland was almost a landlocked country, as the Baltic coastlands, once ruled as Polish Pomerania, had been taken over by colonizing Germans as far as the present-day Baltic republics. The Treaty of Versailles in 1919 granted to Poland a thin strip of land along the lower Vistula (in Polish, Wisla) River to give Poland access to the sea. This prorupt or extended boundary deviated from the ideal compact shape, but the treaty-makers considered it necessary for Poland to have full maritime status. In the process, Germany found itself cut off from East Prussia, though it should be noted that German states rarely had been compact blocks and in fact presented a bewildering crazy-quilt pattern of free states, independent bishoprics, miniature principalities, and disjunct territories.

The Polish Corridor was a strip of land in northern Poland 20 to 70 miles (32–113 kilometers) wide between the former German provinces of Pomerania on the west and East Prussia on the east. The corridor was about 90 miles (145 kilometers) long, extending as far as Danzig (Gdańsk), which was to regain its traditional free trade status. Gdynia was developed as the main Polish port and came to rival Danzig.

These territorial arrangements produced chronic friction between Germany and Poland in the interwar years, especially after the accession to power of the Nazis in 1933. On 21 March 1939,

Hitler—who already had swallowed Austria, the **Sudetes,** and Czechoslovakia—demanded the cession of Danzig and the creation of an extraterritorial German corridor across the Polish Corridor. The unusual condition of an extended political strip was thereby to be interrupted: a proruption was to be prorupted. The demands were rejected and communication between the sides broke down in less than a week. Poland soon obtained French and British guarantees against aggression. With treaties of alliance signed later in the summer, the resistance to the expansion of the Third Reich was strengthened and made irreversible. After Hitler concluded a cynical nonaggression pact with the Soviet Union on 23 August 1939, the stage was set for the invasion of Poland on 1 September, which initiated the war.

The Polish Corridor later disappeared from the map of Europe. After the war, Poland received Danzig and the Baltic coast as far west as the Oder River.

> *Further Reading:* Richard Hartshorne, "The Polish Corridor," *Journal of Geography* 36 (1937), pp. 161–176.

POVOLZHYE

Rising in the **Valdai Hills** northwest of Moscow, the Volga River flows east, then south 2,293 miles (3,690 kilometers) before emptying into the Caspian Sea near Astrakhan. The longest river in Europe, the Volga has played a vital role in Russian history as an eastern corridor for migration, as a trade artery, and, more recently, as a key industrial region beyond the reach of Western armies.

The Mongol invasion of the thirteenth century led to direct control by the Golden Horde just south of the city of Gor'kiy (Nizhni Novgorod), and after the fifteenth century, to the creation of the Tatar khanates of Kazan and Astrakhan. The weakening of Mongol imperial rule, combined with the rise of the Muscovite princes and forays eastward by the cossacks, brought this region under Russian control in the sixteenth century. The Russians established scattered farming communities and towns and attempted to Russify this eastern frontier, but they did not displace non-Russian peoples or mandate complete assimilation. Catherine the Great, of German ancestry, brought a German colony to Saratov that enjoyed political autonomy until the late nineteenth century. The bend of the Middle Volga presents a kind of ethnological museum as well as a political checkerboard within the federated republic of Russia. A variety of Finnish- and Turkic-speaking peoples can be found here. The Tatar autonomous republic dates from 1920 and was one of the first autonomous (in name, at least) territorial units recognized by the Soviet state.

The elongated area stretching east and south from Gor'kiy along the river as far as the Caspian Sea is generally known as the Povolzhye (land along the Volga). Extending from the cool, northern forestlands to the hot, dry deserts of the Caspian, the region is united by a river referred to in Russian folklore as Mother Volga.

The two banks of the Volga present a sharp contrast in topography and in environment. The right or western side of the river has steep bluffs known as the Volga Hills, a resistant edge of inclined sandstone (cuesta). These bluffs stand as high as 500 feet (152 meters) in certain places above the river. The Zhiguli Mountains stand out as another elevated region, where the river is forced to make a sharp turn known as the Samara Bend, reaching its easternmost point at Samara. The left or eastern side of the river is a marshy lowland in transition to the dry steppe farther east. Below Volgograd the contrast between the two banks of the river disappears as it flows through a maze of distributary channels across a desert plain—the former bed of the Caspian Sea.

Just southwest of Volgograd is the Volga-Don Canal, which was opened in 1952. This artificial waterway, passing through an open steppe region, links the lower Volga to the Azov and Black Seas. At the other end of the Volga, the 80-mile (129-kilometer) Moscow Canal joins the Volga to the Russian capital. The Volga-Baltic Waterway, comprising an interlinked reservoir and waterway system, connects the river to St. Petersburg and the Baltic Sea.

Transport accessibility and resource endowment largely explain the rapid industrial development of this key region since the 1930s. The Volga is the most important Russian river for transportation of bulk products, carrying between one-half and two-thirds of all agricultural produce, timber, and oil during the Soviet regime. Although this proportion has declined somewhat due to the increased importance of railway and pipeline transport, the massive Great Volga scheme has created a system of reservoirs, hydroelectric stations, and navigation canals since the 1950s, which has kept the Povolzhye in the front rank as a transport corridor.

Extensive oil fields stretch northeastward from Volgograd to Perm, located on a major left-bank tributary of the Kama River, which drains the flank of the **Ural Mountains.** The Volga-Urals petroleum concentration has been transformed into the major oil- and gas-producing region of Russia, a nation that is self-sufficient in petroleum, in contrast to the United States. Having eclipsed the earlier Baku reserve, the Povolzhye is now being compared to new reserves being discovered in Siberia, where conditions for recovery and transportation are far more difficult because the subsoil is permanently frozen

(i.e., permafrost). Associated petrochemical and plastics industries can be found clustered along the Volga River, and the landscape here is reminiscent of the inland portion of the U.S. Gulf Coast in the Baton Rouge–New Orleans area.

The foundations of steelmaking were laid in the 1930s when Josef Stalin recognized the need to develop an alternative to the heavy industrial region of Ukraine, far enough east to be safe from German invasion. The Donets Basin–Kryvyy Rih region in Ukraine, north of the **Black Sea,** was within easy striking distance of the Nazis, and in fact, it did fall to German forces early in World War II. The Volga-Urals industrial region gained in importance during and after the war as the industrial heartland of Soviet Russia.

The decisive battle of World War II on the Eastern Front was fought in the Povolzhye. In September 1942, Stalingrad (now Volgograd) was subjected to a massive offensive under General Friedrich von Paulus. Paulus failed to conquer the city, and the Russians under Marshal Grigorii Zhukov mounted a counterattack, eventually surrounding the Germans, who had to surrender. The losses on both sides were enormous because Hitler and Stalin, respectively, dictated that the city be taken or kept at any cost. The Germans lost 300,000 men in the Stalingrad campaign alone, and they would never again take the offensive against the Russians.

Further Reading: David J. M. Hooson, "The Middle Volga: An Emerging Focal Region in the Soviet Union," *Geographical Journal* 126 (June 1960), pp. 180–190.

PYRENEES

This formidable mountain range between France and Spain has served not only as an excellent natural frontier and bulwark between these two nation-states but also as a refuge for important ethnic minorities of both countries.

A complexly folded mountain chain, the Pyrenees extend 270 miles (435 kilometers) in a nearly straight line from the Bay of Biscay to the **Mediterranean Sea.** To the west, the mountain range continues as the Cantabrians; the result is that the northern parts of Spain are a nearly continuous wall of mountains facing the

ward position with respect to the prevailing winds, the Spanish borderland has a dry climate similar to that of the steppes. Historically important Spanish settlements occupy the southern margin of the mountains, but the French side has been less a focus of human activity. About two-thirds of the Pyrenees are in Spain.

Though they present beautiful scenery, the Pyrenees do not compare with the

Saint Martin du Cannigon, Pyrenees-Orientales (Roussillon), France *(H.S. Capman/Corbis-Bettmann).*

sea. This is a region defined by moist westerly winds, in contrast to the dry basins and plateaus of the south.

The French and Spanish flanks of the Pyrenees are a study in contrasts. The northern slopes rise up abruptly from the low, undulating French countryside. Due to a humid climate that is the result of accessibility to fresh breezes off the Bay of Biscay, the northern parts of the mountains are covered in coniferous forests as well as oak and beech woods. The southern slopes are much less precipitous, the high peaks being bordered by a belt of elevated basins and sierras. Located in a lee-

Alpine Massif. Higher in average elevation than the Alps (the Pico de Aneto, in the central section, is the highest peak, with an elevation of 11,168 feet or 3,404 meters), the Pyrenees do not present a serrated outline, as glaciation has been less a factor in sculpting them. The Pyrenees are more compact than the Alps and offer few low passes.

In the western part of the mountain chain, between Pamplona in Spain and St.-Jean-Pied-de-Port in France, is the famous pass at Roncesvalles (in Spanish, Puerto de Ibañeta), where the heroic Roland, nephew of Charlemagne, fought to the death in 778, in a rearguard battle against the Gascons (Basques) and Moors, inspiring what is considered the earliest example of French literature, the medieval epic poem *The Song of Roland.* At 3,468 feet (1,057 meters) above sea level, this relatively accessible pass has long been used as an invasion route. During the Middle Ages, it was also used by pilgrims visiting the tomb of St. James at Santiago de Compostela in Spain.

In the central section of the mountains is the difficult, snowbound Somport Pass, at an elevation of 5,354 feet (1,632 meters), beneath which runs the trans-Pyrenean railroad from Saragossa to Pau via Canfranc. One of the few low passes in the Pyrenees can be found in the eastern section, the Col de Perthus, at 915 feet (279 meters), which was used by the Romans. Other passes exist, but in general they have not been as important historically as the various **Alpine Passes**—partly because the Iberian Peninsula is farther removed from the center of Europe, and because there are alternative routes connecting Spain and France along the narrow coastal plain to the east and west of the Pyrenees.

The smaller geographical area of the Pyrenees compared to the Alps, combined with its less complicated structure, has resulted in less differentiation of the massif according to physical basis. On the other hand, different parts of the mountains do correspond to different cultural groups. The province in which Roncesvalles Pass is located, Navarre, occupies the western section of the mountains. Navarre has played an important role in the conflicts between Spain and France from the eighth to the seventeenth centuries. The Basque homelands also occupy the western Pyrenees; the Basque provinces extend westward from Navarre all the way to the Bay of Biscay. The

Basque peoples have survived the incursions of Romans, Visigoths, Moors, and Franks in their mountain refuge without losing their distinctive identity and mysterious tongue. Linguists consider the language of the Basques puzzling not only because it is not Indo-European, but also because it does not appear to have descended from any known language group. (Finnish and Hungarian also are non-Indo-European but are known to have descended from Asiatic languages.)

The central Pyrenees historically have been part of the province (formerly the kingdom) of Aragon. This region, the core of which is in the southern Ebro Basin, is perhaps best known for its part in the unification of Spain, which occurred as a result of the marriage of Ferdinand of Aragon and Queen Isabella of Castile in 1469.

The eastern section of the Pyrenees lies on the northern edge of the province of Catalonia, which was a strong maritime power in the thirteenth and fourteenth centuries and which played an important political role in the Spanish Republic of the 1930s.

The Pyrenees abound in ancient mysteries and folklore. The high degree of artistry of prehistoric man is evident at Altamira and Aurignac, where beautiful cave paintings can be seen. Hannibal crossed the Pyrenees in 218 B.C., on his way to his more celebrated crossing of the Alps with elephants. The Moors were pushed back across the Pyrenees after they reached their northernmost limit in Europe, following the Battle of Poitiers (732). Roland's defeat in Roncesvalles Pass was only a temporary setback for the Christians, who were able to confine the Moors to the Iberian Peninsula for the next seven centuries before driving them across the **Strait of Gibraltar** in 1492.

At the northern foot of the central Pyrenees is Lourdes, where in 1858 a French shepherd girl named Bernadette is said to have had visions of the Mother of Christ, causing this site to be one of the most venerated and visited shrines in Christendom. In the east-central Pyrenees can be found the pocket principality of Andorra, which has prospered of late as a duty-free corridor set in the midst of scenic mountains. The beauty and charm of Old Andorra are legendary: Napoleon is said to have exclaimed upon viewing the town that he wished it could be pre-served as a museum piece. That would be a task impossible to accomplish in the modern world. Andorra, like the rest of the Pyrenees, has been changed irreversibly by the invasion of hydroelectric development and increasing numbers of tourists.

See also: Alpine Passes.

Further Reading: Daniel A. Gómez-Ibáñez, *The Western Pyrenees: Differential Evolution of the French and Spanish Borderland,* Oxford: Clarendon Press, 1975; Peter Sahlins, *Boundaries: The Making of France and Spain in the Pyrenees,* Berkeley: University of California Press, 1989.

RHENISH UPLANDS

The middle course of the Rhine River from Bingen (just downstream from Mainz) to Bonn cuts across a resistant massif that effectively divides northern from southern Germany. The massif consists of a series of compartmentalized terrain units—low, sparsely settled plateaus of undulating relief, contrasting with deep, intervening valleys. The river corridors—both the Rhine and its short tributaries—have been the focus of human population since Roman times. The massif comprises clay-slates, intensively folded during the Hercynian uplift but subsequently lowered and smoothed by erosional forces. The German term for this hill region is Rheinische Schiefergebirge (Rhenish Slate Mountains). The twisting Rhine is constricted here to a narrow channel: the castellated Rhine gorge, with its aura of legend and dark superstition.

From the river the traveler can barely glimpse the upland plains above the cliff-like slopes of the valley. Side slopes of tributary valleys and residual hills are mostly forested today, although planted spruce has replaced the original oak and beech, which was cleared in the Middle Ages. There are a number of distinguishable units of the central **Hercynian Uplands** arranged in a southwest-northeast orientation, with separate regions identified on opposite banks of the river.

To the south, the Hunsrück and Taunus mountains lie respectively to the west and east of the Rhine river. These two regions provide some of the lightest and wildest country in the Rhenish Uplands. Rising to the south, the highest elevations are reached on the ridge that spectacularly overlooks a straight fault-line escarpment that marks the southern boundary of the massif.

Beyond the Mosel, a major left-bank tributary of the Rhine flowing in entrenched meanders, can be found the rugged Eifel region, volcanic in origin, as indicated by numerous volcanic cones, crater lakes, and dammed mountain streams.

Opposing the Eifel on the eastern side of the Rhine is the matching terrain region of the Westerwald, which lies north of the Taunus and beyond the Lahn River. Where the left and right bank tributaries converge on the Rhine, which also happens to be the meeting-place of the Hunsrück, Taunus, Eifel, and Westerwald hill regions, is the site of the industrial town of Koblenz (well named the Confluentes by the Romans), which also benefits from its location at the center of a widening of the Rhine known as the Neuwied Basin.

Farther north are a number of other identifiable units in the Rhenish Uplands (Sauerland, Siegerland, Mark), but here the hills are lower and merge into the industrial Ruhr Valley, with which they are closely associated economically.

The Rhenish Uplands are a physiographic but not a political unit. The traditional capitals are all located on the margins of the region—Trier, in the Mosel valley on the western edge of the hill district; Cologne, in an embayment of the northern plains extending up the Rhine

independent rulers and collect tolls on the river trade passing below. The practice of exacting tolls on Rhine traffic did not end until the historic convention of Mannheim in 1868, three years before the unification of Germany. A major impetus for the creation of a single German state was the need to curb restrictions and lessen tariffs among the numerous German lands. By the nineteenth century

Castles, cathedrals, and vineyards along the Rhine River in the Rhenish Uplands *(Corel Corporation)*.

valley; and Mainz, in the broad plain of the Rhine rift valley (**Rhine Graben**) that bounds the region on the south.

The Rhine (the ancient name of which was Renos, derived from the Celtic root *ri* [to flow]) gives a unity to this region and exerts a continuing hold on the popular imagination. Deeply wooded slopes rise sharply from the valley floor. Rock-held terraces hold vineyards on south-facing slopes near the northern limit of grape cultivation. The numerous castles in the valley were built by Teutonic knights, who fortified the heights so as to establish themselves as

many of the castles had long been abandoned, as witnessed by the poet Byron, who described them as "chiefless castles breathing stern farewells."

The famous Rhine gorge is located on a 35-mile (56-kilometer) stretch of the river known to the Germans as the Gebirgstrecke, or "mountain stretch." Much feared by boatmen and travelers since earliest times, the constricted river has difficult, changeable currents and numerous shoals. The level of the river is subject to large variations, especially as a result of spring flooding in the surrounding hill districts. The Lorelei is the most famous of the imposing cliffs that look down on the Rhine. Formed of resistant quartzite, this mass of rock 433 feet (132 meters) above the river is, according to legend, the home of a beautiful fairy similar to the Greek sirens, who lures rivermen to their deaths in the treacherous currents below. The drowned treasure of the Nibelungs, the Rhinegold, is watched over by the Lorelei, the same treasure that indirectly cost the legendary hero Siegfried his life. Richard Wagner's group of four music dramas, *The Ring of the Nibelungs,* is just one of the many variations on this recurrent theme in German art and literature. Boatmen treat the currents of the Rhine gorge with respect even today: Ships turn over navigation to special pilots in the mountain stretches of the river. Pilots call this stretch *die Schere* (scissors), because the twisting currents of the river can snap a vessel in two just as a scissors cuts a thread. It has been said that the value of all the drowned cargo from the ships that capsized below the Lorelei probably exceeds that of the fabled Rhinegold.

Further Reading: Thomas Henry Elkins, *Germany,* London: Christophers, 1960.

RHINE GRABEN

The Rhine valley between Basel (Switzerland) and Mainz (Germany) is a broad, flat-floored depression (in German, Graben) formed by a system of parallel faults similar in structure to the **Scottish Lowlands.** The borders of the Rhine rift are represented by uplifted portions of the **Hercynian Uplands:** to the west the Vosges, to the east the **Black Forest** (Schwarzwald). From Lake Constance (Bodensee) to Basel, the head of navigation for barge traffic, the east-west flowing Rhine has the characteristics of an Alpine stream—a steep gradient and numerous knickpoints (e.g., rapids). The

river then bends to the north, winding across the fertile valley of the graben, before entering gorges cut into the Rhenish Uplands below Bingen. Some 20–30 miles (32–48 kilometers) wide, the rift valley is surrounded by forested uplands that originated as sharp fractures of the earth's terrain at the same time that the Alps formed. The Rhine forms the political border between France and Germany as far north as Karlsruhe; farther northward, both sides of the river are in German territory.

The upper Rhine valley features Pleistocene terraces formed by deposition of sediments during periods of interglacial warming and elevated sea levels. This corner of southwest Germany contains some of the richest agricultural soils in the country, partly due to a blanket of wind-blown glacial loess. Terraced slopes are covered with rich orchards and vineyards, while the steep slopes from the floodplain to the terrace border are usually wooded. This area was an early focus of Roman-German interaction. That the area had an earlier Celtic base population can be detected by the commonness of Celtic place-names: In fact, *Rhine,* or in the name's ancient form, *Renos,* is derived from the Celtic *ri,* which means "to flow." The Alsatian capital of Strasbourg, located on the west bank of the Rhine, originated as a Celtic encampment.

The north-flowing Rhine cuts across the grain of Germany's "chaos of physiography," integrating a people who, though they shared a common language, did not gain political unification until 1871. Accessibility has been promoted not only along the main river, which has been a thoroughfare since ancient times, but also in a maze of interconnected canals and tributary streams (today also rails, roads, pipelines, and airports) that crisscross the region. In the rift valley the most important tributaries drain from the east: The Neckar (where the cities of Mannheim and Heidelberg are situated) and the Main (Mainz, Wiesbaden, Frankfurt) open up avenues of access across the upland areas to the east of the graben. Although there are few cities in the southern part of the Rhine graben, the small town of Belfort on the west side commands an opening between the Vosges and Jura Mountains through the **Burgundy Gateway,** to southeast France and the Rhône river system.

The Rhine River obviously has played a very special role in German and central European history. For four centuries the river delineated the frontier of the Roman Empire in western Europe (extended in the upper valley to include both sides of the river). Many consider the beginning of the end of the Roman Empire to have occurred on the last day of A.D. 406, when Suevi and Vandal tribes crossed the frozen and defenseless Rhine at Mainz. The Rhine valley constituted the most important part of the Lotharingian Axis: the core area of western Europe extending from southern or lowland England to the Po Plain, along the corridors of the Rhine and Rhône Rivers. The name derives from one of the three grandsons of Charlemagne, Lothair, who inherited most of this domain when the Frankish Empire fragmented around a thousand years ago. The primary rationale of the Franco-Prussian War (1870–1871) was to annex French lands on the west side of the Rhine Graben in Alsace and **Lorraine.** In turn, the world wars of the twentieth century were in part a continuation of the struggle for control of these borderlands. It is no coincidence that the first six countries to join the European Community (Common Market) in 1958—the so-called Inner Six countries of France, Belgium, Netherlands, Luxembourg, West Germany, and Italy—all lie along the Lotharingian Axis. The Rhine valley continues to be the industrial powerhouse of western Europe, including the rift valley, which has been an important center in the manufacture of chemicals, pharmaceuticals, and automobiles.

See also: Agri Decumates.
Further Reading: William Graves, "The Rhine: Europe's River of Legend," *National Geographic,* April 1967, pp. 449–499.

RHÔNE-SAÔNE CORRIDOR
See Burgundy Gateway

RIDGE AND VALLEY PROVINCE
See Blue Ridge

ROCK OF GIBRALTAR
See Gibraltar, Strait of

RONCESVALLES
See Pyrenees

RUHR RIVER
This right-bank tributary of the lower Rhine empties into Europe's greatest river a little south of the Netherlands. Benefiting from both natural and locational advantages, the Ruhr once contained the largest concentration of heavy industry in the world.

Its name derives from the Celtic *Rubro-gilum,* or Red Brook, referring to the red sandstone found in the drainage basin. The district includes the lands north of the Ruhr as far as the Lippe River, and merges toward the south with the industrial belt east and west of Düsseldorf. It embraces a string of cities from Duisberg on the Rhine (now Duisberg-Ruhrort) eastward through Oberhausen, Essen, and Bochum as far as Dortmund.

The Ruhr's industrialization was dependent on its coal deposits, especially the high-quality coking coal necessary for modern steelmaking. Coal measures out-crop at the surface in the southern part of the region in a fringe of hills running from west to east just north of the Ruhr, known as the Haarstrang (hair-string). Farther north lies a portion of the Börde (border) plain that straddles the physiographic contact zone between the **North European Plain** and the **Hercynian Uplands** of central Europe. Here coal lay at some depth, but not so deep that its thick, relatively uniform beds could not be tapped, especially with the advent of modern hydraulic pumping to keep the mine shafts well drained. The Ruhr also benefited from its locational centrality in middle Europe, with access to the Rhine and the North Sea. In time the region would be crisscrossed by all manner of transport links: canals, railroads, highways, pipelines, and air transport.

Industrial development surged ahead in the Ruhr between 1850 and 1913, stimulated by railroad building, the opening up of new markets in Germany and abroad, and technological advances, all within the compass of the expanding ambitions of the German Empire. The growth of the Ruhr's highly integrated coal and steel industrial complex was due also to organizational innovations: Behind protective tariffs designed to support the infant industries, the Krupp and Thyssen concerns grew up to become giant collusive entities that were horizontally and vertically integrated, giving rise to a new term in economic organization, *cartel* (from the German word *Kartell*). These giant combines with intimate links to the German state set production levels for each company, regulated prices, and acted as selling agents. Coal mining advanced northward as old mines in the exposed section were exhausted, but steel-making and metal fabrication remained behind in the southern cities.

Iron and steel production arose out of earlier craft traditions in both metallurgy and textiles. In medieval times an iron and steel industry existed at the towns of Solingen in the hilly Sauerland and Siegerland just south of the Ruhr. Such craft-based industry relied on local iron ore reserves and charcoal-producing forests. With the development of large-scale, mechanized production, the local reserves of iron ore proved insufficient, and after 1871, the newly unified Second Reich of Germany reached out to Sweden, Spain, North Africa, and newly annexed German **Lorraine** for raw material. Complementary flows of iron ore and coking coal passed between Lorraine and the Ruhr, allowing both to take advantage of new methods of production in steel-making; but it should be kept in mind that the Ruhr never depended only on the Lorraine for provision of ore, important though this latter region was as a border area and source of contention between France and Germany. Coal mining and steel production in the region spun off the German chemical and pharmaceutical industries, which—although more concentrated in the southwestern part of Germany, that is, in the upper Rhine valley and in Bavaria—often arose as ancillaries of Ruhr industry.

Failure on the part of Germany to make its reparations payments after World War I led to French and Belgian troops occupying this key industrial region in 1923–1924. This occupation gave Hitler an excuse to foment rebellion against the Weimar Republic, which led to his unsuccessful "Beer-Hall Putsch" of 1923. The foreign troops eventually were evacuated (1925), but the effect of the occupation had been to enflame nationalist feeling and patriotic sentiment during a volatile period of economic collapse. In this context and with the aid of industrialists in the Ruhr, Hitler succeeded in gaining power in 1933.

Heavily targeted as a German military arsenal during World War II, the Ruhr's infrastructure and production capacity were largely wiped out by Allied bombers. But with the aid of the Marshall Plan the region soon regained its industrial position during the postwar years of rapid economic growth. With the declining importance of heavy industry and the increasing role of services in the modern economy, the Ruhr is no longer the dominant German industrial region it once was. Nevertheless, the state of North Rhine–Westphalia, in which the Ruhr is located, is the largest, most populous, and most affluent of the German *Länder*.

Further Reading: Chauncy D. Harris, "The Ruhr Coal-Mining District," *Geographical Review* 36 (1946), pp. 194–221.

SAINT BERNARD PASS
See Alpine Passes

SAINT BRENDAN'S ISLANDS

The islands of Saint Brendan are wrapped in a garb of legend and lore, fact and myth, as closely interwoven as any geographical beliefs in the Western tradition. The life of Brendan, the esteemed Irish monk, needs to be kept separate from the legend of Brendan and his voyages. We know the former was born in southwest Ireland on the Fenit Peninsula, County Kerry, in the last decades of the fifth century A.D.—perhaps in 483 or 489. Raised by his natural parents only for the first year of his life, he then came under the tutelage of Bishop Eirc, who had him baptized, and a foster mother, Saint Ita. Later he was educated by the influential Irish monk Saint Enda. After being ordained in 512, Brendan established a monastery at Ardfert, north of Tralee, and traveled widely in his missionary activities, allegedly visiting the Hebrides, Wales, Brittany, and even the Faeroe Islands—about 520 miles (837 kilometers) from his native Galway and at the limits of the known world of his time.

Navigating the dangerous waters of the north Atlantic, the much-traveled Saint Brendan earned the appellation "the Voyager." He made two trips to the Hebrides, the second in 563 to visit the island Iona, where the venerable Saint Columba lived, who is credited with converting northern Scotland to Christianity. Brendan established the Abbey of Llancarfan in Wales and became its abbot. He founded monasteries in Ireland at Ardfert and Inishdadroum (County Clare) and at Annadown and Clonfert (County Galway). He made a long sea journey accompanied by a number of fellow monks late in his life, which is described for us in the Latin manuscript *Navigatio sancti Brendani Abbatis* (The Voyage of Saint Brendan the Abbot). Brendan returned from this journey to Clonfert, where he died peacefully in 578.

No written account of Saint Brendan's voyages appeared for two and a quarter centuries after his death, and then so much copying and recopying was done in this pre-Gutenberg age that today no less than 120 different Latin manuscripts of the *Navigatio* are extant. To add to the complexity, Brendan was of course a saint, and accounts of his life inevitably are colored by the need of the early Christian authors to portray Brendan in the right spiritual light, as being like John in his asceticism, or Paul in his missionary activities, and so on. Moreover, the voyages of Brendan came to be a literary theme in a secular tale: Embellished with each retelling, the story expanded to accommodate what was known about the geography of the north Atlantic. As various as the versions were, all told of the holy Brendan searching for other worlds during a long sea voyage, in which he encountered many monsters and performed numerous miracles. Islands various and wonderful are depicted: the Island of Sheep, containing flocks of sheep larger than cattle; an island that turned out to be the back of a whale; a Paradise of Birds; a Fiery Mountain. Brendan and his followers, squeezed into a small timber-and-stretched-hide curragh, once even got stuck in a Coagulated Sea. (Depending on whether one takes this to be ice floes or sargasso, the assignment of the latitude of the voyage varies.) The sojourners eventually reach the blessed object of their journey, the Promised Land of the Saints, only to return to tell amazing stories to the awed stay-at-homes.

The account of the seven-year, God-directed wanderings of Saint Brendan reads like the interleaved stories of Homer's *Odyssey,* Virgil's *Aeneid,* and the biblical *Book of Revelation,* with a large dose of Celtic mythology and a smaller dose of medieval geography tossed in. A correlation between the islands described in the *Navigatio* and actual places has been attempted, with some fairly obvious ascriptions—the Island of Sheep as the Faeroes, the Fiery Mountain as Iceland, and so on. But such an approach requires Brendan's travels to have stretched across the entire Atlantic basin, from the volcanic island of Jan Mayen in the Arctic to the Bahamas and Jamaica. It also assumes that Brendan actually made the voyages attributed to him rather than that the story was a fiction pieced together from diverse sources.

The author and sailor Tim Severin in 1976 constructed a traditional curragh and sailed it with several companions from Ireland across the north Atlantic along a stepping-stone route—from Ireland to the Hebrides, then to the Faeroe Islands, to Iceland, Greenland, and finally Newfoundland—to prove that such a voyage *could* have been made, but of course, not proving that such a voyage *did* occur as recounted in the *Navigatio.* (Severin was following in the footsteps of the renowned writer-explorer Thor Heyerdahl in demonstrating the feasibility of pre-Columbian oceanic contacts.)

The islands of Saint Brendan first make their recognizable appearance on a map of the world at Hereford Cathedral made about 1275. Here they are shown as part of the **Canary Islands**, which had been known since ancient times as the Fortunate Islands. By the beginning of the next century, as the Atlantic islands of antiquity were discovered (or rediscovered), a new geography of reality began to displace the map of tradition. The 1339 map of Angelino Dulcert of Majorca shows Saint Brendan's Islands in the position of the **Madeiras.** A map by the Pizzigano brothers of Venice dated 1367 also has the islands of the itinerant monk in the neighborhood of the Madeiras. In the early 1400s, with the rediscovery of the Madeiras, the islands of St. Brendan—still very much believed in—are displaced to the west and north. Martin Behaim's 1492 globe features a large island of Saint Brendan west of the Cape Verde Islands, where no island exists. By 1544 Brendan's Island has been moved far to the north, at about the same latitude as northern Newfoundland. The great cartographer Mercator adopted this location in 1567, as did Ortelius after him in 1571. In general, as geographical knowledge increased in the late medieval period, the Blessed Isles of antiquity, together with more recently "discovered" legendary islands of wealth and equable climate, gradually were displaced to the margins of the map. The island of Saint

Brendan (usually singular on the later maps) came to rest in the far northern waters between Newfoundland and Labrador, keeping company with other mythical islands like Frisland, Demonias, and Verde. Eventually, the island of Saint Brendan resided in the middle of a group of islands within Newfoundland's Bonavista Bay, where it remained until 1884, when it was renamed Cottel Island, the name it bears today. Thus, the search for the islands of the wandering saint, which encompassed thirteen centuries of travel, ends at last, and the name disappears from cartographic history.

Further Reading: Donald S. Johnson, *Phantom Islands of the Atlantic: The Legends of Seven Lands that Never Were,* New York: Walker and Co., 1994; John O'Meara, trans., *The Voyage of Saint Brendan: Journey to the Promised Land,* Dublin: Dolmen Press (in association with Humanities Press of Atlantic Heights, N.J.), 1978; Timothy Severin, *The Brendan Voyage,* New York: McGraw-Hill, 1978 (Avon paperback, 1979).

SAINT GOTTHARD PASS

The Swiss confederation first emerged in the thirteenth century as a defensive league of cantons around Lake Lucerne. Controlling and exploiting this important pass route in the central section of the Alps (Lepontine Alps), the Swiss cantons of Uri, Schwyz, Obwalden, and Nidwalden, the "four forest cantons" formed the initial nucleus of the country of Switzerland as early as the fourteenth century. The Saint Gotthard Pass had emerged as the primary gateway between Italy and the German lands during the previous century. The region is the source of the Rhine, Rhône, Reuss, and Ticino Rivers. At an elevation of 6,935 feet (2,114 meters), the pass was named for St. Godelhardus, who first built shelters here for travelers.

The Romans much earlier had extended their frontier, for defensive purposes, to the crest of the Alps. The stepsons of Augustus, the first emperor, made two bold advances in 15 B.C. into the mountains. Though rivaling the Brenner Pass in the amount of traffic it carried in the Middle Ages, the Saint Gotthard route appears not to have been used much during Roman rule. This may have been due in part to difficulties along its northern section—the difficult gorge of the Reuss near Andermatt and the cliff road along an eastern bay of Lake Lucerne—which were not completely safe until the nineteenth century. Also, the major connecting point to the north is Basel and the navigable Rhine, which were served by other lines of communication across France and western Switzerland.

The collapse of the Roman empire in the fifth century brought German invaders—first the Alemanni and the Burgundii, later the Franks. The route became especially important in the thirteenth century, as the growing trade of a revitalized Europe made the commercial connections between Milan and the Rhineland more important. The Saint Gotthard was the most direct link between rising commercial centers on opposite sides of the Alps. It had the advantage over its competitors of combining large stretches of river and lake transit on both the Italian and Swiss flanks with a single steep ascent. The bridging of the Schöllenen gorge near Andermatt in the thirteenth century has been considered a necessary first step in the establishment of the Saint Gotthard as the preeminent route across the central Alps in the Middle Ages.

Habsburg incursions on the Germanic peoples in the three valleys on the eastern shore of Lake Lucerne led in 1291 to a solemn pact between the cantons of Uri, Schwyz, and Unterwalden to form the first confederation—Bund der Eidgenossen. Gaining allies and achieving military success (armed neutrality only became the official policy of the Swiss after their defeat at the hands of the French in 1515 at Marignano), Switzerland expanded from its core area along the Saint Gotthard route to the north Italian plains, as well as to the east and west. Bern in the west, Glarus in the east, and Zurich in the north came to the aid of the initial nucleus of four forest cantonments, or Waldstätter, and eventually joined the confederation. (Early on, Schwyz assumed leadership among the cantons and gave its name, distorted as Schweiz—Switzerland—to the entire nation.)

Today the St. Gotthard Railway (built between 1872 and 1880) links northern and southern Switzerland through a 9.25-mile (14.9-kilometer) tunnel. Since 1980, the St. Gotthard Road Tunnel, of about the same length, has allowed highway travelers between Switzerland and Italy to cut across this historic route with remarkable ease.

See also: Alpine Passes; Tirol.

Further Reading: H. J. Fleure, "Notes on the Evolution of Switzerland," *Geography* 26 (1941), pp. 169–177.

SAINT HELENA ISLAND

Every schoolchild knows that after Napoleon's defeat, subsequent escape from Elba, and final loss at Waterloo, the British exiled the former emperor and would-be conqueror of Europe to the island of Saint Helena. Very few know much more about this interesting place or the particulars of how Napoleon spent his last days on this south Atlantic island.

Located 1,200 miles (1,931 kilometers) west of Africa and 700 miles (1,126 kilometers) southeast of Ascension Island, the site could not have been better chosen for the safekeeping of Britain's perpetual enemy. A few islands in the Pacific would have made escape more difficult, but the British in the nineteenth century did not control the Pacific as absolutely as they did the Atlantic. England soon transformed Ascension and Tristan da Cunha, today political dependencies of St. Helena, into garrison islands.

The volcanic island of Saint Helena represents the top of the generally submerged Mid-Atlantic Ridge in the south Atlantic in the same way that Iceland does in the north. Elevations rise to a height of 2,685 feet (818 meters) on Mt. Actaeon. Uninhabited when first discovered by the Portuguese navigator João da Nova Castella in 1502, the island features rugged volcanic slopes cut by deep ravines and gushing gorges. In 1633, St. Helena was taken by the Dutch, who never colonized the island. The island's 47 square miles (122 square kilometers) were annexed by the British in 1659 and placed under control of the British East India Company. Not until 1834 did the island become an official crown colony, whose key function was as a stopover and a coaling station for merchant ships and the Royal Navy. During the Boer War the island served as a prison for South African Boers (Afrikaners).

The neighboring islands of Ascension and Tristan da Cunha also merit some attention, because their colonization dates from the period of the detention of Napoleon. Ascension was at this time directly under admiralty rule—commanded just as if it had been a ship. In the later years of Victoria's reign the island became a cable station on the South African line. In 1912 Ascension was attached to St. Helena for administrative purposes. By the time a large BBC transmitter was put in place on Ascension, the island had gone through phases that had taken it from garrison to communications way station. Ascension played an important rule in World War II after a large airfield was built there to serve as a refueling stop for transatlantic flights to southern Europe, North Africa, and the Middle East.

Although Saint Helena served as a place of confinement for assorted colonial rebels and refugees like the sultan of Zanzibar and the Zulu Chief Denizula (1890–1897), its most celebrated prisoner was Napoleon I, who was sent there in 1815 and lived at Longwood, near the capital city and chief port of Jamestown, until his death in 1821. Longwood, the summer seat of the Lieutenant-Governor, stood on a high plateau, ideally suited for security, as it lay some five miles (eight kilometers) from the port and was overlooked by an army encampment. Officially recognized as a general on pension, the former emperor was for the most part free to walk, talk, and socialize as he wanted, but he never gave up hope that he would be allowed to return to France. His life on Saint Helena was not hard; he was attended by his own servants and even flirted with the English ladies. Although his health declined after 1817, when he was diagnosed with hepatitis, a liver disorder common on the island, he remained active, directing large gardening projects with a zeal and discipline he had once applied to the movement of armies. His end came in the dead hours of the early morning of 5 May 1821, his last words incoherent: "France, armée, tête d'armée, Joséphine." In accordance with his wishes, he was buried in Geranium Valley, receiving full military honors from the British.

Further Reading: Julia Blackburn, *The Emperor's Last Island: A Journey to St. Helena,* New York: Vintage, 1991.

SAINT LAWRENCE LOWLANDS

The broad trough of the St. Lawrence cuts diagonally across the **Canadian Shield** from southwest to northeast, separating two elevated massifs—the Laurentian plateau to the northwest and the Appalachian-era highlands to the southeast. Nowhere else in North America does an eastward flowing river penetrate so far into the interior. While the river proper, which begins as an outlet on the northeastern side of Lake Ontario, is only 750 miles (1,207 kilometers) long, its length extends to 2,300 miles (3,701 kilometers) if one counts the distance from the westward end of the most elevated Great Lake, Lake Superior, to the Gulf of St. Lawrence. The river played an important role in the exploration of the continent, received the major influx of French settlement in the early period, and was a major battlefield in the Anglo-French struggle for control of North America.

Jacques Cartier entered the wide mouth of the estuarine river near Cape Gaspé in 1535, thereby establishing French claim to the Saint Lawrence–**Great Lakes** region. Cartier subsequently explored westward, visiting the sites of Quebec City and Montreal, reaching as far as the Lachine Rapids just upstream from Montreal, which he recognized as a major obstacle to navigation. These rapids were so named because the French believed that by sailing up the St. Lawrence and across the Great Lakes (after they were discovered by Champlain in 1615) they would find a route to China. Champlain founded the first French colony at Quebec (present Lower Town), some 300 feet (91 meters) above the river on a bluff that was unassailable from the river but open to attack from the land. The military significance of this gateway to the St. Lawrence continued to be important even after the English occupation: Quebec became known as "the **Gibraltar** of North America." About a half century later, some 200 miles or 322 kilometers upstream, the French established the city of Montreal (originally called Ville-Marie) at the foot of volcanic Mount Royal—for which the city was named—on a large island in the river, at the head of navigation for any vessel larger than a canoe, and also where a major left-bank drainage, the Ottawa River, flowed into the larger river. The city soon outgrew the older city of Quebec, due to its better access to the interior fur trade.

The circumventing of the Lachine Rapids began with canals dug as early as 1825 and continued with other projects to make the upper river more navigable. The culmination of these efforts was the St. Lawrence Seaway, completed in 1959, which opened a channel for oceangoing ships along the entire length of the river from Kingston, Ontario, to Montreal via the Thousand Islands. The seaway transformed the Great Lakes into an arm of the Atlantic Ocean for purposes of trade—a development that only reinforced the nodality of Montreal in the transport network. (The construction of the Montreal-Portland, Maine, rail line in 1853 had made Montreal the major junction of the railroad system.)

The fertile lowlands of the St. Lawrence, extending about 200 miles (322 kilometers) from the Quebec narrows to the island of Montreal, are the heart of French Canada. Hemmed in by highlands to the north and south and isolated by a long and difficult drainage way to the west, the French core region along the lower course of the river lacked a beckoning agricultural frontier to lure settlers outward and onward, such as that possessed by the British colonies along the eastern seaboard of North America. Some idea of the sparsity of early settlement can be seen in the population data: Between 1608 and 1663, only about 2,500 Europeans arrived, and half of these were in fur trading outposts.

The French did manage to establish a distinctive settlement system. The crown granted large parcels of land, or seigneuries, which were surveyed in characteristic long lots extending back from the St. Lawrence and its major tributaries so as to maximize river frontage. Large owners subdivided their tracts into smaller amounts of land that were then occupied by *habitants,* as small farmers called themselves in French Canada. Because the land was surveyed using the now antiquated measure of the arpent (1 arpent = 192 feet), the long lot system came to be known as the arpent system. The distinctive pattern of riverine survey is evident from the air, as it is in another place in North America where it was used—southern Louisiana. Farmsteads and roads aligned themselves along the river levees, which provided the most fertile, best-drained land in the floodplain, producing a linear settlement pattern resembling a straggling village, in sharp contrast to the dispersed pattern of rural settlement in Anglo North America.

The control of the valley, along with the rest of Canada, passed in 1763 to the British, at the conclusion of the French and Indian War (Seven Years War). Without a western outlet and under the political thumb of the British, Lower Canada, as French Canada was known, entered a period of long, slow decline, its inhabitants increasingly adopting defensive, inward-looking postures vis-à-vis the Anglo-settled areas. The economy of French Canada in the nineteenth century was viewed as backward, one of bare subsistence, and its people were characterized as traditional and conservative. However, urban commercial success, especially in Montreal, began as early as the late nineteenth century and has brought renewed confidence to French Canadians. Although many support the movement for an independent French Canada at present (1997), most do not.

Further Reading: R. Cole Harris, *The Seigneurial System in Early Canada: A Geographical Study,* Madison, Wis.: University of Wisconsin Press, 1966.

SALAMIS ISLAND

In the fifth century B.C., the vastly outnumbered forces of classical Greece trounced the powerful Persian Empire in a naval battle fought in the narrow channel between the island of Salamis and mainland Greece.

Benign Persian overlordship of the Greek colonies in Asia Minor (present Turkey) had turned to despotic oppression under the rule of Darius I (521–486 B.C.). After crushing a revolt of Ionian city-states supported by Athens, the mighty Persian Empire turned its attention westward to punish the puny mainland Greeks, whom one historian referred to at this juncture as "a very small nut between the teeth of a mighty nutcracker." Persian rule at the time stretched across the better part of the Middle East to India and included North Africa as far as Cyrenaica, with the friendly and allied Phoenician colony of Carthage beyond, which challenged Greek colonies in Sicily.

An early expedition led to the humiliating defeat of the Persians at **Marathon,** a narrow coastal plain just northeast of Athens. With the death of Darius, it fell to his son, Xerxes, to avenge the Persians' honor with another massive assault on the Greeks. The Hellenes, especially the Athenians, had not slumbered in the interval, as they had built a sizable fleet of 200 warships (triremes) at the recommendation of the Athenian military leader Themistocles. Nevertheless, Persian forces far outnumbered and outshipped the

Greeks, as Xerxes assembled 180,000 men and 750 galleys. Because of intercity rivalry, the Greek fleet was nominally under the command of the Spartan Eurybiades, though Themistocles was effectively in charge of Greek forces.

After the courageous but ultimately unsuccessful Greek resistance at **Thermopylae** in northern Greece, the southern states withdrew behind the security of the **Peloponnese.** The clever Themistocles did not lose faith in sea power, even at this moment of crisis, and he convinced the Athenians to desert Athens for the nearby island of Salamis, located a mile offshore, at the entrance to the Bay of Eleusis. The key to Themistocles' strategy was to lure the larger Persian ships into the narrow strait between the northeast part of the island and the mainland, where the size and number of Persian ships would work against them due to problems of maneuverability.

On 23 September 480 B.C. the battle was joined as the Greeks came out in a line curving across the strait to the east, while an allied Corinthian decoy force retired to the north. The Persians had bottled up the western end of the Bay of Eleusis with 200 Egyptian ships and closed the eastern channel with an Ionian and Phoenician blockade. The main Persian force advanced into the strait, clumsily breaking its three-line formation and reforming into columns to pass the island of Psytallia at the entrance to the strait. Themistocles had calculated on the morning breeze whipping up a swell to make the maneuvering of the larger Persian ships even more difficult. The more mobile Greeks were able to avoid the Persian archers, come alongside, and shear off the enemy's oars.

Seated on a golden throne at an elevated spot on the mainland shore, Xerxes watched the unfolding of the day's battle.

By sunset, 200 Persian ships had been lost, with the Greeks losing only a fifth as many. Xerxes ordered an immediate retreat. A token Persian army left on the mainland met defeat the next year at Plataea, which marked the end of Persia's attempts to conquer Greece. It was the twilight of oriental influence in the Mediterranean region but the dawn of a new day for maritime Greeks.

Further Reading: Ernle Bradford, *Thermopylae: The Battle for the West,* New York: Da Capo, 1993 has several chapters on the naval battle of Salamis as well as background on the Persian Wars; Richard Natkiel and Antony Preston, *Atlas of Maritime History,* New York: Facts on File, 1986.

SALISBURY PLAIN

The site of this undulating plateau in south Wiltshire is a chalk upland at the center of the rim-and-spoke topography of southern or lowland England. The relatively resistant chalk (pure limestone) leaves as a result of processes of erosion steep escarpments (scarps) and more gentle back slopes (downs), the characteristic features of a cuesta-form landscape (see discussion of cuesta in Introduction). Salisbury Plain forms a central open area from which chalk outcrops run southwest, northeast, and east. The **Cotswold Hills,** the Chilterns, and several sections of the Downs are thus accessible to this region in southwestern England, which also abuts the more difficult terrain of the West Country. The plain itself is an area of gentle uplift that has been eroded around its edges to form a highly indented surface. A number of rivers that drain the upland form distinctive clay vales. Rivers such as the Avon and the Wylye provide access southward to the **English Channel** and northward to Bristol Channel (and the Severn system), but significantly, not in the direction of the Thames and the North Sea.

Long barrows of the earliest Neolithic people, from about 4500 B.P., are especially common on limestone uplands of the Cotswolds and of Salisbury Plain. These areas were easily cleared for farming as they were only lightly timbered, in contrast to the heavily forested vales of the Midlands and the Thames valley. The shallow soils of the uplands could be cultivated easily with the scratch plows then available, while the heavier clays of the vales awaited the development of the heavy moldboard plow in the Middle Ages before they would be well settled. Early roads like the Icknield Way avoided the forests of the London Basin and clay vales to the northwest, and instead connected places in the chalkland district, such as the ancient site of Roman St. Albans, to Salisbury Plain.

The result was that the compact chalk upland of the Salisbury Plain was the most densely populated part of the country in prehistoric times. During the Iron Age numerous small rectangular fields were scattered across the plain and adjoining chalkland districts. Surplus grain from this region was shipped to Gaul. It is not surprising that places on the plateau took on a sacred significance, if we remember how indistinguishable at that time were the spheres of economic, political, and religious life.

The most famous antiquity of England and perhaps of all Europe is Stonehenge, which stands on Salisbury Plain about eight miles (13 kilometers) north of the cathedral city of Salisbury and slightly more than two miles (3.2 kilometers) west of Amesbury. This series of stone ruins arranged in concentric circles has inspired countless visitors since the time of the Romans to wonder about its purpose, its meaning, and more practically, how the giant stones were transported there.

The monument consists of several different structures built at various times. The outermost bank and ditch and the outlying Heel Stone, oriented toward the rising midsummer sun, are the oldest parts of Stonehenge, dating from around 2500 B.C. This part of Stonehenge seems to have been made by the same Neolithic folk who scattered long barrows across the downs. The erection of a circle of blue-

the massive Sarsen circle, in which a continuous ring of stone archways (trilithons) lined the perimeter of the central area. The enormous stones that formed the vertical uprights and horizontal lintels of these prehistoric gates (we cannot be certain they acted as gates) are a form of sandstone found nearby on the Marlborough downs. Within the continuous Sarsen ring (now

Stonehenge on Salisbury Plain, as photographed in 1969. One can no longer stroll this close to the megaliths *(photo by Jesse Walker)*.

stones (a variety of types of crystalline rocks transported from Pembrokeshire in southern Wales) around the central area and the extension of a processional avenue toward the northeast in the direction of Avebury were the primary works of the second phase of construction. Radiocarbon dating indicates this part of the monument was built around 2000 B.C. by an early Bronze Age culture, the Beaker people, who had links with European warrior societies.

The last and most conspicuous phase of construction involved the erection of

partly in ruin), a horseshoe of Sarsen trilithons opened outward to the northeast, in the direction of the main axis of the monument. This phase also saw the dismantling of the bluestone ring and the rearrangement of its stones within the Sarsen structures in a pattern duplicating that of the Sarsens but on a smaller scale. This last phase of Stonehenge, dating from about 1500 B.C., was the work of an advanced Wessex culture, a Bronze Age people who served as middlemen in the metal trade between Ireland and the continent.

First sight of Stonehenge often disappoints visitors, such as the American writer Emerson, whose first impression of the rings of stone was that they looked "like a group of brown dwarfs on a wide expanse." This is a common reaction, especially if one approaches the site from the direction of Amesbury, because the stones are diminished by the background of the rolling downlands. But seen close up, silhouetted against the sky with a low sun revealing shades and textures of the stones, the setting is a perfect background for one of Thomas Hardy's Wessex novels—a lowering, tragic landscape that suggests ancient patterns of uncontrollable destiny and fate:

> The couple advanced further into this pavilion of the night till they stood in its midst.
> "It is Stonehenge!" said Clare.
> "The heathen temple, you mean?"
> "Yes, older than the centuries; older than the D'Urbervilles."
> (Thomas Hardy, *Tess of the D'Urbervilles*)

In the early Middle Ages the Germanic West Saxons occupied the rich agricultural districts in the vicinity of the Salisbury Plain, giving it their name in contracted form, Wessex. Although the kingdom of Essex (East Saxons), in the neighborhood of London, fell in the eighth century to Danes invading from the North Sea, the kings of Wessex were able to withstand Viking incursions due to their relatively isolated position. Eventually the West Saxons under Alfred were able to consolidate their rule throughout lowland England in response to the foreign challenge. The region was blessed with superior agricultural soils, access to nearby districts via routeways that cut across the downs, and a defensible inte-

rior location. Salisbury Plain and its immediate environs thus may be considered the core area of the English nation. It was on the margin of the plain that Winchester emerged as the capital of Wessex and later the first capital of England. With the decline in political status of Wessex and Winchester, arable land was converted to pasture and sheep raising became the primary agricultural activity. The location of military training grounds on the plain today indicates yet a further decline in agricultural occupancy and rural settlement.

Further Reading: R. J. C. Atkinson, *Stonehenge,* London: Penguin, 1979 (1958).

SARGASSO SEA

This quiet pool of water extending east of Bermuda in the North Atlantic—a feature of legend and superstition—actually exists. The Sargasso Sea has exerted a powerful influence on the popular imagination since it was first described by Columbus. A persistent high-pressure cell of diverging, spinning air, the Bermuda High, drives the ocean currents in a huge, clockwise spiral of water. The currents are driven ceaselessly in a circular pattern, so that bits of sargassum seaweed, torn from rocks and reefs of Florida and the West Indies, find their way into this zone but are unable to get out. The placid water here is the result of something like what happens in a stream between two swiftly flowing currents, where a quiet, circular eddy may cause a floating leaf or twig to circle for hours. However, the Sargasso Sea is not a small feature: It extends from a little north of Bermuda south as far as the Virgin Islands, at the northern end of the Lesser Antilles, and then eastward out into the mid-Atlantic. This vast sea, roughly 1,000 miles (1,610 kilometers) broad and twice as long, is a marine desert, as precipitation is rare. Winds are also lacking, which has probably been a more important factor than either seaweed or superstition in the avoidance of the region by sailors. However, Columbus, the first recorded visitor to the Sargasso Sea, was struck by its great patches of seaweed.

This area forms part of a region that eventually came to be known as the Horse Latitudes, a zone of calms located at approximately 30° of latitude in both hemispheres. Though navigators usually avoided these areas due to their undependable and veering winds, ships sometimes were becalmed here, and they faced an ordeal that might last several weeks before the winds freshened. These latitudes might have come by their name as a result of precisely such events: As the valuable supplies of fresh water were drawn down, horses and other livestock, major consumers of water on sea voyages, would be thrown overboard to conserve precious water.

Superstitious sailors traded yarns about ships caught in the Sargasso Sea, doomed to sail forever in wide circles, manned by the ghosts of their dead crews. The tales grew in the telling, so for hundreds of years gruesome and detailed accounts of spectral ships trapped in the Sargasso Sea passed back and forth. Another common view was that shipwrecks were spirited away to this region no matter where they occurred on the oceans.

This historical background may relate to that modern spectral phenomenon, the supposed disappearance of planes over the Bermuda Triangle, a zone with approximately the same location. Reports of mystical happenings east of Florida are often couched in more contemporary language (i.e., the effects of a time-space warp), but the result is much the same. These accounts are no more reliable than the sightings of ghost ships in days of yore,

but the imaginative appeal of such stories cannot be denied.

SCILLY, ISLES OF

This archipelago of 140 islands, islets, and rocks lies off southwest England, 28 miles (45 kilometers) from Land's End. Its heather-covered granite hills are a partially submerged extension of the Cornish peninsula. The traditional way of reaching the Isles of Scilly (pronounced as "silly") is by boat from Penzance, some 42 miles (68 kilometers) away on the coast of Cornwall. Five of the islands are inhabited. On the largest, Saint Mary's, is the capital, Hugh Town, where Prince Charles (Charles II) stopped as he fled England on his way to Jersey during the civil war in 1645.

The islands have numerous legends and historical associations. They are identified with the Phoenicians' Cassiterides, or Tin Islands, and Roman and earlier ruins suggest the islands have been visited since the Bronze Age. Legend has it that a land called Lyonnesse once linked the Isles of Scilly to England. The wizard Merlin once saved King Arthur's knights from certain defeat when his magic words caused the connecting land to be submerged, thereby drowning the enemy's soldiers and leaving the knights on the safe, high ground of the isles. The Victorian poet laureate Tennyson drew inspiration in the writing of his Arthurian epic *Idylls of the King* by staring out to sea from the Cornish coast, over the vanished land, in the direction of the Isles of Scilly.

Despite the islands' latitude of 50°, the same as frigid Newfoundland, the Gulf Stream brings them temperate weather and balmy air most of the time. Due to their favorable climate and proximity to the large British market, they have become the "flower garden of England."

Dangerous rocks and shoals and deceptive crosscurrents have made the area a graveyard for many ships. One particular disaster earned the islands a certain place in history: The worst navigational disaster in the annals of the Royal Navy took place off the western end of the Isles of Scilly in 1707. A fleet returning from the Mediterranean lost its bearings in the fog, and three men-of-war and 2,000 sailors were lost at sea. The error was essentially a technical one—a miscalculation of longitude. Six years later Parliament announced a contest that fired the imaginations of a generation of scientists, navigators, and mapmakers. The designer of the first instrument that could determine longitude to within a half degree of accuracy would receive a prize of 20,000 British pounds, a considerable fortune in the eighteenth century. The contest was eventually won by an amateur inventor, John Harrison (1693–1776), a Yorkshire mechanic who designed what was in essence an extremely accurate timepiece that would become the basis of the ship's chronometer.

Thus, a wreck off the Isles of Scilly led to the solution of the old problem of calculating longitude. Before this time, mariners had only lines of latitude to guide them, but they lacked angular distances east or west—longitude. Time was the key to measuring longitude. If a navigator could compare the precise time at a standard location whose longitude he knows to his own time at, say, noon when the sun lies due south, he can determine how far east or west he is of the standard location. The problem came about because the motion of a tossing ship at sea threw off the common pendulum clocks of the day and made the accurate determination of time impossible.

However, this was not the last sea disaster associated with the isles. In March 1967 the supertanker *Torrey Canyon* broke apart on a nearby reef, the largest ship at the time ever to go aground. Thirty-five million gallons of crude oil flowed into the **English Channel,** which lies just to the east, blackening holiday beaches up and down the south coast of England and reaching as far as the coasts of Brittany and Normandy, 220 miles (354 kilometers) away. Favorable winds and currents spared the Scillies, but the furor over the spill fueled the growing environmental movement of the late 1960s.

Further Reading: Dava Sobell, *Longitude: The True Story of a Lone Genius Who Solved the Greatest Scientific Problem of His Time,* New York: Walker and Co., 1995; Alan Villiers, "England's Scillies: The Flowering Isles," *National Geographic,* July 1967, pp. 126–145.

SCOTTISH HIGHLANDS

Tourist itineraries often include a stop in this physiographic region. The rugged mountains and elongated lakes of the northernmost region in Britain are the setting of breathtaking views. The Scottish Highlands exhibit a conspicuous northeast-to-southwest trend, which is evident in the alignment of the massive rounded ridges and the ribbon lakes. The graininess of the land has been produced by the same processes of faulting that yield a similar corrugated terrain in northern Wales and in peripheral parts of Ireland.

The Scottish Highlands comprise three major units: the Grampian Mountains in the south, overlooking the heavily populated **Scottish Lowlands;** the wild and desolate Northwest Highlands at the northern tip of Britain, which are lower and less compact than the Grampians; and the deep cleft of Glen More, separating these two massives. The Great Glen runs some 60 miles (96 kilometers) from Fort William at its southwestern end—originally a British fort to keep the recalcitrant Scots in line—to Inverness at the northeastern end at the head of the deep embayment of Moray Firth (a Scottish firth is essentially the same as a Norwegian fjord). The highest peak in the British Isles can be found southeast of Fort William at Ben Nevis (4,406 feet or 1,343 meters).

The Caledonian Canal now links a series of lakes in the Great Glen, making navigation between coasts possible. Leg-

Prince Charlie finally met defeat at the hands of the British redcoats in 1746, during the reign of King George II. The aftermath of Culloden was the destruction of the Highland culture and the depopulation of the region. The enclosure of Highland territories in the late eighteenth and nineteenth centuries for sheep pastures and hunting preserves was but one part of this lengthy process. It is said

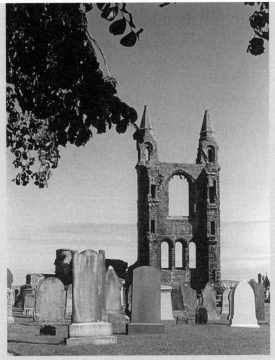

Though perhaps better known for the Royal and Ancient Golf Club, Saint Andrews, near the border with the Scottish highlands, also features the prominent medieval ruins of this major church and its cemetery *(photo by Jesse Walker).*

end has it that one of the lakes occupying the faulted trench of the Great Glen—Loch Ness—is inhabited by a long-necked sea monster. The first reported sight of the creature took place in the sixth century, when St. Columba, a pioneer evangelist from Christian Ireland (Scotia), made the sign of the cross here and saved a swimmer from the monster.

Inverness has been called the Capital of the Highlands. Nearby, on Culloden Moor, the Highland Scots under Bonnie

that the major Scottish export during this time was people, as many Scots emigrated to Canada, the United States, and Australia.

A precise demarcation of the Highlands is difficult. The west coast, with its deep fjords and rugged adjoining mountains, is very different from the smooth, unindented east coast, with its broad coastal plain. Many would thus consider the northeastern coast non-Highland in character. The Highland boundary is perhaps less a matter of geology than of anthropology. A traditional delineation would include the mainland territory of the crofting Gaels and exclude the island groups of the Orkneys, the Shetlands, and the Hebrides, although they are similar in landform. Crofts are small subsistence farms with traditional land tenure arrangements guaranteed by the government. They are most common on the raised beaches and elevated terraces along the narrow coastal strip on the west coast. A croft consists of a small patch of cropland with an associated right to pasture. Typically, a crofter raises vegetables and oats on an intensively cultivated *inbye,* while permission to graze a certain number of sheep on common hill grazing land represents the *souming* of the croft. The crofting system is as much a form of domestic architecture as of land management. The dwelling house and cow barn were combined in one structure, the *black house,* with the dividing wall between the two parts of the house rising only to the eaves. Similar to a cottage in Ireland, the crofter's residence received a regular coat of whitewash but was nonetheless called a black house because the inside was blackened by peat fires.

Further Reading: Calum I. Maclean, *The Highlands,* London: B. T. Batsford, 1959; Kenneth MacLeish, "The Highlands: Stronghold of Scottish Gaeldom," *National Geographic,* March 1968, pp. 398–435.

SCOTTISH LOWLANDS

The central corridor of the Scottish population between Glasgow and Edinburgh is not really a lowland in the sense of a plain, as it includes many hills formed by faulting, glacial deposition, and vulcanism. Nonetheless, little of its land is much above sea level, and the two major fjord-like indentations of its coastline, the Firth of Forth to the east and the Firth of Clyde

to the west, approach each other to within 31 miles (50 kilometers). Scotland's midland valley is a structural depression that has formed from the foundering of a block of the earth's crust between parallel faults. The boundaries of the *graben* are sharp and evident in the landscape, especially the line of the Highland boundary fault to the northwest, where the Grampian block rises 900 feet (274 meters) above the central valley. Old Red Sandstones and rocks from the Carboniferous period can be found within the sagging trough between the two fault boundaries, with the Old Red Sandstones exposed on the outer margin of the depression and the coal-rich Carboniferous rocks lying in the center. Volcanic intrusions add to the complexity of the landscape, and in some cases they provide urban sites, as at Edinburgh, where the nucleus of the medieval town is the volcanic neck (Castle Rock) on which Edinburgh castle stands.

Although some three-quarters of Scotland's highly urbanized population live in the midland vale, the region still has a reputation for agricultural prosperity and innovation. Grain growing used to be dominant in the drier east, as on the Fife Peninsula (between the firths of Tay and Forth). In the rainier west, dairying has long been a specialty, as in Ayrshire, home of the famous breed of the same name. Market gardening, poultry and pig farms, and fruit growing all have their niche. The fruit for the celebrated jams and marmalades of Dundee used to come from the nearby Carse of Gowrie, just upstream on the Tay along a strip of low-lying, sheltered coastlands; but today, large quantities of foreign fruit are brought in.

Coal has been worked here since the Middle Ages, but the rise of export trade in the sixteenth century and the beginning of large-scale metalworking at the end of the eighteenth led to rapid urban growth and development similar to that in northern England. The major seams of coal are scattered throughout the midland valley and include the Ayrshire field, adjoining a low sandy shore in the west, with few inlets; the Lanark field, straddling the middle Clyde and extending northeastward toward the Forth; the Fife and Clackmannan field, west of Kirkcaldy; and the Midlothian field, southeast of Edinburgh.

The decline in coal production in the region was a result of the long-term maturation of Western economies, which led to technological developments in steelmaking and lowered the consumption of coal. It also is related to the quality of the coal reserves. Scottish splint worked well for charging early hot-blast furnaces but is not much good in modern steelmaking with its requirements for high-quality coking coals. (Scotland's coal is now mostly used for electric power generation.)

The rise of Glasgow to the rank of major port and industrial city dates from the early 1700s, when its merchants forged trading links between the Clyde and the American colonies. The passage of the Act of Union of 1707, which joined the English and Scottish parliaments and created the United Kingdom, caused many Scottish nationalists to echo their bard Robert Burns, saying that Scotland had been sold for English gold (England paid a financial compensation to Scotland). However, the Act of Union did grant the Scots the right to trade with English colonies. Scotland took advantage of its geographical position, which afforded shorter transatlantic crossings. Glasgow's traders organized the lucrative economy of the tobacco colonies of the **Chesapeake Bay,** which were underserviced by cities, and provided various services also to Caribbean plantations, serving as distributors of their sugar. Scottish tobacco princes gave way to cotton kings and then to iron and steel magnates. Glasgow became the preferred point of departure for transatlantic passengers. The smaller but culturally preeminent city of Edinburgh held onto its banking and service community and its prestigious university, functioning much as would a national capital; but record-breaking vessels were launched from Clydeside. British launchings in the period between the two world wars amounted to between one-third and one-half of the world total, and the deeply dredged Clyde was easily the most important site of British shipbuilding.

The son and grandson of renowned lighthouse engineers, Robert Louis Stevenson was also a resident of Edinburgh. His classic tales of adventure *(Treasure Island* and *Kidnapped),* portrait of psychological distress in an urban setting *(Dr. Jekyll and Mr. Hyde),* and warm, sensitive children's verse *(Child's Garden of Verses)* display the fertile imagination of a true son of the Scottish Lowlands.

See also: Scottish Highlands.
Further Reading: George Scott-Moncrieff, *The Lowlands of Scotland,* London: Batsford, 1939.

SEINE RIVER
See Paris Basin

SEMMERING PASS
See Alpine Passes

SEVEN SEAS
Almost everyone talks of the Seven Seas, but no one seems to be able to name them. In ancient times, the *Seven Seas* referred to seven large bodies of water that writers considered arms of a single, circumambient **Ocean Sea.** These included the **Mediterranean Sea,** the Red Sea, the China Sea, the

West African Sea, the East African Sea, the Indian Ocean, and the Persian (Arabian) Gulf. Other ancient writers identified the Seven Seas as seven supposed saltwater lagoons on the east coast of Italy, including the **Venetian Lagoon.** The phrase often went undefined, however, lending it an air of exoticism and mystery.

With the discovery of new lands and seas, the antique reference fell out of favor. In 1896, however, the popular writer Rudyard Kipling titled a book of poems *The Seven Seas,* and due to his influence (he was preeminently the poet of empire, which was then at high tide), the description came back into use. The following bodies of water would be identified today as the Seven Seas: the North Atlantic Ocean, the South Atlantic Ocean, the North Pacific Ocean, the South Pacific Ocean, the Indian Ocean, the Arctic Ocean, and the Antarctic Ocean. The division of the Atlantic and Pacific Oceans into two parts might seem somewhat artificial, but there is a justification for it. Near the equator is a belt of calm air known as the doldrums (avoided by early sailors), which separates winds and ocean currents of opposite direction in the two hemispheres.

The term continues to refer as much to the world of legend as that of fact: Despite the common listing of the Antarctic Ocean today as one of the Seven Seas, *there is no Antarctic Ocean.* A look at a world map will show that the waters surrounding the south polar continent of Antarctica do not constitute a separate ocean but rather are the southern extension of the Atlantic, Pacific, and Indian Oceans.

SEVEN WONDERS OF THE ANCIENT WORLD

Though more strictly architectural than geographical, these awe-inspiring structures from antiquity have impressed un-told numbers of people since ancient times. The list originally compiled by such ancient writers as Antipater of Sidon and Philo of Byzantium is in part traditional. The persistence of these ancient monuments in the collective memory of mankind is all the more remarkable in that only one survives to the present, and some lasted for only a short time. A better title for the list might be the Seven Wonders of the Ancient Western World, as it only includes remarkable works known to the ancient Greeks and Romans. Clustered around or near the eastern **Mediterranean Sea,** the following grouping includes two statues, two tombs, a temple, a garden, and a lighthouse:

1. Great Pyramid of Giza, Egypt

The oldest and only surviving of the Seven Wonders, the tomb of Khufu (in Greek, Cheops), fourth dynasty (ca. 2650 B.C.), was built to guarantee the pharaoh a secure journey into the afterworld. The food, furniture, and other royal possessions placed inside the pyramid—although most would be removed by vandals in the course of the centuries—were meant to ensure that the intact body (the mummy) and the spiritual double pass safely into the afterlife. The Great Pyramid, located on the Nile near Memphis, is as tall as a 42-story skyscraper. Its base is cardinally oriented (north-south and east-west), giving rise to countless speculations that the tomb was an ancient astronomical observatory or had some other utilitarian function. Herodotus, Caesar, and Napoleon all gazed on this pyramid in wonder. The nearby, eastward-facing Sphinx, with its lion's body and human face only added to the mystery of the site.

2. Hanging Gardens of Babylon

The eight-gated city of Babylon, situated on the Euphrates River in

Mesopotamia, featured splendid processional ways and elaborate ziggurats (winding towers), such as the infamous Tower of Babel, but it is best remembered for the gardens that graced its citadel. The gardens, not actually hanging but rather planted on flats like balconies or arboreal terraces supported by arches, included trees as well as flowers. Tradition has it that Nebuchadnezzar II (605–562 B.C.) built the gardens to console his wife, who was from the humid eastern land of Media. An elaborate hydraulic system irrigated the gardens with extensive piping and pump works. At a height of 350 feet (107 meters), this wonder was almost certainly seen by Alexander the Great, who added Mesopotamia to his world empire and died in the city of Babylon, perhaps in sight of the famous gardens.

3. Statue of Zeus at Olympia, Greece

Within Olympia's shrine of Zeus, built in the fifth century B.C., was a huge statue of the ruler of the heavens. Located at the southern end of Greece on the **Peloponnese** peninsula, Olympia was the site of the most honored athletic contests of the ancient Greeks, a people who admired the grace and beauty of the body as much as they celebrated the mind. Today's Olympic Games derive from the regular series of contests held at ancient Olympia. We know of the gigantic Zeus statue only from its description by ancient writers, such as Pausanias, and from coins that bear its image. The statue, the work of the famous sculptor Phidias, was of gold and ivory. Zeus, the ruler of the gods but also the protector of cities and the god of hospitality, held a wreath as a symbol of victory in his right hand and a scepter in his left. The fate of the statue is unknown.

4. Temple of Artemis at Ephesus

Diana's temple was begun about 350 B.C. in this Hellenistic city in Asia Minor. The temple, built with the help of donations from Croesus, was in the classical Greek style, resembling the Parthenon in Athens. The archaeologist John Wood unearthed sixty-foot-high columns from this structure during the course of a famous dig in the late nineteenth century. Herodotus considered the temple so magnificent that he compared it to the pyramids of Egypt. Partly demolished by Goths in 262, the temple was later set afire by a madman. Parts of the columns and sculpture are preserved in the British Museum.

5. Mausoleum at Halicarnassus

Artemisia, queen of Caria, ordered a tomb to be built for her deceased husband, King Mausolus, in 350 B.C. at Halicarnassus (today's Bodrum, in Turkey). The structure was 140 feet (43 meters) in height, 440 feet (134 meters) in circumference, and comprised three sections: a podium base; a 360-columned temple as a middle section; and a pyramidal roof, topped by a marble four-horse chariot. It took approximately three years to complete the construction. Later, the need to build defensive fortresses nearby led to the dismantling of the tomb, but a horse and several friezes are still preserved at the British Museum. This king's name and tomb gave rise to the English word mausoleum.

6. Colossus of Rhodes

Perhaps the most mysterious of the Seven Wonders is this giant bronze statue, which stood at the entrance to the harbor of the Aegean Island of Rhodes. An earthquake that erupted in 226 B.C., only a half century after its raising, toppled the statue. Nearly 110 feet (34 meters) tall, the statue honored Helios, the Greek sun-god, who represented the unification of the Rhodian kingdom. The legs of the Colossus did not stand astride the harbor, permitting ships to go between, as portrayed in medieval times and described by Shakespeare ("Ye Gods, he doth bestride the world like a Colossus," Antony says of Caesar). The entrance to the harbor was too wide—1,300 feet (396 meters)—and such a large statue, with legs set apart (during the Renaissance, it was commonly portrayed as standing on two separate pedestals), would have crumbled even without an earthquake.

The Greek geographer and historian Strabo described the toppling of the statue, saying that the statue broke at its knees, with the head, torso, and thighs lying where they fell. The Romans left the ruins where they lay. In 672, by which time Arabs had taken control of the island, the remains held little meaning for local inhabitants, and the metal was sold for scrap and hauled off to Asia, reputedly by 900 camels. When the French decided to design a statue to commemorate America's commitment to freedom, the inspiration for the Statue of Liberty, which now stands at the entrance to New York's harbor, was one of the conceptions of this ancient statue current at the time—with one arm upheld, bearing a lamp or torch.

7. Pharos Lighthouse, Alexandria

Alexander the Great put his stamp on a newly conquered Egypt (332 B.C.) by establishing the gridiron town of Alexandria at the western end of the Nile Delta, along a limestone spur that jutted out from the mainland. Access to the Mediterranean and an excellent natural harbor were the primary factors in Alexander's choice of location for his city. The choice proved well founded, as Alexandria quickly gained a reputation as a cosmopolitan trading center.

A few years later, during the reign of Ptolemy II, known also as Philadelphus (285–246 B.C.), a lighthouse was built on an island at the tip of this spur or peninsula. Between four and five hundred feet (122–152 meters) in height, the four-storied, gleaming white tower sent out a bright beacon, warning ships at sea of limestone reefs and other dangers, such as the treacherous Bull's Horn rocks at the harbor entrance. The lighthouse was designed by the architect Sostratus (a contemporary of the mathematician Euclid) and made use of new and advanced technology, such as polished metal mirrors.

The lighthouse continued to function until 641, after which the Arab conquerors of Alexandria used remnants of the structure as a mosque. In 1375 an earthquake completely destroyed the lighthouse. However, to this day, in modern romance languages the word *pharos* and variations thereof are used to signify a lighthouse (e.g., in Spanish, *faro*).

In an imitative vein, the American civil engineering society in 1994 designated the outstanding U.S. engineering achievements the "Seven Wonders of the United States." Among the most significant structural wonders are counted the Golden Gate Bridge, Hoover Dam, the interstate highway system, Kennedy Space Center, **Panama Canal**, Trans-Alaska Pipeline, and the World Trade Center. (The Panama Canal is no longer under U.S. ownership, but it was built by the United States.)

Further Reading: Peter A. Clayton and Martin J. Price, *The Seven Wonders of the Ancient World,* New York: Barnes and Noble, 1988; John and Elizabeth Romer, *The Seven Wonders of the Ancient World,* New York: Henry Holt, 1996; Lowell Thomas, *Seven Wonders of the Ancient World,* Garden City, N.Y.: Hanover House, 1956.

SIERRA MADRE OCCIDENTAL

The chief mountain system of Mexico—the Sierra Madre—encloses the **Mexican Plateau** on the east, west, and south, and is only open to the north, in the direction of the United States. The Sierra Madre Occidental is the rugged western border of the plateau surface, a forbidding mountain mass that parallels the Gulf of California and the Pacific. The range widens to the south, increasing in breadth from around 100 miles (161 kilometers) in the states of Sonora and Chihuahua (south of Arizona) to around 300 miles (483 kilometers) farther south, where it merges with the transverse volcanic axis of the Cordillera Anáhuac. This volcanic cordillera crosses the plateau in a series of snow-topped peaks south of Mexico City. The elevations of the Sierra Madre increase from north to south, with individual mountains reaching 7,000–8,000 feet (2,134–2,438 kilometers) and some peaks rising as high as 14,000 feet (4,267 meters).

Both the sierra and the western side of the plateau have been built up from large amounts of volcanic material that has issued from vents. Westward-flowing streams have cut deep valleys along the margins of the plateau, producing characteristic steep-sided canyons, or barrancas, which have blocked passage between the narrow strip of coastal lowlands and the plateau. Some of these barrancas, such as that of El Cobre, are as deep and spectacular as the Grand Canyon of the Colorado. In the southern section of the sierra, in Jalisco, lies Lake Chapala, the largest lake in Middle America.

The western sierra is both more elevated and broader than the sierra that flanks the plateau on the east. Impassable barrancas, steep slopes, and mountain barriers have rendered access from the coast extremely difficult, and not until 1945 was an auto highway completed across the sierra from Mazatlán on the Pacific coast to Durango on the plateau. The first railroad to cross the escarpment was finished in 1962, connecting Chihuahua City in the north to Topolobampo. As a result, the wealth that has come from exploitation of the rich mineral resources of the sierra—silver, lead, copper, gold, and iron—has not led to the growth of a major Pacific port but rather has augmented the provincial economy or been siphoned off to Mexico City, or earlier, to Spain.

Initial Spanish conquest of Mexico focused on the densely populated centers of the Mesa Central and on the well-populated Valley of Oaxaca to the south. Not until the expeditions of the infamous Nuño de Guzmán (1531 and 1532) was the western edge of the plateau explored and its native peoples conquered. Although Guzmán found some silver and gold deposits in the western foothills of the escarpment, his more important work was the founding of the towns of Guadalajara and Compostela, on the western side of the plateau. After the Mixton War (1541) an approach opened northward from Guadalajara into the grassland district of Zacatecas. This in turn led to the accidental discovery in 1546 of the vast silver deposits of Zacatecas, which set off a rush of Spanish wealth seekers. A northern frontier was extended primarily along a line of outcropping silver-bearing ores in the eastern foothills of the Sierra Madre Occidental. Within 20 years, rich silver-mining communities sprang up at Durango and elsewhere, reaching as far north as the Santa Bárbara mines in southern Chihuahua.

The great Silver Belt in northern Mexico, in the land of the Chichimecs, lay within a semiarid zone of grassland, bordered on the west by the mixed pine-and-oak forest of the sierra. Livestock raising and irrigated grain cultivation arose as economic activities ancillary to mining. Connections across the steep escarpment to the west did not exist during the colonial period, and silver, the chief export, had to find another outlet. Silver eight-real pieces, and later, pesos, streamed from the mints at Zacatecas, Mexico City, and a number of other places, entering into international commerce as the preferred medium of ex-

Coahuila and Nuevo León south of the Rio Grande as far as Orizaba, at about 19° N, where it merges with the volcanic belt. Elevations increase to the south, with the snow-capped peak of Orizaba, or Citlaltépetl, at 18,700 feet (5,700 meters) the highest point in Middle America. Unlike the western sierra, this range does not display volcanic landforms but rather consists of a series of elongated

Sierra Madre Oriental mountains from Highway 60, west of Lináres, San Luis Potosí state *(photo by Robert C. West)*.

change. These dollar-sized "pieces of eight" were legal tender in the United States until 1857, and were important in the creation of a dollar-based currency in the first place. Colonial Spain derived most of its wealth from the string of silver mines along the eastern foothills of the Sierra Madre Occidental, stretching from Zacatecas and Guanajuato northward to the Chihuahua mines of Santa Eulalia.

SIERRA MADRE ORIENTAL

The eastern flank of Mexico's central plateau extends from the barren hills of

limestone ridges that are oriented north-south and closely resemble the folded mountains of the Appalachians. Elevations commonly reach 7,000–8,000 feet (2,134–2,438 meters), with some peaks rising above 13,000 feet (3,962 meters). Viewed from the plateau, the mountains do not present dramatic relief but appear rather like the upturned lip of the plateau. From the Gulf coastal plain, however, the range rises in tiers of parallel ridges and valleys to create a dramatic escarpment. At their northern end, the folded mountains veer westward near the site of Monterrey, which lies on a plain at their base.

The conquest of central Mexico between 1519 and 1521 required the Spaniard Cortés to traverse the eastern escarpment of the Sierra Madre Oriental on his route from Veracruz to the Aztec capital of Tenochtitlán (Mexico City). Although mineral deposits, especially silver, were more abundant on the western flank of the plateau, fertile grasslands along the western margins of the sierra attracted a pastoral element among the Spanish early on. Saltillo was founded in 1577 as a result of a group of Spanish colonists crossing the arid northern interior from the western silver belt. The discovery of small silver and lead mines drew Spanish settlers farther north to Monclova and east across the escarpment to the sites of Monterrey and Cerralvo, overlooking the narrow coastal plain. Missionaries and stockmen pressed forward and crossed the Rio Grande into the grassy interior coastal plain of Texas, founding San Antonio in 1718. This line of Spanish advance eventually reached as far as the Sabine River, an informal boundary separating Spanish Texas from French Louisiana.

SIERRA NEVADA (U.S.)

This nearly 400-mile (644-kilometer) wall of mountains, most of it located in eastern California, has been variously a barrier, a region of mineral extraction, and a refuge from urban civilization.

The largest fault-block mountain range in the United States, the Sierra Nevada—from Sp. *sierra* (sawtooth mountain) and *nevada* (snowy)—is tilted so that the eastern edge rises sharply from the **Great Basin,** while the western slope gradually descends to the floor of the **Central Valley** in rolling foothills and grassy valleys. The southern end of the

Sierras is at Tehachapi Pass, southeast of Bakersfield, where the transverse Tehachapi Mountains curve to the southwest to meet the Coast Ranges. To the north, the mountains end at the gap south of the volcanic cone of Lassen Peak. The highest elevation in the lower forty-eight states is attained at Mt. Whitney (el. 14,495 feet or 4,418 meters), overlooking the eastern margin of the Sierras near Lone Pine. The Sierra Nevada has spectacular mountain scenery, especially in the High Sierras south of Lake Tahoe and at the national parks of Yosemite, Sequoia, and Kings Canyon.

It might surprise some to learn that gold was first discovered in California not in the northern part of the state but near Los Angeles, where a mine was in operation at San Fernando in 1842. Though attracting some attention, this discovery was small compared to the flood of publicity, much of it wildly exaggerated, following the discovery of gold in the western foothills of the Sierra Nevada in 1848. The site was a dry streambed along the south fork of the Río de los Americanos (the name was quickly changed to the American River), which was then being used as a millrace for a sawmill under construction. This initial discovery was on a tributary of the Sacramento River, 40 miles (64 kilometers) upriver from Sutter's Fort, which was established in 1839 by John Sutter, a Swiss, as a central location for a diversified farming and ranching community. The discovery of gold literally washed away Sutter's pastoral dream. Tens of thousands of prospective miners infected with gold fever roamed up and down the western edge of the Sierras along streams that drained the foothills. Miners inspected and sifted through river sand and dirt looking for the gleaming specks, flakes, and nuggets of their dreams. Camps sprang up (and often just as quickly disappeared) along streams that can still be traced on a modern map: American, Yuba, Cosumnes, Mokelumme. The forty-niners searched for ore-bearing deposits in a belt that extended nearly 300 miles (483 kilometers) north and south. Eventually, prospectors searched all of the alluvial deposits of the Sacramento and San Joaquin Rivers as well.

means of individual miners or even a group. Miners rightly assumed that the small flecks and larger nuggets they had been seeking in the streambeds had eroded from rocks in places farther upstream. The bedrock source of rich veins of gold—the so-called mother lode—was east of Sacramento in a narrow belt extending up and down the foothills (the area northwest of Mariposa was especially

Glacial polished granite with erratic boulders in the high country of Yosemite in the Sierra Nevada (*photo by Jesse Walker*).

Placer-type mining (pronounced "plasser") originally prevailed, by which alluvial sediments were washed in a pan, rocker, or trough to separate the bright glints of gold from the washings. By the mid-1850s such crude hand techniques had given way to the application of capital and expertise (and environmental damage) in the form of hydraulic mining, using hose-and-nozzle methods. Sometimes miners removed entire hillslopes to more easily get at pay dirt. The construction of elaborate flumes and aqueducts followed, but they were beyond the

rich). Shafts had to be sunk to bedrock, and the expensive process of underground mining of quartz rock began.

By 1860 most of the pickers-and-panners had either quit or drifted to other mining regions in Idaho or Colorado. Most of the forty-niners never struck it rich in the gold fields; more of them made money selling supplies and provisions to the miners. The Golden State received an enormous influx of population at midcentury—from 15,000 in 1848 to half a million by 1857. Almost overnight, shanties and tents had become substantial

Victorian frame houses and Sacramento and San Francisco were transformed into respectable cities, functioning respectively as the outfitting and distribution center for the northern mines and as the center of California's international trade. If today's automobile travelers are bold enough to leave the interstates, they can follow the twists and turns of California State Highway 49 the entire length of the gold country, from Oakhurst in the south (near Yellowstone National Park) to Vinton, north of Lake Tahoe.

Further Reading: John Walton Caughey, *The California Gold Rush,* Berkeley: University of California Press, 1975 (1948); Earl Pomeroy, *The Pacific Slope: A History of California, Oregon, Washington, Idaho, Utah, and Nevada,* New York: Knopf, 1965.

SKAGGERAK

See Danish Straits

SOUTH PASS (ROCKY MOUNTAINS)

Influenced by the mistaken notion that the boundary between east- and west-flowing streams in the mountainous western United States was a single continuous ridge, explorers Lewis and Clark (1804–1806) followed the Missouri River and its tributaries across the **Continental Divide** at Lemhi Pass (Idaho) before descending the Pacific slope. The route of this famous exploring party commissioned by President Thomas Jefferson crossed the divide well north of the only major breach of the Rockies— South Pass—which lies in a broad, level valley in southwestern Wyoming, at the south end of the Wind River Range, at an elevation of about 7,550 feet (2,301 meters). Within only a few years of this epochal expedition fur traders found the southern route across the Rockies (1812–1813) that would later be followed by so many western migrants.

South Pass is not a narrow defile like the **Alpine Passes** but rather a broad (and elevated) corridor, winding across widely separated ranges. Bounded by the Wind River Range to the north and Antelope Hills to the south, the pass is a semiarid plain with scattered sagebrush, and represents the only crossing of the Rockies with a gentle grade in the presence of water and grass.

The historic Oregon Trail, discovered in 1824 and first used by Captain Benjamin Bonneville's exploring party of 1832, crossed the divide here near Lander, Wyoming. One of the major landmarks along the trail, Independence Rock, overlooks the Sweet Water valley, which emigrants followed after leaving the North Platte near Casper. Travelers hoped to see this conspicuous erosional remnant by the fourth of July if they were to make their crossing before winter snows closed off passes farther west. Arriving later, they feared "seeing the elephant," slang for the perils of the journey. Although travelers may have envisioned South Pass as a narrow opening through the mountains with steep walls on both sides, they were already in the pass once their route paralleled the Sweet Water.

The 2,000-mile (3,219-kilometer) emigrant road connecting Independence, Missouri, at the junction of the Missouri and the North Platte, and Oregon City near where the Willamette River joins the Columbia, was used primarily between 1841 and 1869. During this period, an estimated 350,000 emigrants followed the Oregon Trail in what has been considered the largest peaceful mass migration in history.

Beyond South Pass the trail split in two directions: The Mormon Trail branched toward the Great Salt Lake; the California-bound left the Snake River and headed southwest along one of the few perennial streams in Nevada, the Humboldt, in the direction of the formidable **Sierra Nevada.** Travelers heading for Oregon followed the hot, dry Snake River Plain, where water was just out of reach at the bottom of a black basaltic canyon, and eventually crossed the Blue Mountains to reach the Columbia at the Dalles, where the Cascades are breached.

who first explored its islands and bordering mainlands had difficulty choosing a proper name for it.

As a result of an error on Toscanelli's map of 1474, Columbus believed that a large island, **Antillia** (island in front of [Asia]), lay in the western Atlantic and would serve as a good stopping-off point in his proposed western voyage. Later, as geographic knowledge increased, the

Independence Rock on the Oregon Trail, a conspicuous landmark for travelers on the way to South Pass *(Corel Corporation).*

The Union Pacific Railroad, completed in 1869, also crossed the Rockies at South Pass. This railway made the long, dangerous emigrant road obsolete. Most of the Oregon Trail in Kansas and Nebraska has been plowed under; but in ranch country the landscape is slow to change, and hundreds of miles of ruts can still be seen, especially in Wyoming. South Pass today is designated a U.S. national historic landmark.

SPANISH MAIN

Although the Caribbean Sea was the best-known sea of the New World, the Spanish

name of this legendary island came to be applied to the very real islands between Trinidad and the Bahamas. Columbus's original authorization of 30 April 1492 spoke of the discovery of *islas y tierra firme* in what was then believed to be a single, circumambient **Ocean Sea.** By 1500 it was apparent that Cuba was not Japan, nor the Central American coastlands China, as Columbus had believed. Balboa's crossing of **Darién** (1513) in southeastern Panama had revealed another sea, the South Sea. The newfound sea having been given this name, the other thereafter came to be called Mar del Norte, or North Sea. The east-west orientation of the **Isthmus of Panama** (formerly called the Isthmus of Darién) led to the labeling of the two great oceans as northern and southern, which was the prevailing Spanish usage of the time. So the Caribbean Sea was an arm of the Mar del Norte, just as the Gulf of Mexico, which the Spanish distinguished from the Caribbean, was another arm. The discoverers of new land required names for the varying topography of the coast and lands, but navigators of the continuous seas did not need to name smaller parts of the sea except at reentries marking the termini of routes or at constriction points. The Caribbean had broad approaches to the east through widely scattered islands, and the **Straits of Florida** connecting it to the Gulf of Mexico were hardly a **Gibraltar**-like control point.

Major challenges to Spanish hegemony came at the end of the sixteenth century, with the rise of English freebooting and privateering by men like Drake and Hawkins, who preyed on Spanish fleets and bases. The defeat of the Armada off the **English Channel** (1588) has often been considered to represent a sea change in political power, but of course this judgment has been made in hindsight, following the development of English industrial and naval supremacy in later centuries. In the seventeenth century, north European powers—England, the Netherlands, and France—established toeholds of influence in the Caribbean, in their colonization of the Lesser Antillean island arc in the southeastern part of the basin, which the Spanish avoided because it had no gold (but did have hostile tribes). To isolated freebooting were added elements of adventurism, and buccaneering and piracy became endemic in the region, reaching as far north as the **Chesapeake Bay.**

The term Spanish Main—shorthand for Spanish *tierra firma,* or for Spanish Mainland—became the common English usage referring to the southern littoral of the Caribbean from the isthmus of Panama to the mouth of the Orinoco River in Venezuela. Most of the northern coastlands of South America are dry and inhospitable, consisting of thorn scrub and salt pans, but beyond Cartagena rainfall increases until a dense tropical rain forest characterizes the Darién region on the border between Colombia and Panama. Valuable silver passed from Peru to the ports of the Spanish Main. From the north end of the Isthmus of Panama, initially at Nombre de Dios, later at Portobelo, the once-yearly treasure fleets set out for Havana, Cuba, whence they were escorted by armed convoy across the Atlantic to Seville.

The town of Maracaibo, at the entrance to the lake of the same name, was sacked no less than five times in the seventeenth century. Portobelo became the focus of English freebooters after Drake sacked Nombre de Dios (1572) and forced the Spanish to relocate their major transshipment point farther up the coast. Drake had more success plundering slow-moving mule trains and taking lesser ports of the Spanish Main than he had conquering the Spanish stronghold at Portobelo. In his last expedition he failed to take the town and died, and was secretly buried at sea off Portobelo. Later buccaneers like William Parker in 1601, Sir Henry Morgan in 1688, and Admiral Edward Vernon in 1739 were able to sack Portobelo, which the Spanish had believed impregnable.

Pirate havens shifted from island to island, as the rule of law was established in the West Indies, finally occupying the Bahamas at the northern edge of the region, in what strictly speaking was not a part of the Caribbean. Writers of romance then appropriated the name Spanish Main to refer to the entire Caribbean region, whose history had given rise to so many colorful stories and personalities.

Further Reading: Carl Ortwin Sauer, *The Early Spanish Main,* Berkeley: University of California Press, 1969.

SUDETES

Extending some 185 miles (300 kilometers) between the upper courses of the Elbe and Oder Rivers, this hilly borderland between the Czech Republic and Poland has long been occupied by Germanic and Slavic peoples, whose struggles have sometimes featured in history, most significantly in the period just before World War II.

The Sudetes (Czech *Sudety;* German, *Sudeten*) are part of the belt of deeply incised plateaus running across central Europe. To the west the Sudetes are continued by the Saxon hill lands of the Erzgebirge (Ore Mountains); while to the east, beyond the Moravian Gate, are the **Carpathian Mountains,** the major mountain system of eastern Europe, of a later geological era and standing higher in places but presenting an aspect similar to that of the Sudetes.

The Sudetes comprise a number of distinct units: Bordering on southeastern Germany are the Lusatian (Polish Luzické) Mountains; along the border of southwest Poland are, from west to east, the Isergebirge, the Riesengebirge (Polish Krkonose)—the central and highest range of the Sudetes, reaching 5,259 feet (1,603 meters) in the Schneekoppe—the Adlergebirge, and the Hrubý Jeseník Mountains. The mineral resources of the Sudetes are varied but not so rich as either the extensive silver-bearing ores of the Erzgebirge to the west or the abundant Silesian coal deposits found east of the Oder; so the in-

habitants of the Sudetes have placed emphasis on home industries, especially the production of glass, porcelain, and textiles.

The region has traditionally been German speaking. It has long been recognized as a borderland whose historical antecedents lie in the late medieval thrust of German colonization to the rim of the **Bohemian Basin.** All of the German-speaking population in the regions of Czechoslovakia bordering on Germany were known as Sudeten Germans. The Sudetenland, home of these Germans for centuries, has been for the most part under the political control of Bohemia (after 1918, Czechoslovakia). In the interwar years, the alleged mistreatment of Germans in this borderland was added to the list of German grievances. After Hitler came to power in 1933, the Sudeten Germans, with the active support and interference of the German National Socialists, or Nazis, formed a home front (later, party) modeled on the Nazis and devised the Carlsbad Program (1938) to address issues of equality, autonomy, and reparations for discrimination suffered after 1918.

Already in September 1936 at the Nazi party's annual convention held in Nürnberg (Nuremberg) Hitler had stated the need for additional *Lebensraum* (living-space) for an expanding Germany. His preoccupation with gaining lands already settled by Germans was well known. In spring 1938 the Anschluss, or unification of Austria with the German Reich, took place, which although affirmed by a plebiscite was clearly a power grab by Hitler and the Nazis. The next pawn was given up in the infamous attempt at appeasement by British Prime Minister Chamberlain at Munich in September 1938, by which Hitler was given the Sudetenland in exchange for his worthless promise that this was his final demand.

Within six months German troops occupied Czechoslovakia and established the German-controlled protectorates of Bohemia and Slovakia; six months after that, Germany attacked Poland, initiating World War II.

After the capitulation of Germany in 1945, the Potsdam Conference sanctioned the expulsion of Germans from east European territories, including the Sudetenland. Despite the exchange of national minorities and attempts at repatriation, the Sudetes experienced a decline in population and almost a total loss of native Germans.

See also: Hercynian Uplands.

TEHUANTEPEC, ISTHMUS OF

For the Spanish, the first few decades of the sixteenth century in the Americas were taken up in attempts to discover a strait connecting the Atlantic and Pacific Oceans. Beginning with Columbus's fourth voyage (1502), which explored the Caribbean coast of the Central American landmass from Honduras to the Gulf of Darien (Panama), the Spanish sought a water opening across the isthmus that would link their far-flung empire stretching from Patagonia to California, from the Philippine Islands to the **Canaries.**

After Balboa crossed the narrow **Isthmus of Darién** and discovered the South Sea, there was renewed hope that a transisthmian water passage would be discovered. However, the Spanish would continually be disappointed, and the lack of an easy route across the Americas would persist through the sixteenth and seventeenth centuries as a thorny difficulty in trade between Spain and her colonies. Cortés thought the search for a strait across the isthmus was so important that he traversed the narrow waist of southern Mexico—the Isthmus of Tehuantepec—in search of a riverine passage and pioneered a land trail even before he subdued Tenochtitlán (Mexico City). The conquistador spent two decades trying to develop this land route across Tehuantepec in hopes of developing a ship-building

center at the Pacific terminus of the route that could trade with the Orient and Peru. The arduous roads across central Mexico linking Acapulco to Mexico City to Veracruz, over which so many bulky commodities traveled, would thereby be avoided.

The Tehuantepec constriction has the two essential characteristics of a transisthmian crossing: narrowness and low elevation. Only about 125 miles (201 kilometers) separate the Bay of Campeche, an arm of the Gulf of Mexico, on the north from the Gulf of Tehuantepec on the southern (Pacific) terminus. The region is mostly tropical lowlands, lying north of the Chiapan Highlands yet south of the main zone of convergence of the sierras of northern and central Mexico. Traveling from the north and the Gulf of Mexico, the Spanish were able to follow the broad estuarine river of the Coatzacoalcos more than a third of the way across the isthmus before they had to choose from among a number of tributaries draining the low continental divide. During the rainy season canoes could travel two-thirds of the distance across the isthmus before they reached a landing at the fall line, where overland transportation commenced.

The future conqueror of the Aztecs might well have crossed at the most convenient point, the Chivela pass, which can be reached by ascending the Almoloya valley, a tributary of the Coatzacoalcos, but we can never know for sure. This pass lies at about 800 feet (244 meters) above sea level. From there a number of streams cross the Pacific slope and the narrow coastal plain before reaching the lagooned coast at the present-day port of Salina Cruz or the nearby city of Tehuantepec. Despite his heroic efforts of two decades, Cortés failed to establish an interoceanic transport route here. The major stumbling block was the use of imposed labor services on the Indians despite the Crown's prohibition, which led Cortés to forfeit his rights to boatbuilding, after which he was, in effect, demoted.

An 1850 survey reported no cart road over the continental divide, only a mule path. The route was seriously considered as an alternative to the **Panama Canal** by James B. Eads—best known for his bridging of the Mississippi River at St. Louis—who was engaged in a project in the late 1870s and early 1880s that involved the construction of a ship-railway across the Tehuantepec isthmus. The accuracy of the vision of such luminaries as Hernán Cortés, James Eads, and Alexander von Humboldt (who also reviewed the isthmus's suitability as a crossing) was borne out when a transisthmian railroad was completed across the narrow neck in 1907, crossing at Chivela pass. Today's motorists follow Mexico's Highway 185 through a nearby pass at Mazahua.

Further Reading: Max L. Moorhead, "Hernán Cortés and the Tehuantepec Passage," *Hispanic American Historical Review,* Aug. 1949, pp. 370–379.

TENOCHTITLÁN

See Mexican Plateau

THAMES ESTUARY

The narratives of English life flow as easily as the Thames River, along whose wil-low-shaded banks English history has largely been written. Not one of the longest rivers of the world, the Thames winds for only 236 miles (380 kilometers) from its head west of Oxford on the eastern slopes of the **Cotswold Hills** to its outlet at The Nore. The river is navigable for 210 miles (338 kilometers) as far as Lechlade, but the upper river today is used mostly for pleasure boating. Ships to 800 tons can reach as far as London Bridge, the traditional head of navigation for large ships that were prevented from going farther upstream by the narrow arches of the old bridge. The upper course of this noble river meanders through picturesque meadows, loops around the town boasting the oldest university in a well-educated domain as well as a bustling Leland auto manufacturing plant (formerly, Morris), passes royal estates and regatta yards, and reaches London from the west, in a cozy bungalow belt. The upper river justifies its Celtic name, Tamese, which means tranquil water.

The birthplace of England and empire, however, has been the tidal Thames. The stretch of river from Teddington to below the capital city twice daily receives, then releases water from its North Sea reservoir. Kipling described the river in his poem "The River's Tale" as being like a watchman who walks his beat past London, five hours up and seven down:

Up I go till I end my run
At Tide-end-town, which is
    Teddington.
Down I come with the mud in my
    hands
And plaster it over the Maplin
    Sands.

The swiftness of the river (as much as four knots) and its tidal range (21 feet or 6.4 meters at London Bridge) forces navigators and watermen alike to mesh their work carefully with the tidal turnings of the river.

Flooding on the lower Thames is more the result of high tides coming up from the coast than of surplus water overflowing its banks as it flows seaward. Most feared is an exaggerated high tide known as a surge tide, caused by a combination of a low-pressure system lifting the water (just as it raises air), and gale winds whip-

and even its tranquil upper course is regulated by a large number of weirs to maintain an even level.

The Thames once flowed across a broad valley to join the Rhine, until about 8000 B.C., when rising sea levels caused by the melting of the Pleistocene ice sheets flooded the valley that is now the North Sea and severed Britain from the continent. Julius Caesar crossed the Thames in

Cranes line the sides of the historic Tilbury dock on the Thames, still in heavy use as recently as 1987, as shown here *(Adam Woolfitt/Corbis)*.

ping up the North Sea. Higher embankments protecting against this threat tend to obscure a view of the land as they seal off the river. As an alternative, the ingenious Thames Barrier has been put in place eight miles downstream from London, at Woolwich. The barrier is a giant, retractable flood gate (actually, a series of interlinked gates) that normally lies flush with the riverbed, unlike a vertical, guillotine-type gate, and revolves upward to a vertical position only when needed. Thus, like most great rivers of the world, the Thames does not flow freely to the sea,

54 B.C. in his conquest of the Britons; but not until a century later did troops of Emperor Claudius lay out the routes, still in use today, that branch out from the farthest fordable site downstream on the river—the first structures in what would become the Roman city of Londinium, present-day London. Only one bridge crossed the river until the eighteenth century—the London Bridge—but today 28 bridges span the tideway between Teddington and the Tower of London.

The history-haunted river has witnessed the departure of the Romans; the arrival of the Saxons, and later, the Danes and the Normans; and great wars with the French in the late medieval period and again as a prelude to the nineteenth century. The rise of the British empire, dating from the Renaissance era, brought to a fore the need to increase the number of mercantile ships as well as of Royal Navy vessels. This focused attention on the Port of London, which extends from London Bridge to Blackwall in a stretch of the river known as The Pool. In addition, a row of docks below London once served to attach Britain to its far-flung colonies: the West India, East India, and Millwall Docks, within a wide meander just below the city; the Royal Docks, including the Victoria and Albert Docks, opened in 1885 and 1880, and the King George V Docks, added in 1921 (it has been said that this combined group of Royal Docks includes the largest collective sheet of impounded dock water in the world); and the Tilbury Docks, opened in 1886 farther downriver. The need for these extensive docks arose from the high tidal range of the river and the congestion of wharfside traffic. The trend in new dock construction has been toward larger basins, located farther downstream. While the two India docks and Millwall are served by rail, Tilbury Docks has good road connections, accommodates big ships with containers, and allows roll-on, roll-off transshipment.

The enclosed world of the docks, where the aroma of spices and spirits, grain and lumber long scented the air, had fallen into disuse by the 1950s. The once bustling warehouses and wharves were derelict, to employ a common British usage that is applied to places rather than people. Redevelopment schemes converted the abandoned space into pricey residences and office blocks that can hardly be afforded by people in working-class communities of the East End.

Oceangoing vessels carrying containers today are likely to need only transshipment with no warehouse storage, and are best served by Tilbury Docks, which have become an outport for London, with Gravesend reduced to an annex of the metropolis. No longer is London, in the words of the poet John Masefield, a "great street paved with water, filled with shipping." Cocklers along the foreshore and exposed flats have been replaced by "mud larks," modern-day prospectors seeking with the aid of clicking metal detectors (a beep signals a find) the assorted spawn of history buried beneath the silt of the shifting river.

Further Reading: George H. Dury, *The British Isles: A Systematic and Regional Geography,* 5th ed., London: Heinemann, 1973, pp. 316–330; Mervyn Savill, *Tide of London: A Study of London and Its River.* London: Brittannicus Liber, 1951.

THERMOPYLAE

The pass at Thermopylae is a narrow corridor between Mt. Oeta (7,200 feet or 2,195 meters) and the Gulf of Malis in northern Greece. In ancient times the routeway that passed here was the main land link between Thessaly and central Greece. Large armies like the Persian force that invaded Greece in 480 B.C., after crossing Hellespontus (today's **Dardanelles**) on a bridge of ships, could not follow the narrow, highly indented coastline all the way south but had to cross into the interior: Not only was fresh water often lacking along the coast, but the troops would have had to form into narrow files that would have needed weeks to cross an inlet.

The Persians under Darius had come earlier, in 490 B.C., and had been beaten decisively at **Marathon** by Athenians. But now, led by the despot Xerxes, Persia assembled the largest army and navy ever seen in history in its drive to conquer the West (historians estimate the army had about 200,000 men). Athens used its new wealth from the silver mines of Laurium to build triremes for its navy, which would finally triumph at **Salamis.** A small troop of 300 elite warriors from Sparta were sent to hold the Thermopylae pass in the late summer of 480 B.C.

The pass had two narrow gates at either end and a middle gate (referring to a level tract of land allowing passage through hill lands). Herodotus, the chronicler of the Persian Wars, visited the site and reported that it was wide enough for a single carriage. Under the command of one of Sparta's kings, Leonidas (by tradition, elite Spartiates had to be led by a king), the heavily armored Spartan hoplites chose to defend the Middle Gate, both because the people of Phocis had left a defensive wall built against the Thessalians and because the corridor was broad enough to allow the establishment of a solid line, which was the most efficient use of Spartan arms and armor.

A sulphurous spring that gave the place its name—literally, Hot Gates—poured out of the base of the mountain about a mile to the northwest of the Middle Gate. The right flank of the Spartan line was the Malian Gulf; the left, the steep slope of Kallidromos. Today the Malian Gulf has silted up and the modern coastline lies several miles from the scene of battle. The pass was an ideal place to deploy a hoplite line, being unturnable at either end, or so it seemed.

On 18 August, Xerxes threw wave after wave of the Persian army—Medes, the men of Susa, and finally, the crack division of the Immortals, ten thousand elite soldiers personally selected by the great king—into the narrows, but the Spartans held the line. For two days the Spartans fought valiantly though they were greatly outnumbered, as they had been taught since childhood that to die in battle was better than to return home disgraced by defeat. On the night before the third day a traitor showed the Persians a track ascending a steep ravine that reached a high pass around the side of the mountain and the Spartan army. (The Greek betrayer Ephialtes occupies the same position in Greek history that Judas does in Christianity.) Outflanked on the third day and knowing that their destiny was sealed, the Spartans fought on valiantly to the end. They died to a man, according to the iron law of Lycurgus, by which they had lived since childhood.

Their loss had not only slowed the Persians and demonstrated the almost superhuman valor of the Spartans, but the battle came on the heels of major losses of Persian ships due to a storm and an engagement with the Greeks off Artemisium. Perennially at odds with one another, the individualist Greeks began to form a broader Greek sympathy and to view a victory together against the alien invaders as more important then their local grudges and identities. The death of the Spartan king Leonidas and his 300 men at the Hot Gates became a torch, not to fire a funeral pyre, but to light the way of unity among the fractious but freedom-loving Greeks, and to show the way of freedom to the heirs of the Greek legacy.

See also: Dardanelles.
Further Reading: Ernle Bradford, *Thermopylae: The Battle for the West,* New York: Da Capo, 1993 (1980).

THULE

This ancient name, given to the most northerly land of Europe, is of unknown origin but has been found in both Greek and Latin historical writings. It is first mentioned in Polybius's account of the voyage of the Greek navigator Pytheas (ca. 310 B.C.), who sailed six days northward of Britain and discovered what he believed was the most northern region in the world. The island he encountered has been variously identified as Iceland, Norway, or one of the Shetland Islands. Pliny and Tacitus (who both believed the island to be in the Shetlands), Boethius, and Chaucer all refer to this last isle of the sea.

By the time of the Renaissance the name was regularly employed as a metaphor for the utmost geographical limits, as in Sylvester's *Du Bartas:* "From Africa to Thule's farthest Flood." Use of the Latin phrase *ultima Thule* (farthest Thule) became common during the Restoration and the eighteenth century, at least among the educated, to denote an ultimate goal of human endeavor or a land remote beyond all reckoning. A reporter in a 1784–1785 gazette referred to Cook's recently discovered Sandwich Islands (Hawaii) as "the Thule of the Southern hemisphere." In the nineteenth century a fop could be caricatured as "the *ultima Thule* of extravagant frippery" (1828).

Even as eloquent usage converted the ancient island into a figure of speech, a very real place arose bearing the name at the north end of Greenland. Just north of Cape York, Arctic explorer Knud Rasmussen of Denmark founded in 1910 the small settlement of Thule, which was meant to serve as a trading post. The name also came to be applied to the nearby Etah Eskimos, who inhabited the vast region stretching from Alaska to Greenland. The United States built an air force base here during World War II, which in 1951, after an agreement with Denmark, was expanded to provide for additional operations. Thule is now the most important U.S. defense outpost in Greenland as well as a base for Danish and U.S. scientific investigations on the ice cap and on Peary Land.

It is of note that the name Thule also has been applied to the lustrous, silver-white element Thulium, the rarest of the metallic rare earth elements—atomic weight 69—named in 1879 by P. T. Cleve for "the ancient name of Scandinavia," as well as to the rare, peach-blossom-colored mineral thulite, a sample of which was reportedly found in 1820 at Telemark, Norway.

Further Reading: Jack and Harriet Frye, *North to Thule: An Imagined Narrative of the Famous "Lost" Sea Voyage of Pytheas of Massalia in the Fourth Century B.C.,* Chapel Hill, N.C.: Algonquin Books of Chapel Hill, 1985.

THURINGIA

The nearly continually shifting boundary of the German state of Thüringen can be pinned down to a single physiographic region—the Thuringian Basin. The basin has for its boundaries the edges of scarps formed as cuestas (see Introduction). The inclined sedimentary formations of the basin lie like reverse shingles on the crystallines of the adjoining regions: the **Harz Mountains** to the north, and the Bohemian Massif to the southeast. The Saale and Werra drain the east and west sides of the region, respectively. The center of the basin is an undulating plain developed on a fertile marl. Leipzig, the nearest large city, lies just north of the basin.

The Thuringian Forest (in German, Thüringer Wald) is a forested upland that lies to the south and forms one of the boundaries of the basin. It is an extension of the Bohemian crystallines, forming an element of the belted **Hercynian Uplands.** Presenting a mountainous appearance (though of relatively low elevation), the Thuringian Forest extends approximately 80 miles (129 kilometers) from southeast to northwest, rising to 3,222 feet (982 meters) in the Grosser Beerberg. Noted for its scenic beauty and numerous resorts (e.g., Eisenach and Oberhof), the Forest is an attractive ornament gracing the fertile agricultural basin and its prosperous industrial centers—Gotha, Erfurt, Jena, and Mühlhausen.

ber of quasi-independent duchies, principalities, and free cities, helping to produce the characteristic crazy-quilt pattern of German political geography that lasted well into the nineteenth century.

Thuringia was an important center of the Protestant Reformation. Martin Luther studied at the university of Erfurt and took his vows as an Augustinian friar at its monastery. Mühlhausen was an An-

Flower fields, Erfurt, Thuringia *(Corel Corporation)*.

The ancient Thuringians were a Germanic tribe occupying central Germany between the Elbe and the Danube. Defeated by the Franks in 531 at Burgscheidungen, they came under the rule of Frankish dukes and were converted to Christianity in the eighth century by St. Boniface. Charlemagne made Thuringia into a march (or frontier) against Slavic advances. In the eleventh century the landgraves of Thuringia established themselves as princes of the Holy Roman Empire and ruled over much of the modern territory of Thuringia. In the late Middle Ages the region fragmented into a num-

abaptist center dominated during the Peasants' War (1524–1526) by Thomas Münzer, who was executed there in 1525. In the late eighteenth century Goethe and his followers turned the Thuringian city of Weimar, the capital of the duchy of Saxe-Weimar, into the literary capital of Europe. (Earlier, Johann Sebastian Bach had contributed to the cultural preeminence of the city by serving as court organist and concertmaster.) In the nineteenth century, Thuringia sided with the hegemonic claims of nearby Prussia, joining the German Empire in 1871. The Thuringian states, which had been divided since the fifteenth century, were only reunited as a *land* or state of the Weimar Republic in 1920. This short-lived republic took its name from a 1919 national assembly that had been held in the Thuringian city of Weimar to determine the form of government of post–World War I Germany.

The mixed cultural legacy of Thuringia can perhaps best be illustrated by focusing on Weimar: The city is the site of numerous monuments to Goethe, Schiller, and other cultural heroes, but there is also a memorial at Buchenwald village, near Weimar, where 56,000 died in the Nazi concentration camp.

TIBER RIVER
See Latium

TIERRA DEL FUEGO

At the extreme southern end of the tapering South American continent, poleward of about 55° S, lies an inhospitable zone of isolated islands, glacial peaks, and barren fjord coastlines. Located south of the **Strait of Magellan,** the archipelago is shared by Argentina and Chile. It extends as far as Horn Island at the southernmost tip of South America, on which is located **Cape Horn.** The island chain consists of one main island, called sometimes Tierra del Fuego or Great Island; five smaller but sizable islands; and innumerable small islands, islets, and rocks, separated by many inlets and channels. The western or Chilean portion of the archipelago, in the province of Magallanes, represents the southern extension of the **Andes,** rising to Mount Sarmiento (7,500 feet or 2,286 meters) and Mount Darwin (7,005 feet or 2,135 meters). East of 68°36'38" the Argentine National Territory of Tierra del Fuego is a continuation of the windswept Patagonian tableland, of which it is sometimes considered a part.

Ferdinand Magellan discovered the archipelago in 1520 and gave the region its name (Land of Fire) because he observed that the natives, a primitive people who wore no clothes, set signal fires on the mountain peaks at night. Early explorers and users of the strait often referred to the fierceness and primitiveness of the native Fuegians. Charles Darwin visited Tierra del Fuego during his famous voyage aboard the *Beagle,* reporting that the country was "a broken mass of wild rocks, lofty hills and useless forests," and that the local population was so debased that "what a scale of improvement is comprehended between the faculties of a Fuegian savage and a Sir Isaac Newton!"

Nevertheless, the voyage of the *Beagle* and Darwin's theory of evolution, formulated in response to his observations on the trip, might not have come about were it not for the Fuegians. Lord FitzRoy, commander of the *Beagle,* had visited this remote land on a previous scientific expedition. Returning home to England, he brought four Fuegian natives for an experiment in improving the "savages." They were introduced to English manners, language, and religion, and it was one of the main purposes of FitzRoy's *Beagle* expedition, for which he employed the young, unproven Darwin as a naturalist and ship's companion, to set up a mission at the tip of South America and return the Fuegians to their homeland to see if their improved ways persisted. The paternalistic experiment failed miserably: One of the Fuegians died of smallpox before returning, and two others immediately escaped from the civilizing effects of the mission, taking the opportunity to abscond with valuables. The Europeans soon abandoned the project, discovering later that the fourth Fuegian had reverted to his native ways. Fortunately for us, Darwin's original thoughts on this expedition related to the organic descent of plants and animals rather than to the biased, Victorian cultural observations that he reserved for his diaries.

See also: Galápagos Islands.
Further Reading: Stephen Jay Gould, "The Moral State of Tahiti—and of Darwin," pp. 262–274 in *Eight Little Piggies: Reflections in Natural History,* by Stephen Jay Gould, New York: Norton, 1993; Richard Lee Marks, *Three Men of the Beagle,* New York: Alfred A.

scape. The major river, the Inn, has a south-west-to-northeast course across the region. The site of the capital, Innsbruck, can be detected in its name: The town lies at a bridgeable point on the Inn, where the river has been displaced to one side of a broad glaciated valley. At about 4,500 feet (1,372 meters), the tributaries of the Inn, descending off the northern slopes, approach the Eisack River flowing south. This

Pala Mountains, south Tirol *(Corel Corporation).*

Knopf, 1991 (mostly set in Tierra del Fuego).

TIROL

Straddling a key **Alpine Pass,** this ancient mountainous region located between Austria and Italy is an important cultural and political borderland. Tirol guards both sides of the Brenner Pass, linking the **Bavarian Plateau** to the **Po Plain** of Italy. The western Alps of the Tirol, in Switzerland, have higher peaks, more deeply incised valleys, and larger remnant glaciers; in upper Austria, the peaks are lower and the longitudinal or east-west valleys open up the land-

low divide, located in the southern part of Austrian Tirol, forms the Brenner Pass. As traveler Ludwig Steub wrote in 1875, "The roof of the Brenner Post House is the watershed where drippings from one gutter flow to the Black Sea and from the other gutter to the Adriatic."

Altitude is everything in Tirolean life, especially as it affects land use. An *alp* or an *alm* is actually a high meadow where cattle are grazed or hay is harvested. Initial occupancy of the region was along the lower part of the terraces and slopes, just below tree line and away from the marshes and dangerous valley floors.

Only when residents learned to drain the wet valley bottoms could the cities of Innsbruck, Brixen, and Merano be established. In the South Tyrol (Südtirol), located in Italy, ethnic groups sort along altitudinal lines: Italians tend to dwell in the major cities of the valley, a legacy of the Roman emphasis on urbanism, while the agricultural Germans live higher up, on the slopes.

The Romans annexed the Alpine area to their empire around 15 B.C. and called it Rhaetia, after the tribes that lived there. They built on strategic hills and in low valleys, intent on controlling the roads through Brenner Pass and Reschen Pass, which linked outposts of the empire. Germanic tribes, including the Baiuoarii and the Lombards, invaded the region in the sixth century, followed by the Franks, who held all of Tirol by the eighth century. The northern section (present-day Tirol) fragmented into a number of different counties before being united under the Counts of Tirol, who eventually passed it to Austria and the Habsburgs (1363). Much of South Tirol came under the rule of the Bishops of Trent and the Bishops of Brixen from the eleventh century to 1802–1803.

After about A.D. 1000 Tirol flourished, as the valley floor became a thoroughfare of a revitalized Europe. Cotton, silk, spices, and glass passed through the low corridor from Venice, while merchants from the north sent linen, wool, furs, iron tools, and precious metals south to Italy. Armies, crusaders, traders, gypsies, and even the plague crossed the Alps here. The food-producing Germans established a string of towns along the historic routeway to serve travelers. To the transit trade was added a booming mining industry in the 1500s, focused on silver and copper, profits from which promoted the European expansion of the

Habsburg dynasty. The economic dislocations of this time and the control of the region by outsiders (the Fugger family of Augsburg controlled most of the mines) contributed to the Peasant War of 1525–1526, in which the Tirolean peasant leader, Michael Gaismair, was assassinated.

Subsequently, the life of Tirol turned inward as the region defined itself increasingly in terms of Catholicism, conservatism, communalism, and traditional craft livelihoods. Following Napoleon's brief attachment of the region to one or another of his allies—at one time it was ruled by Bavaria, at another by Italy—the entire region passed to Austria at the Congress of Vienna (1815). After World War I, in 1919, the Treaty of Saint-Germain awarded South Tirol (predominantly German-speaking Bolzano and Italian-speaking Trento) to Italy. Tirol proper, also known as Bundesland Tirol, today is a province of Austria, including the part where Innsbruck is located, which is separated from a small but fertile piece of East Tirol by a corridor belonging partly to the province of Salzburg and partly to Italy. Coercive attempts by the Fascists to Italianize German-speaking South Tiroleans during the period between the two world wars led to so much friction that the Italian constitution of 1947, supplemented by later agreements, guarantees the autonomy of South Tirol and protects the rights of its minority population.

Further Reading: John W. Cole and Eric R. Wolf, *The Hidden Frontier: Ecology and Ethnicity in an Alpine Valley,* New York: Academic Press, 1974; Martha C. Ward, *The Hidden Life of Tirol,* Prospect Heights, Ill.: Waveland, 1993.

TORDESILLAS LINE

In the fifteenth century the north-central Spanish city of Valladolid replaced Toledo as the chief residence of the Kings of Castile. The choice of this city for the marriage of Ferdinand and Isabella in 1469 added to its prestige, due in large part to the presence of a university almost as old as Oxford's (more pertinently, almost as old as Salamanca's) and several ornate medieval palaces and churches. Located at the confluence of the Pisuerga and Esgueva Rivers, just above their

leagues west of the Cape Verde Islands—thereby legalizing the Portuguese claim to Brazil. Calculated at three miles to the league, the north-south line lies at approximately 47° W longitude, passing just east of the mouth of the Amazon. So drawn, the official line only encloses the eastern third of Brazil. Because Spain and Portugal were ruled by a unified monarchy in the period 1580–1640 and both

A Brazilian 400-reis circulating coin, 1932, commemorating the four hundredth anniversary of the colonization of Brazil by the Portuguese and showing the Tordesillas Line (vertical line) *(courtesy of the American Numismatic Association).*

meeting with the Douro River—the major river of northwest Spain draining west to the Atlantic past Porto, Portugal—the town was not only rich in cultural monuments but also was the center of an important cereal-growing area.

Just eighteen miles (29 kilometers) southwest of Valladolid, at the small Douro River village of Tordesillas, on 7 June 1494 an agreement was signed between ambassadors representing Ferdinand and Isabella of Spain and King John II of Portugal, dividing the world's newly discovered lands into two equal halves along a line of longitude. Although the demarcation of Spanish and Portuguese spheres followed in principle the papal bull issued in 1493 by Pope Alexander VI, the Tordesillas treaty moved the dividing line west—from 100 to 370

were Catholic countries, the westward thrust of the Portuguese *bandeirantes,* who combined the functions of frontiersmen and military conquerors, was able to extend the Portuguese overseas lands in America to include about half of the South American continent.

These considerations were probably not in the minds of the treaty makers in 1494, as Brazil was not officially discovered until Pedro Álvars Cabral's voyage of 1500. However, some claim that a possible earlier discovery of Brazil, obscured by the Portuguese policy of secrecy, led to the revisions between the 1493 papal decree and the 1494 Tordesillas treaty so as to include Brazil in the Portuguese zone. The more obvious reason for a reconsideration of the 1493 line was the return of Columbus from his first voyage in the spring of 1493 and the tumultuous reception of his discoveries, which almost led to war between Spain and Portugal.

Later analyses, calculations, and endorsements were more concerned with the location of the treaty's line of demarcation in the East Indies, particularly with respect to the Spice Islands, or the Moluccas. Absent a method to accurately determine longitude at sea—an obstacle that was not overcome until the invention of the ship's chronometer in the eighteenth century—there was no way to know precisely where the papal division was in the east. Nevertheless, the region was parceled out, and the Spanish colonial empire lying west of the Tordesillas line stretched from South and Central America across the Pacific to the Philippines, while the Portuguese sphere east of the line included Brazil, Africa, India, and most of the East Indies (today, Indonesia).

North European powers—the English, French, and Dutch—took little notice of this amicable division of lands among the Iberian countries. As early as 1497, John Cabot sailed from Bristol to take possession for his king of Newfoundland and potentially the entire eastern seaboard of North America. In 1541 the Frenchman Jacques Cartier explored the Gulf of Saint Lawrence and claimed the adjacent lands for his country. In the early years of the seventeenth century the Dutch managed to oust the Portuguese from the East Indies and even occupied northeastern Brazil for a while. Previous Portuguese dominance in the east can be detected by the relic political territories of Portuguese India (such as Goa, which was seized by India in 1961) and the trading port of Macao, which is to be returned to China in December 1999.

On 7 June 1994 the 500th anniversary of the Tordesillas agreement was celebrated by Juan Carlos of Spain and President Mario Soares of Portugal, who visited the two fifteenth-century buildings where the historic signing had occurred, commemorating an event whose legacy is felt by millions of people from Spanish-speaking America to Portuguese-speaking Angola, Mozambique, and Macao.

Further Reading: Samuel Eliot Morison, *Portuguese Voyages to America in the Fifteenth Century,* Cambridge, Mass.: Harvard University Press, 1940.

TRAFALGAR, CAPE

Following the resumption of hostilities between France and Britain in 1803, Napoleon's grand scheme was to draw a vast Army of England (a division of the army meant to conquer England) toward Boulogne so that he could launch a successful cross-channel assault. His navy had to pursue a feinting strategy, withdrawing to the Caribbean, in order to draw Britain's traditional strength away from its near impregnable bottleneck of the **English Channel.** Admiral Nelson, the British commander, who had already exhibited feats of heroism in the previous battles of Cape St. Vincent (1797), the Nile (1798), and Copenhagen (1801), now had the primary mission (1805) of tracking the French ships in the **Mediterranean Sea** under the command of Pierre-Charles de Villeneuve and of preventing other forces from uniting with them. After a wild goose chase around the Mediterranean, Villeneuve's fleet slipped out of Toulon on 30 March and shortly afterward passed **Gibraltar** on its way to the Caribbean. Although Nelson was aware of the purpose of the French decoy, he gave earnest enough pursuit that the French plans for a rendezvous in Martinique were disrupted. Villeneuve returned across the Atlantic and put in at Vigo, off the northwest coast of Spain, after an indecisive battle off Cape Finisterre (22 July). By August, Villeneuve had slipped down the coast to Cádiz, now with 30 ships of the line, held there by 25 British ships. Nelson meanwhile had returned to Brest, to reinforce the Channel squadron.

Villeneuve's mysterious move to the south rather than the north can be explained: By late summer, Napoleon had abandoned his plans to cross the Channel and was now pulling his troops out of Boulogne in preparation for moving them eastward against Austria and Russia. Villeneuve's new orders were to proceed to the Mediterranean.

On 15 September, Nelson set sail from England with a bold plan of attack. Lying off Cádiz on 27 September, he held the 17 British ships under his command 50 miles (80 kilometers) out at sea, beyond the sight of the French. He drew the large fleet of 33 French and Spanish ships out of the harbor on the morning of 20 October. The Spanish ships, staying near the coast, were heading south for the Gibraltar Strait, hoping to escape into the Mediterranean. Nelson pursued a course parallel to the coast and the Spanish ships, 20 miles to the west, so as not to reveal the full British force of 27 ships. He now lay near the western entrance to the Strait of Gibraltar, off Cape Trafalgar. Early in the morning of 21 October, with the wind at his back and with no harbors nearby should Villeneuve decide to run, Nelson prepared to do battle: He would turn his two formations directly into the French fleet, which was strung out four miles across the ocean in front of his lines. The details of the ferocious fighting at close range and the feats of heroism have been recounted numerous times elsewhere. The eventual result—a resounding victory for the British, who lost no ships, while the French lost 18—was one of the high points in British naval history. The French and Spanish forces had been swept from the seas, which henceforth would be controlled by the English. When a mortally wounded and expiring Nelson (he had taken a gunshot through the lungs and into the spine, from a French sharpshooter) was informed of the success of the battle, he replied, "That is well, but I bargained for 20." He asked that his body not be thrown overboard. At 4:30 P.M. he passed from this world. His body was eventually interred at Westminster Abbey, in a place of honor.

Nelson's victory at Trafalgar was the greatest British victory since the rout of the Armada. Fighting continued for another ten years, but Britain's control of the waves was never again seriously challenged. Its maritime preeminence in the nineteenth century stemmed in no small part from Nelson's bravery and his success. No naval hero is held in higher esteem, as is suggested by the placement on the busiest square in London of a monument commemorating Nelson and his victory at Trafalgar.

Further Reading: Alan Schom, *Trafalgar: Countdown to Battle, 1803–1805,* New York: Oxford University Press, 1990; Oliver Warner, *Trafalgar,* New York: Macmillan, 1959.

TRANSYLVANIAN ALPS
See Carpathian Mountains

TRONDHEIM FJORD
This arm of the Atlantic Ocean extends some 80 miles (129 kilometers) into north-central Norway along the west coast. The fjord is considered a natural boundary between northern and southern Norway. Located just north of the Dovre Mountains, the Trøndelag district forms a depression of relatively soft Cambro-Silurian schists. Higher sea levels resulting from the melting of Pleistocene ice sheets

not only inundated the center of the depression, producing the fjord, but also reached the present-day 650-foot (198-meter) contour, depositing a fertile layer of sands and clays along the eastern shore of the fjord and in the lower courses of streams draining into the fjord. The inner margin of Trondheim Fjord is thus one of the most fertile agricultural regions in mountainous Norway. The postglacial

the evergreen forest creeps downslope from the surrounding uplands. Western or Outer Trøndelag, in contrast, is a resistant block of ancient Caledonian rocks that falls from about 2,500 feet (762 meters) in elevation near the western shore of Trondheim Fjord to an extensive, rocky skerry along the Norwegian Sea. A narrow gap in the coastal mountains links the fjord to the sea.

The ancient capital city of Trondheim sits on the banks of the River Nid along Trondheim Fjord, Norway *(Adam Woolfitt/Corbis).*

sands and gravels form numerous terraces along the fjord's eastern shore and in tributary valleys. There is very little truly level land in Inner Trøndelag, as the streams flowing into the fjord have carved up the lowland into a number of small districts. Farms are relatively large and prosperous; but even here, in the midst of one of Norway's most fertile agricultural landscapes,

Trondheim (Trondhjem) is the third largest city in Norway (and the early medieval capital), and has for its site the mouth of the short Nid River, on a peninsula in the fjord. The city lies 250 miles (402 kilometers) north of Oslo and is thus relatively inaccessible from the capital city. A sea route was the only way between the two until a direct railroad link was built in

1877. The core of the medieval state, the Trondheim region took advantage of its inaccessibility and interior location, much as Moscow did in Russia at this time, to consolidate its position in an incipient state. Isolation, fertile soils, and an ice-free port all help explain the development of this Scandinavian hearth. Founded in 997 by Olaf I, the first Christian king of Norway, Trondheim was the political and religious capital of the state in the Middle Ages. Known as Nidaros, the city benefited from one of the few low passes across the Norwegian Mountains, the Trøndelag-Jämtland Gap, which connected eastward to the Swedish town of Östersund. From its status as an important port and an economic center, Trondheim declined in the fourteenth century, as the Hanseatic League directed its trade more toward Bergen.

Trondheim is famous today for its Gothic cathedral, erected over the tomb of Olaf I (St. Olaf). Rebuilt many times after fires, the church in its modern form, a blue soapstone and marble edifice, is the result of construction that began in 1869. The Archbishop of Nidaros resisted the Reformation in 1537 but finally was forced to flee the country. At the same time, the city adopted its new name. This blow to the religious ascendancy of the city furthered its decline, until Trondheim reemerged as a trade center in the mid-nineteenth century, a development reinforced by the arrival of the railroad a few decades later. The coronation of the first king of modern, independent Norway, Haakon VII, at Nidaros Cathedral in 1906 did much to enhance the prestige of the city and its region.

UKRAINIAN STEPPE

Open grasslands north and east of the **Black Sea** extend from the **Carpathian Mountains** in the west across most of the Ukrainian republic into southern Russia and the northern rim of central Asia. As with comparable places in the United States (e.g., the prairies of the **Great Plains**), the treeless area is a response to semiarid climatic conditions. Since most of the grassland has been brought under the plow, the most salient feature of the steppe today is its rich black-earth soil, or *chernozem*. The fertile soils of this region have been responsible for its reputation as a bread belt, first of czarist Russia, then of the Soviet Union. The eastern parts of the steppe, from the Volga River east across northern Kazakhstan as far as southern Siberia, receive more variable precipitation, and it is here that the Russians focused their post-1950s agricultural push known as the Virgin Lands Project, whose success was as checkered as the region's rainfall. As the climate becomes drier to the east in the Caspian-Aral depression, soils change from the black earths to the less fertile chestnut soils of the sparse semidesert. To the north a narrow transitional belt of wooded steppe is encountered stretching from the Ukrainian capital of Kiev across the southern end of the **Ural Mountains** as far as Novosibirsk.

The peopling of the steppe lands was not the result of migration from old Greek trading towns on the Black Sea or ancient settlements in central Asia but rather took place as the Slavic peoples of eastern Europe followed the major rivers of the Russian plain downstream, especially the **Dnieper**, crossing from the forested north, with its maze of interconnected lakes, rivers, and peat marshes, to the treeless southern steppe. Kiev was the earliest and most successful of the settlements to organize this region as early as the seventh century A.D. Located on the steppe at the edge of the forest lands, Kiev became the first focus of Russian identity.

The grasslands were always prey to invading tribes of nomadic horsemen, who issued in irregular pulses from the vastness of interior Asia, with their different languages and their conquering ways. Mongol invasions of 1237–1240 put an end to the Kievan state. As Russian peoples regrouped farther north and east within the security of the forest, the steppe came under the control of the Lithuanian kingdom, which at the time extended from the Baltic almost to the Black Sea. After the union of Poland and Lithuania in 1569, Poland asserted increasing control of the southern region. A group of hardy, independent people, many of whom had escaped from Polish serfdom, sought haven on the steppe border, particularly beyond the lower Dnieper rapids. There they established a military order called the Zaporozhye Sich (the Clearing Beyond the Rapids), and became known to the Ottoman Turks as cossacks, or *kozaki,* an adaptation of the Turkish word *kzakh* (outlaw or adventurer). The cossacks were even able to form an independent kingdom briefly after 1649, but thereafter ensured their survival, albeit sometimes in dependence, by making alliances with the powerful rising state of Muscovite Russia.

Ukraïna means frontier, and its usage dates from the sixteenth century, when the region was a contested frontier between Poland and Muscovite Russia. Many Westerners say *the* Ukraine, which is disliked by Ukrainians because it implies their homeland is just a place of passage, a borderland. After all, the region stretches across 1,000 miles (1,609 kilometers), from the Carpathians to the rivers Don and Volga—hardly a narrow belt!

Briefly independent during the civil war that followed the Bolshevik revolution of 1917, the region was incorporated into the Union of Soviet Socialist Republics (U.S.S.R., Soviet Union) in 1920. The homelands of the proud cossacks once again attained political independence in 1991, after the breakup of the Soviet Union. However, the new republic of Ukraine is still affiliated with Russia by the loose, confederal arrangements of the Commonwealth of Independent States (CIS).

See also: Dnieper River.

UMBRIA

See Apennine Mountains

URAL MOUNTAINS

The Turkish word *ural* (belt or girdle), is an appropriate metaphor for these mountains separating Europe from Asia. Lo-

cated in west-central Russia, the north-south trending Urals extend about 1,300 miles (2,092 kilometers) from the bend of the Ural River, north of the Caspian Sea, almost to the Arctic (if the map of Europe and Asia were a person, this "waistline" would indicate a rather stout and ungainly physique). Of low average elevation, the Urals seldom exceed 6,000 feet (1,829 meters) and are better described as hills than mountains. The south-central section of the Urals presents a number of low passes, descending to 1,345 feet (410 meters) in the gap taken by the Trans-Siberian Railroad west of Sverdlovsk. The highest elevation is attained at Naroda (or Narodnaya) Peak, which rises to 6,184 feet (1,885 meters).

The Urals resemble the **Hercynian Uplands** of central Europe in geological structure and age, but possess some important differences in mineralization. Large reserves of iron ore, copper, manganese, nickel, platinum, and gold—in fact, nearly all the metallic minerals—contrast with the paucity of coal deposits, at least of the quality needed in modern steelmaking. In the 1930s, Stalin began to promote frontier industrialization of new regions in the southern Urals, northern Kazakhstan, and southern Siberia that were accessible by the Trans-Siberian mainline or by short feeder routes branching to the north or south. Freight trains hauled iron ore from the Urals to selected coal-rich frontier zones, such as Karaganda in northeastern Kazakhstan or the Kuznetsk Basin west of Lake Baikal, and returned to the Urals industrial cities with coal. In this way, two iron-making regions were at the same time linked and promoted, and Stalin was able to count on heavy industrial concentrations beyond the reach of invading armies. This policy proved prescient, as the Ukrainian steelmaking region, including the Donets

Basin (coal) and Kryvyy Rih (iron ore), was occupied by the Nazis throughout most of World War II.

The Urals have never been a major obstacle to east-west migration, but they do represent an important watershed between the Ob-Irtysh river system, draining western Siberia north to the Arctic Ocean, and the Volga-Kama, draining the western flanks of the divide south into the Caspian Sea. The Urals also constitute a significant climatic barrier: Lands east of the Urals have a severe continental climate, barred as they are from moderating airmasses flowing off the Atlantic.

Russian fur hunters from Novgorod reached the northern Urals as early as the twelfth century. An industry based on extensive iron-ore deposits and a seemingly inexhaustible forest for charcoal-making was introduced in the sixteenth century. In the following two centuries, ironworking was the foremost industry in Russia and, apart from grain, the leading export.

By 1800, Russia was the world leader in production of pig and bar iron. The focus of the industry was in the southern Urals' centers of Yekaterinburg (Sverdlovsk) and Nizhniy Tagil. Bar iron from the Urals was shipped west to fabricating centers to be converted to steel.

In the late nineteenth century, iron production in the Urals fell behind that in Ukraine and other European centers due to its lack of high-quality coal and its relative inaccessibility. In the 1930s the communist regime was able to subsidize industry where it chose, and inaccessibility was an important locational factor. Russia was successful in developing heavy industrial regions beyond the reach of the invading Nazis, and with the aid of steel and armaments made in the Urals, it succeeded in rolling back the advancing German army.

Further Reading: Craig and Osleeb ZumBrunnen, *The Soviet Iron and Steel Industry,* Totowa, N.J.: Rowman and Littlefield, 1986.

VALDAI HILLS

Northwest of Moscow, about halfway to the Baltic, is a low hill region attaining elevations of about 1,100 feet (335 meters). Pleistocene glaciation has overridden and modified the underlying rock structure, with the typical landscape being one of low, morainic hills, shallow lakes, marshy plains, and peat bogs. The look of the land is similar to that of the lake districts of northern Minnesota and northern Wisconsin. The region is more accurately described as an upland, since only the northwest approach is noticeably steep, while the rise is gradual from all other directions. The Massachusetts-sized area contains the headwaters of European Russia's major rivers—the Volga, **Dnieper,** and Western Dvina—as well as the sources of the rivers flowing into Lake Ilmen. This plateau has derived its historical significance from its strategic location, linking various river systems and forming axes of communication across the great Russian plain.

Rivers served as the primary means of movement during the winter and summer months in Russia, and only during the brief spring and fall seasons were the watercourses blocked. Not until the nineteenth century did sled traffic give way to barges, which in turn were limited by short summers and low waters. In the absence of well-developed overland roads the key factor in traditional Russia was the skillful use of the rivers and knowledge of the connecting portages (later, canals).

The maze of minor waterways and interconnected lakes and marshes in the Valdai was explored and thoroughly mastered by early migrants. Agriculturally minded Slavs often passed through the Valdai rather than stopping, as the region does not possess the best farmland. The sparsity of population today in the Valdai, however, is the result of the destruction of many villages during World War II, which were never rebuilt.

Rather than carrying light canoes over portages in the manner of American Indians, Russian pioneers usually dragged or rolled a river boat across connecting links. The Russian term *volok* for portages connotes dragging more than carrying, and numerous place-names in the region testify to the early importance of transit points: Vyshniy Volochek (Upper Portage) on the Tvertsa River; Vologda on the Vologda River, at the head of navigation on the Northern Dvina river system; Volok on the Msta River.

The Valdai as a major river divide was located along the routes linking the Baltic to the upper Volga and Oka Rivers, and beyond, to the Caspian Sea. The region also lies at a strategic place along the north-south routes connecting the Baltic to the

Black Sea via the Dnieper and Don Rivers. The second major hearth of Russian culture after Kiev (on the Dnieper) rose to the southeast of the Valdai Hills, namely at Yaroslavl, Suzdal, Vladimir, and, later, Moscow, and the Valdai provided a natural gateway to this growing region. The fur-trading center and member of the Hanseatic League, Novgorod, located just north of the Valdai, relied on portages across the divide for trade with grain-producing southern districts. The boundaries of emerging principalities (city-states) were often defined by control of key portages.

The Mongol invasion of 1237–1240 was a cataclysm that overthrew the gradually evolving system of Russian principalities. With the rise of Muscovy in the sixteenth century and the establishment of a unitary Russian state, trade and migration naturally shifted eastward away from the easily blocked Baltic–Dnieper–Black Sea route, which was often controlled by the Lithuanian-Polish power or Sweden in the sixteenth and seventeenth centuries. An alternative trade route was pioneered in the sixteenth century by the English, proceeding due north from Moscow to the **White Sea.** The elimination of Moscow's major rival of Novgorod preparatory to overthrowing the Tatar yoke was made easier by its assertion of control over the vital portages of the Valdai, by which Novgorod received its grain.

Further Reading: David J. M. Hooson, "The Geographical Setting," pp. 1–48 in Robert Auty and Dimitri Obolensky, eds., *An Introduction to Russian History,* Companion to Russian Studies 1, Cambridge: Cambridge University Press, 1976.

VALERIAN WAY

See Apennine Mountains

VARDAR-MORAVA CORRIDOR

This traditional routeway across the rugged Balkans has been the primary connection between the Danube plain and the Aegean Sea. It has been a crossroads for diverse, often clashing cultures throughout history as well as the core of the Serbian and Macedonian states, which are located at opposite ends of the corridor.

Two rivers come together to form this north-south structural depression in the Balkans, which divides the northeast-southwest-trending mountains and ranges of the Dinaric Alps in the west from the west-east-trending Rhodope and Balkan Mountains in the east. In contrast to the major riverine access from the western Mediterranean into interior Europe along the Rhône-Saône Corridor, which consists of two rivers flowing in the same direction, with one a tributary of the other, here the rivers diverge and flow in opposite directions: The Vardar flows toward the southeast, emptying into the head of the Aegean at the western end of the neck of the Chalcidic Peninsula, while the Morava, heading at about the same place, flows northward out of the highlands across the Pannonian Plain before reaching the Danube River near Belgrade, the capital of the former state of Yugoslavia. At the opposite end of this trough lies Thessaloníki (Salonika), Greece's second largest city and a major port and industrial center. The rivers come close together at the Macedonian capital of Skopje, the birthplace of Mother Theresa. Since ancient times the passage across the low divide between the drainage basins has allowed settlers and soldiers, raiders and traders, to pass back and forth between Mediterranean Europe and Danubian Central Europe. The building of the railroad system only reinforced these ancient patterns, as Skopje became the most accessible place in a network of roads and rail lines fanning outward across low points in the surrounding crystalline schists.

Cultural historians often argue about whether major changes in culture and technology are the results of the activity of indigenous peoples or of the external influences of foreign settlement and conquest. In the Balkans, there can be little doubt about which force has been more important. As a meeting ground between two continents, the region has been crossed and recrossed by invaders and conquerors throughout history. The corridor was open to the north for the steppe-dwelling Scythians who invaded the Balkans and controlled this route from the eighth to the fourth centuries B.C., overtaking the indigenous Thracian elements, and in turn being repulsed by Greeks and Persians. Today's Macedonia, occupying a border area between Greece, Bulgaria, and the former Yugoslavia, corresponds roughly to the ancient Kingdom of Macedon, of which Alexander the Great became king in 336 B.C. Anchored in the Vardar region at the head of the Aegean, the Macedonians, who were less sea-minded than the Greeks, demonstrated a genius for continental organization in their administration of the vast lands of Alexander's conquests, an empire stretching as far as India, to which they introduced the essentially Greek Hellenistic culture.

The crusaders likewise took advantage of the gateway of the Morava and Vardar Rivers in their invasion of the region, as did the Serbian state in its southward expansion. A curious problem in the ethnographic puzzle of the Balkans is whether Macedonia is Greek or Slavic (particularly Bulgar). It is likely that only by making a study valley by valley, village by village, could an intelligent opinion be formed. The Balkans received a mixture of southward-moving Slavic peoples around A.D. 1000 who either conquered the native peoples or assimilated into their society.

At the north end of the corridor, Serbs established themselves as one of the most numerous and powerful south Slavic groups, maintaining a major state in the Middle Ages, until they met defeat at the hands of the Turks in 1389 at the battle of Kosovo. Not until the end of the nineteenth century, with the Russian victory over the Turks in 1878 and the gradual decay of Ottoman influence in the area, did Serbian political independence again become an issue of pressing importance.

South of Belgrade, the rich plain of Sumadja gradually rises southward in the direction of the lower Morava. A century ago a dense forest of oak and beech covered the Sumadja (*suma* means forest), providing hiding-places from the Turks, but most of the forest has since been removed to provide space for intensive agriculture. To the southeast the Morava valley shrinks to a narrow corridor between high cliffs. Transhumant cattle and sheep raising result in grazing of the upper slopes. Nish is the most important town along this route, benefiting from its location at the junction of the Morava and the Nishava, the latter providing an opening to the high basin of Sofia, and beyond, the Maritsa valley and the Turkish Straits.

On the banks of the upper Vardar lies Skopje, the capital of Yugoslavian Macedonia. A distinctly Mediterranean climate and associated cultural elements are found here. The climate is less continental, with dry summers and less severe winters. The presence of mosques with minarets in the landscape is evidence that the Middle East is not far away. Once the Skopje plain was freed of malaria in the modern period, a productive agriculture developed, and farther downstream rich orchards and fields of tobacco find export to Western Europe. Skopje was almost completely destroyed by an earthquake in

July 1963, but the city was rebuilt with international aid.

The topographic complexity of the Balkans (Turkish for wooded heights), with its rugged mountains and difficult communication, has undoubtedly contributed to the ethnographic and political fragmentation of the region. The relationship between history and topography is complex, though: To rise as a nationality, a group must emerge from its mountain redoubts, which fostered and preserved its sense of identity, and establish a foothold in one of the more accessible valleys with enough good soil to permit intensive agriculture and a greater population density. These conditions can only be attained in a few locations along the coast or in major valleys like the Vardar-Morava trough. Therefore, the political map depends on the isolation of often backward-looking cultural groups; but these archaic forms are set in motion against one another in the major cities and at control points in the landscape. Political turmoil and instability are the predictable results, in a meeting ground not only between north and south but also between east and west. (The western Slavic groups, such as the Slovenes and the Croats, have been more influenced by western Europe, especially Catholic Italy and Austria, while eastern groups like the Serbs within the Greek sphere of influence have adopted the Eastern Orthodox religion.) Treaty makers at the end of World War I cobbled together a new political unit, Yugoslavia or South Slavs, on the basis of a presumed similar culture in the southernmost extension of Slavic peoples. But religion, language (including the adopted alphabet, whether Roman or Cyrillic), and shared memory have proven more important than race in distinguishing peoples in this political shatter belt of southeastern Europe. Yugoslavia was held together in

the post–World War II period by Cold War geopolitical alignments, and its dissolution into its component ethnic nations was an almost inevitable result of the collapse of the Soviet Union in the early 1990s.

Further Reading: Robert D. Kaplan, *Balkan Ghosts: A Journey through History,* New York: St. Martin's, 1993; Rebecca West, *Black Lamb and Grey Falcon: A Journey through Yugoslavia,* New York: Viking, 1941.

VENICE, LAGOON OF

Small islets in a coastal lagoon at the head of the Adriatic Sea form the magnificent but endangered site of historic Venice. Screened from the sea by sand spits (of which the Lido is the best known) and separated from the continent by water, the islands were a refuge from marauders in late classical times. By the Middle Ages, Venice had become a city of palaces and churches—a place of prestige and beauty. The reputation of the city for visual attractions persists today, as the city exudes an almost dream-like intensity of color and light.

The archipelago of 118 small islands lies opposite an inaccessible stretch of coast near the center of a saltwater lagoon 31 miles (50 kilometers) wide. The Romans founded a large colony at Aquileia, farther up the coast about six miles (ten kilometers) inland, northwest of present-day Trieste. The eastern **Alpine Passes** branched out here to the Venetian plain (Venetio today includes a mainland strip as well as the islands). Aquileia and nearby Padua (Roman Patavium) conducted a brisk overland trade between northern Italy and newly conquered lands.

In the fifth century A.D. inhabitants of Aquileia fled before the onslaught of the Huns and Avars and took refuge on the Venetian islands. By A.D. 697, the peo-

ples of these scattered islands had organized themselves into a confederation
under the centralized rule of a doge (from
Latin *dux* [leader]). The haven proved an
excellent place for trading, as Venice's location at the head of the Adriatic and
near the major eastern pass routes made it
a highly accessible place for trade, not
only that between Italy and the Danubian
lands but also between the eastern

diplomatic service by making the presence of its ambassadors felt in all the
courts of the world. The great traveler
Marco Polo represented the enterprising
spirit of the Queen of the Seas, as Venice
was known in the thirteenth and fourteenth centuries. The acme of Venetian
power was reached in the fifteenth century, when all of mainland Venice had
been conquered and strategic points in

Canal, boats, and bridges in Venice *(photo by Jesse Walker)*.

Mediterranean and the rest of Europe.
Venice early recognized the importance of
its eastern connections, especially those to
the Byzantine Empire, and the gorgeous
mosaics and gilt domes of its churches, as
exemplified by Saint Mark's Basilica,
show the treasured influence of the east.

In the late medieval period, Venice
became the dominant sea power in the
Mediterranean and the economic capital
of Europe. It controlled the north Italian
trade and the transalpine pass routes;
colonized the Adriatic shores of Dalma-
tia; led the host in the fourth crusade;
and established the basis of the modern

the Aegean and eastern Mediterranean
had been taken.

Venice is best known for its many
palaces, churches, and elegant residences
lining the canals (in Italian, *canale*) that
serve as streets. The old town has 150
canals crossed by some 400 bridges, including the picturesquely named Bridge
of Sighs, which connects the fourteenth-
to-fifteenth-century Gothic Palace of the
Doges on St. Mark's Square to the former
prisons. The canals are deepened waterways separating the original islands. Most
of the canals are narrow, but the Grand
Canal, shaped like the letter S, is the main

traffic artery, with its main bridge, the Rialto, named after the island that was once the city's nucleus.

Venice grew to become an unusual political entity, neither feudal nor seignorial; it became a republic. The need to protect the lagoonal site, especially from silting, fostered a strong collective identity, a deference to authority, and a lack of factionalism. The Venetians contrived an ingenious method to channel the flow of the major rivers, such as the Brenta, into the lagoon to prevent silting. The tide flowed into the lagoon through three porti or inlets, including Porta di Lido, opposite Saint Mark's Square; Porta di Malamocco, the deepest spot in the north Adriatic Sea, which is located farther south; and farther south yet, near the end of the lagoon, Porta di Chioggia. Sewage was released directly into the lagoon until very recently, because the tides flushed and cleaned the system on a regular basis.

The conquest of Constantinople by the Turks (1453), the pioneering of an all-sea route to India by Vasco da Gama (1497–1499), and the discovery of new, western routes to the Orient in the sixteenth century led to the decline of the Venetian empire. The rich aristocratic culture that had sponsored the art of Titian, Tintoretto, and Bellini went against the tide of rising bourgeois sensibilities of the rest of Europe. By the Treaty of Campo Formio (1797), a cynical Napoleon gave Venice to the Austrian Habsburgs, thereby ending the 1,100-year history of the independent republic. Four bronze horses were lifted from St. Mark's Basilica and shipped to Paris to adorn the Arc de Carrousel in the Tuileries Gardens. Though Venice was independent again for a short time during the 1848 Revolution, the republic was taken again by Austria and remained in Habsburg hands until its incorporation into a newly unified Italy in 1866.

The greatest problem Venice faces today is high water. In the past century, the levels of the high tide (Italian *acqua alta*) have risen by 1.3 feet. Doorways along the canals have had to be rebuilt at higher positions. More than half of this rise is due to subsidence, or sinking of the land, caused by overpumping of underground aquifers, leading to slumping (such pumping is now drastically curtailed). The other cause of high water is the modification of the lagoon and its inlets and the effects on tides. Large areas of the lagoon have been reclaimed for fish ponds, known as *valli,* as well as for agriculture, industry, and building. The destruction of *barene,* or mudflats, has proceeded at a rapid rate. Inlets have been deepened, with the result that rising tides advance more quickly past the Lido into the shallow lagoon. The ratio between lagoonal area and tidal inlets thus has decreased, and higher flood stages result. Especially to be feared is the combination of high tides and southeastern sirocco winds, which drive the water in a surge against the north Adriatic coast. In the presence of a high precipitation event, these conditions threaten to inundate the treasures of the city.

Possible solutions now under consideration include blocking the inlets with gates that could be put in place during a flood, which is the commonly favored solution, although it would aggravate pollution from agricultural runoff and industrial discharge; returning the inlets to their original, shallower condition; opening the *valli* to floodwater; and elevating the city even further on giant stilts. Only the last would not exacerbate pollution. However, no one has come forward with what would surely be a controversial design for raising a city that already looms precariously—though beautifully—above the water. The art collector and connoisseur Bernard Berenson once described Venice as "man's most beautiful artifact." Until something is done, Venetians must endure the *acqua alta,* interleaving the various levels of their houses with sheets of impermeable lead to prevent the upward movement of moisture, waging a desperate war—not with Turkish marauders or infidel pirates this time, but with the slow, sad creep of humidity.

Further Reading: John Julius Norwich, *Venice: The Greatness and the Fall,* London: Allen Lane, 1981; and by the same author, *Venice: The Rise to Empire,* London: Allen Lane, 1977.

VICHY
See Massif Central

VIENNA BASIN
This narrow belt of lowlands along the Danube near Vienna (in German, Wien) is a meeting point between the Alps and the **Hercynian Uplands,** which dominate topography to the north, west, and east, and the **Hungarian Basin** (or Pannonian plain), which lies to the southeast. The easternmost Alpine range of the Wienerwald (Vienna Woods) reaches the Danube just outside Vienna. East of the Danube the **Carpathian Mountains** continue the Alpine orogeny (see Introduction) in a crescent-shaped arc across Czechoslovakia, Poland, and Romania. Just above Vienna, the Danube skirts the crystallines of the Bohemian Forest (Böhmerwald). Not as extensive or fertile as the **Paris Basin,** the Vienna lowlands are situated in extreme eastern Austria, lending today's Vienna a relatively peripheral location for a capital city. However, it must be remembered that as the capital of the Austro-Hungarian Empire until World War I, Vienna controlled an extensive hinterland downstream on the Danube.

The Vienna Basin comprises two sections subdivided by the west-to-east-flowing Danube. The southern half, drained by the Leitha River, is today mostly an urban region, with Vienna sited on the western rim, on an elevated gravel terrace. To the north of the Danube lies the low, flat, and flood-prone Marchfeld, drained by the March River. A rural region today, the Marchfeld originally functioned as a march, or frontier, between Germanic Austria and the Hungarian plains, as did much of the land on the opposite bank of the Danube. Vienna is situated where the Danube widens and braids as it emerges from a constriction produced by the river cutting through the sandstone Wienerwald. River regulation and confinement of the Danube's bed has resulted in not one but three Danubes in this ancient city: the Canal, the boundary of Old Vienna on its northern side; the old Danube, suitable for water-based sports; and the Danube proper, which has been straightened and channelized since 1868.

Controlling more than its immediate hinterland, the largest city on the Danube lies at one end of the most important routeway across the eastern Alps—the Brenner Pass. Connecting the Mediterranean cities of Venice and Trieste with the Danube lands, the Brenner is the major gateway between Italy and Central Europe. Upstream on the Danube lies the **Bavarian Plateau;** downstream is the Hungarian Basin. Access to Poland and the **North European Plain** can be gained through the Moravian Gate, cutting across the Carpathians between the **Bohemian Basin** and Slovakia.

Originally a Celtic settlement, Vienna grew in the first century B.C. as a Roman camp along the Danube frontier. A civil settlement arose alongside the Roman garrison at the town of Vindobona. It was the home in the second century A.D. of one of the last great Roman emperors, the meditative yet strong Marcus Aurelius.

After the decline of Rome, barbarian peoples overran the region from the eastern steppes (Huns, Avars). By 1000 the Vienna district represented the Ostmark, or eastern frontier, of Bavaria, which under the Habsburg family (beginning in 1822) became Österreich (Austria, or the Eastern Empire). The Vienna Basin is thus the core area of the modern nation of Austria, even though the city lies on the periphery of Austrian territory.

As early as 1100, German settlement had pushed eastward from Vienna to Burgenland, on the margins of the Hungarian plains, and into the Morava valley, where it was repulsed by Hungarians and thus turned toward the southern frontier, into the Alpine borderlands and forelands. The Danube region in the vicinity of Vienna was an important Crusader route, and Richard the Lionhearted was imprisoned just upstream at Dürnstein before being discovered by his minstrel, Blondel. Three times, in 1529, 1532, and again in 1683, the Turks were turned back from the gates of Vienna and European civilization thus preserved.

VOLGA RIVER
See Povolzhye

WALACHIAN PLAIN

This historic region lying between the Transylvanian Alps and the Danube River is the core of the modern Romanian state.

The Oltul River, a tributary of the Danube, divides Greater Walachia, or Muntenia, in the east, from Lesser Walachia, or Oltenia, in the west. This division has been of geopolitical importance in the parceling out of the Danubian territories between rival powers. For example, Austria in the seventeenth century was able to wrest control of Little Walachia from the Ottoman Turks. In the nineteenth century, Russia secured access and indirect control of Walachia from the moribund Turks. After 1862, the Sultan recognized the union of Walachia with its sister principality of Moldavia, the latter being the easternmost province of Romania, bordering on Moldova, the ethnically similar republic that was formerly part of the Soviet Union.

The Walachian Plain is an example of an interior plain or basin that has formed as a result of a block of the earth's crust foundering and then being filled with sediments sluiced from the surrounding hills and mountains. In this respect the Walachian Plain is similar to the **Rhine Graben** or the **Hungarian Basin.** The plains of the lower Danube were once a gulf of the **Black Sea** that gradually was filled by materials washed down from the

Transylvanian Alps. Subsequent uplift has raised the basin to an average elevation of about 150 feet (46 meters). The plain extends from the southern foothills of the Transylvanian Alps to the piedmont of the Balkan ranges. To the east the region is bounded by the Dobruja, a steppe tableland that blocks the straight course of the Danube and forces it northward. Moldavia is a similar steppe tableland on the region's eastern border.

Much of the Walachian Plain and the Hungarian Basin was once covered with grass before it was planted with crops; but because trees will grow well there if planted, some have concluded that these grasslands were created by a prehistoric removal of forests akin to the destruction of the Mediterranean forest. The plain is the breadbasket of Romania, and combined with the Ploieşti oil fields and the Bucharest urban area, it furnishes most of the nation's employment.

The native peoples are descended from a mixed Slavic and Latin stock, the latter element coming from Roman inhabitants of the province of Dacia. To close off the Carpathian passes and restrict access to the Danubian lands from marauding steppe dwellers, the Romans extended their usual Danubian frontier to incorporate much of the area that is now Romania. With the end of the Latin imperium, Romanized natives sought refuge in the northern mountains. Following a series of invasions, the last by the Mongols, these mountain peoples descended to the plains and founded the principality of Walachia around 1290, under the leadership of Radu Negru, or Rudolf the Black. They were called Vlachs (or Walachs) by their Slavic neighbors. A turbulent history characteristic of the political shatter belt of eastern Europe ensued, establishing various overlords in the region, alternating between the Turks, Austrians, Magyars, and Russians. By the mid-nineteenth century, the Ottoman Turks maintained a nominal suzerainty over an increasingly independent people, and the history of modern Romania had begun.

Further Reading: H. Seton-Watson, *The 'Sick Heart' of Modern Europe: The Problem of the Danubian Lands,* Seattle, Wash.: University of Washington Press, 1975; D. Turnock, *The Romanian Economy in the Twentieth Century,* New York: St. Martin's, 1986.

WASATCH MOUNTAINS

See Great Basin

WEIMAR

See Thuringia

WESSEX

See Salisbury Plain

WHITE SEA

An inlet of the Barents Sea in northwestern European Russia, this relatively warm, navigable body of water formed an early trade route between the Muscovite state and western Europe.

The northern section of the White Sea (in Russian, Beloye More), between the Kola and Kanin peninsulas, is linked to the embayed southern section by a strait 30–35 miles (48–56 kilometers) wide and about 100 miles (160 kilometers) long. The Mezen, the Northern Dvina, and the

Onega Rivers empty into large bays in the deep, southern section. Near the Northern Dvina's outlet is located the major port of Arkhangelsk (Archangel). Shipping takes place throughout the year from Arkhangelsk but requires the assistance of icebreakers in winter. Today a canal 140 miles (225 kilometers) long links Belomorsk on the White Sea to St. Petersburg on the Baltic.

The White Sea was known by the people of Novgorod, an important early Russian trading town, as early as the eleventh century, but not until the mid-sixteenth century did west Europeans discover this far northern arm of the Arctic Ocean. The elusive search for a **Northeast Passage,** a high latitude shortcut around northern Europe and Siberia to Marco Polo's Cathay (China), drew Europeans ineluctably to the growing Russian domain. In 1553, and again in 1555, under two successive monarchs, an English stock company received a charter to benefit from possible trade resulting from an eastern voyage. The full name of this organization, which came to be known as the Muscovy or Russian Company, reveals something of its intentions: The Merchants Adventurers of England for the Discovery of Lands, Territories, Isles, Dominions and Seignories Unknown.

On the recommendation of navigator Martin Frobisher, respected historian and geographer Richard Hakluyt, and Renaissance polymath and sometime practitioner of the black arts John Dee, who had set his sights firmly on a British Empire (an expression he may have invented), an expedition of three ships under Sir Hugh Willoughby departed from England in 1553. The flagship and one other ship wintered off Lapland, and all aboard perished, their emaciated and frozen bodies discovered the next spring by Russian fishermen. The ship commanded by Richard Chancellor entered the White Sea and landed at Archangel. Chancellor traveled overland to Moscow and obtained permission from Ivan the Terrible for his company to open avenues of commerce with Russia. The Muscovite Company remained profitable until the Hanseatic League's overland enterprises undercut it. Meanwhile, Chancellor led a second expedition in 1556, but the ship was wrecked on the coast of Scotland. A third party, sent out the same year under the command of Captain Stephen Borough in the *Serchthrift,* reached as far as Vaigats Island and contacted Samoyed reindeer people before turning back. Muscovite Company traders reached the Caspian Sea and the important Islamic center of Bokhara in 1557, establishing trade with the shah of Persia only a few years later. The rise of the Ottoman Turks cut off these distant enterprises.

The lasting influence of the Muscovite Company, which did not finally go out of business until 1917, was that it set the pattern for later, highly successful trading companies, such as the East India Company (chartered 1600), and imparted knowledge of distant yet essentially European lands. The Russians, in turn, got their first glimpse of entrepreneurial Englishmen, and one suspects they never quite forgot it.

WINDWARD ISLANDS

The southern end of the Lesser Antillian island arc includes *Dominica, St. Lucia, St. Vincent and the Grenadines,* and *Grenada.* Aside from the coral cays of the Grenadines, these islands are mountainous and bristle with volcanic peaks. St. Lucia is crowned with two striking examples, the Pitons, that have been poetically described as "miniature wooded Matterhorns above the water." Washed on one side by the broad swells of the Atlantic and on the other by the gentle Caribbean, the islands are thickly overgrown with tropical vegetation and exude an Edenic quality: Streams rush toward the coast through deep, wooded valleys, and white, sparkling beaches attract visitors from the gray north.

A paradise to the tourist, these islands were once fiercely contested by the northwest European powers, especially the French and British, during a series of eighteenth-century wars. Ships' bells and bugles once sounded where now quiet water relaxes the muscles of the overwrought. Most of these islands passed back and forth between the French and the British numerous times. The control of St. Lucia, for instance, passed between these two countries 14 times before British supremacy was finally established. St. Lucia became an important naval base and imperial coaling station after the British won it for good in 1814.

These islands were the last refuge of the hostile Carib Indians. From their stronghold in *Martinique,* the French in the late 1650s revenged themselves on a previous attack by Caribs from St. Lucia in a general slaughter of the remaining Indians on the island. By a 1660 treaty signed by the British and the French, St. Vincent and Dominica were set aside as a refuge for the Caribs.

The Treaty of Paris (1763) at the end of the French and Indian War (known in Europe as the Seven Years War) was the highwater mark of the old mercantilist British Empire. The treaty is best known for its granting of Canada and India to the British, but it also gave possession of the formerly neutral islands of Dominica and St. Vincent, as well as Grenada, the Grenadines, and Tobago to the British. St. Lucia was returned to the French, but British forces returned to occupy the island in 1778, and again in 1794 and

1796, only to return it once again to the French in the Treaty of Versailles (1783) and the Treaty of Amiens (1802). Taken in 1803, St. Lucia finally passed to the British with the Treaty of Paris in 1814.

Why so much interest in St. Lucia and the corresponding changes in political control of such a small island during the numerous Caribbean wars between England and France in the late eighteenth century? St. Lucia (pronounced "LOO-shah") was the key to the command of the Caribbean. It had an excellent, deep-water harbor at Castries, at the northwest end of the island. From there the British in the nineteenth century could survey the principal French base at Fort Royal (today Fort-de-France), Martinique: From a point a mile or so from Government House, on the plateau of the Morne above Castries, the island of Martinique, the birthplace of Napoleon's Josephine, could be glimpsed on a clear day. The admiral who took St. Lucia for Britain in 1762, George Brydges Rodney, once said, "His Majesty's squadrons stationed in St. Lucia will not only have it in their power to block every port in Martinique, but likewise the cruisers from St. Lucia can always stretch to windward of all the other islands and intercept any succours intended for them." Hence, perhaps, the name assigned to "the Windwards," although the consensus of opinion seems to be that the names of the West Indian island groups are not based on wind direction but are arbitrary designations, because the average wind direction here is from the east, and the Windward Islands lie to the south, not to the east of the **Leewards.**

Rodney sailed from St. Lucia to win the decisive Battle of the Saints in 1782, which turned the tide against the French and prevented their planned invasion of Jamaica. The battle was named after the

small islands in the narrow channel between Dominica and Guadeloupe (Les Saintes).

As a result of the Napoleonic wars, the British established supremacy in the Windwards as in so many other places around the world. Dissatisfied with what was perceived as foot-dragging on the slavery issue, the British replaced former representative governments on these islands with direct rule from England, appointing the governor and other top officials and designating the local assembly, which was usually dominated by Creole landowners, to an advisory position. The Windwards thus became a small division of the enormous British Empire, and the name comes down to us as a governing unit of empire rather than as a natural territory or a wind-designated region. The whole island group was represented by a single governor, although individual administrators also were assigned to the larger islands. Lacking any significant element of self-government, the islands were known as Crown Colonies and so remained until the great period of nation building began in the 1960s. Only after the failure of the British-supported West Indies Federation (1958–1962) did the individual islands of the Windwards gain independence.

Taken from the French during the wars of the eighteenth century, St. Lucia, St. Vincent, Dominica, and Grenada became sovereign nations in the 1970s.

Further Reading: Cyril Hamshere, *The British in the Caribbean,* Cambridge, Mass.: Harvard University Press, 1972.

WÜRM (WISCONSINAN) GLACIATION

Sometimes the most important thing is the most obvious. The fundamental character of the terrain in northern Europe, the northern United States, and Canada derives from the effects of the continental ice sheets of the Pleistocene epoch (Ice Age), which lasted from about two million B.P. until about 10,000 B.P.

The glaciers generally had a moderating influence on relief, filling in valleys and eroding high points in the landscape. Where mountains lay near the sea, valley glaciers steepened the valley walls and gouged out broad, flat-floored bottoms. As sea levels rose with the melting of the ice sheets, river mouths were inundated to produce the well known, spectacular *fjords,* most of which are on the west coasts in the higher midlatitudes of Norway, British Columbia, and Alaska.

More characteristic landforms of deposition form in less mountainous areas farther south. A ground moraine is a rolling, irregular plain composed of jumbled sand, silt, and cobbles (till) deposited directly from melting ice and giving the look of a pioneer washboard. A chain of low hills comprising the same unstratified materials—an end moraine—marks the limit of glacial movement or a pause in its activity. Loops of hills extend across the upper Midwest and northern Pennsylvania in the United States, reaching the east coast at a point just north of New York City. In Europe these hills run from the **Jutland** peninsula of Denmark across northern Germany and Poland, then southward past the Baltic republics and into Russia. The development of the languages of Baltic peoples, which are distinguished from the tongues of their Slavic neighbors, has been partly attributed to their isolation behind the Baltic Hills, the local name for the end moraine.

Along the margin of the ice sheet, meltwater channels changing courses frequently laid out a broad sheet of sorted sediments in the form of an outwash plain. Much land in the **North European Plain** was formed in this manner and consists of sterile and sandy ground, as in the infertile pasturelands of Friesland east of IJsselmeer (in English, Lake Ijssel) and in the extensive Lüneburger Heath south of Hamburg, which is overgrown with pine and heather. Elsewhere, thick deposits of windblown silt, known as loess, were the result of the settling out from the air of a sort of glacial flour—rock materials that were ground so fine that the wind picked them up. Soils derived from loess, whether located on the east side of the Mississippi River in Illinois or Wisconsin, or on the historically important German Börde, the border between the northern plains and the **Hercynian Uplands,** are particularly fertile and suitable for cultivation. Early German settlement shunned the infertile *Geest* of the sandy outwash plains and concentrated on a corridor in the better agricultural zone of the loessial border. In central Belgium and parts of the **Paris Basin,** reworked and retransported silt, or *limon,* added a significant boost of fertility to the soils.

The last advance of the Pleistocene ice attained its maximum geographical extent and thickness at ca. 18,000 B.P. The ice covered the upper midwestern United States as far south as southern Wisconsin, in a looping boundary between Madison and Janesville—hence the term Wisconsinan glaciation. In Europe, Würm glaciation of the same period covered the Baltic, the Scandinavian Peninsula, Finland, and northwest Russia (as far as the Smolensk-Moscow Plateau, just northwest of Moscow). Only a narrow strip in Germany and Poland was glaciated, while a larger area in Russia received the influence of this last gasp of Pleistocene glaciation. The eastern side of the Jutland peninsula was glaciated, but the western side, receiving as it does the moderating influence of the North Sea, was not. The British Isles, though receiving glacial action as far south as London in earlier periods of glaciation, were without ice during the Würm glaciation except perhaps on a few high points.

Pleistocene glaciation disrupted the drainage pattern of preexisting streams. Many of the north-flowing rivers of northern Europe, such as the Vistula and the Rhine, had their outlets blocked by ice and veered to the west before emptying into the sea. The right-angled bends in the lower courses of many rivers of the northern plains is quite evident today. Sometimes rivers resumed their original courses, and the abandoned lateral channels could be used for easily dug canals linking the north-flowing streams. The best-known example of this is the Mittelland Kanal, or Midland Canal, across northern Germany.

Interrupted drainage also produces numerous lakes, marshes, peat bogs, sloughs, and generally lands of poor drainage. The effects of the upper Midwest's irregular drainage, particularly its extensive wetlands, played an important role in delaying settlement of the Great Lakes plains. The overland route across the plains of northern Europe was probably the shortest migration path in prehistoric times, but it was also the least used, because swollen streams blocked early migrants' paths, and intervening lands more often than not bore the sodden legacy of the Ice Age.

Even as important a geographical feature as the Mississippi River can be related to glaciation. Before the Pleistocene epoch, an ancestral river flowed north toward Canada, emptying either into Hudson Bay or into the Saint Lawrence valley. The maximum extent of Pleistocene glaciation reached almost as far south as the Ohio River east of the Mississippi, and more approximately, the Missouri River west of the Mississippi. An enormous ice plateau stretching all the way to Canada blocked the north-flowing Mississippi, and meltwaters along the glacier's edge collected to form the Ohio and Missouri Rivers, which emptied south into the main channel of the Mississippi, which also now flowed south. The present course of the Mississippi River is not of Wisconsinan age but dates from earlier stages of the Pleistocene, when colder conditions resulted in southern advance of the ice. The sites of a number of towns along the Mississippi River, all the way from Baton Rouge, Louisiana, to La Crosse, Wisconsin, were chosen in part because of their location on dry alluvial terraces (there are sometimes more than one, the first being called the "second bottom"). These terraces formed as the river cut down to a new, lower level in response to lower sea levels created by the locking up of much of the earth's water in glacial ice.

YUCATÁN PENINSULA

This squat thumb extends out from the mainland of southeastern Mexico, pointing across the Gulf of Mexico in the direction of Florida. Separating the Gulf from the Caribbean Sea, the Yucatán consists primarily of a low, flat limestone tableland similar to that of peninsular Florida but with a very different landscape, due to its predominantly dry climate and to the cultural influence of the ancient Mayas, from whom the local population is descended. The northern part of the peninsula is completely arid and bears only a scrub forest or a savanna. To the south, rainfall increases and a dense rain forest covers the land, extending into the Petén of Guatemala. The northern end of the east coast has low cliffs, while the southern coastline is indented by bays and paralleled by islands and cays. Cozumel is the largest island. Elevation also increases to the south, rising to around 500 feet (150 meters). Irregular transverse ranges cross the peninsula at intervals. To the northwest the plain continues as the Campeche Bank, which stretches about 150 miles (240 kilometers) out to sea from the low, sandy shoreline.

Surface water is almost nonexistent in the north, as it is swallowed by the porous limestone. The pre-Columbian people of the classical period (ca. 100 B.C.–A.D. 630) thrived by tapping as their water source the steep-sided sinkholes known as *cenotes*. The hilly southern part of the peninsula, with more nearly adequate water, was the center of classical Mayan culture. Much-visited pre-Columbian sites on the Yucatán include Chichén Itzá, Uxmal, and Uaxactún. There are many impressive Mayan traits and evidences: flat-topped pyramids; towers, plazas, and ball courts (the ball game played was rather like soccer, but you couldn't use your feet or hands, a ring substituted for a net, and the losers, alas, lost their lives); an advanced knowledge of astronomy that predicted some periodic events in the heavens not fully understood until recently; and an intricate style of glyph stone writings, the meaning of which only began to be deciphered in the twentieth century. Perhaps the most distinguishing characteristic of the Mayan cultural hearth is that it is located in the lowland Tropics. Unlike the transitional Toltecs, or the Aztec tribes encountered by the Spanish, the Mayans were not attracted to the cool plateau lands or mountains.

The once well-populated center of the Mayan culture was long a remote, relatively unimportant part of Spanish America. Depopulated long before the conquest, the southern rain forest served as a barrier to human migration and settlement. Cortés made his epic march across the base of the peninsula to Honduras in 1524–1525. Already in 1517 Francisco Hernándo de Córdoba skirted the coast from Cape Catoche to the Bay of Campeche on a voyage of discovery. The subjugation of the indigenous population was carried out between 1527 and 1546 by the two Franciscos de Montejo, first the father, then the son. Though not as

place. The turn of the century saw the first planting of henequen around the major settlement of Mérida, which previously had been a Spanish ranching district. It was hoped that this plantation crop would replace producing areas like the Philippines that were lost during the Spanish-American War. A species of yucca, henequen yields a coarse fiber suitable for the spinning of strong twine

Many ruins of temples, cities, and pyramids may be found on the Yucatán Peninsula and in adjoining Guatemala (here Chichén Itzá) *(photo by Jesse Walker)*.

restive as their distant relatives to the south, the Lacandan Mayans of the Chiapas highlands, Yucatecas have not always been peaceful. In 1857 they rose up against the *hacendados* who had appropriated their best lands, and Mexico and the estate owners only narrowly escaped losing the peninsula to the Indians.

Natives crop small patches of ground in traditional slash-and-burn dibble farming. Despite the limitations of the thin, red soil and inadequate water, some agricultural specialization has taken

or rope. The Yucatán has in the past provided more than half of the henequen used in the United States and has been the world's largest producer of cheap twine. Following the Mexican Revolution (1910–1920), agrarian reform led to the carving up of the henequen plantations into collective *ejidos* run by the Indians.

The former Mexican territory (now, state) of Quintana Roo occupies the eastern part of the peninsula. It has been the major provider of *chicle,* the latex of the *chicosapote* tree *(Achras sapota),* used for chewing gum, which has been widely used in the United States since the 1890s. Mayan *chicleros* wander the unsettled forests to tap trees for latex, rather like the *seringueiros* who once gathered wild rubber in the **Amazon Basin.** The labor is not strictly agricultural as it involves gathering rather than cultivating, but it is important nevertheless.

Far more wealth today comes from the exploitation of the Cantarel oil field along the northwest coast near Mérida. Peripheral to the major fields along Mexico's east coast from Tampico to Tabasco, the Yucatán field could extend south across the peninsula as far as Guatemala, and widespread development would have a significant effect on the landscape and economy of the region. To rope, chewing gum, and petroleum must be added another economic activity directed toward satisfying the outsider: tourism. Not only U.S. citizens but Europeans and growing numbers of middle-class Hispanics flock to the Mayan ruins and the Edenic beaches of the east coast, in movements better described in the language of commodity flows and financial exchanges than in the time-honored fashion of travelers, who count on some discomforts in their experience of foreign lands.

Further Reading: Roland Chardon, *Geographic Aspects of Plantation Agriculture in Yucatan,* National Research Council Publication, no. 876, Washington, D.C.: National Research Council, 1961.

ZUIDER ZEE

The Dutch have waged a long and stubborn struggle to overcome a difficult physical environment. When the Romans first visited this distant part of Europe around 50 B.C., they found nothing but bogs and marshes, defended against the ravages of the North Sea by a slender row of sand dunes stretching from Belgium to Denmark. Openings in the dunes allowed the deltaic rivers of the Rhine, Maas, and Scheldt to reach the sea, pouring their sediments now here, now there, creating a shifting pattern of islands and terra firma. And so it remained until well into the Middle Ages. A single stormy night in the thirteenth century caused seventy villages and almost a hundred thousand people to disappear.

The reclamation of a large part of the land under the Zuider Zee, or Southern Sea, is just the latest event in a centuries-long saga of Dutch successes in creating land as well as holding back the tides. No longer on the map, the Zuider Zee was once a shallow inlet of the North Sea about 80 miles (130 kilometers) long, indenting the northeastern coast of the Netherlands. Known to the Romans as Flevo Lacus, it was joined to the North Sea during a series of storms from 693 to 1237 that cut through the narrow ribbon of land separating the lake from the Waddenzee, the shallow, salt-water portion of the North Sea between the Frisian Islands and the coast.

A large reclamation project begun in 1920 split the old Zuider Zee into the IJsselmeer, south of the earthen dam, and the Waddenzee, between the dam and the West Frisian Islands. Subsequently, much of the IJsselmeer has been converted to polders, or reclaimed land, in a process of engineering that for any other people would be well nigh miraculous but to the Dutch came naturally. Large, roughly rectangular blocks of the former sea bed were surrounded by dikes and an encircling canal was dug to carry surplus water to the sea. Windmills were erected on the dikes and hooked up to pumping machines powered by wind or gasoline, so drainage could proceed automatically and uninterruptedly. When all the water had been pumped out of the lake, a series of parallel ditches were laid out to ensure good drainage. After a few years' rains sufficiently had washed the salt from the soil, intensive cultivation of the land for agriculture or for urban plats could begin. The largest of the reclaimed lands is the Northeast Polder, and all that remains of the IJsselmeer today is the northern part.

When the light-hearted Dutch genius Hendrik Willem Van Loon wrote his classic *Van Loon's Geography* (1932)—I used to think the author's name was a hoax—the 19-mile (31-kilometer) dam, really a sea dike carrying a roadway between North Holland and Friesland, had just been completed. The age-old process of poldering, which Van Loon described, had not yet begun on the former bed of the Zuider Zee, but the Dutch had a long history of building such dikes (a thirteenth-century ruler of the western province of Holland was even known as William the Diker), and aided by newer technologies and bigger pumps it was not long before the Dutch added another patch to their patrimony. Van Loon's book was a world survey, not of "statistics about the import and export of raw cotton and canned kangaroo tails," but about places that really mattered and had something to do with us as inhabitants of a small object entirely surrounded by space. I can only hope that my own book, written in the same spirit as that of the Dutchman, has contributed as much to its readers' understanding and appreciation of the world.

Further Reading: Audrey M. Lambert, *The Making of the Dutch Landscape: An Historical Geography of the Netherlands,* London: Seminar Press, 1971; Hendrik Willem Van Loon, *Van Loon's Geography: The Story of the World We Live In,* New York: Simon and Schuster, 1932.

BIBLIOGRAPHY

General and Reference Works

Atlas of World History. Chicago: Rand McNally, 1992.

Beazley, C. Raymond. *The Dawn of Modern Geography.* 3 vols., 1897–1906. Reprint. New York: P. Smith, 1949.

Bridges, E. M. *World Geomorphology.* Cambridge: Cambridge University Press, 1990.

Brown, Lloyd A. *The Story of Maps.* New York: Dover, 1977 (1949).

Butzer, Karl W., ed. *The Americas before and after 1492: Current Geographical Research.* Special Issue, *Annals of the Association of American Geographers,* vol. 82, no. 3, September 1992.

Cambridge World Gazetteer: A Geographical Dictionary. David Munro, ed. Cambridge: Cambridge University Press, 1988.

Cameron, Ian. *Lodestone and Evening Star: The Epic Voyages of Discovery, 1493 B.C.–1896 A.D.* New York: Dutton, 1966.

Canby, Courtlandt. *The Encyclopedia of Historic Places.* 2 vols. New York: Facts on File, 1984.

Cavendish, Richard, Rosemary Burton, and Bernard Stonehouse. *Journeys of the Great Explorers.* New York: Facts on File, 1992.

Clayton, Peter A., and Martin J. Price. *The Seven Wonders of the Ancient World.* New York: Barnes and Noble, 1988.

Columbia Encyclopedia, The. 5th ed. New York: Columbia University Press, 1993.

Crosby, Alfred W., Jr. *The Columbian Exchange: Biological and Cultural Consequences of 1492.* Westport, Conn.: Greenwood, 1972.

———. *Ecological Imperialism: The Biological Expansion of Europe, 900–1900.* Cambridge: Cambridge University Press, 1986.

Davis, Kenneth C. *Don't Know Much about Geography.* New York: Avon, 1992.

De Blij, H. J., and Peter O. Muller. *Geography: Regions and Concepts.* 7th ed. New York: Wiley and Sons, 1994.

Demko, George J. *Why in the World: Adventures in Geography.* New York: Anchor Books, 1992.

Dupuy, R. Ernest, and Trevor N. Dupuy. *The Harper Encyclopedia of Military History: From 3500 B.C. to the Present.* 4th ed. New York: HarperCollins, 1993.

East, W. Gordon. *The Geography behind History.* New York: Norton, 1965.

Espenshade, Edward B., Jr., ed. *Goode's World Atlas.* 19th ed. Chicago: Rand McNally, 1995.

Fernandez-Armesto, Felipe. *The Times Atlas of World Exploration.* New York: HarperCollins, 1991.

Fritze, Ronald H. *Legend and Lore of the Americas before 1492: An Encyclopedia of Visitors, Explorers, and Immigrants.* Santa Barbara, Calif.: ABC-CLIO, 1993.

Glassner, Martin Ira. *Political Geography.* New York: Wiley and Sons, 1993.

Gould, Stephen Jay. *Eight Little Piggies: Reflections in Natural History.* New York: Norton, 1993.

Harder, Kelsie B. *Illustrated Dictionary of Place Names: United States and Canada.* New York: Van Nostrand Reinhold, 1976.

Harley, J. B., and David Woodward. *The History of Cartography.* Vol. 1, *Cartography in*

Prehistoric, Ancient, and Medieval Europe and the Mediterranean. Chicago: University of Chicago Press, 1987; vol. 2, book 1, *Cartography in the Traditional Islamic and South Asian Societies,* 1992; vol. 2, book 2, *Cartography in the Traditional East and Southeast Asian Societies,* 1994.

Huston, Kenneth. *Cambridge Guide to Historical Places of Great Britain and Ireland.* Cambridge: Cambridge University Press, 1990.

Illustrated Encyclopedia of World Geography. 11 vols., 1990–1993. Oxford: Oxford University Press.

Ingpen, Robert, and Philip Wilkinson. *Encyclopedia of Mysterious Places: The Life and Legends of Ancient Sites around the World.* Bergenfield, N.J.: Viking Studio Books, 1990.

International Geographical Encyclopedia and Atlas. Boston: Houghton Mifflin, 1979.

Laqueur, Walter, ed. *A Dictionary of Politics.* New York: Free Press, 1971 (rev. ed. 1973).

Larousse Encyclopedia of World Geography. New York: Odyssey, 1964.

Lobeck, Armin K. *Things Maps Don't Tell Us: An Adventure into Map Interpretation.* Chicago: University of Chicago Press, 1956 (1993).

Marsh, George Perkins. *Man and Nature: Or Physical Geography as Modified by Human Action.* New York: Charles Scribner, 1864.

Martin, Geoffrey J., and Preston E. James. *All Possible Worlds: A History of Geographical Ideas.* 3d ed. New York: Wiley and Sons, 1993.

Morison, Samuel Eliot. *The European Discovery of America: The Northern Voyages, A.D. 500–1600.* New York: Oxford University Press, 1971.

———. *The European Discovery of America: The Southern Voyages, A.D. 1492–1616.* New York: Oxford University Press, 1974.

———. *Portuguese Voyages to America in the Fifteenth Century.* Cambridge, Mass.: Harvard University Press, 1940.

Natkiel, Richard, and Antony Preston. *Atlas of Maritime History.* New York: Facts on File, 1986.

Parry, J. H. *The Age of Reconnaissance: Discovery, Exploration, and Settlement, 1450 to 1650.* Berkeley: University of California Press, 1963.

———. *The Establishment of the European Hegemony, 1415–1715: Trade and Exploration in the Age of the Renaissance.* 3d ed. New York: Harper Torchbooks, 1966.

Ramsay, Raymond H. *No Longer on the Map: Discovering Places that Never Were.* New York: Viking, 1972.

Russell, Jeffrey Burton. *Inventing the Flat Earth: Columbus and Modern Historians.* New York: Praeger, 1991.

Russell, Richard Joel, and Fred Bowerman Kniffen. *Culture Worlds.* New York: Macmillan, 1951.

Seltzer, Leon E., ed. *The Columbia Lippincott Gazetteer of the World.* New York: Columbia University Press, 1952 (1961 supplement).

Sobell, Dava. *Longitude: The True Story of a Lone Genius Who Solved the Greatest Scientific Problem of His Time.* New York: Walker and Co., 1995.

Stamp, Sir Dudley, ed. *Dictionary of Geography.* New York: Wiley and Sons, 1966.

Stewart, George R. *Names on the Land: A Historical Account of Place-Naming in the United States.* New York: Random House, 1945.

Thomas, Lowell. *Seven Wonders of the Ancient World.* Garden City, N.Y.: Hanover House, 1956.

Thrower, Norman J. W. *Maps and Civilization: Cartography in Culture and Society.* Chicago: University of Chicago Press, 1996.

Van Loon, Hendrik Willem. *Van Loon's Geography: The Story of the World We Live In.* New York: Simon and Schuster, 1932.

Von Engeln, O. D., and Jane McKelway Urquhart. *The Story Key to Geographic Names.* Port Washington, N.Y.: Kennikat, 1924.

Webster's New Geographical Dictionary. 3d ed. Springfield, Mass.: Merriam-Webster, 1997.

Westermann Lexikon der Geographie. 4 vols. Braunschweig: Georg Westermann, 1968.

Wilford, John Noble. *The Mapmakers: The Story of the Great Pioneers in Cartography from Antiquity to the Space Age.* New York: Vintage, 1981.

Wilson, Edward O. *The Diversity of Life.* New York: Norton, 1992.

Regional Studies

Abbey, Edward. *Desert Solitaire.* New York: McGraw-Hill, 1968.

Aitken, R. "Routes of Transhumance on the Spanish Meseta." *Geographical Journal* 106 (1945): 59–62.

Allen, John Logan. *Lewis and Clark and the Image of the American Northwest.* New York: Dover, 1991 (1975).

Ambrose, Stephen E. *D-Day, June 6, 1944: The Climactic Battle of World War II.* New York: Simon and Schuster, 1994.

Ardagh, John, and Colin Jones. *Cultural Atlas of France.* New York: Facts on File, 1991.

Ascherson, Neal. *Black Sea.* New York: Hill and Wang, 1995.

Atkinson, R. J. C. *Stonehenge.* London: Penguin, 1979.

Attenborough, David. *The First Eden: The Mediterranean World and Man.* London: Collins/BBC Books, 1987.

Auden, W. H. *Collected Shorter Poems, 1927–1957.* New York: Random House, 1966.

Auty, Robert, and Dimitri Obolensky. *An Introduction to Russian History.* Companion to Russian Studies 1. Cambridge: Cambridge University Press, 1976.

Babcock, William H. "Atlantic and Antillia." *Geographical Review* 3 (1917): 392–395.

———. *Legendary Islands of the Atlantic: A Study in Medieval Geography.* American Geographical Society Research Series, no. 8. New York: American Geographical Society, 1922.

Barber, R. L. N. *The Cyclades in the Bronze Age.* Iowa City: University of Iowa Press, 1987.

Barry, John M. *Rising Tide: The Great Mississippi Flood of 1927 and How It Changed America.* New York: Simon and Schuster, 1997.

Bentley, James. *Bavaria.* London: Aurum, 1950.

Berton, Pierre. *The Klondike Fever: The Life and Death of the Last Great Gold Rush.* New York: Carroll and Graf, 1958.

Blackburn, Julia. *The Emperor's Last Island: A Journey to St. Helena.* New York: Vintage, 1991.

Blair, Peter Hunter. *Roman Britain and Early England: 55 B.C.–A.D. 871.* New York: Norton, 1963.

Blanchard, Raoul. "Flanders." *Geographical Review* 4 (1917): 417–433.

Bowman, Isaiah. *The Andes of Southern Peru: Geographical Reconnaissance along the Seventy-third Meridian.* New York: Henry Holt and Company, 1916.

Bradford, Ernle. *Thermopylae: The Battle for the West.* New York: Da Capo, 1993 (1980).

Braudel, Fernand. *The Mediterranean and the Mediterranean World in the Age of Philip II.* 2 vols. Paris: A Colin, 1966 (1949).

Brill, Edith. *Portrait of the Cotswolds.* London: Robert Hale, 1964.

Bronson, William. *The Last Great Adventure.* New York: McGraw-Hill, 1977.

Brown, Ralph H. *Historical Geography of the United States.* New York: Harcourt, Brace and World, 1948.

———. *Mirror for Americans: Likeness of the Eastern Seaboard, 1810.* American Geographical Society Special Publication, no. 27. New York: American Geographical Society, 1943.

Burghardt, Andrew F. *Borderland: A Historical and Geographical Study of Burgenland, Austria.* Madison, Wis.: University of Wisconsin Press, 1962.

Burtenshaw, David. *Saar-Lorraine.* London: Oxford University Press, 1976.

Cary, Max. *The Geographic Background of Greek and Roman History.* Oxford: Clarendon Press, 1949.

Caughey, John Walton. *The California Gold Rush.* Berkeley: University of California Press, 1975 (1948).

Cerruti, James. "The Cotswolds, 'Noicest Parrt o' England'," *National Geographic,* June 1974, pp. 846–869.

Chardon, Roland. *Geographic Aspects of Plantation Agriculture in Yucatan.* National Research Council Publication, no. 876. Washington, D.C.: National Research Council, 1961.

Chatwin, Bruce. *In Patagonia.* New York: Penguin, 1988 (1977).

Clout, Hugh D. *The Massif Central.* Oxford: Oxford University Press, 1973.

Cole, John W., and Eric R. Wolf. *The Hidden Frontier: Ecology and Ethnicity in an Alpine Valley.* New York: Academic Press, 1974.

Colinvaux, Paul A. "The Past and Future Amazon." *Scientific American,* May 1989, pp. 102–108.

Cook, Joel. *The Mediterranean and Its Borderlands.* 2 vols. Philadelphia: John C. Winston, 1910.

Creighton, Donald. *The Story of Canada.* Toronto: Macmillan, 1959.

Crist, Raymond E. "Along the Llanos-Andes Border in Venezuela: Then and Now." *Geographical Review* 46 (1956): 187–208.

Cronon, William. *Nature's Metropolis: Chicago and the Great West.* New York: Norton, 1991.

Darby, H. C. "The Regional Geography of Thomas Hardy's Wessex." *Geographical Review* 38 (1948): 426–443.

Darwin, Charles R. *Journal of Researches into the Natural History and Geology of the Countries Visited during the Voyage of H.M.S. Beagle round the World, under the Command of Capt. Fitz Roy, R.N.* London: John Murray, 1839.

Davenport, William. "Living the Good Life in Burgundy." *National Geographic,* June 1978, pp. 794–817.

Davies, Arthur. "Geographical Factors in the Invasion and Battle of Normandy." *Geographical Review* 36 (1946): 613–631.

De Roos, Willy. *North-West Passage.* Camden, Maine: Maine Publishing, 1979.

Dean, Warren. *Brazil and the Struggle for Rubber: A Study in Environmental History.* Cambridge: Cambridge University Press, 1987.

DeCosta, William. "Around the Horn: The Journal of a Voyage to San Francisco." *Missouri Review* 15 (1992): 93–121.

Dickenson, John. *Brazil.* London: Longman, 1982.

Dickinson, Robert E. *Germany: A General and Regional Geography.* London: Methuen, 1953.

Dunn, Richard. *Sugar and Slaves: The Rise of the Planter Class in the English West Indies, 1624–1713.* New York: Norton, 1973.

Durrenberger, Robert. "The Colorado Plateau." *Annals of the Association of American Geographers* 62 (1972): 211–236.

Dury, George H. *The British Isles: A Systematic and Regional Geography.* 5th ed. London: Heinemann, 1973.

Earle, Carville. "Environment, Disease, and Mortality in Early Virginia." *Journal of Historical Geography* 5 (1979): 365–390.

————. *Geographical Inquiry and American Historical Problems.* Stanford: Stanford University Press, 1992.

Elkins, Thomas Henry. *Germany.* London: Christophers, 1960.

Fagan, Brian M. *The Great Journey: The Peopling of Ancient America.* London: Thames and Hudson, 1987.

Fetterman, John. "The People of Cumberland Gap." *National Geographic,* Nov. 1971, pp. 591–621.

Fisher, Raymond H. *Bering's Voyages: Whither and Why.* Seattle, Wash.: University of Washington Press, 1977.

Fleure, H. J. "Notes on the Evolution of Switzerland." *Geography* 26 (1941): 169–177.

Floyd, Calvin J. "The Sound Dues." *American-Scandinavian Review* (Winter 1962): 386–396.

Franck, Harry A. *Vagabonding down the Andes: Being the Narrative of a Journey, Chiefly Afoot, from Panama to Buenos Aires.* New York: The Century Company, 1917.

Freise, Friedrich W. "The Drought Region of Northeastern Brazil." *Geographical Review* 28 (1938): 363–378.

Fullerton, Brian, and Alan F. Williams. *Scandinavia.* 2d ed. London: Chatto and Windus, 1975.

Gallois, Lucien. "The Origin and Growth of Paris." *Geographical Review* 13 (1923): 345–367.

Gómez-Ibáñez, Daniel A. *The Western Pyrenees: Differential Evolution of the French and Spanish Borderland.* Oxford: Clarendon Press, 1975.

Gottman, Jean. *A Geography of Europe.* 4th ed. New York: Holt, Rinehart and Winston, 1969.

Graves, William. "The Rhine: Europe's River of Legend." *National Geographic,* April 1967, pp. 449–499.

Hamshere, Cyril. *The British in the Caribbean.* Cambridge, Mass.: Harvard University Press, 1972.

Haring, Clarence. *The Spanish Empire in America.* New York: Oxford University Press, 1947.

———. *Trade and Navigation between Spain and the Indies.* Gloucester, Mass.: Peter Smith, 1964.

Harris, Chauncy D. "The Ruhr Coal-Mining District." *Geographical Review* 36 (1946): 144–221.

Harris, R. Cole. *The Seigneurial System in Early Canada: A Geographical Study.* Madison, Wis.: University of Wisconsin Press, 1966.

Harris, R. Cole, and John Warkentin. *Canada before Confederation: A Study in Historical Geography.* New York: Oxford University Press, 1974.

Hartshorne, Richard. "The Polish Corridor." *Journal of Geography* 36 (1937): pp. 161–176.

Haskin, Frederic J. *The Panama Canal.* Garden City, N.Y.: Doubleday, Page and Co., 1913.

Herlihy, Peter H. "Opening Panama's Darién Gap." *Journal of Cultural Geography* 9 (1989): 41–59.

Hoffman, George W., ed. *Europe in the 1990s: A Geographic Analysis.* 6th ed. New York: Wiley and Sons, 1990.

Hooson, David J. M. "The Middle Volga: An Emerging Focal Region in the Soviet Union." *Geographical Journal* 126 (1960): 180–190.

Hopkins, D., et al., eds. *The Paleoecology of Beringia.* New York: Academic Press, 1982.

Horton, Tom. *Bay Country.* Baltimore: The Johns Hopkins University Press, 1987.

Hugo, Victor. *The Toilers of the Sea.* New York: Heritage, 1961 (orig. ed. 1866).

Hunt, Charles B. *Natural Regions of the United States and Canada.* San Francisco: W. H. Freeman, 1974.

Innis, H. A. *The Cod Fisheries: The History of an International Economy (The Relations of Canada and the United States)* New Haven: Yale University Press (Toronto: Ryerson Press), 1940.

James, Preston E. *Latin America.* New York: Lee and Shepard, 1942.

Johnson, Donald S. *Phantom Islands of the Atlantic: The Legends of Seven Lands that Never Were.* New York: Walker and Co., 1994.

Jordan, Terry G. *The European Culture Area: A Systematic Geography.* 3d ed. New York: HarperCollins, 1995.

Kaplan, Robert D. *Balkan Ghosts: A Journey through History.* New York: St. Martin's, 1993.

Keating, Bern. *The Northwest Passage: From the Mathew to the Manhattan, 1497–1969.* Chicago: Rand McNally, 1970.

Kohl, J. G. "Asia and America." American Antiquarian Society *Proceedings,* October 1911, pp. 284–338.

Krypton, Constantine. *The Northern Sea Route: Its Place in Russian Economic History before 1917.* New York: Research Program on the U.S.S.R., 1953.

La Fay, Howard. "Andalusia: The Spirit of Spain." *National Geographic,* June 1957, pp. 833–856.

Lambert, Audrey M. *The Making of the Dutch Landscape: An Historical Geography of the Netherlands.* London: Seminar Press, 1971.

Lippman, David H. "Bastogne Belatedly Besieged." *Military History,* Dec. 1994, pp. 30–37.

Lovering, T. S., and E. N. Goddard. *Geology and Ore Deposits of the Front Range, Colorado.* U.S. Geological Survey Professional Papers, no. 223. Washington, D.C.: Government Printing Office, 1951.

Mack, Gerstle. *The Land Divided: A History of the Panama Canal and Other Isthmian Canal Projects.* New York: Octagon, 1974.

Maclean, Calum I. *The Highlands.* London: B. T. Batsford, 1959.

MacLeish, Kenneth. "The Highlands: Stronghold of Scottish Gaeldom." *National Geographic,* March 1968, pp. 398–435.

Malin, James L. *Grassland Historical Studies: Natural Resources Utilization in a Background of Science and Technology.* Vol. 1, *Geology and Geography.* Lawrence, Kans. (self-published), 1950.

———. *History and Ecology: Studies of the Grassland.* Ed. Robert P. Swierenga. Lincoln, Nebr.: University of Nebraska Press, 1981.

Margary, Ivan Donald. *Roman Roads in Britain.* London: Baker, 1967.

Margolis, Mac. *The Last New World: The Conquest of the Amazon Frontier.* New York: Norton, 1992.

Martin, John. "Location Factors in Lorraine Iron and Steel Industry." *Institute of British Geographers, Transactions and Papers,* no. 23 (1957): 191–212.

Martonne, Emmanuel de. "The Carpathians: Physiographic Features Controlling Human Geography." *Geographical Review* 3 (1917): 417–437.

McCullough, David. *The Path between the Seas: The Creation of the Panama Canal, 1870–1914.* New York: Simon and Schuster, 1977.

McDowell, Bart. "Hungary." *National Geographic,* April 1971, pp. 443–483.

McIntyre, Loren. "Amazon: The River Sea." *National Geographic,* Oct. 1972, pp. 445–494.

McPhee, John A. *Basin and Range.* New York: Farrar, Straus, and Giroux, 1981.

Mead, William R. *The Scandinavian Northlands.* Oxford: Oxford University Press, 1974.

Meigs, Peveril. "Some Geographical Factors in the Peloponnesian War." *Geographical Review* 51 (1961): 370–380.

Meinig, D. W. *The Great Columbia Plain: A Historical Geography, 1805–1910.* Seattle, Wash.: University of Washington Press, 1968.

———. "The Mormon Culture Region: Strategies and Patterns in the Geography of the American West, 1847–1964." *Annals of the Association of American Geographers* 55 (1965): 191–220.

———. *The Shaping of America: A Geographical Perspective on 500 Years of History.* Vol. 1, *Atlantic America, 1492–1800.* New Haven: Yale University Press, 1986.

———. *The Shaping of America: A Geographical Perspective on 500 Years of History.* Vol. 2, *Continental America, 1800–1867.* New Haven: Yale University Press, 1993.

Millward, Roy. *Scandinavian Lands.* London: Macmillan, 1964.

Mitchell, Robert D., and Paul A. Groves. *North America: The Historical Geography of a Changing Continent.* Totowa, N.J.: Rowman and Littlefield, 1987.

Moorehead, Alan. *Gallipoli.* New York: Harper and Brothers, 1956.

Moorhead, Max L. "Hernán Cortés and the Tehuantepec Passage." *Hispanic American Historical Review,* August 1949, pp. 370–379.

Moser, Don. "The Azores: Nine Islands in Search of a Future." *National Geographic,* Feb. 1976, pp. 261–288.

Mutton, Alice F. A. "The Black Forest: Its Human Geography." *Economic Geography* 14 (1938): 131–153.

Myres, John L. *Geographical History in Greek Lands.* Westport, Conn.: Greenwood, 1974 (orig. pub. Oxford: Clarendon Press, 1953).

Nicholas, David. *Town and Countryside: Social, Economic, and Political Tensions in Fourteenth-Century Flanders.* Bruges: De Tempel, 1971.

Norwich, John Julius. *Venice: The Greatness and the Fall.* London: Allen Lane, 1981.

———. *Venice: The Rise to Empire.* London: Allen Lane, 1977.

O'Meara, John, trans. *The Voyage of Saint Brendan: Journey to the Promised Land.* Dublin: Dolmen Press (in association with Humanities Press of Atlantic Heights, N.J.), 1978.

Parsons, James J. "A Geographer Looks at the San Joaquin Valley." *Geographical Review* 76 (1986): 371–389.

———. "Human Influences on the Pine and Laurel Forests of the Canary Islands." *Geographical Review* 71 (1981): 253–271.

Pomeroy, Earl. *The Pacific Slope: A History of California, Oregon, Washington, Idaho, Utah, and Nevada.* New York: Knopf, 1965.

Pounds, N. J. G. *An Historical Geography of Europe.* Cambridge: Cambridge University Press, 1990.

Powell, John Wesley. *Report on the Lands of the Arid Region of the United States.* U.S. House of Representatives, Executive Document 73, 45th Congress, 2nd Session. Washington, D.C.: U.S. Government Printing Office, April 3, 1878.

Prebble, John. *The Darien Disaster.* Edinburgh: Mainstream, 1978 (orig. pub. Martin Secker and Warburg, 1968).

Prunty, Merle C., and Charles S. Aiken. "The Demise of the Piedmont Cotton Region." *Annals of the Association of American Geographers* 62 (1972): 283–306.

Richmond, I. A. *Roman Britain.* 2d ed. Harmondsworth, Middlesex: Penguin, 1963 (orig. ed. 1955).

Robertson, C. J. "Agricultural Regions of the North Italian Plain." *Geographical Review* 28 (1938): 573–596.

Rogers, Francis M. *Atlantic Islanders of the Azores and Madeiras.* North Quincy, Mass.: Christopher, 1979.

Rogozinski, Jan. *A Brief History of the Caribbean: From the Arawak and the Carib to the Present.* New York: Meridian, 1992.

Romer, John, and Elizabeth Romer. *The Seven Wonders of the Ancient World.* New York: Henry Holt, 1996.

Rowe, Vivian. *The Great Wall of France: The Triumph of the Maginot Line.* London: Putnam, 1959.

Ruge, Sophus. *Fretum Anians.* Dresden, 1888.

Rugg, Dean S. *Eastern Europe.* London: Longman Scientific and Technical, 1986.

Sahlins, Peter. *Boundaries: The Making of France and Spain in the Pyrenees.* Berkeley: University of California Press, 1989.

Salway, Peter. *Roman Britain.* Vol. 1a, *Oxford History of England.* Oxford: Clarendon Press, 1981.

Sauer, Carl Ortwin. *The Early Spanish Main.* Berkeley: University of California Press, 1969.

———. "The Personality of Mexico." *Geographical Review* 31 (1941): 353–364.

Savill, Mervyn. *Tide of London: A Study of London and Its River.* London: Brittannicus Liber, 1951.

Sawyer, Birgit, and Peter Sawyer. *Medieval Scandinavia: From Conversion to Reformation, circa 800–1500.* Minneapolis: University of Minnesota Press, 1993.

Schom, Alan. *Trafalgar: Countdown to Battle, 1803–1805.* New York: Oxford University Press, 1990.

Scott-Moncrieff, George. *The Lowlands of Scotland.* London: Batsford, 1939.

Semple, Ellen Churchill. *The Geography of the Mediterranean Region: Its Relation to Ancient History.* New York: Henry Holt, 1931.

Seton-Watson, Hugh. *The 'Sick Heart' of Modern Europe: The Problem of the Danubian Lands.* Seattle, Wash.: University of Washington Press, 1975.

Severin, Timothy. *The Brendan Voyage.* New York: McGraw-Hill, 1978 (Avon paperback, 1979).

———. *Explorers of the Mississippi.* New York: Knopf, 1968.

———. *The Golden Antilles.* New York: Knopf, 1970.

Smith, C. T. *An Historical Geography of Western Europe before 1800.* Revised ed. London: Longman, 1978.

Spry, Irene M. *The Palliser Expedition: The Dramatic Story of Western Canadian Exploration, 1857–1860.* Saskatoon, Sask.: Fifth House, 1995 (1963).

Stegner, Wallace. *Beyond the Hundredth Meridian: John Wesley Powell and the Second Opening of the West.* New York: Penguin, 1992 (Boston: Houghton Mifflin, 1954).

Strassler, Robert B., ed. *The Landmark Thucydides: A Comprehensive Guide to the Peloponnesian War.* New York: Free Press, 1996.

Stutz, Bruce. *Natural Lives, Modern Times: People and Places of the Delaware River.* New York: Crown, 1992.

Taylor, Griffith. "Trento to the Reschen Pass: A Cultural Traverse of the Adige Corridor." *Geographical Review* 30 (1940): 215–237.

Thomas, Roger. "Offa's Dyke." *British Heritage,* Feb. 1997, pp. 40–45.

Thomson, George Malcolm. *The Search for the North-West Passage.* New York: Macmillan, 1975.

Thuroczy, Janos. *Chronicle of the Hungarians.* Bloomington, Ind.: Indiana University Press, Research Institute for Inner Asian Studies, 1991.

Turnock, D. *The Romanian Economy in the Twentieth Century.* New York: St. Martin's, 1986.

Ullman, Edward L. "Rivers as Regional Bonds: The Columbia-Snake Example." *Geographical Review* 41 (1951): 210–225.

Unger, Leonard. "Rural Settlement in the Campania." *Geographical Review* 43 (1953): 506–524.

United States Environmental Protection Agency and Environment Canada. *The Great Lakes: An Environmental Atlas and Resource Book.* Chicago and Toronto, 1987.

Uttley, John. *A Short History of the Channel Islands.* New York: Praeger, 1966.

Villiers, Alan. "England's Scillies: The Flowering Isles," *National Geographic,* July 1967, pp. 126–145.

Wainwright, A. *A Pennine Journey: The Story of a Long Walk in 1938.* London: Penguin, 1986.

Walker, D. S. *The Mediterranean Lands.* London: Methuen, 1960.

Wallace, Elisabeth. *The British Caribbean: From the Decline of Colonialism to the End of Federation.* Toronto: University of Toronto Press, 1977.

Ward, Martha C. *The Hidden Life of Tirol.* Prospect Heights, Ill.: Waveland, 1993.

Warkentin, John, ed. *Canada: A Geographical Interpretation.* Toronto: Methuen, 1968.

Warner, Oliver. *Trafalgar.* New York: Macmillan, 1959.

Warner, William W. *Beautiful Swimmers: Watermen, Crabs, and the Chesapeake Bay.* New York: Penguin, 1977.

Wauchope, Robert. *Lost Tribes and Sunken Continents: Myth and Method in the Study of American Indians.* Chicago: University of Chicago Press, 1962.

Wauchope, Robert, and Robert C. West, eds. *Handbook of Middle American Indians, Vol. I: Natural Environment and Early Cultures.* Austin: University of Texas Press, 1964.

Webb, Walter Prescott. *The Great Plains.* Boston: Ginn, 1931.

Weigend, Guido G. "Effects of Boundary Changes in South Tyrol." *Geographical Review* 40 (1950): 364–375.

Weiner, Jonathan. *The Beak of the Finch: A Story of Evolution in Our Time.* New York: Knopf, 1994 (reprinted by Vintage, 1995).

West, Rebecca. *Black Lamb and Grey Falcon: A Journey through Yugoslavia.* New York: Viking, 1941.

West, Robert C., and John P. Augelli. *Middle America: Its Lands and Peoples.* 3d ed. Englewood Cliffs, N.J.: Prentice-Hall, 1989.

Wheeler-Bennett, John. *The Wooden Titan: Hindenburg in Twenty Years of German History, 1914–1934.* New York: Morrow, 1936.

William-Olsson, W. "Stockholm: Its Structure and Development." *Geographical Review* 30 (1940): 420–438.

Williams, G. "Welsh Settlers and Native Americans in Patagonia." *Journal of Latin American Studies* 11 (1979): 41–66.

Williams, Stephen. *Fantastic Archaeology: The Wild Side of North American Prehistory.* Philadelphia: University of Pennsylvania Press, 1991.

Williamson, James A. *The English Channel: A History.* London: Collins, 1959.

Wilson, John. "Drought Bedevils Brazil's Sertão." *National Geographic,* Nov. 1972, pp. 704–723.

Wishart, David J. "Settling the Great Plains, 1850–1930: Prospects and Problems." In Robert D. Mitchell and Paul A. Groves, eds., *North America: The Historical Geography of a Changing Continent,* pp. 255–278. Totowa, N.J.: Rowman and Littlefield, 1987.

Wolf, Eric R. *Sons of the Shaking Earth.* Chicago: University of Chicago Press, 1959.

Worster, Donald. *Rivers of Empire: Water, Aridity, and the Growth of the American West.* New York: Pantheon, 1985.

Wright, John Kirtland. *The Geographical Basis of European History.* New York: Henry Holt, 1928.

————. *The Geographical Lore of the Time of the Crusades: A Study in the History of Medieval Science and Tradition in Western Europe.* New York: Dover, 1965 (1925).

Yeadon, David. "To Scotland Afoot along the Pennine Way." *National Geographic,* March 1986, pp. 388–418.

ZumBrunnen, Craig, and Osleeb ZumBrunnen. *The Soviet Iron and Steel Industry.* Totowa, N.J.: Rowman and Littlefield, 1986.

INDEX